SIR PHILIP SIDNEY

PHILIP SIDNEY was born on 30 November 1554. He was educated at Shrewsbury School and Christ Church, Oxford; he may have spent some time also at Cambridge. In 1572 he set out for three years of foreign travel. He was in Paris at the time of the St Bartholomew's Day Massacre of Protestants; he also stayed in Frankfurt, Vienna, Padua, and Venice (where Veronese painted his portrait, now lost), and made a brief excursion into Hungary. In 1577 he went to the Continent again, as an ambassador to the Imperial Court at Prague. Soon after his return he may have begun to write the *Old Arcadia*, which he finished in 1580. *The Defence of Poesy* probably belongs to 1581, and the sonnet sequence *Astrophil and Stella* to 1581–3. Soon after this he began to recast his *Arcadia* on epic lines, a revision which he never completed. In 1583 he married Frances Walsingham, whose father was Secretary of State to the Queen. Though he was appointed royal cup-bearer in 1576, and in 1583 was knighted, he held no major office until in 1585 he was appointed Governor of the Dutch port of Flushing. In September 1586 he was shot in the thigh during a battle against the Spanish near Zutphen and died of infection just over three weeks later.

KATHERINE DUNCAN-JONES was educated at King Edward VI High School for Girls, Birmingham, and St Hilda's College, Oxford, where she obtained the Charles Oldham Shakespeare Prize and the Matthew Arnold Memorial Prize. After a year of teaching in Cambridge she was elected to a fellowship at Somerville College, Oxford. In 1972 she edited (with J. van Dorsten) *Miscellaneous Prose of Sir Philip Sidney* for the Clarendon Press; her paperback *Selected Poems of Sir Philip Sidney* (also Clarendon Press) was published in 1973. She delivered the 1980 Chatterton Lecture to the British Academy on Sidney's poetry. Her biography *Sir Philip Sidney: Courtier Poet* was published by Hamish Hamilton in 1991; her Arden edition of *Shakespeare's Sonnets* in 1997; and her biographical study *Ungentle Shakespeare* (Arden) 2001.

OXFORD WORLD'S CLASSICS

*For over 100 years Oxford World's Classics have brought
readers closer to the world's great literature. Now with over 700
titles—from the 4,000-year-old myths of Mesopotamia to the
twentieth century's greatest novels—the series makes available
lesser-known as well as celebrated writing.*

*The pocket-sized hardbacks of the early years contained
introductions by Virginia Woolf, T. S. Eliot, Graham Greene,
and other literary figures which enriched the experience of reading.
Today the series is recognized for its fine scholarship and
reliability in texts that span world literature, drama and poetry,
religion, philosophy and politics. Each edition includes perceptive
commentary and essential background information to meet the
changing needs of readers.*

OXFORD WORLD'S CLASSICS

Sir Philip Sidney
The Major Works

Edited with an Introduction and Notes by
KATHERINE DUNCAN-JONES

OXFORD
UNIVERSITY PRESS

OXFORD
UNIVERSITY PRESS

Great Clarendon Street, Oxford OX2 6DP

Oxford University Press is a department of the University of Oxford.
It furthers the University's objective of excellence in research, scholarship,
and education by publishing worldwide in

Oxford New York

Auckland Bangkok Buenos Aires Cape Town Chennai
Dar es Salaam Delhi Hong Kong Istanbul Karachi Kolkata
Kuala Lumpur Madrid Melbourne Mexico City Mumbai Nairobi
São Paulo Shanghai Singapore Taipei Tokyo Toronto

with an associated company in Berlin

Oxford is a registered trade mark of Oxford University Press
in the UK and in certain other countries

Published in the United States
by Oxford University Press Inc., New York

First published 1989
First published, with revisions, as an Oxford World's Classics paperback 2002
Reissued 2008

British Library Cataloguing in Publication Data

Data available

Library of Congress Cataloging in Publication Data

Sidney, Philip, Sir, 1554–1586.
[Selections, 1989]
Sir Philip Sidney/edited by Katherine Duncan-Jones.
p. cm.—(Oxford world's classics)
"Selections from the writings of Sir Philip Sidney"
Bibliography: p. Includes index.
I. Duncan-Jones, Katherine. II. Title. III. Series.
821'.3—dc19   PR2341.D8 1989 88–37444

ISBN 978-0-19-953841-6

7

Printed in Great Britain by
Clays Ltd, St Ives plc

CONTENTS

INTRODUCTION

WHETHER we approach Sidney primarily through his literary works or his biography, the fact of his soldier's death in 1586 at the early age of thirty-one stops us short, casting long shadows back over all the rest. The inevitability of this is accepted in the present collection, in which some of the documents relating to Sidney's death and its impact on his contemporaries are included in the Appendices. They comprise an obituary by his father's secretary, Edmund Molyneux, which has never been reprinted in modern times; a rather idealized account of his last days by an unknown clergyman; three out of the two hundred or more[1] elegies which appeared in the decade after his death; and his friend Fulke Greville's account of the skirmish at Zutphen and Sidney's wounding. This extract includes the famous, but almost certainly spurious, anecdote of the wounded Sidney passing a water bottle to a common soldier with the words 'Thy necessity is yet greater than mine' (329).

However, the fact of his early death, so obvious to us, was not available to Sidney himself. His last letter (313) shows him still desperate for life the night before he died, and must modify the credence we give to some of the accounts of his death-bed. If Sidney's works are suffused with melancholy and a sense of sudden, inconclusive endings, the reasons must be sought elsewhere. Indeed, in leaving the manuscript of his revised *Arcadia* with Fulke Greville when he left England for the Netherlands in November 1585, Sidney was probably declaring a private determination to return to his literary work in progress at a future date. The half-sentence with which the revised portion ends may have been a deliberate device to aid his memory when he got back to work on it. This ambitious, wide-ranging, and boldly exploratory romance (from which four extracts are included here, 253–73) marks the point Sidney had reached when he left England for active political and military service. Yet the long *New Arcadia* fragment leaves him, as a writer, still on the middle ground; still in process of self-discovery; still, perhaps, in quest of both the genre and the audience which would bring his powers to their greatest fulfilment.

The question of audience—for whom did Sidney write?—is an important one to ask, though a hard one to answer, for it must have a bearing on a yet more fundamental question: why did Sidney write at all?

[1] According to the *DNB*.

There is no evidence that he intended any of his works except his intemperate *Defence* of his uncle, the Earl of Leicester,[2] to see print: it is to the accident of his death that we owe the fact of their publication during the 1590s (see Chronology). Sidney's nearest contemporaries, writers such as Gascoigne, Spenser, and Lyly, wrote and published poetry in the hope of attracting or consolidating patronage, or of gaining secure employment and/or reputation at Court. Sidney did not need these things in quite the same way. He had plenty of 'business', as he often complains in letters, and if writing poetry and fiction was one of the things that kept him frequently for longish spells away from Court, as Letters [4] and [9] in the present collection may hint, literary activity may even have hindered his chances of lucrative preferment. While other Elizabethans, Shakespeare included, wrote at least partly for money, Sidney may actually have lost money by writing, in so far as absorption in literary projects kept him out of the Queen's eye when offices were being filled. A sense of career opportunities lost filters into several of the sonnets of *Astrophil and Stella*, such as *AS* 18:

> . . . my wealth I have most idly spent.
>   My youth doth waste, my knowledge brings forth toys,
> My wit doth strive those passions to defend
> Which for reward spoil it with vain annoys.
> I see my course to lose itself doth bend . . .

As a young courtier, rather than as a poet, Sidney appeared to have everything to play for. Unlike Spenser, who had to carve out a career for himself through diligent and loyal service to his employers (one of whom may have been Sidney's father), Sidney was from birth beset by more 'great expectation' (*AS* 21.8) than can have been altogether comfortable. Philip II, his godfather, is said to have enjoyed dandling his infant namesake,[3] and as he grew up into a period in which many courtiers of the older generation were either unmarried, like Hatton or Dyer, or, like Leicester and Walsingham, had the utmost difficulty in producing male heirs, Sidney became a kind of universal 'nephew' figure. He was actual nephew to his two childless uncles, the Earls of Warwick and Leicester; and later son-in-law and heir to Sir Francis Walsingham. He filled similar roles abroad. William of Orange hoped that he might marry one of his daughters; and he clearly inspired more than fatherly devotion in the bachelor diplomat Hubert Languet. It is not

[2] Sidney, *Misc. Prose*, 129–41.
[3] Moffet, *Nobilis*, 7, 71.

clear that any of these avuncular figures knew that the promising young Protestant courtier wrote poems and stories, or would have thought the better of him if they had. In imagination, at least, the 'heir apparent' role extended yet further. Reaching adulthood in the period of Queen Elizabeth's advancing middle age, with the last hopes of her producing either a consort or an heir to the throne collapsing at the end of the second Alençon courtship in 1582, Sidney became in the eyes of some almost a crown prince. In a surprisingly frank elegy in which he admits that in life he refrained from praising Sidney, as 'the rising sun', Sir Walter Ralegh was to celebrate his 'princely lineage' (326). For much of his life Sidney's father, Sir Henry Sidney, was Lord Deputy Governor of Ireland, which came out in Latin as 'Pro-Rex'. As the son of a quasi-king he could be viewed, and on the Continent often was, as a quasi-prince. It also probably did not escape the notice of his Continental admirers that one of Sidney's aunts by marriage, Lady Jane Grey, had actually ascended the throne, albeit briefly. However, it does seem largely to have escaped their notice that the young 'baron Sidney' (he was given the title in Paris when he was only 17) was a poet.

Why, then, did Sidney write poetry? In *A Defence of Poesy* he describes himself as having, in his 'not old years', 'slipped into the title of a poet' (212), and there may be some truth in this. He hints elsewhere in the *Defence*, and suggests more explicitly in both the *Old Arcadia* and *Astrophil and Stella*, that it was the experience of falling passionately in love that compelled Sidney/Philisides/Astrophil to relieve pent-up anguish in verse. There may be truth in this, too; we shall probably never know. But whether love or other factors were the catalyst, there may indeed have been something partly accidental in Sidney's self-discovery as a poet. What we know for sure is that after his return from three years of European travel in 1575 Sidney played an increasingly public role in Elizabethan high society as a deviser of and participant in what Molyneux calls 'royal pastimes' (314). These included tiltyard appearances, playlets, and allegorical displays of lesser or greater sophistication, ranging from the probably very early 'pastoral show' at Wilton in which the love-lorn rustic Dick lamented his woes in poulter's measure to his even more naïve companion Will (1–2), by way of the attractive pastoral mini-drama *The Lady of May* (1578 or 1579) to the elaborate, and in detail rather mysterious, *Triumph of the Four Foster Children of Desire* (1581), which made use of elaborate machinery, lavish costumes and armour, caparisoned horses, and 'special effects' on a grand scale. The fullest surviving account of the *Triumph* is included in the present collection (299–311). Sidney's fame as a tilter and a deviser of courtly spectacles spread well beyond the circle of those who actually saw them.[4] If he had left no other literary works, his fame as an up-market Master of the Revels would probably have lingered. But despite such minor legacies from the entertainments as the possible influence of the pedantic schoolmaster Rombus in *The Lady of May* on Shakespeare's Holofernes in *Love's Labour's Lost*, Sidney would scarcely have qualified as an 'Oxford Author' on the strength of these alone.

More obliquely, Sidney's 'public entertainer' role penetrated most of his other literary works. For instance, the four sets of Eclogues or 'pastorals' in the *Old Arcadia* (all included in the present collection, 42–133) consist of elegant poetic recreations before an assembled audience which may reflect real-life debates and discussions between Sidney and his friends on such issues as love, marriage, the social order, and versification. Though Philisides, the Sidney figure, is by no means central, his role is comparable with that of Chaucer the pilgrim—the poor or limited versifier who is, on another level, the versatile author of the whole wide-ranging entertainment. In *Astrophil and Stella* the poet-lover Astrophil shares many of Sidney's public functions and is, in particular, an outstanding tilter, who claims that Stella's presence on occasion makes him perform even better (*AS* 41). The *New Arcadia* is full of spectacular armed combats of lesser or greater degrees of seriousness, such as the 'Iberian jousts' (included here, 258–61), which probably reflect the actual Accession Day Tilts in which Sidney participated. In Book 3 of the revised *Arcadia* Sidney develops a new and more momentous kind of theatricality, as, for instance, when the heroine Philoclea gazes down, as so many unhappy courtiers did in the sixteenth century, at a solemnly staged execution in the courtyard below her window. The relatively lightweight and conventional discussions of love and friendship that characterized earlier books of the *Old Arcadia* give way, in the final book of the *New*, to serious debates on marriage and on the existence of Divine Providence, not the least remarkable feature of which is that they are conducted by female characters (261–6, 266–73).

Although in the *Defence* Sidney seems to align himself more or less with the Puritan Stephen Gosson in his disapproval of the licentiousness of the public theatres—the 'abuse' of poetry—a feeling for drama and dramatic effect characterizes many of his own works. Such a feeling may have been fostered early on by his education at Shrewsbury School,

[4] For instance, an Italian Protestant refugee, Scipio Gentili, suggested in the preface to his *Davidis Psalmos epicae paraphrases* (1584) that Sidney's most praiseworthy achievements in his maturity were his elaborately devised spectacles and equestrian events.

where the regular acting of comedies was part of the curriculum for older boys, and where scholars also took part in the annual outdoor staging of morality plays in a large natural arena, 'The Quarry'. Under the direction of Sidney's headmaster, Thomas Ashton, these Whitsuntide plays drew audiences of thousands.[5] Sidney's Oxford college, Christ Church, was also rich in dramatic activity, and included the dramatist George Peele among its members while Sidney was there.

Yet much of Sidney's most powerful and characteristic writing has little to do with public displays, whether at school, college, Court, or in great houses such as Wanstead and Wilton. Early requirements to participate in public entertainments of various kinds—learned, sporting, or courtly—may have helped Sidney to discover his own extraordinary creative facility. But he soon developed it in other directions, and for much more restricted audiences. There seems little doubt that the *Arcadia*, in its earliest form, was for family entertainment only, among the younger Sidneys and Herberts. As he said to his sister, 'Now it is done only for you, only to you'. The audience he envisaged for *Astrophil and Stella* may have been smaller still. We do not know to what extent it was composed for the immediate perusal of Stella's real-life model, Penelope Rich—she would certainly have been capable of appreciating it.[6] But characteristically the 'felt' audience within individual sonnets is intensely private. Astrophil seems frequently alienated both from his friends and from Stella, hammering out his obsessions in neurotic solitude—'As good to write, as for to lie and groan' (*AS* 40)—which brings us back to the subject of love. Whether or not it dominated Sidney's life as a young man, it certainly dominated his poetry.

To one of the earliest and best of Sidney's modern critics, it seemed that Sidney wrote too much about love and that his verse was not sufficiently varied, especially as compared with Spenser's. Yet he saw the power and originality of Sidney's lyric gift as inseparable from his emotionality:

Once the poet has set himself the task of writing an amorous complaint, that deep melancholy which lay beneath the surface of glamour of Elizabethan existence, and which was so characteristic of Sidney himself, begins to fill the conventional form with a more than conventional weight. It surges through the magical adagio of the lines; they have that depth of reverberation, like the sound of gongs beaten under water, which is sometimes characteristic of Sidney as of no other Elizabethan, not even Shakespeare.[7]

[5] Wallace, 44.
[6] Cf. 'Lady Rich', 182–90.
[7] Theodore Spencer, 'The poetry of Sir Philip Sidney', *ELH*, xii (1945), 267.

This is an eloquent account of a paradox at the heart of Sidney's writing. The splendid rhetorical show of the public courtier conceals inward torment, though for some of his audience the concealment may be effective. As Sidney said bitterly of the Queen, 'so long as she sees a silk doublet upon me her Highness will think me in good case' (Letter [9]). But the attentive reader will find that time and again deep misery is welling up beneath the bright, witty, metrically assured surface of Sidney's verse lines. His literary theory, in the *Defence*, celebrates artistic freedom and joyous creativity—the free imagination of the poet 'ranging only within the zodiac of his own wit' as he delivers the 'golden world' of art (216). But this is not how it feels in many of his own lyrics or passages of prose fiction, which offer us repeated images of paralysis and stagnation. Tellingly, Sidney's own persona, Philisides, is described on his first appearance as disabled by unhappiness:

Another young shepherd named Philisides . . . neither had danced nor sung with them, and had all this time lain upon the ground at the foot of a cypress tree, leaning upon his elbow, with so deep a melancholy that his senses carried to his mind no delight from any of their objects [55].

The avuncular Geron attempts to rouse him to activity with a store of good advice, but is rejected as a tedious old fool, rather as Polonius is snubbed by the love-mad-seeming Hamlet (*Hamlet*, II. ii. 171–219). Time and again in Sidney's lyrical poems, culminating in *Astrophil and Stella*, the speakers lock themselves into positions of emotional and rhetorical impasse. Gifted, like Sidney/Philisides, with exceptional linguistic skills, they are left either with nothing to say or no one to say it to, or both.

For instance, *Lamon's Tale* (139–52), a poem which forms a bridge between the *Old Arcadia* and *Astrophil and Stella*, describes the two shepherds Strephon and Klaius falling in love with the celestial-sounding shepherdess Urania. Having come, rather slowly, to apprehend the nature of their own feelings, they proceed to bewail their inner torment at great length and with astounding emotional intensity. But like so many of Sidney's literary projects, *Lamon's Tale* is unfinished, breaking off before Klaius has had his say, which, to match that of Strephon, needs to be at least a hundred lines long. The compiler of the Eclogues in the 1593 composite text tells us that the hearers, 'not knowing when Lamon would end, being even now stepped over to a new matter', decide it is time for bed. It is not surprising that even other characters in the fiction are imagined as lacking patience to hear the 'tale' out, since Strephon and Klaius, alarmingly solipsistic, seem to be going nowhere unless towards bedlam (rather than bed). In their long and intricate outpourings, both here and in the Fourth Eclogues (117–20), they use hyperboles which travel close to the verge of madness, as their minds' landscapes blot out external reality:

> Me seems I hear, when I do hear sweet music,
> The dreadful cries of murdered men in forests [117].

Astrophil and Stella, unusual among Sidney's works in being apparently finished and fully shaped, ends likewise with emotional impasse. In the Eleventh Song, Astrophil is forced to 'run away' from Stella's window, his dialogue with her unresolved; and in the last sonnet the final image given us is of Astrophil's everlasting and inescapable emotional imprisonment:

> Ah what doth Phoebus' gold that wretch avail
> Whom iron doors do keep from use of day? [211].

The only escape, as the penultimate sonnet hints, is for Sidney to drop the 'Astrophil' persona altogether and begin writing in a quite different genre.

This he clearly tried to do. The dates of his various works of translation—from Aristotle's *Rhetoric*, Du Plessis Mornay's treatise on the truth of the Christian religion, Du Bartas's *Sepmaine sainte*, and the Psalms—are not known; but he may have undertaken them at various times to channel his writing energies into serious, un-amorous projects. If so, the attempt was probably not very successful. All that survive are metrically skilled versions of the first forty-two Psalms, of which five are included here (274–8). If the other translations had been anything like finished they would surely have been preserved and published by Sidney's literary executors, who were all only too anxious to provide evidence of his moral seriousness: it seems likely that he did not get very far with any of these enterprises. Writing *A Defence of Poesy*, which lays so little stress on love poetry and so much on the freedom and power of heroic or epic modes, might perhaps be expected to unlock Sidney, as a writer, from his compulsive drift towards emotional paralysis. Certainly it is, *per se*, a confident, celebratory, in many ways prophetic work, which lays down the theoretical basis for a richly inventive heroic narrative. Yet it does not seem fully to have released Sidney from his habitual tendency to journey towards deadlock. The revised *Arcadia* certainly has a wealth —perhaps even an excess—of interlaced and inset narratives, such as the story of the 'Paphlagonian unkind king', which was to provide Shakespeare with the sub-plot of *King Lear* (253–8); but it also has yet more images of impasse. Amphialus, a character newly conceived in the revised *Arcadia*, is yet another tragic lover, an 'accidental man' trapped in concentric circles of impossible situations, the inmost of which is an agonized love melancholy even more intense than that of his predecessors in Sidney's work, Dick, Philisides, Strephon, Klaius, or Astrophil. It provokes him to an extreme never considered by them: suicide. The *New Arcadia* breaks off with three of its five principal characters (Pamela, Philoclea, Pyrocles) literally in prison, as well as locked emotionally in the toils of love. The other two, Musidorus and Amphialus, also in love, are trapped in misguided and violent conflict based on misunderstanding, and both are grievously wounded, Amphialus near death. John Carey has written powerfully of the 'constant impulse towards deadlock in the rhetoric' in the *New Arcadia*, and of Sidney's accounts of 'the space in which the characters move, full of vacillation and ambivalence'.[8] Cruelty, misunderstanding, corruption, and a besieged fortress seem strangely to prefigure situations that Sidney was to experience in real life in the Netherlands in 1585–6, except that in the *New Arcadia* love is the central source of all these things. If Sidney tried to bid farewell to the splendid trifles of human passion in his latest literary work, he clearly did not succeed.

The melancholy and stagnation of Sidney's lovers may have psychological roots which will never yield themselves to our scrutiny; they may form part of an artistic strategy to lend 'forcibleness' to his poetry; or they may express a deliberate pose, part aesthetic, part didactic, assumed to show the vanity of human wishes and the emptiness of merely human longings. Fulke Greville, who played down the dominance of love in Sidney's writings, would no doubt have supported the last view:

The truth is, his end was not writing even while he wrote . . . but both his wit and understanding bent upon his heart to make himself and others, not in words or opinion, but in life and action, good and great.[9]

However, there may be yet another reason for the recurring images of deadlock in which Sidney's young men find themselves. They may echo the frustrations of his own unique personal position in Elizabethan society. Despite, or even because of, the high hopes placed on him both at home and abroad, life was not particularly comfortable for Sidney. He does not seem, for instance, to have had a house he could call his own. He

---

[8] John Carey, 'Structure and rhetoric in Sidney's *Arcadia*', Kay, 246–64.
[9] Greville, *Prose Works*, 12.

clearly spent as much time as possible at Wilton, his brother-in-law's house, and after his marriage he lived in the house of his father-in-law, Sir Francis Walsingham. He was always short of money. The enormous wealth of his uncles, Leicester and Warwick, was not freely available to him; his immediate resources as a young man were most often determined by the poverty and consequent frugality of his father, Sir Henry Sidney. The office of Royal Cup-bearer, which he held from 1576, was poorly remunerated and carried little status. His embassy to the Holy Roman Emperor Rudolph II was splendidly successful, but was not followed up with any further commission of comparable status. The glittering career as the Queen's ambassador which seemed to lie before him at the age of 22, never really took off, for several reasons. One was the Queen's caution. Sidney may have been rather *too* successful on the Continent for her liking, as he could not be trusted not to take independent initiative. Another handicap was the modified admiration felt for him by the Queen's favourite, the Earl of Leicester. Greville describes a conversation with Leicester after Sidney's death:

[He] told me ... that when he undertook the government of the Low Countries ... he carried his nephew over with him as one among the rest, not only despising his youth for a counsellor, but withal bearing a hand upon him as a forward young man.[10]

Letters written in the immediate aftermath of Sidney's wounding and death make it poignantly clear that it was only during the Netherlands campaign that Leicester came fully to appreciate his nephew's worth.[11] As a recurrent reminder to him of his own childlessness (his only legitimate child, Lord Denbigh, died in July 1584 at the age of about 4) Sidney must inevitably have aroused rather mixed feelings in Leicester's ambitious bosom, and he may well have put a damper on some of Sidney's bids for preferment. In addition to all this, an element of sheer bad luck seemed often to frustrate his chances of worthwhile employment.

For instance, in July 1584 Sidney was commissioned to visit the King of France to negotiate with him over the protection of the Low Countries and was allocated an unusually generous £1,500 for the expenses of this important mission. However, news came that the King was travelling to Lyons, where he would be unable to receive ambassadors, and the

---

[10] Ibid. 18.
[11] Cf. John Bruce, *The Leycester Correspondence*, Camden Society xxvii (1844), 445 and *passim*.

project terminated after only eight days without Sidney and his train leaving British soil.[12] It was only in 1583 that Sidney was knighted (his French barony was not recognized in England), and this was more part of a diplomatic mopping-up operation than a tribute to his worth. Someone was needed to stand proxy for the installation, *in absentia*, of the German Prince Casimir as a Knight of the Garter, and Sidney, as a friend of Casimir's, was suitable. The honour done to him personally was almost accidental.

There is no need, then, to suggest that Sidney foresaw his early death in order to explain the recurrent melancholy and frustration evoked in his literary works, which may have had multiple causes, internal and external. By the last months of his life, as he said to Walsingham, he had indeed foreseen the inglorious collapse of Leicester's Netherlands campaign: 'be not troubled with my trouble, for I have seen the worst in my judgement beforehand, and worse than that cannot be' (295). But we should not read the weary tone of this letter back into the years of Sidney's creativity, from 1577 to 1584/5. During these seven years he was rich in promise but—for a man of his exceptional talent and energy—severely underemployed and underappreciated, at least in England. His greatest happiness was probably experienced in the company of his sister, for whom he wrote the first *Arcadia*. He is said also to have written her numerous letters, both in prose and verse.[13] If these were ever to come to light they might show us a more relaxed, humorous Philip than the one we meet in correspondence with statesmen and humanists. We probably come nearest to their tone in surviving letters to his younger brother Robert (cf. [7] and [8])—'Lord, how I have babbled!'—and in some of the lyrics in *Certain Sonnets* (14–38), such as the sonnet on a naïve satyr written in answer to one by his friend Edward Dyer (*CS* 16a, 16). However, 'that deep melancholy which lay beneath the surface glamour of Elizabethan existence', as Theodore Spencer called it, remains the prevailing mood of Sidney's surviving work.

If obsessive melancholy and a tendency to write himself into a corner are negative features of Sidney's writing, something should be said, briefly, of its abundant positive characteristics. The first and perhaps most overwhelming is his use of language. It was not for nothing that Dr Johnson chose Sidney as his earliest quarry for examples in the *Dictionary*, especially for 'the dialect of poetry and fiction'. The breadth, originality, and flexibility of Sidney's diction is scarcely surpassed even

[12] Wallace, 308–10; Bodleian MS Tanner 78, fo. 90.
[13] Moffet, *Nobilis*, 12, 74.

by Shakespeare. Often, like Chaucer, he uses words which seem easy and accessible to us, so that we may not readily appreciate the fact that he is using them for the first time, or for the first time in a still-current sense. His linguistic legacy to English language and culture is not now often acknowledged or noticed, yet is considerable, ranging from the popular phrase 'my better half', to denote a spouse, which comes from a passage of high tragedy in the *New Arcadia*, to the name 'Pamela', adopted from Sidney by Richardson, or such a half-explicit allusion as Dickens's use of the title *Great Expectations* (cf. *AS* 21.8) for a novel overshadowed by the obsessive passion of a hero called Philip for an unattainable lady called [E]stella. More recent titles derived from Sidney are Philip Larkin's 'Sad Steps', a meditation on moonlight and the unreachableness of love whose title and initial point of reference come from *Astrophil and Stella* 31 [14], and a recent travel book on France, *That Sweet Enemy*, derived from *Astrophil and Stella* 41.4.[15].

Also easy to overlook is Sidney's originality in genre. The two *Arcadias* are so innovatory, in fact, that they have never been satisfactorily pigeon-holed either as 'novel', 'romance', 'comedy', or 'heroic poem'. The difficulty of classification, along with the problem of the disunity of the composite text, has probably been one of the factors contributing to their long period of neglect from the eighteenth to the early twentieth centuries. Because of its date of publication, *Astrophil and Stella* does not look so original as it was. It was to be followed by dozens of sonnet sequences in the 1590s, but it must be remembered that when Sidney wrote it there were no other sonnet sequences in English, unless we count the pedantic and wholly un-'forcible' *Hekatompathia* of Thomas Watson (1581/2), in eighteen-line stanzas, which may indeed have stimulated some of Sidney's attacks on derivative and unconvincing love poets (*AS* 3,6,15). Sidney's is not only the earliest English sonnet sequence properly so described: it is also arguably the best, in terms of assured poetic technique, richness of tone, and subtlety of organization.

Then, again, *A Defence of Poesy* stands head and shoulders above all the other theoretical treatises of the Elizabethan period, such as those of Gascoigne, Webbe, Puttenham, Campion, and Daniel, both because it is consistently entertaining, which the others are not, and because Sidney carries the debate back to first principles—the value of the imagination itself—and tackles Plato head-on. If some of his critical assumptions, most notably those about drama, seem somewhat limited, we should

---

[14] Philip Larkin, *High Windows* (1974), 32.
[15] Christopher Sinclair Stevenson, *That Sweet Enemy* (1987).

remind ourselves that his own death was not the only event on the horizon that Sidney could not foresee. The *Defence* was probably written, or at least begun, in 1580, when Shakespeare was 16. At this date others who were to light up the literary landscape in the last years of Elizabeth's reign were Marlowe, who was also 16; Nashe, who was 13; Donne, who was 8; and Ben Jonson, who was 7. If Sidney had lived to be 60, he could have seen all of Shakespeare's plays. Dying, as he did, at 32, he saw none.

The present collection, which ranges more widely through Sidney's works than any previous volume of selections has done, is intended to illustrate the whole spectrum of Sidney's literary achievements, pointing not only to 'what might have been', but to what was.

ACKNOWLEDGEMENTS

MY FIRST and most substantial debts are to Sidney's previous Oxford editors: the late Jan van Dorsten, the late W. A. Ringler, Miss Jean Robertson, and Dr Victor Skretkowicz. Jean Robertson has also given unfailing personal help and guidance. Lord De L'Isle generously showed me the manuscript of Sidney's *Defence* at Penshurst. Mr John Buxton speedily furnished new translations from Latin of five of Sidney's letters. Miss Lucinda Coventry brought her classical knowledge to bear on some previously untraced tags and allusions. Others to whom I am indebted in various ways include the unfailingly good-humoured staff of Duke Humphrey's Library and the following individuals: Miss Helen Cobb, Mr Charles Cottrell-Dormer, Dr B. E. Juel-Jensen, Dr Dennis Kay, Professor S. W. May, Dr Judith Priestman, Mrs Christina Roaf, Mr Daniel Waissbein, Professor Germaine Warkentin, and Dr H. R. Woudhuysen.

Finally, I would like to thank the General Editor for his help, advice, and judgement.

CHRONOLOGY

1554   Sidney born at Penshurst, Kent, 30 November, eldest child of Sir Henry Sidney and Lady Mary, sister of Robert Dudley, Earl of Leicester. Philip II, who had married Mary Tudor in July, was his godfather.

1564   Enrolled at Shrewsbury School 17 October, along with his friend and future biographer Fulke Greville (1554–1628).

1565   Sir Henry Sidney began the first of three terms of office as Lord Deputy Governor of Ireland.

1566   Visited Kenilworth and Oxford, where he witnessed splendid entertainments for the Queen (August and September).

1567/8   Became an undergraduate at Christ Church, Oxford, where his contemporaries included William Camden, George Peele, Richard Hakluyt, Walter Ralegh, Thomas Bodley, Richard Hooker, and perhaps John Lyly.

1572   Began European tour as part of the train of the Earl of Lincoln (May); witnessed the massacre of Protestants in Paris, 24 August (St Bartholomew's Day); met the Protestant diplomat Hubert Languet in Strasbourg; spent winter in Frankfurt.

1573   Travelled to Venice by way of Heidelberg and the imperial court at Vienna.

1574   Studied in Padua and Venice, where his portrait (now lost) was painted by Paolo Veronese (February); visited Genoa and Florence (March); at Vienna with Hubert Languet, apart from an excursion to Poland in October (August–January).

1575   Returned to England by way of Brno, Prague, Dresden, Frankfurt, Heidelberg, and Antwerp, reaching London in June. With his parents and sister accompanied the Queen on progress to Kenilworth, Lichfield, Chartley, Stafford, Chillington, Dudley, and Worcester. Accompanied his father to Shrewsbury; returned to Court (August).

1576   Joined his father in Ireland (August–October), possibly travelling home with the body of Walter Devereux, 1st Earl of Essex, whose dying wish had been that his daughter Penelope ('Stella') should marry Philip. Succeeded his father as 'Cup-bearer' to the Queen.

1577   Sent as ambassador to the newly acceded Emperor Rudolph in Prague (February–June), renewing European contacts en route and meeting Don John of Austria, Edmund Campion, and (May) William of Orange. Visited Wilton, Wiltshire, where his sister Mary was newly married to the 2nd Earl of Pembroke (August–September); here he may have written 'A dialogue between two shepherds' and may have begun the 'Old' *Arcadia*. Wrote a defence of his father's policies in

Ireland (*Misc. Prose*, 8–12). Participated in Accession Day Tilt, 17 November, and wrote songs for it.

1578   Possibly wrote *The Lady of May* for the Queen's visit to the Earl of Leicester at Wanstead (May); possibly accompanied the Queen on her summer progress, which included a visit to Audley End where she was entertained by representatives of the University of Cambridge.

1579   Visit to England by Hubert Languet and the German Protestant prince John Casimir (February); the latter was made a Knight of the Garter by the Queen. Quarrelled with the Earl of Oxford while playing tennis at Court (August); this dispute may have been connected with Sidney's opposition to the Queen's projected marriage to the Duke of Alençon, against which he argued at length in a widely circulated *Letter* (*Misc. Prose*, 33–57). Spenser dedicated *The Shepheardes Calender* to him (December).

1580   Probably completed the 'Old' *Arcadia*.

1581   Gave the Queen New Year's gift of 'a whip garnished with small diamonds'. Divided his time between London and Wilton. Became a Member of Parliament (April). Devised and participated in *The Triumph of the Four Foster Children of Desire* (May). Penelope Devereux married Lord Rich (1 November). Sidney perhaps wrote 'Lamon's Tale' and began to write *Astrophil and Stella* and *The Defence of Poesy* about this time.

1582   Among large party of nobility and gentry which accompanied the Duke of Alençon to Antwerp (February); took an increasingly active interest in schemes to colonize America.

1583   Stood proxy for the absent Prince Casimir at his official installation as Knight of the Garter at Windsor Castle (see above, 1579), and as a result, became a knight (January). Married Frances, daughter and heir of the Queen's Secretary of State Sir Francis Walsingham (21 September). Perhaps began to revise the *Arcadia*.

1584   Worked in the Ordnance Office, with special interest in the fortification of Dover. Appointed to abortive diplomatic mission to France (July; see Introduction, xv–xvi). Wrote a *Defence* of his uncle, the Earl of Leicester, in response to a libel on him (*Misc. Prose*, 123–41).

1585   Unfinished literary projects on which he may have worked in the earlier part of the year include the 'New' *Arcadia* and translations of the Psalms, of Du Plessis Mornay's *De la verité de la religion chrestienne*, and of Du Bartas's *La semaine ou Creation du monde* (1578). Appointed Joint Master of the Ordnance (July). Travelled to Plymouth with Sir Francis Drake in the hope of accompanying him to the West Indies (September); peremptorily recalled by the Queen, who appointed him governor of the cautionary town of Flushing, in the Netherlands; Leicester had just been appointed lieutenant general of the English troops sent out to support the Dutch provinces which had revolted against Spanish rule. Daughter Elizabeth born. Arrived in Flushing (November).

1586   Leicester enraged the Queen by accepting the title of Governor General of the Netherlands (January). Sir Henry Sidney died at Worcester (May). Sidney made a successful night attack on the town of Axel (July). Lady Mary Sidney died (August). Leicester, Sidney, and others made an early morning raid on a Spanish baggage train approaching the besieged city of Zutphen in which Sidney was wounded with a musket shot in the thigh (22 September); he died of infection at Arnhem (17 October).

1587   Funeral at St Paul's (16 February), eight days after the execution of Mary, Queen of Scots. Publication of Arthur Golding's translation of Du Plessis Mornay, claimed as a completion of Sidney's.

1590   First publication of the 'New' *Arcadia*, the manuscript of which Sidney had entrusted to Greville in 1585.

1591   First publication of *Astrophil and Stella*, in a poor text, with a preface by Thomas Nashe.

1593   Publication of 'New' *Arcadia* with Books 3–5 of the 'Old' version appended.

1595   Publication of *The Defence of Poesy* (two editions, one with title *An apology for poetry*).

1598   Publication of the first 'complete Sidney', probably under the supervision of the Countess of Pembroke, including *CS, AS, DP*, and *LM* in addition to the composite *Arcadia*. Ten further editions during the seventeenth century.

1599   The Countess of Pembroke completed her translation of the Psalms, left unfinished by her brother.

1652   Fulke Greville's *Life of Sidney* (composed c. 1610–14) published.

1907   Bertram Dobell discovered that *OA* survived in complete form in manuscript. Nine manuscripts are now known.

NOTE ON THE TEXT

TEXTS of Sidney's literary works are based when possible on previous Oxford editions, as is the short extract from Fulke Greville. The letters have as far as possible been collated with the originals. Latin letters have been newly translated by John Buxton. Modernization, where necessary, and some regularization of punctuation, have been carried out silently, but substantive emendations are recorded in the Notes.

Sidney's poems are referred to according to the system of reference devised by Ringler: see Abbreviations.

The degree sign (°) indicates a note at the end of the book. More general headnotes are not cued.

A dialogue between two shepherds, uttered in a pastoral show at Wilton

Will: Dick, since we cannot dance, come, let a cheerful voice
 Show that we do not grudge° at all when others do rejoice.
Dick: Ah Will, though I grudge not, I count it feeble glee
 With sight made dim with daily tears another's sport to see.
 Who ever lambkins saw (yet lambkins love to play)
 To play when that their loved dams are stolen or gone astray?
 If this in them be true, as true in men, think I,
 A lustless° song, forsooth, thinks he, that hath more lust to cry.
Will: A time there is for all, my mother often says,
 When she with skirts tucked very high with girls at stoolball°   10
 plays.
 When thou hast mind to weep, seek out some smoky room;
 Now let those lightsome sights we see° thy darkness overcome.
Dick: What joy the joyful sun gives unto bleared eyes,
 That comfort in these sports you like, my mind his comfort
 tries.
Will: What, is thy bagpipe broke, or are thy lambs miswent,
 Thy wallet or thy tar-box° lost, or thy new raiment rent?
Dick: I would it were but thus, for thus it were too well.
Will: Thou seest my ears do itch at it; good Dick, thy sorrow
 tell.
Dick: Hear then, and learn to sigh: a mistress I do serve
 Whose wages makes me beg the more, who feeds me till I   20
 starve,
 Whose livery is such as most I freeze, apparelled most,
 And looks so near unto my cure that I must needs be lost.
Will: What? These are riddles, sure; art thou then bound to her?
Dick: Bound as I neither power have, nor would have power to
 stir.
Will: Who bound thee? *Dick*: Love my lord. *Will*: What
 witnesses thereto?
Dick: Faith in myself, and worth in her, which no proof can
 undo.
Will: What seal? *Dick*: My heart deep graven. *Will*: Who made
 the band so fast?
Dick: Wonder that by two so black eyes the glittering stars be
 passed.

Will: What keepeth safe thy band?   *Dick*: Remembrance is the
    chest,°
    Locked fast with knowing that she is of worldly things the   30
    best.
Will: Thou late of wages 'plained'st;° what wages may'st thou
    have?
Dick: Her heavenly looks, which more and more do give me
    cause to crave.
Will: If wages make you want, what food is that she gives?
Dick: Tears' drink, sorrows' meat, wherewith, not I, but in me
    my death lives.
Will: What living get you then?   *Dick*: Disdain; but just disdain;
    So have I cause myself to plain, but no cause to complain.
Will: What care takes she for thee?   *Dick*: Her care is to
    prevent
    My freedom, with show of her beams, with virtue my content.
Will: God shield us from such dames; if so our downs be sped,°
    The shepherds will grow lean, I trow, their sheep will ill be   40
    fed.
    But, Dick, my counsel mark: run from the place of woe;
    The arrow being shot from far doth give the smaller blow.
Dick: Good Will, I cannot take thy good advice, before
    That foxes leave to steal, because they find they die therefore.
Will: Then Dick, let us go hence, lest we great folks annoy,
    For nothing can more tedious be than plaint in time of joy.
Dick: O hence! O cruel word, which even dogs do hate;°
    But hence, even hence, I needs must go, such is my dogged
    fate.

Two songs for an Accession Day Tilt

Philisides,° the shepherd good and true,
    Came by Menalcas'° house, the husbandman,
With songs of love, and praise of Mira's° hue,
    Whose fair sweet looks make him look pale and wan.
It early was; Menalcas forth was bound
    With horse and man, to sow and till the ground.

'Menalcas', soft this shepherd to him says,
    'Wilt thou with work this holy time defile?

This is the chief of Cupid's Sabbath days,°
　The wake of those that honour Samos' isle,°   10
Where great and small, rich, poor, and each degree
　Yield faith, love, joy, and prove what in them be.'

Menalcas, who of long his thoughts had tilled
　With fancy's plough, that they might pleasure bear,
And with his love the empty furrows filled
　Which always sprang to him again in fear,
Was well content the plough and all to yield
　Unto this Sabbath day, and sacred field.

And on is past by course amongst the rest
　With lays of joy, and lyrics all of praise,   20
His heart as theirs in service of the best;
　For other saints, he knoweth not their days.
If any joust, his whip must be his spear,
　And of his team, the till horse° must him bear.

When he runs well,° then well to her betide;
　When ill, then ill a plain faith is expressed;
If neither well nor ill light on his side
　His course is yet rewarded with the best:
For of all runners this the fortune is
　That who runs best is fortuned once to miss.°   30

This was to be said by one of the Ploughmen after that I had passed the
tilt with my rustical music, and this freeman's song° that followeth:

　　　　　Sing, neighbours, sing; hear you not say
　　　　　　　This Sabbath day
　　　　　A Sabbath is reputed
　　　　　　　Of such a royal saint
　　　　　As all saints else confuted
　　　　　　　Is love without constraint?

　　　　　Let such a saint be praised
　　　　　　　Which so her worth hath raised: 40
　　　　　From him that would not thus
　　　　　　　Good Lord, deliver us.°

Sound up your pipes, do you not see
    That yond is she,
Even she that most respecteth
    The faithful loving minds,
And no one thought rejecteth
    That upon honour binds.

Let such a saint be praised
    Which so her worth hath raised: 50
From him that would not thus
    Good Lord, deliver us.

Show forth your joy, let mourning stay;
    This is her day!
Her day, on which she entered,°
    When with her entered Peace,
Which she hath not adventured°
    But kept for our increase.

Let such a saint be praised
    Which so her worth hath raised: 60
From him that would not thus
    Good Lord, deliver us.

All joy is full, like for no mo;°
    Let sorrow go!
Let sorrow go despised
    And mirth be made a queen,
The heavens highly praised
    That we this day have seen.

Let such a saint be praised
    Which so her worth hath raised: 70
From him that would not thus
    Good Lord, deliver us.

The *impresa*° to this should have been a harrow, and this word, *Nec habent occulta sepulchra.*°

THE LADY OF MAY

Her most excellent Majesty walking in Wanstead Garden, as she passed down into the grove, there came suddenly among the train one apparelled like an honest man's wife° of the country; where, crying out for justice, and desiring all the lords and gentlemen to speak a good word for her,° she was brought to the presence of her Majesty, to whom upon her knees she offered a supplication, and used this speech:

The Suitor. Most fair lady; for as for other your titles of state, statelier persons shall give you, and thus much mine own eyes are witnesses of: take here the complaint of me, poor wretch, as deeply plunged in misery, as I wish to you the highest point of happiness. One only daughter I have, 10 in whom I placed all the hopes of my good hap, so well had she with her good parts recompensed my pain of bearing her, and care of bringing her up. But now, alas, that she is come to the time that I should reap my full comfort of her, so is she troubled with that notable matter, which we in the country call matrimony, as I cannot choose but fear the loss of her wits, at least of her honesty.° Other women think they may be unhappily cumbered with one master husband; my poor daughter is oppressed with two, both loving her, both equally liked of her, both striving to deserve her. But now lastly (as this jealousy, forsooth, is a vile matter) each have brought their partakers° with them, and are at this present, without your 20 presence redress it, in some bloody controversy; my poor child is among them. Now, sweet lady, help; your own way guides you to the place where they encumber her. I dare stay here no longer, for our men say here in the country, the sight of you is infectious.°

And with that she went away a good pace, leaving the supplication with her Majesty, which very formally contained this:

Supplication°

Most gracious Sovereign:

To one whose state is raised over all,
Whose face doth oft the bravest sort enchant,
Whose mind is such, as wisest minds appal,
Who in one self these diverse gifts can plant:
   How dare I, wretch, seek there my woes to rest,
   Where ears be burnt, eyes dazzled, hearts oppressed?
Your state is great, your greatness is our shield,

30

Your face hurts oft, but still it doth delight,
Your mind is wise, your wisdom makes you mild;
Such planted gifts enrich even beggars' sight:
　　So dare I, wretch, my bashful fear subdue,
40　　And feed mine ears, mine eyes, mine heart in you.

Herewith, the woman suitor being gone, there was heard in the woods a confused noise, and forthwith there came out six shepherds, with as many fosters,° haling and pulling to whether side they should draw the Lady of May, who seemed to incline neither to the one nor other side. Among them was Master Rombus,° a schoolmaster of a village thereby, who, being fully persuaded of his own learned wisdom, came thither with his authority to part their fray; where for an answer he received many unlearned blows. But the Queen coming to the place, where she was seen of them, though they knew not her estate, yet something there was which made them startle° aside and gaze upon her: till old father Lalus° stepped forth
50　*(one of the substantiallest shepherds) and making a leg or two, said these few words:*

Lalus the old shepherd. May it please your benignity to give a little superfluous intelligence to that which, with the opening of my mouth, my tongue and teeth shall deliver unto you. So is it, right worshipful audience, that a certain she-creature, which we shepherds call a woman, of a minsical° countenance, but by my white lamb, not three quarters so beauteous as yourself, hath disanulled the brain-pan of two of our featioust° young men. And will you wot how? By my mother Kit's soul,° with a certain fransical° malady they called 'love'; when I was a young
60　man they called it flat folly. But here is a substantial schoolmaster can better disnounce the whole foundation of the matter, although in sooth, for all his loquence° our young men were nothing duteous to his clerkship. Come on, come on, Master Rombus, be not so bashless;° we say that the fairest are ever the gentlest. Tell the whole case, for you can much better vent the points of it than I.

Then came forward Master Rombus, and with many special graces made this learned oration:

Now the thunderthumping Jove transfund his dotes° into your excellent formosity, which have with your resplendent beams thus segregated the
70　enmity of these rural animals. I am, *Potentissima Domina*, a schoolmaster; that is to say, a pedagogue; one not a little versed in the disciplinating of the juvental fry,° wherein (to my laud I say it) I use such geometrical proportion, as neither wanteth mansuetude° nor correction, for so it is described:

Parcere subjectis et debellare superbos.°

Yet hath not the pulchritude of my virtues protected me from the contaminating hands of these plebeians; for coming, *solummodo,°* to have parted their sanguinolent° fray, they yielded me no more reverence than if I had been some *Pecorius Asinus:°* I, even I, that am, who I am. *Dixi. Verbum sapiento satum est.°* But what said that Trojan Aeneas, when he 80 sojourned in the surging sulks of the sandiferous seas:° *Haec olim meminisse iuvabit.°* Well well, *ad propositos revertebo;°* the purity of the verity is, that a certain *pulchra puella profectò,* elected and constituted by the integrated determination of all this topographical region, as the sovereign lady of this, Dame Maia's month, hath been *quodammodo°* hunted, as you would say, pursued, by two, a brace, a couple, a cast° of young men, to whom the crafty coward Cupid had *inquam* delivered his dire doleful digging dignifying dart.

But here the May Lady interrupted his speech, saying to him:

Away, away you tedious fool, your eyes are not worthy to look to yonder 90 princely sight, much less your foolish tongue to trouble her wise ears.

At which Master Rombus in a great chafe cried out:

O Tempori, O Moribus!° In profession a child, in dignity a woman, *in ceteris* a maid, should thus turpify° the reputation of my doctrine with the superscription of a fool! *O Tempori, O Moribus!*

But here again the May Lady, saying to him:

Leave off, good Latin fool, and let me satisfy the long desire I have had to feed mine eyes with the only sight this age hath granted to the world.

The poor schoolmaster went his way back, and the lady kneeling down said in this manner: 100

Do not think, sweet and gallant lady, that I do abase myself thus much unto you because of your gay apparel; for what is so brave as the natural beauty of the flowers? nor because a certain gentleman hereby° seeks to do you all the honour he can in this house; that is not the matter; he is but our neighbour, and these be our own groves; nor yet because of your great estate, since no estate can be compared to be the Lady of the whole month of May, as I am. So that since both this place and this time are my servants, you may be sure I would look for reverence at your hands, if I did not see something in your face which makes me yield to you. The truth is, you excel me in that wherein° I desire most to excel, and that 110

makes me give this homage unto you, as the beautifullest lady these
woods have ever received. But now, as old father Lalus directed me, I will
tell you my fortune, that you may be judge of my mishaps, and others'
worthiness. Indeed so it is that I am a fair wench, or else I am deceived,
and therefore by the consent of all our neighbours have been chosen for
the absolute Lady of this merry month. With me have been° (alas I am
ashamed to tell it) two young men, the one a forester named Therion,° the
other Espilus° a shepherd, very long even in love forsooth. I like them
both, and love neither. Espilus is the richer, but Therion the livelier.
120 Therion doth me many pleasures, as stealing me venison out of these
forests, and many other such like pretty and prettier services; but withal
he grows to such rages, that sometimes he strikes me, sometimes he rails
at me. This shepherd, Espilus, of a mild disposition, as his fortune hath
not been to do me great service, so hath he never done me any wrong; but
feeding his sheep, sitting under some sweet bush, sometimes, they say,
he records my name in doleful verses. Now the question I am to ask you,
fair lady, is whether the many deserts and many faults of Therion, or the
very small deserts and no faults of Espilus be to be preferred. But before
you give your judgement (most excellent lady) you shall hear what each of
130 them can say for themselves in their rural songs.

*Thereupon Therion challenged Espilus to sing with him, speaking these six
verses:*

Therion: Come, Espilus, come now declare thy skill,
          Show how thou canst deserve so brave desire,
          Warm well thy wits, if thou wilt win her will,
          For water cold did never promise fire:
               Great sure is she, on whom our hopes do live,
               Greater is she, who must the judgement give.

But Espilus, as if he had been inspired with the Muses, began forthwith to sing,
140 *whereto his fellow shepherds set in with their recorders, which they bare in their*
bags like pipes; and so of Therion's side did the foresters, with the cornets they
wore about their necks like hunting horns in baldrics.°

Espilus: Tune up, my voice, a higher note I yield:
          To high conceits the song must needs be high;
          More high than stars, more firm than flinty field
          Are all my thoughts, in which I live or die:
               Sweet soul, to whom I vowed am a slave,
               Let not wild woods so great a treasure have.

Therion: The highest note comes oft from basest mind,
 As shallow brooks do yield the greatest sound;   150
 Seek other thoughts thy life or death to find;
 Thy stars be fall'n, ploughed is thy flinty ground:
  Sweet soul, let not a wretch that serveth sheep
  Among his flock so great a treasure keep.

Espilus: Two thousand sheep I have as white as milk,
 Though not so white as is thy lovely face;
 The pasture rich, the wool as soft as silk,
 All this I give, let me possess thy grace:
  But still take heed, lest thou thyself submit
  To one that hath no wealth, and wants his wit.   160

Therion: Two thousand deer in wildest woods I have,
 Them can I take, but you I cannot hold:°
 He is not poor, who can his freedom save,
 Bound but to you, no wealth but you I would:
  But take this beast, if beasts you fear to miss,
  For of his beasts the greatest beast he is.

Espilus kneeling to the Queen:

 Judge you, to whom all beauty's force is lent.

Therion: Judge you of love, to whom all love is bent.

But as they waited for the judgement her Majesty should give of their deserts, the 170
shepherds and foresters grew to a great contention whether of their fellows had
sung better, and so whether the estate of shepherds or foresters were the more
worshipful. The speakers were Dorcas, an old shepherd, and Rixus,° a young
forester, between whom the schoolmaster Rombus came in as moderator.

Dorcas the old shepherd: Now all the blessings of mine old grandam (silly
Espilus) light upon thy shoulders for this honeycomb singing of thine.
Now, by mine honesty, all the bells in the town could not have sung
better. If the proud heart of the harlotry° lie not down to thee now, the
sheep's rot° catch her, to teach her that a fair woman hath not her fairness
to let it grow rustish.   180

Rixus the foster: O Midas,° why art thou not alive now to lend thine ears to
this drivel? By the precious bones of a huntsman, he knows not the
blaying° of a calf from the song of a nightingale. But if yonder great
gentlewoman be as wise as she is fair, Therion, thou shalt have the prize;

and thou, old Dorcas, with young master Espilus, shall remain tame fools, as you be.

Dorcas: And with cap and knee be it spoken, is it your pleasure, neighbour Rixus, to be a wild fool?

Rixus: Rather than a sheepish dolt.

190 *Dorcas*: It is much refreshing to my bowels, you have made your choice; for my share, I will bestow your leavings upon one of your fellows.

Rixus: And art not thou ashamed, old fool, to liken Espilus, a shepherd, to Therion, of the noble vocation of huntsmen, in the presence of such a one as even with her eye can give the cruel punishment?

Dorcas: Hold thy peace, I will neither meddle with her nor her eyes. They say in our town, they are dangerous both. Neither will I liken Therion to my boy Espilus, since one is a thievish prowler, and the other is as quiet as a lamb that new came from sucking.

Rombus the schoolmaster: Heu, Ehem, Hei, Insipidum, Inscitium vulgorum et
200 populorum.° Why, you brute nebulons,° have you had my *corpusculum* so long among you, and cannot yet tell how to edify° an argument? Attend and throw your ears to me,° for I am gravidated with child, till I have indoctrinated your plumbeous cerebrosities.° First you must divisionate your point, *quasi* you should cut a cheese into two particles—for thus I must uniform my speech to your obtuse conceptions; for *prius dividendum oratio antequam definiendum, exemplum gratia*:° either Therion must conquer this, Dame Maia's nymph, or Espilus must overthrow her; and that *secundum* their dignity, which must also be subdivisionated into three equal *species*, either according to the penetrancy of their singing, or the
210 meliority of their functions, or lastly the superancy of their merits. *De* singing *satis*. *Nunc* are you to argumentate of the qualifying of their estate first, and then whether hath more infernally, I mean deeply, deserved.

Dorcas: O poor Dorcas, poor Dorcas, that I was not set in my young days to school, that I might have purchased the understanding of Master Rombus' mysterious speeches. But yet thus much my capacity doth conceive of him, that I must give up from the bottom of my stomach what my conscience doth find in the behalf of shepherds. O sweet honey milken lambs, and is there any so flinty a heart, that can find about him to speak against them, that have the charge of so good souls as you be,
220 among whom there is no envy, but all obedience; where it is lawful for a man to be good if he list, and hath no outward cause to withdraw him from it; where the eye may be busied in considering the works of nature,

and the heart quietly rejoiced in the honest using them? If contemplation, as clerks say, be the most excellent, which is so fit a life for a templer° as this is, which is neither subject to violent oppression, nor servile flattery? How many courtiers, think you, I have heard under our field in bushes make their woeful complaints, some of the greatness of their mistress' estate, which dazzled their eyes and yet burned their hearts; some of the extremity of her beauty mixed with extreme cruelty; some of her too much wit, which made all their loving labours folly? O how often have I 230 heard one name sound in many mouths, making our vales witnesses of their doleful agonies! So that with long lost labour, finding their thoughts bare no other wool but despair, of young courtiers they grew old shepherds. Well, sweet lambs, I will end with you, as I began. He that can open his mouth against such innocents, let him be hated as much as a filthy fox; let the taste of him be worse than musty cheese, the sound of him more dreadful than the howling of a wolf, his sight more odible than a toad in one's porridge.

Rixus: Your life indeed hath some goodness.

Rombus the schoolmaster: O *tace, tace*, or all the fat will be ignified. First let 240 me dilucidate° the very intrinsical marrowbone of the matter. He doth use a certain rhetorical invasion into the point, as if indeed he had conference with his lambs; but the truth is, he doth equitate° you in the mean time, master Rixus, for thus he saith: that sheep are good, *ergo* the shepherd is good: an *enthymeme a loco contingentibus*,° as my finger and my thumb are *contingentes*. Again, he saith, who liveth well is likewise good: but shepherds live well, *ergo* they are good; a syllogism in Darius King of Persia° *a coniugatis*: as you would say, a man coupled to his wife, two bodies but one soul. But do you but acquiescate to my exhortation, and you shall extinguish him. Tell him his *major* is a knave, his *minor* is a fool,° 250 and his conclusion both: *et ecce homo blancatus quasi lilium*.

Rixus: I was saying the shepherd's life had some goodness in it, because it borrowed of the country quietness something like ours. But that is not all; for ours, besides that quiet part, doth both strengthen the body, and raise up the mind with this gallant sort of activity. O sweet contentation, to see the long life of the hurtless trees; to see how in straight growing up, though never so high, they hinder not their fellows; they only enviously trouble, which are crookedly bent. What life is to be compared to ours, where the very growing things are ensamples of goodness? We have no hopes, but we may quickly go about them, and going about them, we soon 260 obtain them; not like those that, having long followed one (in truth) most excellent chase, do now at length perceive she could never be taken; but that if she stayed at any time near her pursuers, it was never meant to tarry with them, but only to take breath to fly further from them. He therefore that doubts that our life doth not far excel all others, let him also doubt that the well deserving and painful Therion is not to be preferred before the idle Espilus, which is even as much to say, as that roes are not swifter than sheep, nor stags more goodly than goats.

Rombus: *Bene, bene, nunc de questione propositus*: that is as much to say, as
270 well, well, now of the proposed question, that was, whether the many great services and many great faults of Therion, or the few small services and no faults of Espilus, be to be preferred, incepted or accepted the former.

The May Lady: No, no, your ordinary brains shall not deal in that matter; I have already submitted it to one whose sweet spirit hath passed through greater difficulties, neither will I that your blockheads lie in her way. Therefore, O lady, worthy to see the accomplishment of your desires, since all your desires be most worthy of you, vouchsafe our ears such happiness, and me that particular favour, as that you will judge whether
280 of these two be more worthy of me, or whether I be worthy of them; and this I will say, that in judging me, you judge more than me in it.

This being said, it pleased her Majesty to judge that Espilus did the better deserve her; but what words, what reasons she used for it, this paper, which carrieth so base names, is not worthy to contain. Sufficeth it that upon the judgement given, the shepherds and foresters made a full consort of their cornets and recorders, and then did Espilus sing this song, tending to the greatness of his own joy, and yet to the comfort of the other side, since they were overthrown by a most worthy adversary. The song contained two short tales, and thus it was:

Espilus: Sylvanus° long in love, and long in vain,
290   At length obtained the point of his desire,
        When being asked, now that he did obtain
        His wished weal, what more he could require:
          'Nothing', said he, 'for most I joy in this,
          That goddess mine, my blessed being sees.'

Therion: When wanton Pan,° deceived with lion's skin,
        Came to the bed, where wound for kiss he got,
        To woe and shame the wretch did enter in,
        Till this he took, for comfort of his lot:
          'Poor Pan', he said, 'although thou beaten be,
300   It is no shame, since Hercules was he.'

Espilus: Thus joyful I in chosen tunes rejoice,
              That such a one is witness of my heart,
              Whose clearest eyes I bliss, and sweetest voice,
              That see my good, and judgeth my desert.

Therion: Thus woeful I in woe this salve do find,
              My foul mishap came yet from fairest mind.

The music fully ended, the May Lady took her leave in this sort:

Lady your self, for other titles do rather diminish than add unto you: I and my little company must now leave you. I should do you wrong to beseech you to take our follies well, since your bounty is such as to 310 pardon greater faults. Therefore I will wish you good night, praying to God, according to the title I possess, that as hitherto it hath excellently done, so henceforward the flourishing of May, may long remain in you and with you.

And so they parted, leaving Master Rombus, who presented her Majesty with a chain of round agates° something like beads, first beginning in a chafe:

Videte these obscure barbarons,° *perfidem perfide*; you were well served to be vapilated,° relinquishing my dignity before I have valedixed this nymph's serenity. Well, *alias* I will be vindicated. But to you, Juno, Venus, Pallas *et profecto plus*,° I have to ostend a mellifluous fruit of my 320 fidelity. *Sic est*, so it is, that in this our city we have a certain neighbour, they call him Master Robert of Wanstead. He is counted an honest man, and one that loves us doctified men *pro vita*; and when he comes to his ædicle° he distributes *oves, boves et pecora campi*° largely among the *populorum*. But so stays the case, that he is foully commaculated with the papistical enormity, *O heu Aedipus Aecastor*.° The *bonus vir* is a huge *catholicam*, wherewith my conscience being replenished, could no longer refrain it from you, *proba dominus doctor, probo inveni*. I have found *unum par*, a pair, *papisticorum bedorum*, of Papistian beads, *cum quos*, with the which, *omnium dierum*, every day, next after his *pater noster* he *semper* saith 330 'and Elizabeth',° as many lines as there be beads on this string. *Quamobrem*, I say, *secundum* the civil law,° nine hundredth paragroper of the 7. ii. code in the great Turk Justinian's library,° that he hath deponed all his juriousdiction° therein, and it is forfeited *tibi dominorum domina:*° *accipe* therefore, for he will never be so audacious to reclamat it again, being *iure gentiorum*° thus manumissed. Well, *vale, vale, felissima, et me ut facias ama*: that is, to love me much better than you were wont. And so *iterum valeamus et plauditamus:*° PLAUDITAMUS ET VALEAMUS.

CERTAIN SONNETS

I

Since, shunning pain, I ease can never find;
Since bashful dread seeks where he knows me harmed;
Since will is won, and stopped ears are charmed;
Since force doth faint, and sight doth make me blind;
Since loosing long, the faster still I bind;
Since naked sense can conquer reason armed;
Since heart in chilling fear with ice is warmed;°
In fine, since strife of thought but mars the mind:
I yield, O love, unto thy loathed yoke,
Yet craving law of arms, whose rule doth teach   10
That hardly used, whoever prison broke,
In justice quit, of honour made no breach:°
   Whereas, if I a grateful guardian° have,
   Thou art my lord, and I thy vowed slave.

2

When love, puffed up with rage of high disdain,
Resolved to make me pattern of his might,
Like foe, whose wits inclined to deadly spite,
Would often kill, to breed more feeling pain;
He would not, armed with beauty only, reign
On those affects which easily yield to sight,
But virtue sets so high, that reason's light,
For all his strife, can only bondage gain:
So that I live to pay a mortal fee,
Dead-palsy-sick of all my chiefest parts;   10
Like those whom dreams make ugly monsters see,
And can cry 'Help!' with nought but groans and starts.
   Longing to have, having no wit to wish,
   To starving minds such is god Cupid's dish.

3°

To the tune of *Non credo gia che piu infelice amante*

The fire to see my wrongs for anger burneth;
The air in rain for my affliction weepeth;
The sea to ebb for grief his flowing turneth;
The earth with pity dull the centre keepeth;
  Fame is with wonder blazed;
  Time runs away for sorrow;
  Place standeth still amazed,
  To see my night of evils, which hath no morrow.
    Alas, all only she no pity taketh
    To know my miseries, but, chaste and cruel.   10
    My fall her glory maketh:
    Yet still her eyes give to my flames their fuel.

Fire, burn me quite, till sense of burning leave me;
Air, let me draw no more thy breath in anguish;
Sea, drowned in thee, of tedious life bereave me;
Earth, take this earth, wherein my spirits languish.
  Fame, say I was not born;
  Time, haste my dying hour;
  Place, see my grave uptorn;
  Fire, air, sea, earth, fame, time, place, show your power. 20
    Alas, from all their helps I am exiled;
    For hers am I, and death fears her displeasure.
    Fie, death, thou art beguiled;
    Though I be hers, she makes of me no treasure.

4°

To the same tune

  The nightingale, as soon as April bringeth
Unto her rested sense a perfect waking,
While late bare earth, proud of new clothing, springeth,
Sings out her woes, a thorn her song-book making,
  And mournfully bewailing
  Her throat in tunes expresseth
  What grief her breast oppresseth
  For Tereus' force on her chaste will prevailing.

O Philomela fair, O take some gladness,
That here is juster cause of plaintful sadness: 10
Thine earth now springs, mine fadeth;
Thy thorn without, my thorn my heart invadeth.

Alas, she hath no other cause of anguish
But Tereus' love, on her by strong hand wroken;
Wherein she, suffering all her spirits' languish,
Full woman-like, complains her will was broken.
  But I, who daily craving
  Cannot have to content me,
  Have more cause to lament me,
  Since wanting is more woe than too much having.°   20
    O Philomela fair, O take some gladness,
    That here is juster cause of plaintful sadness;
    Thine earth now springs, mine fadeth;
    Thy thorn without, my thorn my heart invadeth.

5°

O my thoughts' sweet food, my my only owner,
O my heaven's foretaste by thy heavenly pleasure,
O the fair nymph born to do women honour,
    Lady my treasure:

Where be now those joys that I lately tasted?
Where be now those eyes, ever inly piercers?
Where be now those words never idly wasted,
    Wounds to rehearsers?

Where is, ah, that face, that a sun defaces?
Where be those welcomes, by no worth deserved?   10
Where be those movings, the delights, the graces?
    How be we swerved?

O hideous absence, by thee am I thralled;
O my vain word gone, ruin of my glory!
O due allegiance, by thee am I called
    Still to be sorry.

But no more words, though such a word be spoken,
Nor no more wording, with a word to spill me:
Peace, due allegiance; duty must be broken
    If duty kill me.   20

Then come, O come; then do I come, receive me,
Slay me not, for stay; do not hide thy blisses,
But between those arms; never else do leave me;
    Give me my kisses.

O my thoughts' sweet food, my my only owner,
O my heaven's foretaste by thy heavenly pleasure,
O the fair nymph born to do women honour,
    Lady my treasure.

6°

To the tune of *Basciami vita mia*

Sleep, baby mine, desire; nurse beauty singeth;
Thy cries, O baby, set mine head on aching:
The babe cries: 'Way,° thy love doth keep me waking.'

Lully, lully, my babe; hope cradle bringeth,
Unto my children alway good rest taking:
The babe cries: 'Way, thy love doth keep me waking.'

Since, baby mine, from me thy watching springeth;
Sleep then a little, pap content is making:
The babe cries: 'Nay, for that° abide I waking.'

7

To the tune of the Spanish song, *Si tu señora no dueles de mi*°

    O fair, O sweet, when I do look on thee,
    In whom all joys so well agree,
    Heart and soul do sing in me.
        This you hear is not my tongue,
        Which once said what I conceived,
        For it was of use bereaved,

sleep Baby myne desyre, nurse beauty singeth
Thy cryes o Baby sett my head on akinge
The Babe cryes vaye, thy love doth keep me waking

Lully lully my babe, hope crauls bringeth
vnto my babes, alway god rest thinkinge
The babe cryes vaye, thy love doth keep me waking

Since Baby myne frome me thy watching sprunge
slepe then a little pray "aktende is making
thy Babe cryes vaye, for it is aye it wakinge

The only poem by Sidney surviving in his own hand. CS 6, inscribed on the last leaf of Jean Bouchet's *Les Annales d'Aquitaine* (Poitiers 1557). Reproduced by permission of the Bibliotheca Bodmeriana, Cologny, Geneva.

With a cruel answer stung.
  No, though tongue to roof be cleaved°
  Fearing lest he chastised be,
  Heart and soul do sing in me.   10

O fair, O sweet, when I do look on thee,
In whom all joys so well agree,
Heart and soul do sing in me.
  Just accord all music makes;
  In thee just accord excelleth,
  Where each part in such peace dwelleth,
  One of other beauty takes.
    Since then truth to all minds telleth
    That in thee lives harmony,
    Heart and soul do sing in me.   20

O fair, O sweet, when I do look on thee,
In whom all joys so well agree,
Heart and soul do sing in me.
  They that heaven have known, do say
  That who so that grace obtaineth
  To see what fair sight there reigneth,
  Forced are to sing alway:
    So then, since that heaven remaineth
    In thy face I plainly see,
    Heart and soul do sing in me.   30

O fair, O sweet, when I do look on thee,
In whom all joys so well agree,
Heart and soul do sing in me.
  Sweet, think not I am at ease
  For because my chief part singeth:
  This song from death's sorrow springeth,
  As to swan in last disease;
    For no dumbness nor death bringeth
    Stay to true love's melody:
    Heart and soul do sing in me.   40

8

These four following sonnets were made when his lady had pain in her face°

The scourge of life, and death's extreme disgrace,
　　The smoke of hell, the monster called Pain,
Long shamed to be accursed in every place
　　By them who of his rude resort complain,
Like crafty wretch, by time and travel taught
　　His ugly evil in others' good to hide,
Late harbours in her face, who nature wrought
　　As treasure house, where her best gifts abide.
And so, by privilege of sacred seat,
　　A seat where beauty shines and virtue reigns,
He hopes for some small praise, since she hath great, 10
　　Within her beams wrapping his cruel stains.
　　　　Ah, saucy Pain, let not thy error last;
　　　　More loving eyes she draws, more hate thou hast.

9

Woe, woe to me, on me return the smart;
　　My burning tongue hath bred my mistress pain;
For oft in pain, to pain, my painful heart
　　With her due praise did of my state complain.
I praised her eyes, whom never chance doth move;
　　Her breath, which makes a sour answer sweet;
Her milken breasts, the nurse of child-like love;°
　　Her legs (O legs!), her aye well-stepping feet.
Pain heard her praise, and full of inward fire,
　　(First sealing up my heart as prey of his) 10
He flies to her, and boldened with desire
　　Her face (this age's praise) the thief doth kiss.
　　　　O Pain, I now recant the praise I gave,
　　　　And swear she is not worthy thee to have.

10

Thou Pain, the only guest of loathed constraint,
　　The child of curse, man's weakness' foster-child,
Brother to woe, and father of complaint;
　　Thou Pain, thou hated Pain, from heaven exiled,

How holdest thou her, whose eyes constraint doth fear,
   Whom cursed do bless, whose weakness virtues arm,
Who others' woes and plaints can chastely bear,
   In whose sweet heaven angels of high thoughts swarm?
What courage strange hath caught thy caitiff heart?
   Fear'st not a face that oft whole hearts devours,   10
Or art thou from above bid play this part,
   And so no help 'gainst envy of those powers?
     If thus, alas; yet while those parts have woe,
     So stay her tongue that she no more say 'No'.

11

And have I heard her say, 'O cruel Pain!'
   And doth she know what mould her beauty bears?
Mourns she in truth, and thinks that others fain?
   Fears she to feel, and feels not others' fears?
Or doth she think all pain the mind forebears?°
   That heavy earth, not fiery sprites, may plain?
That eyes weep worse than heart in bloody tears?
   That sense feels more than what doth sense contain?
No, no, she is too wise, she knows her face
   Hath not such pain as it makes others have;   10
She knows the sickness of that perfect place
   Hath yet such health, as it my life can save.
     But this she thinks: our pain high cause excuseth,
     Where her, who should rule pain, false pain abuseth.

12°

Translated out of Horace, *which begins* Rectiùs vives

You better sure shall live, not evermore
   Trying high seas, nor while sea rage you flee,
   Pressing too much upon ill-harboured shore.

The golden mean who loves, lives safely free
   From filth of foreworn house, and quiet lives,
   Released from court, where envy needs must be.

The wind most oft the hugest pine-tree grieves;
   The stately towers come down with greater fall;
   The highest hills the bolt of thunder cleaves;°

Ill haps do fill with hope, good hopes appal   10
   With fear of change the courage well prepared;
   Foul winters, as they come, away they shall.

Though present times and past with evils be snared,
   They shall not last; with cithern silent muse
   Apollo wakes, and bow hath sometime spared.

In hard estate with stout show valour use,
   The same man still in whom wisdom prevails;
   In too full wind draw in thy swelling sails.

13°

Out of Catullus

Nulli se dicit mulier mea nubere malle
   Quam mihi non si se Iupiter ipse petat.
Dicit sed mulier Cupido quae dicit amanti,
   In vento aut rapida scribere oportet aqua

Unto no body my woman saith she had rather a wife be
   Than to myself, not though Jove grew a suitor of hers.
These be her words: but a woman's words to a love that is eager
   In wind or water stream do require to be writ.

14°

Qui sceptra saevus duro imperio regit,
Timet timentes, metus in authorem redit.

Fair, seek not to be feared, most lovely beloved, by thy servants;
   For true it is, that they fear many whom many fear.

15°

Upon the device of a seeled dove, with this word of Petrarch: *Non mi vuol e non
mi trahe d'impaccio*

Like as the dove which seeled-up doth fly,
    Is neither freed, nor yet to service bound,
But hopes to gain some help by mounting high
    Till want of force do force her fall to ground;
Right so my mind, caught by his° guiding eye,
    And thence cast off, where his sweet hurt he found,
Hath neither leave to live, nor doom to die,
    Nor held in evil, nor suffered to be sound,
But with his wings of fancies up he goes
    To high conceits, whose fruits are oft but small,   10
Till wounded, blind, and wearied spirits lose
    Both force to fly, and knowledge where to fall.
        O happy dove, if she no bondage tried;
        More happy I, might I in bondage bide.

16a°

Edward Dyer

Prometheus, when first from heaven high
    He brought down fire, till then on earth not seen,
Fond of delight, a satyr standing by
    Gave it a kiss, as it like sweet had been.
Feeling forthwith the other burning power,
    Wood° with the smart, with shouts and shrieking still,
He sought his ease in river, field and bower,
    But for the time his grief went with him still.
So silly I, with that unwonted sight,
    In human shape, an angel from above,   10
Feeding mine eyes, th'impression there did light,
    That since I run and rest as pleaseth love.
        The difference is, the satyr's lips, my heart;
        He for a while; I evermore have smart.

16°

A satyr once did run away for dread
  With sound of horn which he himself did blow;
Fearing and feared, thus from himself he fled,
  Deeming strange evil in that he did not know.
Such causeless fears when coward minds do take
  It makes them fly that which they fain would have:
As this poor beast, who did his rest forsake,
  Thinking not why, but how, himself to save.
Even thus might I, for doubts which I conceive
  Of mine own words, my own good hap betray,   10
And thus might I for fear of maybe,° leave
  The sweet pursuit of my desired prey.
    Better I like thy satyr, dearest Dyer,
    Who burnt his lips to kiss fair shining fire.

17°

My mistress lours, and saith I do not love;
I do protest, and seek with service due
In humble mind a constant faith to prove;
But for all this I cannot her remove
From deep vain thought that I may not be true.

If oaths might serve, even by the Stygian lake°
Which poets say the gods themselves do fear,
I never did my vowed word forsake:
For why should I, whom free choice slave doth make,
Else what in face, than in my fancy bear?   10

My muse therefore—for only thou canst tell—
Tell me the cause of this my causeless woe,
Tell how ill thought disgraced my doing well,
Tell how my joys and hopes thus foully fell
To so low ebb, that wonted were to flow.

O this it is: the knotted straw is found
In tender hearts; small things engender hate;
A horse's worth laid waste the Trojan ground;
A three-foot stool in Greece made trumpets sound;
An ass's shade ere now hath bred debate.°   20

If Greeks themselves were moved with so small cause
To twist those broils, which hardly would untwine,
Should ladies fair be tied to such hard laws
As in their moods to take a lingering pause?
I would it not, their metal is too fine.

My hand doth not bear witness with my heart;
She saith, because I make no woeful lays
To paint my living death and endless smart;
And so for one that felt god Cupid's dart
She thinks I lead and live too merry days.°   30

Are poets then the only lovers true,
Whose hearts are set on measuring a verse,
Who think themselves well bless'd, if they renew
Some good old dump° that Chaucer's mistress knew,
And use but you for matters to rehearse?

Then, good Apollo, do away thy bow;
Take harp, and sing, in this our versing time;
And in my brain some sacred humour flow,
That all the earth my woes, sighs, tears may know:
And see you not that I fall now to rhyme?   40

As for my mirth: how could I but be glad,
Whilst that, methought, I justly made my boast
That only I the only mistress had?
But now, if e'er my face with joy be clad,
Think Hannibal did laugh when Carthage lost.°

Sweet lady, as for those whose sullen cheer,
Compared to me, made me in lightness found;°
Who stoic-like in cloudy hue° appear;
Who silence force, to make their words more dear;
Whose eyes seem chaste, because they look on ground;   50
   Believe them not, for physic true doth find
   Choler adust° is joyed in womankind.

18°

In wonted walks, since wonted fancies change,
Some cause there is, which of strange cause doth rise:
For in each thing, whereto mine eye doth range,
Part of my pain, me seems, engraved lies.
The rocks, which were of constant mind the mark,
In climbing steep now hard refusal show;
The shading woods seem now my sun to dark,
And stately hills disdain to look so low.
The restful caves now restless visions give;
In dales I see each way a hard ascent;   10
Like late mown meads, late cut from joy I live;
Alas, sweet brooks do in my tears augment:°
  Rocks, woods, hills, caves, dales, meads, brooks, answer me:
  Infected minds infect each thing they see.

19°

If I could think how these my thoughts to leave,
  Or, thinking still, my thoughts might have good end;
  If rebel sense would reason's law receive,
  Or reason, foiled, would not in vain contend;
    Then might I think what thoughts were best to think;
    Then might I wisely swim or gladly sink.

If either you would change your cruel heart,
  Or, cruel still, time did your beauty stain;
  If from my soul this love would once depart,
  Or for my love some love I might obtain;   10
    Then might I hope a change or ease of mind
    By your good help, or in myself, to find.

But since my thoughts in thinking still are spent
  With reason's strife, by senses overthrown;
  You, fairer still, and still more cruel bent;
  I, loving still a love that loveth none;
    I yield and strive, I kiss and curse the pain
    Thought, reason, sense, time, you and I maintain.

20°

A Farewell

Oft have I mused, but now at length I find
Why those that die, men say they do depart;
'Depart', a word so gentle to my mind,
Weakly did seem to paint death's ugly dart.
But now the stars with their strange course do bind
Me one to leave, with whom I leave my heart,
I hear a cry of spirits faint and blind,
That, parting thus, my chiefest part I part.
Part of my life, the loathed part to me,
Lives to impart my weary clay some breath;   10
But that good part, wherein all comforts be,
Now dead, doth show departure is a death,
    Yea, worse than death; death parts both woe and joy;
    From joy I part, still living in annoy.

21

Finding those beams, which I must ever love,
    To mar my mind, and with my hurt to please,
I deemed it best some absence for to prove,
    If further place might further me to ease.
Mine eyes thence drawn, where lived all their light,
    Blinded forthwith in dark despair did lie,
Like to the mole, with want of guiding sight
    Deep plunged in earth, deprived of the sky.
In absence blind, and wearied with that woe,
    To greater woes by presence I return,   10
Even as the fly which to the flame doth go,
    Pleased with the light that his small corse° doth burn.
        Fair choice I have, either to live or die
        A blinded mole, or else a burned fly.

22°

The Seven Wonders of England

Near Wilton sweet,° huge heaps of stone are found;
But so confused, that neither any eye

Can count them just, nor reason reason try
What force brought them to so unlikely ground.

To stranger weights my mind's waste soil is bound,
Of passion's hills, reaching to reason's sky,
From fancy's earth passing all number's bound,
Passing all guess whence into me should fly
    So mazed a mass; or if in me it grows,
    A simple soul should breed so mixed woes.   10

The Breretons have a lake,° which when the sun
Approaching warms—not else—dead logs up sends,
From hidd'nest depth, which tribute when it ends,
Sore sign it is the lord's last thread is spun.

My lake is sense, whose still streams never run,
But when my sun her shining twins there bends;
Then from his depth with force in her begun,
Long drowned hopes to watery eyes it lends;
    But when that fails my dead hopes up to take,
    Their master is fair warned his will to make.   20

We have a fish,° by strangers much admired,
Which, caught, to cruel search yields his chief part,
With gall cut out, closed up again by art;
Yet lives until his life be new required.

A stranger fish myself, not yet expired,
Though rapt with beauty's hook, I did impart
Myself unto th'anatomy desired,
Instead of gall, leaving to her my heart;
    Yet live with thoughts closed up, till that she will
    By conquest's right, instead of searching, kill.   30

Peak hath a cave° whose narrow entries find
Large rooms within, where drops distil amain,
Till knit with cold, though there unknown, remain,
Deck that poor place with alabaster lined.

Mine eyes the strait, the roomy cave my mind,
Whose cloudy thoughts let fall an inward rain

Of sorrow's drops, till colder reason bind
Their running fall into a constant vein
  Of truth, far more than alabaster pure;
  Which, though despised, yet still doth truth endure.   40

A field there is,° where, if a stake be pressed
Deep in the earth, what hath in earth receipt
Is changed to stone, in hardness, cold, and weight;
The wood above doth soon consuming rest.

The earth, her ears; the stake is my request;
Of which, how much may pierce to that sweet seat,
To honour turned, doth dwell in honour's nest,
Keeping that form, though void of wonted heat;
  But all the rest, which fear durst not apply,
  Failing themselves, with withered conscience die.   50

Of ships by shipwreck cast on Albion coast,
Which rotting on the rocks their death do die,
From wooden bones, and blood of pitch, doth fly
A bird° which gets more life than ship had lost.

My ship, desire, with wind of lust long tossed,
Brake on fair cleeves of constant chastity;
Where, plagued for rash attempt, gives up his ghost,
So deep in seas of virtue beauties lie.
  But of his death flies up a purest love,
  Which, seeming less, yet nobler life doth move.   60

These wonders England breeds; the last remains,
A lady, in despite of nature chaste,
On whom all love, in whom no love is placed,
Where fairness yields to wisdom's shortest reins.

An humble pride, a scorn that favour stains;
A woman's mould, but like an angel graced;
An angel's mind, but in a woman cast;
A heaven on earth, or earth that heaven contains;
  Now thus this wonder to myself I frame;
  She is the cause that all the rest I am.   70

23°

To the tune of Wilhelmus van Nassouwe &c.

Who hath his fancy pleased
With fruits of happy sight,
Let here his eyes be raised
On nature's sweetest light:
A light which doth dissever
And yet unite the eyes,
A light which, dying never,
Is cause the looker dies.

She never dies, but lasteth
In life of lover's heart;   10
He ever dies, that wasteth
In love his chiefest part.
Thus is her life still guarded
In never dying faith;
Thus is his death rewarded,
Since she lives in his death.

Look then, and die; the pleasure
Doth answer well the pain;
Small loss of mortal treasure,
Who may immortal gain.   20
Immortal be her graces,
Immortal is her mind;
They fit for heavenly places,
This heaven in it doth bind.

But eyes these beauties see not,
Nor sense that grace descries;
Yet eyes deprived be not
From sight of her fair eyes;
Which, as of inward glory
They are the outward seal,   30
So may they live still sorry
Which die not in that weal.

But who hath fancies pleased
With fruits of happy sight
Let here his eyes be raised
On nature's sweetest light.

24°

To the tune of 'The Smokes of Melancholy'

Who hath ever felt the change of love
And known those pangs that the losers prove
  May paint my face without seeing me,
  And write the state how my fancies be
  The loathsome buds grown on sorrow's tree:
But who by hearsay speaks, and hath not fully felt
What kind of fires they be in which those spirits melt
  Shall guess, and fail, what doth displease;
  Feeling my pulse, miss my disease.

O no, O no; trial only shows   10
The bitter juice of forsaken woes,
  Where former bliss present ills do stain—
  Nay, former bliss adds to present pain,
  While remembrance doth both states contain.
Come, learners, then, to me, the model of mishap,
Engulfed in despair, slid down from fortune's lap;
  And as you like my double lot,
  Tread in my steps, or follow not.

For me, alas, I am full resolved
Those bands, alas, shall not be dissolved,   20
  Nor break my word, though reward come late,
  Nor fail my faith in my failing fate,
  Nor change in change, though change change my state:
But always one myself with eagle-eyed truth° to fly
Up to the sun, although the sun my wings do fry:
  For if those flames burn my desire,
  Yet shall I die in Phoenix' fire.°

25°
– ∪ ∪ – ∪ – –

When to my deadly pleasure,
When to my lively torment,
Lady, mine eyes remained,
Joined, alas, to your beams,
With violence of heavenly
Beauty tied to virtue,

Reason abashed retired,
Gladly my senses yielded.
Gladly my senses yielding
Thus to betray my heart's fort   10
Left me devoid of all life.
They to the beamy suns went,
Where, by the death of all deaths,
Find to what harm they hastened;
Like to the silly sylvan
Burned by the light he best liked,
When with a fire he first met.
Yet, yet, a life to their death,
Lady, you have reserved;
Lady, the life of all love;   20
For though my sense be from me,
And I be dead, who want sense;
Yet do we both live in you;
Turned anew by your means
Unto the flower that aye turns,°
As you, alas, my sun bends.
Thus do I fall, to rise thus;
Thus do I die, to live thus;
Changed to a change, I change not.
Thus may I not be from you;   30
Thus be my senses on you;
Thus what I think is of you;
Thus what I seek is in you;
All what I am, it is you.

26°

To the tune of a Neapolitan song which beginneth: 'No, no, no, no'

    No, no, no, no, I cannot hate my foe:
    Although with cruel fire
    First thrown on my desire
    She sacks my rendered sprite:
      For so fair a flame embraces
        All the places
      Where that heat of all heats springeth
        That it bringeth

To my dying heart some pleasure,
  Since his treasure   10
Burneth bright in fairest light: no, no, no, no.

No, no, no, no, I cannot hate my foe;
  Although with cruel fire
  First thrown on my desire
  She sacks my rendered sprite:
    Since our lives be not immortal,
      But to mortal
    Fetters tied, do wait the hour
      Of death's power,
    They have no cause to be sorry   20
      Who with glory
End the way where all men stay: no, no, no, no.

No, no, no, no, I cannot hate my foe;
  Although with cruel fire
  First thrown on my desire
  She sacks my rendered sprite:
    No man doubts, whom° beauty killeth,
      Fair death feeleth;
    And in whom fair death proceedeth,
      Glory breedeth;   30
    So that I, in her beams dying,
      Glory trying,
Though in pain, cannot complain: no, no, no, no.

27°

To the tune of a Neapolitan villanelle

All my sense thy sweetness gained,
Thy fair hair my heart enchained,
My poor reason thy words moved,
So that thee like heaven I loved:
    Fa la la leridan, dan dan dan deridan,
    Dan dan dan deridan deridan dei:
      While to my mind the outside stood
      For messenger of inward good.

Now thy sweetness sour is deemed,
Thy hair not a hair esteemed;   10
Reason hath thy words removed,
Finding that but words they proved:
  Fa la la leridan, dan dan dan deridan,
  Dan dan dan deridan deridan dei:
    For no fair sign can credit win
    If that the substance fail within.

No more in thy sweetness glory;
For thy knitting hair be sorry;
Use thy words but to bewail thee,
That no more thy beams avail thee: 20
  Fa la la leridan, dan dan dan deridan,
  Dan dan dan deridan deridan dei:
    Lay not thy colours more to view
    Without the picture be found true.

Woe to me, alas, she weepeth:
Fool in me, what folly creepeth?
Was I to blaspheme enraged
Where my soul I have engaged?
  Fa la la leridan, dan dan dan deridan,
  Dan dan dan deridan deridan dei: 30
    And wretched I must yield to this;
    The fault I blame her chasteness is.

Sweetness, sweetly pardon folly;
Tie me, hair, your captive wholly;
Words, O words, of heavenly knowledge,
Know my words their faults acknowledge:
  Fa la la leridan, dan dan dan deridan,
  Dan dan dan deridan deridan dei:
    And all my life I will confess,
    The less I love, I live the less.   40

28°

Translated out of Diana of Montemayor in Spanish, where Sireno, a shepherd, pulling out a little of his mistress Diana's hair, wrapped about with green silk, who now had utterly forsaken him, to the hair he thus bewailed himself:

What changes here, O hair,
I see since I saw you:

How ill fits you this green to wear,
For hope the colour due.°
Indeed, I well did hope,
Though hope were mixed with fear,
No other shepherd should have scope
Once to approach this hair.

Ah hair, how many days,
My Dian made me show,   10
With thousand pretty childish plays
If I ware you, or no:
Alas, how oft with tears,
O tears of guileful breast,
She seemed full of jealous fears,
Whereat I did but jest.

Tell me, O hair of gold,
If I then faulty be
That trust those killing eyes I would,
Since they did warrant me.   20
Have you not seen her mood,
What streams of tears she spent,
Till that I sware my faith so stood
As her words had it bent?

Who hath such beauty seen
In one that changeth so?
Or where one's love so constant been,
Who ever saw such woe?
Ah hair, are you not grieved,
To come from whence you be,   30
Seeing how once, you saw, I lived,
To see me as you see?

On sandy bank of late
I saw this woman sit,
Where, 'Sooner die than change my state',°
She with her finger writ:
Thus my belief was stayed—
Behold love's mighty hand!—
On things were by a woman said
And written in the sand.°   40

29°

The same Sireno in Montemayor, holding his mistress's glass before her, looking upon her while she viewed herself, thus sang:

> Of this high grace, with bliss conjoined,
>   No further debt on me is laid,
> Since that in self-same metal coined,
>   Sweet lady, you remain well paid.
>   For if my place give me great pleasure,
>   Having before me nature's treasure,
>   In face and eyes unmatched being,
>   You have the same in my hands, seeing
>   What in your face mine eyes do measure.

> Nor think the match unev'nly made,   10
>   That of those beams in you do tarry
> The glass to you but gives a shade,
>   To me mine eyes the true shape carry;
>   For such a thought, most highly prized,
>   Which ever hath love's yoke despised,
>   Better than one captived perceiveth:
>   Though he the lively form receiveth,
>   The other sees it but disguised.

30°

> Ring out your bells, let mourning shows° be spread,
>   For love is dead:
>   All love is dead, infected
>   With plague of deep disdain,
>   Worth as naught worth rejected,
>   And faith fair scorn doth gain.
>   From so ungrateful° fancy,
>   From such a female franzy,
>   From them that use men thus:
>   Good lord, deliver us.°   10

> Weep, neighbours, weep: do you not hear it said
>   That love is dead?
>   His death-bed peacock's folly,
>   His winding-sheet is shame,

His will false-seeming holy,
His sole executor blame.
　　From so ungrateful fancy,
　　From such a female franzy,
　　From them that use men thus:
　　Good lord, deliver us.　　　　　　　　　　20

Let dirge be sung, and trentals° rightly read,
　For love is dead.
　　Sir wrong his tomb ordaineth,
　　My mistress' marble heart,
　　Which epitaph containeth:
　　'Her eyes were once his dart.'
　　　From so ungrateful fancy,
　　　From such a female franzy,
　　　From them that use men thus:
　　　Good lord, deliver us.　　　　　　　　30

Alas, I lie: rage hath this error bred;
　Love is not dead.
　　Love is not dead, but sleepeth°
　　In her unmatched mind,
　　Where she his counsel keepeth
　　Till due desert she find.
　　　Therefore from so vile fancy,
　　　To call such wit a franzy
　　　Who love can temper thus:
　　　Good lord, deliver us.　　　　　　　　40

31

Thou blind man's mark, thou fool's self-chosen snare,
Fond fancy's scum, and dregs of scattered thought,
Band° of all evils, cradle of causeless care,
Thou web° of will, whose end is never wrought;
Desire, desire, I have too dearly bought,
With price of mangled mind, thy worthless ware;
Too long, too long, asleep thou hast me brought,
Who should my mind to higher things prepare.
　But yet in vain thou hast my ruin sought:
　In vain thou madest me to vain things aspire,　　10

In vain thou kindlest all thy smoky fire;
For virtue hath this better lesson taught,
Within myself to seek my only hire,
Desiring naught but how to kill desire.

32

Leave me, O love which reachest but to dust,
And thou, my mind, aspire to higher things;
Grow rich in that which never taketh rust;
What ever fades, but fading pleasure brings.
Draw in thy beams, and humble all thy might
To that sweet yoke° where lasting freedoms be,
Which breaks the clouds, and opens forth the light
That doth both shine, and give us sight to see.
O take fast hold, let that light be thy guide
In this small course which birth draws out to death,   10
And think how ill becometh him to slide,
Who seeketh heaven, and comes of heavenly breath:
    Then farewell, world; thy uttermost I see;
    Eternal love, maintain thy life in me.

                        Splendidis longum valedico nugis°

'The lad Philisides'

The lad Philisides
Lay by a river's side,
In flowery field a gladder eye to please;
His pipe was at his foot,
His lambs were him beside;
A widow turtle near on bared root
Sate wailing without boot;
Each thing, both sweet and sad,
Did draw his boiling brain
To think, and think with pain,   10
Of Mira's beams, eclipsed by absence bad.
And thus, with eyes made dim
With tears, he said, or sorrow said for him:

'O earth, once answer give:
So may thy stately grace
By north or south still rich adorned live;
So Mira long may be
On thy then blessed face,
Whose foot doth set a heaven on cursed thee;
I ask—now answer me—   20
If th'author of thy bliss,
Phoebus, that shepherd high,
Do turn from thee his eye,
Doth not thyself, when he long absent is,
Like rogue all ragged go,
And pine away with daily wasting woe?

'Tell me, you wanton brook:
So may your sliding race
Shun loathed-loving banks with cunning crook;
So in you ever new   30
Mira may look her face,
And make you fair with shadow of her hue,
So when to pay your due
To mother sea you come,
She chide you not for stay,
Nor beat you for your play:
Tell me, if your diverted streams become
Absented quite from you,
Are you not dried? Can you yourself renew?

'Tell me, you flowers fair,   40
Cowslip and columbine:
So may your make,° this wholesome spring-time air,
With you embraced lie,
And lately thence untwine,
But with dew-drops engender children high;°
So may you never die,
But pulled by Mira's hand
Dress bosom hers, or head,
Or scatter on her bed:
Tell me, if husband spring-time leave your land, 50
When he from you is sent,
Wither not you, languished with discontent?

'Tell me, my seely pipe:
So may thee still betide
A cleanly cloth thy moistness for to wipe;
So may the cherries red
Of Mira's lips divide
Their sugared selves to kiss thy happy head;
So may her ears be led,
Her ears, where music lives,   60
To hear, and not despise,
Thy liribliring cries:
Tell, if that breath which thee thy sounding gives
Be absent far from thee,
Absent alone canst thou then piping be?

'Tell me, my lamb of gold:
So may'st thou long abide
The day well fed, the night in faithful fold;
So grow thy wool of note
In time, that, richly dyed,
It may be part of Mira's petticoat;   70
Tell me, if wolves the throat
Have caught of thy dear dam,
Or she from thee be stayed,
Or thou from her be strayed,
Canst thou, poor lamb, become another's lamb?
Or rather, till thou die,
Still for thy dam with bea-waymenting° cry?

'Tell me, O turtle true:
So may no fortune breed   80
To make thee, nor thy better-loved, rue;
So may thy blessings swarm
That Mira may thee feed
With hand and mouth; with lap and breast keep warm:
Tell me, if greedy arm
Do fondly take away
With traitor lime the one,
The other left alone;
Tell me, poor wretch, parted from wretched prey,
Disdain not you the green,   90
Wailing till death; shun you not to be seen?

'Earth, brook, flowers, pipe, lamb, dove,
Say all, and I with them:
'Absence is death, or worse, to them that love.'
So I, unlucky lad,
Whom hills from her do hem,
What fits me now but tears, and sighings sad?
O fortune too too bad:
I rather would my sheep
Th'had'st killed with a stroke,   100
Burnt cabin, lost my cloak,
Than want one hour those eyes which my joys keep.
O, what doth wailing win?
Speech without end were better not begin.

'My song, climb thou the wind
Which Holland sweet now gently sendeth in,
That on his wings the level thou may'st find
To hit, but kissing hit,
Her ears, the weights of wit.
If thou know not for whom thy master dies.   110
These marks shall make thee wise:
She is the herdess fair that shines in dark,
And gives her kids no food but willow's bark.'°

This said, at length he ended
His oft sigh-broken ditty,
Then rase; but rase on legs with faintness bended,
With skin in sorrow dyed,
With face the plot of pity,
With thoughts, which thoughts their own tormentors tried,
He rase, and straight espied   120
His ram, who to recover
The ewe another loved
With him proud battle proved:
He envied such a death in sight of lover,
And always westward eyeing,°
More envied Phoebus for his western flying.

THE OLD ARCADIA

THE FIRST ECLOGUES

THE manner of the Arcadian shepherds was, when they met together, to pass their time, either in such music as their rural education could afford them, or in exercise of their body and trying of masteries. But, of all other things, they did especially delight in eclogues; wherein sometimes they would contend for a prize of well singing, sometimes lament the unhappy pursuit of their affections, sometimes, again, under hidden forms utter such matters as otherwise were not fit for their delivery. Neither is it to be marvelled that they did so much excel other nations in that quality since, from their childhood, they were brought up unto it, and were not such base shepherds as we commonly make account of, but the very owners of the sheep themselves,° which in that thrifty world the substantiallest men would employ their whole care upon. And when they had practised the goodness of their wit in such sports, then was it their manner ever to have one who should write up the substance of that they said; whose pen, having more leisure than their tongues, might perchance polish a little the rudeness of an unthought-on song. But the peace wherein they did so notably flourish, and especially the sweet enjoying of their peace to so pleasant uses, drew divers strangers, as well of great as of mean houses, especially such whom inward melancholies made weary of the world's eyes, to come and live among them, applying themselves to their trade: which likewise was many times occasion to beautify more than otherwise it would have been this pastoral exercise. But nothing lifted it up to so high a key as the presence of their own duke who, not only by looking on but by great courtesy and liberality, animated the shepherds the more exquisitely to seek a worthy accomplishment of his good liking, as this time after the valiant killing of the beasts by the two disguised princes performed. The duke (because Cleophila so would have it) used the artificial day of torches to lighten the sports their inventions could minister. And yet, because many more shepherds were newly come than at the first were, he did, with a gentle manner, chastise the cowardice of the fugitive shepherds with making them for that night the torch bearers; and the others later come, he willed, with all freedom of speech and behaviour, to keep their accustomed method; which they prepared themselves to do, while he sat himself down, having on the one side the duchess, but of his heart side the fair Cleophila. To whom speaking in looks (for as yet his tongue was not come to a thorough boldness), he sought to send the first ambassade of his passions—little marked of Cleophila whose eyes seemed to have changed sight with Philoclea's eyes (whom Gynecia had of purpose placed by herself), so attentive looks were mutually fixed between them, to the greatest corrosive° to Gynecia that can be imagined, whose love-open sight did more and more pierce into the knowledge of Cleophila's counterfeiting, which likewise more and more fortified her unlawful desires; yet with so great and violent a combat with herself as the suppression of a long-used virtue comes to. But another place shall serve to manifest her agonies; this, being dedicated only to pastorals, shall bend itself that way, and leave all those princely motions to their considerations that, untold, can guess what love means—whereof the princess Pamela, that sat next to Cleophila, was most free, having in her mind used Dorus's baseness as a shield against his worthiness. But they being set in order, Dametas, who much disdained (since his late authority) all his old companions, brought his servant Dorus in good acquaintance and allowance of them; and himself stood like a director over them, with nodding, gaping, winking or stamping, showing how he did like or mislike those things he did not understand. The first sports the shepherds showed were full of such leaps and gambols as (being accorded to the pipe which they bare in their mouths even as they danced) made a right picture of their chief god Pan and his companions, the satyrs. Then would they cast away their pipes and, holding hand in hand, dance as it were in a brawl by the only cadence of their voices, which they would use in singing some short couplets; whereto the one half beginning, the other half answered; as, the one half saying:

> We love, and have our loves rewarded.

The others would answer:

> We love, and are no whit regarded.

The first again:

> We find most sweet affection's snare.

With like tune, it should be (as in a choir) sent back again:

> That sweet, but sour despairful care.

A third time likewise thus:

> Who can despair whom hope doth bear?

The answer:

> And who can hope who feels despair?

Then, all joining their voices, and dancing a faster measure, they would conclude with some such words:

As without breath no pipe doth move,
No music kindly without love.

Having thus varied both their songs and dances into diverse sorts of inventions, their last sport was one of them to provoke another to a more large expressing of his passions: which Lalus, a shepherd accounted one of the best singers among them, having marked in Dorus's dancing no less good grace and handsome behaviour than extreme tokens of a troubled mind, he began first with his pipe, and then with his voice, thus to challenge Dorus; and was by him answered in the underwritten sort:

Lalus. Come, Dorus, come,° let songs thy sorrows signify;
    And if, for want of use, thy mind ashamed is,
    That very shame with love's high title dignify.
  No style is held for base where love well named is:
    Each ear sucks up the words a true love scattereth,
    And plain speech oft than quaint phrase better framed is.

Dorus. Nightingales seldom sing, the pie° still chattereth;
    The wood cries most before it throughly kindled be;
    Deadly wounds inward bleed, each slight sore mattereth;°
  Hardly they herd which by good hunters singled be;   10
    Shallow brooks murmur most, deep silent slide away,
    Nor true love loves his loves with others mingled be.

Lalus. If thou wilt not be seen, thy face go hide away,
    Be none of us, or else maintain our fashion:
    Who frowns at others' feasts doth better bide away.
  But if thou hast a love, in that love's passion,
    I challenge thee, by show of her perfection,
    Which of us two deserveth most compassion.

Dorus. Thy challenge great, but greater my protection:
    Sing, then, and see (for now thou hast inflamed me)   20
    Thy health too mean a match for my infection.
  No, though the heav'ns for high attempt have blamed me,
    Yet high is my attempt. O muse, historify°
    Her praise, whose praise to learn your skill hath framed
      me.

Lalus. Muse, hold your peace! But thou, my god Pan, glorify
    My Kala's gifts, who with all good gifts filled is.
    Thy pipe, O Pan, shall help, though I sing sorrily.
  A heap of sweets she is, where nothing spilled is,

Who, though she be no bee, yet full of honey is:
    A lily field, with plough of rose, which tilled is.   30
Mild as a lamb, more dainty than a cony is:
    Her eyes my eyesight is, her conversation
    More glad to me than to a miser money is.
What coy account she makes of estimation!
    How nice to touch, how all her speeches peised be!°
    A nymph thus turned, but mended in translation.

Dorus. Such Kala is; but ah, my fancies raised be
    In one whose name to name were high presumption,
    Since virtues all, to make her title, pleased be.
O happy gods, which by inward assumption   40
    Enjoy her soul, in body's fair possession,
    And keep it joined, fearing your seat's consumption.
How oft with rain of tears skies make confession
    Their dwellers rapt with sight of her perfection,
    From heav'nly throne to her heav'n use digression.
Of best things then what world can yield confection
    To liken her? Deck yours with your comparison:
    She is herself of best things the collection.

Lalus. How oft my doleful sire cried to me, 'tarry son',
    When first he spied my love? How oft he said to me,   50
    'Thou art no soldier fit for Cupid's garrison.
My son, keep this that my long toil hath laid to me:
    Love well thine own; methinks, wool's whiteness passeth
        all:
    I never found long love such wealth hath paid to me.'
This wind he spent; but when my Kala glasseth° all
    My sight in her fair limbs, I then assure myself,
    Not rotten sheep, but high crowns she surpasseth all.
Can I be poor, that her gold hair procure myself
    Want I white wool, whose eyes her white skin garnished?
    Till I get her, shall I to keep inure myself?   60

Dorus. How oft, when reason saw love of her harnished°
    With armour of my heart, he cried, 'O vanity,
    To set a pearl in steel so meanly varnished!
Look to thyself; reach not beyond humanity;
    Her mind, beams, state, far from thy weak wings banished;
    And love which lover hurts is inhumanity.'

Thus reason said: but she came, reason vanished;
   Her eyes so mast'ring me that such objection
   Seemed but to spoil the food of thoughts long famished.
Her peerless height my mind to high erection   70
   Draws up; and if, hope failing, end life's pleasure,
   Of fairer death how can I make election?

Lalus. Once my well-waiting eyes espied my treasure,
   With sleeves turned up, loose hair, and breasts enlarged,°
   Her father's corn (moving her fair limbs) measure.
'O', cried I, 'of so mean work be discharged:
   Measure my case, how by thy beauty's filling
   With seed of woes my heart brim-full is charged.
Thy father bids thee save, and chides for spilling.
   Save then my soul, spill not my thoughts well heaped,   80
   No lovely praise was ever got with killing.'
These bold words she did hear, this fruit I reaped,
   That she, whose look alone might make me blessed,
   Did smile on me, and then away she leaped.

Dorus. Once, O sweet once,° I saw, with dread oppressed,
   Her whom I dread; so that with prostrate lying
   Her length the earth in love's chief clothing dressed.
I saw that richess fall, and fell a-crying:
   'Let not dead earth enjoy so dear a cover,
   But deck therewith my soul for your sake dying.   90
Lay all your fear upon your fearful lover:
   Shine eyes on me, that both our lives be guarded;
   So I your sight, you shall yourselves recover.'
I cried, and was with open rays rewarded;
   But straight they fled, summoned by cruel honour,
   Honour, the cause desert is not regarded.

Lalus. This maid, thus made for joys, O Pan, bemoan her,
   That without love she spends her years of love:
   So fair a field would well become an owner.
And if enchantment can a hard heart move,   100
   Teach me what circle may acquaint her sprite,
   Affection's charms in my behalf to prove.
The circle is my round-about-her sight:
   The power I will invoke dwells in her eyes:
   My charm should be she haunt me day and night.

Dorus. Far other care, O muse, my sorrow tries,
    Bent to such one, in whom, myself must say,
    Nothing can mend one point that in her lies.
  What circle, then, in so rare force bears sway?
    Whose sprite all sprites can spoil, raise, damn, or save: 110
    No charm holds her, but well possess she may;
  Possess she doth, and makes my soul her slave:
    My eyes the bands, my thoughts the fatal knot.
    No thralls like them that inward bondage have.

Lalus. Kala, at length, conclude my ling'ring lot:
  Disdain me not, although I be not fair.
  Who is an heir of many hundred sheep
  Doth beauties keep, which never sun can burn,
  Nor storms do turn: fairness serves oft to wealth.
  Yet all my health I place in your goodwill: 120
  Which if you will (O do) bestow on me,
  Such as you see, such still you shall me find:
  Constant and kind. My sheep your food shall breed,
  Their wool your weed: I will you music yield
  In flow'ry field; and as the day begins
  With twenty gins we will the small birds take,
  And pastimes make, as nature things hath made.
  But when in shade we meet of myrtle° boughs,
  Then love allows, our pleasures to enrich,
  The thought of which doth pass all worldly pelf.   130

Dorus. Lady yourself, whom neither name I dare,
  And titles are but spots to such a worth,
  Hear plaints come forth from dungeon of my mind:
  The noblest kind rejects not others' woes.
  I have no shows of wealth: my wealth is you,
  My beauty's hue your beams, my health your deeds;
  My mind for weeds your virtue's liv'ry wears.
  My food is tears; my tunes waymenting yield;
  Despair my field; the flowers spirit's wars;
  My day new cares; my gins my daily sight,
  In which do light small birds of thoughts o'erthrown.
  My pastimes none; time passeth on my fall.
  Nature made all, but me of dolours made.
  I find no shade, but where my sun doth burn;
  No place to turn; without, within, it fries;
  Nor help by life or death who living dies.

Lalus. But if my Kala this my suit denies,
 Which so much reason bears,
 Let crows pick out mine eyes which too much saw.
 If she still hate love's law,   150
 My earthy mould doth melt in wat'ry tears.

Dorus. My earthy mould doth melt in wat'ry tears,
 And they again resolve
 To air of sighs, sighs to the heart's fire turn,
 Which doth to ashes burn;
 Thus doth my life within itself dissolve.

Lalus. Thus doth my life within itself dissolve,
 That I grow like the beast
 Which bears the bit a weaker force doth guide,
 Yet patient must abide;   160
 Such weight it hath which once is full possessed.

Dorus. Such weight it hath which once is full possessed
 That I become a vision,
 Which hath in other's head his only being
 And lives in fancy's seeing.
 O wretched state of man in self-division!

Lalus. O wretched state of man in self-division!
 O well thou say'st! A feeling declaration
 Thy tongue hath made of Cupid's deep incision.   170
 But now hoarse voice doth fail this occupation,
 And others long to tell their loves' condition:
 Of singing thou hast got the reputation.

Dorus. Of singing thou hast got the reputation
 Good Lalus mine; I yield to thy ability:
 My heart doth seek another estimation.
 But ah, my muse, I would thou hadst facility
 To work my goddess so by thy invention
 On me to cast those eyes, where shine nobility:
 Seen and unknown; heard, but without attention.   180

The eclogue° betwixt Lalus and Dorus of every one of the beholders received great commendations, saving only of the two grave shepherds, Geron and Dicus, who both plainly protested it was pity wit should be employed about so very a toy as that they called love was—Geron thereto the more inclined, as that age, having taken from him both the thoughts and fruits of that passion, wished all the world proportioned to himself. But Dicus, whether for certain mischances of his own, or out of a better judgement, which saw the bottom of things, did more detest and hate love than the most envious man doth in himself cherish and love hate. Which, as he did at all times publicly profess, so now he came, as a man should say, armed to show his malice; for in the one hand he bare a whip, in the other a naked Cupid, such as we commonly set him forth. But on his breast he ware a painted table, wherein he had given Cupid a quite new form, making him sit upon a pair of gallows, like a hangman, about which there was a rope very handsomely provided; he himself painted all ragged and torn, so that his skin was bare in most places, where a man might perceive all his body full of eyes, his head horned with the horns of a bull, with long ears accordingly, his face old and wrinkled, and his feet cloven. In his right hand, he was painted holding a crown of laurel, in his left a purse of money; and out of his mouth hung a lace which held the pictures of a goodly man and an excellent fair woman. And with such a countenance he was drawn as if he had persuaded every man by those enticements to come and be hanged there. The duke laughed when he saw Dicus come out in such manner, and asked him what he meant by such transforming the gentle Cupid. But Dicus, as if it had been no jesting matter, told him plainly that long they had done the heavens wrong to make Cupid a god, and much more to the fair Venus to call him her son—indeed, the bastard of false Argus,° who, having the charge of the deflowered Io (what time she was a cow), had traitorously in that shape begot him of her; and that the naughtiness of men's lust had given him so high a title. Everyone of the company (except old Geron) began to stamp with their feet, and hiss at him, as thinking he had spoken an unpardonable blasphemy. But Geron, well backing him in it, Dicus boldly stepped forth and, after having railed at the name of Cupid as spitefully as he could devise, calling to Pan to help his song in revenge of his losing the fair Syrinx,° he thus, tuning his voice to a rebeck, sang against him:

> Poor painters oft° with silly poets join
> To fill the world with strange but vain conceits:
> One brings the stuff, the other stamps the coin,
> Which breeds naught else but glosses of deceits.
>   Thus painters Cupid paint, thus poets do,
>   A naked god, blind, young, with arrows two.
>
> Is he a god, that ever flies the light?
> Or naked he, disguised in all untruth?
> If he be blind, how hitteth he so right?

Or is he young, that tamed old Phoebus' youth?   10
　　But arrows two, and tipped with gold or lead:
　　Some hurt, accuse a third with horny head.°

No, nothing so; an old false knave he is,
By Argus got on Io, then a cow,
What time for her Juno her Jove did miss,
And charge of her to Argus did allow.
　　Mercury killed his false sire for this act,
　　His dam, a beast, was pardoned beastly fact.

With father's death, and mother's guilty shame,
With Jove's disdain at such a rival's seed,   20
The wretch compelled, a runagate became,
And learned what ill a miser state doth breed;
　　To lie, to steal, to pry, and to accuse,
　　Naught in himself, each other to abuse.

Yet bears he still his parents' stately gifts,
A horned head, cloven foot, and thousand eyes,
Some gazing still, some winking wily shifts,
With long large ears where never rumour dies.
　　His horned head doth seem the heav'n to spite:
　　His cloven foot doth never tread aright.   30

Thus half a man, with man he easily haunts,
Clothed in the shape which soonest may deceive:
Thus half a beast, each beastly vice he plants
In those weak hearts that his advice receive.
　　He prowls each place still in new colours decked,
　　Sucking one's ill, another to infect.

To narrow breasts he comes all wrapped in gain:
To swelling hearts he shines in honour's fire:
To open eyes all beauties he doth rain;
Creeping to each with flatt'ring of desire.   40
　　But for that love is worst which rules the eyes,
　　Thereon his name, there his chief triumph lies.

Millions of years this old drivel Cupid lives;
While still more wretch, more wicked he doth prove:
Till now at length that Jove him office gives
(At Juno's suit who much did Argus love),
　　In this our world a hangman for to be
　　Of all those fools that will have all they see.

He had not fully ended his last words of his invective song when a young shepherd named Histor who, while Dicus was singing, sometimes with his eyes up to heaven, sometimes seeming to stop his ears, did show a fearful mislike of so unreverent reproaches, with great vehemency desired all the hearers to take heed how they seemed to allow any part of his speech against so revengeful a god as Cupid was, who had even in his first magistracy showed against Apollo the heat of his anger. 'But', said he, 'if you had heard or seen such violence of his wrath as I even yesterday, and the other day, have, you would tremble at the recital of his name.'

The duke and all the rest straight desired him to tell what it was; and he (seeming loath, lest his words might disgrace the matter) told them that, as he was two days before sitting in the shade of a bush, he did hear the most wailful lamentation of an Iberian nobleman called Plangus (uttered to the wise shepherd Boulon) that he thought any words could express; and all touching a pitiful adventure, the ground and maintenance whereof was only Cupid. 'And that song', said he, 'for in a song I gathered it, would I let you hear but that, for the better understanding, I must first repeat the subject thereof. This Plangus, when no persuasion of the wise Boulon could keep him from the pitiful complaining of his sorrows, yet yielded so much to my request as to harbour with me these last days in my simple cabin where, with much entreaty, he told me this pitiful story:°

That of late there reigned a king of Lydia who had for the blessing of his marriage his only daughter Erona, a princess worthy for her beauty as much praise as beauty may be praised. This Erona being fourteen years old, seeing the country of Lydia so much devoted to Cupid as that in each place his naked pictures and images were superstitiously adored, procured so much of her father (either moved thereunto by the hate of that god, or the shamefast consideration of such nakedness) utterly to deface and pull down all those pictures of him; which how terribly he punished quickly after appeared. For she had not lived a year longer when she was stricken with most obstinate love to a young man, but of mean parentage, in her father's court, named Antiphilus; so mean as that he was but the son of her nurse, and by that means came known of her. And so ill could she conceal this fire, and so wilfully persevered she in it, that her father offering her the marriage of the great Otanes, king of Persia (who desired her more than the joys of heaven), she, for Antiphilus's sake, refused him. Many ways her father did seek to withdraw her from it; sometimes persuasions, sometimes threatenings, sometimes hiding Antiphilus and giving her to understand he was fled the country; lastly making a solemn execution to be done of another under the name of Antiphilus, whom he kept in prison. But neither she liked persuasions, nor feared threatenings, nor changed for absence; and when she thought him dead, it was manifestly seen she sought all means, as well by poison as knife, to follow him. This so brake the father's heart with grief that, leaving things as he found them, he shortly after died. Then forthwith Erona, being seized of the crown, sought to satisfy her mind with Antiphilus's marriage.

But before she could accomplish it, she was overtaken with a cruel war the king Otanes made upon her, only for her person, towards whom, for her ruin, love had kindled his cruel heart: indeed cruel and tyrannous; for being far too strong in the field, he spared not man, woman, nor child, but with miserable tortures slew them, although his fair sister Artaxia (who accompanied him in the army) sought all means to mollify his rage; till lastly he besieged Erona in her best city, vowing he would have her either by force or otherwise. And to the extremity he had brought her when there landed in Lydia, driven thither by tempest, two excellent young princes, as Plangus named them, Pyrocles, prince of Macedon, and Musidorus, duke of Thessalia (at these words, a man might easily have perceived a starting and blushing, both in Cleophila and Dorus; but being utterly unsuspected to be such, they were unmarked). Those two princes, as well to help the weaker as for the natural hate the Grecians bare the Persians, did so much with their incomparable valour as that they gat into the city, and by their presence much repelled Otanes' assaults. Which he understanding to be occasioned by them, made a challenge of three princes in his retinue against those two princes and Antiphilus; and that thereupon the matter should be decided, with compact that neither should help his fellows, but of whose side the more overcame, with him the victory should remain. Of his side was Barzanes, lord of Hyrcania against Pyrocles; Nardes, satrapas° of Mesopotamia, to fight with Musidorus; and against Antiphilus he placed this same Plangus, second son to the king of Iberia, who served him with dear estimation. And so it fell out that Pyrocles and Musidorus overcame both their adversaries, but of the other side Plangus took Antiphilus prisoner. Under which colour, as though the matter had been equal (though indeed it was not), Otanes continued his war; and to bring Erona to a compelled yielding, sent her one day word that the next morrow he would, before the walls of her town, strike off Antiphilus's head, if she yielded not to his desire.

Then, lo, was Cupid's work well seen; for he had brought this miserable princess to such a case as she had love against love. For if she loved him (as unmeasurably she did), then could she condescend to no other; again, if she loved him, then must she save his life; which two things were impossible to be joined together. But the matchless courage of those two princes prevented him, and preserved her; for the same night, with a desperate camisado,° they pierced into the midst of his army where Otanes, valiantly defending himself, was by Pyrocles slain, and Antiphilus by Musidorus rescued. Plangus, seeing no other remedy, conveyed in safety to her country the fair Artaxia, now queen of Persia, who, with the extremest lamentations could issue out of a woman's mouth, testified to the world her new greatness did no way comfort her in respect of her brother's loss; whom she studied all means possible to revenge upon every one of the occasioners.

But thus was Antiphilus redeemed, and (though against the consent of all the Lydian nobility) married to Erona. In which case the two Greek princes left them, being called away by one of the notablest adventures in the world. But the vindicative° Cupid, who had given Erona only so much time of sweetness as to make the miseries more cruel that should fall upon her, had turned Antiphilus's heart while he was Otanes' prisoner quite from her to queen Artaxia; insomuch that, longing to have the great crown of Persia on his head and, like a base man suddenly advanced, having no scope of his insolence, made Artaxia secretly understand (who, he knew, mortally hated Erona) that, if she would reward his vehement loving of her with marriage, he would either by poison or otherwise make away the beautiful Erona, and so, with the might of Persia, easily join those two kingdoms together. The wise Artaxia, that had now a good entrance to her desires, finely handled the vile Antiphilus and brought his heart to such a wicked paradise that one day, under colour of hunting, he enticed abroad the excellent Erona to a place where he had laid some of Artaxia's men in ambushment, and there delivered both himself and her into their hands; who conveying them to their mistress, Antiphilus was justly rewarded of his expected marriage. For she presently gave him into the hands of four valiant gentlemen, who dearly had loved their master Otanes, to be slain with as many deaths as their wit and hate could find out. Which accordingly was done, and he held a whole month together in continual wretchedness, till at last his life left him, rather with continuance of the miserable pain than any violent stroke added unto him. As for Erona, she put her in prison, swearing that, if by that time two year she did not bring Pyrocles and Musidorus to fight with those four (who would prove upon them they had traitorously killed her brother Otanes), she should be publicly burned at a stake; which likewise she should be, if Pyrocles and his fellow were overcome. But if they would take the matter upon them, then should they have a free camp granted them to try the matter in the court of the king of Parthia, because they might hold hers for suspected. This did she hoping that the courage of the two young princes would lead them to so unequal a match, wherein she rested assured their death, and so consequently her revenge, should be fully performed. But Erona, because she might exceed even misery with misery, did not, for all the treachery of Antiphilus (able to make any love a mortal hatred), nor yet for his death (the breaker of all worldly fancies), leave to love Antiphilus and to hate herself since she had lost him. And in respect of his revenge upon those four his murderers (not for her own life, which she was weary of), she desired that Pyrocles and Musidorus might against the day be brought thither, having such confidence in the notable proofs she had seen of their virtue that those four should not be able to withstand them, but suffer death for killing her (in spite of hate) beloved Antiphilus. But whom to send for their search she knew not, when Cupid (I think for some greater mischief) offered this Plangus unto her, who from the day of her first imprisonment was so extremely enamoured of her that he had sought all means how to deliver her. But that being impossible, for the narrow watch was of her, he had (as well he might, being greatly trusted of Artaxia) conference with Erona; and, although she would promise no affection in reward (which was finished absolutely in Antiphilus), yet he took upon him the quest of those two heroical princes who, in this mean time, had done such famous acts that all Asia was full of their histories. But he, having travelled a whole year after them, and still hearing their doings notably recounted, yet could never (being stayed by many misadventures) fully overtake them; but was newly come into Egypt after they had shipped themselves thence for Greece; and into Greece likewise followed, taking this country in his way because mariners had told him such a ship had touched upon the south part of Peloponnesus, where it was my hap to hear him make the pitifullest lamentation that ever before came into mine ears. Neither could the wise Boulon (who had found him making the like doleful complaints, as his mind otherwise occupied led him contrary to these woods) anything mitigate his agonies; but, as he told us (having likewise at our request recounted the full story of those two rare princes), his purpose was to go into Thessalia and Macedon where, if he cannot hear of them, he will return into Persia, and either find some way to preserve Erona or burn at the stake with her.'

Great was the compassion Cleophila and Dorus conceived of the queen Erona's danger—which was the first enterprise they had ever entered into; and therefore (besides their noble humanity) they were loath their own worthy work should be spoiled. Therefore, considering they had almost a year of time to succour her, they resolved as soon as this their present action (which had taken full possession of all their desires) were brought to any good point they would forthwith take in hand that journey; neither should they need in the meantime anything reveal themselves to Plangus (who, though unwittingly, had now done his errand). To which they thought themselves in honour bound, since Artaxia laid treason to their charge. But how that fancy was stopped shall be after told.

Now Dorus desired Histor to repeat the lamentable song he first spake of; and Histor was ready to do it when out starts old Geron and said it was very undecent° a young man's tongue should possess so much time, and that age should become an auditor. And therefore, bending himself to another young shepherd named Philisides° who neither had danced nor sung with them, and had all this time lain upon the ground at the foot of a cypress tree, leaning upon his elbow, with so deep a melancholy that his senses carried to his mind no delight from any of their objects, he strake him upon the shoulder with a right old man's grace that will seem livelier than his age will afford him; and thus began his eclogue unto him:

Geron   Philisides   Histor

Geron. Up, up, Philisides, let sorrows go,
  Who yields to woe doth but increase his smart.
  Do not thy heart to plaintful custom bring,
  But let us sing, sweet tunes do passions ease,
  An old man hear, who would thy fancies raise.

Philisides. Who minds to please the mind drowned in annoys
  With outward joys, which inly cannot sink,
  As well may think with oil to cool the fire;
  Or with desire to make such foe a friend,
  Who doth his soul to endless malice bend.   10

Geron. Yet sure an end to each thing time doth give,
  Though woes now live, at length thy woes must die.
  Then virtue try, if she can work in thee
  That which we see in many time hath wrought,
  And weakest hearts to constant temper brought.

Philisides. Who ever taught a skill-less man to teach,
  Or stop a breach, that never cannon saw?
  Sweet virtue's law bars not a causeful moan.
  Time shall in one my life and sorrows end,
  And me perchance your constant temper lend.   20

Geron. What can amend where physic is refused?
  The wits abused with will no counsel take.
  Yet for my sake discover us thy grief.
  Oft comes relief when most we seem in trap.
  The stars thy state, fortune may change thy hap.

Philisides. If fortune's lap became my dwelling place,
  And all the stars conspired to my good,
  Still were I one, this still should be my case,
  Ruin's relic,° care's web, and sorrow's food;
  Since she, fair fierce, to such a state me calls,   30
  Whose wit the stars, whose fortune fortune thralls.

Geron. Alas, what falls are fall'n unto thy mind
  That there where thou confessed thy mischief lies
  Thy wit dost use still still more harms to find?
  Whom wit makes vain, or blinded with his eyes,
  What counsel can prevail, or light give light,
  Since all his force against himself he tries?
  Then each conceit that enters in by sight
  Is made forsooth a jurat of his woes:
  Earth, sea, air, fire, heav'n, hell, and ghastly sprite.   40
  Then cries to senseless things which neither knows
  What aileth thee, and if they knew thy mind
  Would scorn in man (their king) such feeble shows.
  Rebel, rebel, in golden fetters bind
  This tyrant love; or rather do suppress
  Those rebel thoughts which are thy slaves by kind.
  Let not a glitt'ring name thy fancy dress
  In painted clothes, because they call it love.
  There is no hate that can thee more oppress.
  Begin (and half the work is done) to prove   50
  By raising up, upon thyself to stand;
  And think she is a she that doth thee move.
  He water ploughs, and soweth in the sand,°
  And hopes the flick'ring wind with net to hold,
  Who hath his hopes laid up in woman's hand.
  What man is he that hath his freedom sold?
  Is he a manlike man that doth not know man
  Hath power that sex with bridle to withhold?
  A fickle sex, and true in trust to no man;
  A servant sex, soon proud if they be coyed;   60
  And to conclude, thy mistress is a woman.

Histor. Those words did once the loveliest shepherd° use
    That erst I knew, and with most plainful muse;
    Yet not of women judging, as he said,
    But forced with rage, his rage on them upbraid.

Philisides. O gods, how long this old fool hath annoyed
    My wearied ears! O gods, yet grant me this,
    That soon the world of his false tongue be void.
    O noble age who place their only bliss
    In being heard until the hearer die,
    Utt'ring a serpent's mind with serpent's hiss! 70
    Then who will hear a well authorized lie
    (And patience hath), let him go learn of him
    What swarms of virtues did in his youth fly
    Such hearts of brass, wise heads, and garments trim
    Were in his days: which heard, one nothing hears,
    If from his words the falsehood he do skim.
    And herein most their folly vain appears,
    That since they still allege, *When they were young*,
    It shows they fetch their wit from youthful years. 80
    Like beast for sacrifice where, save the tongue
    And belly, naught is left; such sure is he,
    This 'live-dead man in this old dungeon flung.
    Old houses are thrown down for new we see;
    The oldest rams are culled from the flock;
    No man doth wish his horse should aged be;
    The ancient oak well makes a fired block;
    Old men themselves do love young wives to choose;
    Only fond youth admires a rotten stock.
    Who once a white long beard well handle does 90
    (As his beard him, not he his beard, did bear),
    Though cradle-witted, must not honour lose.
    O when will men leave off to judge by hair,
    And think them old that have the oldest mind,
    With virtue fraught and full of holy fear?

Geron. If that thy face were hid, or I were blind,
    I yet should know a young man speaketh now,
    Such wand'ring reasons in thy speech I find.
    He is a beast that beast's use will allow
    For proof of man who, sprung of heav'nly fire, 100
    Hath strongest soul when most his reins do bow.

But fondlings fond know not your own desire,
Loath to die young, and then you must be old,
Fondly blame that to which yourselves aspire.
But this light choler that doth make you bold,
Rather to wrong than unto just defence,
Is passed with me, my blood is waxen cold.
Thy words, though full of malapert° offence,
I weigh them not, but still will thee advise
How thou from foolish love mayst purge thy sense   110
First, think they err that think them gaily wise
Who well can set a passion out to show;
Such sight have they that see with goggling eyes.
Passion bears high when puffing wit doth blow,
But is indeed a toy; if not a toy,
True cause of ills, and cause of causeless woe.
If once thou mayst that fancy gloss destroy
Within thyself, thou soon wilt be ashamed
To be a player of thine own annoy.
Then let thy mind with better books be tamed,   120
Seek to espy her faults as well as praise,
And let thine eyes to other sports° be framed.
In hunting fearful beasts do spend some days,
Or catch the birds with pitfalls, or with lime,
Or train the fox that trains so crafty lays.
Lie but to sleep, and in the early prime
Seek skill of herbs in hills, haunt brooks near night,
And try with bait how fish will bite sometime.
Go graft again, and seek to graft them right,
Those pleasant plants, those sweet and fruitful trees,   130
Which both the palate and the eyes delight.
Cherish the hives of wisely painful bees;
Let special care upon thy flock be stayed;
Such active mind but seldom passion sees.

Philisides. Hath any man heard what this old man said?
Truly, not I who did my thoughts engage
Where all my pains one look of hers hath paid.

Histor. Thus may you see how youth esteemeth age,
And never hath thereof arightly deemed,
While hot desires do reign in fancy's rage,   140
Till age itself do make itself esteemed.

Geron was even out of countenance, finding the words he thought
were so wise win so little reputation at this young man's hands; and
therefore, sometimes looking upon an old acquaintance of his called
Mastix, one of the repiningest fellows in the world, and that beheld
nobody but with a mind of mislike (saying still the world was amiss, but
how it should be amended he knew not), sometimes casting his eyes to
the ground, even ashamed to see his grey hairs despised, at last he spied
his two dogs, whereof the elder was called Melampus, and the younger
Lælaps (indeed the jewels he ever had with him), one brawling with the
other. Which occasion he took to restore himself to his countenance, and
rating Melampus, he began to speak to his dogs as if in them a man
should find more obedience than in unbridled young men:

Geron   Mastix

Geron. Down, down, Melampus; what? your fellow bite?
   I set you o'er the flock I dearly love
   Them to defend, not with yourselves to fight.
   Do you not think this will the wolves remove
   From former fear they had of your good minds,
   When they shall such divided weakness prove?
   What if Lælaps a better morsel finds
   Than thou erst knew? Rather take part with him
   Than jarl: lo, lo, even these how envy blinds!
   And thou, Lælaps, let not pride make thee brim°   10
   Because thou hast thy fellow overgone,
   But thank the cause, thou seest, when he is dim.
   Here, Lælaps, here; indeed, against the foen
   Of my good sheep thou never truce-time took:
   Be as thou art, but be with mine at one.
   For though Melampus like a wolf do look
   (For age doth make him of a wolvish hue),
   Yet have I seen when well a wolf he shook.
   Fool that I am that with my dogs speak Grew.°
   Come narr, good Mastix, 'tis now full tway° score   20
   Of years (alas) since I good Mastix knew.
   Thou heardst e'en now a young man sneb° me sore
   Because I red° him as I would my son.
   Youth will have will, age must to age therefore.

Mastix. What marvel if in youth such faults be done,
   Since that we see our saddest° shepherds out
   Who have their lesson so long time begun?

Quickly secure, and easily in doubt,
Either asleep be all if naught assail,
Or all abroad if but a cub start out.   30
We shepherds are like them that under sail
Do speak high words when all the coast is clear,
Yet to a passenger will bonnet vail.
'I con thee thank'° to whom thy dogs be dear,
But commonly like curs we them entreat,
Save when great need of them perforce appear,
Then him we kiss whom late before we beat
With such intemperance, that each way grows
Hate of the first, contempt of later feat.
And such discord 'twixt greatest shepherds flows,   40
That sport it is to see with how great art
By justice' work they their own faults disclose;
Like busy boys to win their tutor's heart,
One saith he mocks; the other saith he plays;
The third his lesson missed; till all do smart.
As for the rest, how shepherds spend their days
At blow point, hot cockles, or else at keels,°
While, 'Let us pass our time', each shepherd says.
So small account of time the shepherd feels,
And doth not feel that life is naught but time,   50
And when that time is past, death holds his heels.
To age thus do they draw their youthful prime,
Knowing no more than what poor trial shows,
As fish sure trial hath of muddy slime.
This pattern good unto our children goes,
For what they see their parents love or hate
Their first caught sense prefers to teacher's blows.
These cocklings cockered° we bewail too late
When that we see our offspring gaily bent,
Women manwood,° and men effeminate.   60

Geron. Fie, man; fie, man; what words hath thy tongue lent?
Yet thou art mickle warse than ere was I,
Thy too much zeal I fear thy brain hath spent.
We oft are angrier with the feeble fly
For business where it pertains him not
Than with the pois'nous toads that quiet lie.
I pray thee what hath e'er the parrot got,
And yet they say he talks in great men's bow'rs?

A cage (gilded perchance) is all his lot.
Who off his tongue the liquor gladly pours   70
A good fool called with pain perhaps may be,
But e'en for that shall suffer mighty lours.
Let swan's example° sicker serve for thee,
Who once all birds in sweetly singing passed,
But now to silence turned his minstrelsy.
For he would sing, but others were defaced:
The peacock's pride, the pie's pilled flattery,
Cormorant's glut, kite's spoil, kingfisher's waste,
The falcon's fierceness, sparrow's lechery,
The cuckoo's shame, the goose's good intent,   80
E'en turtle touched he with hypocrisy.
And worse of other more; till by assent
Of all the birds, but namely those were grieved,
Of fowls there called was a parliament.
There was the swan of dignity deprived,
And statute made he never should have voice,
Since when, I think, he hath in silence lived.
I warn thee therefore (since thou mayst have choice)
Let not thy tongue become a fiery match,
No sword so bites as that ill tool annoys.   90
Let our unpartial eyes a little watch
Our own demean, and soon we wonder shall
That, hunting faults, ourselves we did not catch.
Into our minds let us a little fall,
And we shall find more spots than leopard's skin.
Then who makes us such judges over all?
But farewell now, thy fault is no great sin,
Come, come, my curs, 'tis late, I will go in.

And away with his dogs straight he went, as if he would be sure to have
the last word, all the assembly laughing at the lustiness of the old fellow,
who departed muttering to himself he had seen more in his days than
twenty of them. But as he went out, Dorus seeing a lute lying under the
princess Pamela's feet, glad to have such an errand to approach her, he
came, but came with a dismayed grace, all his blood stirred betwixt fear
and desire; and playing upon it with such sweetness as everybody
wondered to see such skill in a shepherd, he sang unto it with a sorrowing
voice these elegiac verses:

– – – – – ∪ ∪ – ∪ ∪ – ∪ ∪ – –
– – – ∪ ∪ – – ∪ ∪ – ∪ ∪ –

Dorus. Fortune, Nature, Love, long have contended about me,
    Which should most miseries cast on a worm that I am.
Fortune thus gan say: 'Misery and misfortune is all one,
    And of misfortune, Fortune hath only the gift.
With strong foes on land, on seas with contrary tempests,
    Still do I cross this wretch, what so he taketh in hand.'
'Tush, tush', said Nature, 'this is all but a trifle, a man's self
    Gives haps or mishaps, e'en as he ord'reth his heart.
But so his humour I frame, in a mould of choler adusted,°
    That the delights of life shall be to him dolorous.'   10
Love smiled, and thus said: 'Want joined to desire is
    unhappy.
But if he naught do desire, what can Heraclitus° ail?
None but I works by desire; by desire have I kindled in his
    soul
Infernal agonies unto a beauty divine,
Where thou, poor Nature, left'st all thy due glory to Fortune.
    Her virtue is sovereign, Fortune a vassal of hers.'
Nature abashed went back; Fortune blushed, yet she replied
    thus:
'And e'en in that love shall I reserve him a spite.'
Thus, thus, alas! woeful in nature, unhappy by fortune,
    But most wretched I am now love awakes my desire.

Nota°

The rules observed in these English measured verses be these:

Consonant before consonant always long, except a mute and a liquid (as *rēfrain*), such indifferent.

Single consonants commonly short, but such as have a double sound (as *lăck, wĭll, tĭll*) or such as the vowel before doth produce long (as *hāte, debāte*).

Vowel before vowel or diphthong before vowel always short, except such an exclamation as *ōh*; else the diphthongs always long and the single vowels short.

Because our tongue being full of consonants and monosyllables, the vowel slides away quicklier than in Greek or Latin, which be full of vowels and long words. Yet are such vowels long as the pronunciation makes long (as *glōry, lādy*), and such like as seem to have a diphthong sound (as *shōw, blōw, dīe, high*).

Elisions, when one vowel meets with another, used indifferently as the advantage of the verse best serves; for so in our ordinary speech we do (for as well we say *thou art* as *th'art*), and like scope doth Petrarch take to himself sometimes to use apostrophe, sometimes not.

For the words derived out of Latin and other languages, they are measured as they are denizened in English and not as before they came over sea (for we say not *fortŭnate* though the Latin say *fortūna*, nor *usŭry* but *ūsury* in the first); so our language hath a special gift in altering them and making them our own.

Some words especially short.

Particles used now long, now short (as *bŭt, ŏr, nŏr, ŏn, tŏ*).

Some words, as they have diverse pronunciations, to be written diversely, (as some say *thŏugh*, some pronounce it *thō*).

As for *wĕe, thĕe, shĕe*, though they may seem to be a double vowel by the wrong orthography, be here short, being indeed no other than the Greek iota; and the like of our *o*, which some write double in this word *dŏo*.

Dorus, when he had sung this, having had all the while a free beholding of the fair Pamela (who could well have spared such honour, and defended the assault he gave unto her face with bringing a fair stain of shamefastness unto it), let fall his arms and remained so fastened in his thoughts as if Pamela had grafted him there to grow in continual imagination. But Cleophila espying it, and fearing he should too much forget himself, she came to him and took out of his hand the lute; and laying fast hold of Philoclea's face with her eyes, she sang these sapphics,° speaking as it were to her own hope:

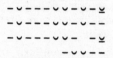

Cleophila. If mine eyes can speak to do hearty errand,
　　　　Or mine eyes' language she do hap to judge of,
　　　　So that eyes' message be of her received,
　　　　　　　　Hope, we do live yet.

　　　　But if eyes fail then, when I most do need them,
　　　　Or if eyes' language be not unto her known,
　　　　So that eyes' message do return rejected,
　　　　　　　　Hope, we do both die.

　　　　Yet dying, and dead, do we sing her honour;
　　　　So become our tombs monuments of her praise;   10
　　　　So becomes our loss the triumph of her gain;
　　　　　　　　Hers be the glory.

　　　　If the senseless spheres do yet hold a music,
　　　　If the swan's sweet voice be not heard, but at death,
　　　　If the mute timber when it hath the life lost,
　　　　　　　　Yieldeth a lute's tune,

Are then human minds privileged so meanly
As that hateful death can abridge them of power
With the voice of truth to record to all worlds
    That we be her spoils?   20

Thus not ending, ends the due praise of her praise;
Fleshly veil consumes, but a soul hath his life,
Which is held in love; love it is that hath joined
    Life to this our soul.

But if eyes can speak to do hearty errand,
Or mine eyes' language she do hap to judge of,
So that eyes' message be of her received,
    Hope we do live yet.

Great was the pleasure of Basilius, and greater would have been Gynecia's but that she found too well it was intended to her daughter. As for Philoclea, she was sweetly ravished withal; when Dorus, desiring in a secret manner to speak so of their cases as perchance the parties intended might take some light of it, making low reverence to Cleophila, he began this provoking song in hexameter verse unto her. Whereunto she, soon finding whither his words were directed (in like tune and like verse), answered as followeth:

Dorus   Cleophila

   – ◡ ◡ – ◡ ◡ – ◡ ◡ – – – ◡ ◡ – –

Dorus. Lady, reserved by the heav'ns to do pastors' company
    honour,
  Joining your sweet voice to the rural muse of a desert,
  Here you fully do find this strange operation of love,
  How to the woods love runs as well as rides to the palace,
  Neither he bears reverence to a prince nor pity to beggar,
  But (like a point in midst of a circle) is still of a nearness,
  All to a lesson he draws, nor hills nor caves can avoid him.

Cleophila: Worthy shepherd, by my song to myself all favour is
    happened,
  That to the sacred muse my annoys somewhat be revealed,
  Sacred muse, who in one contains what nine do in all them.   10
  But O, happy be you which safe from fiery reflection
  Of Phoebus' violence in shade of stately cypress tree,
  Or pleasant myrtle, may teach th'unfortunate Echo
  In these woods to resound the renowned name of a goddess.

Happy be you that may to the saint, your only Idea
(Although simply attired), your manly affection utter.
Happy be those mishaps which, justly proportion holding,
Give right sound to the ears, and enter aright to the
    judgement;
But wretched be the souls which, veiled in a contrary subject,
How much more we do love, so the less our loves be believed.   20
What skill serveth a sore of a wrong infirmity judged?
What can justice avail to a man that tells not his own case?
You, though fears do abash, in you still possible hopes be:
Nature against we do seem to rebel, seem fools in a vain suit.
But so unheard, condemned, kept thence we do seek to abide
    in,
Self-lost and wand'ring, banished that place we do come
    from,
What mean is there, alas, we can hope our loss to recover?
What place is there left we may hope our woes to recomfort?
Unto the heav'ns? our wings be too short, th'earth thinks us a
    burden;
Air, we do still with sighs increase; to the fire? we do want   30
    none.
And yet his outward heat our tears would quench, but an
    inward
Fire no liquor can cool: Neptune's seat would be dried up
    there.
Happy shepherd, with thanks to the gods, still think to be
    thankful,
That to thy advancement their wisdoms have thee abased.

Dorus: Unto the gods with a thankful heart all thanks I do
    render,
    That to my advancement their wisdoms have me abased.
But yet, alas! O but yet, alas! our haps be but hard haps,
Which must frame contempt to the fittest purchase of honour.
Well may a pastor plain, but alas his plaints be not esteemed.
Silly shepherd's poor pipe, when his harsh sound testifies our   40
    woes.
Into the fair looker-on, pastime, not passion, enters.
And to the woods or brooks, who do make such dreary recital
What be the pangs they bear, and whence those pangs be
    derived,

Pleased to receive that name by rebounding answer of Echo,
And hope thereby to ease their inward horrible anguish,
Then shall those things ease their inward horrible anguish
When trees dance to the pipe, and swift streams stay by the
music,
Or when an echo begins unmoved to sing them a love song.
Say then what vantage do we get by the trade of a pastor?
(Since no estates be so base, but love vouchsafeth his arrow, 50
Since no refuge doth serve from wounds we do carry about
us,
Since outward pleasures be but halting helps to decayed
souls)
Save that daily we may discern what fire we do burn in.
Far more happy be you, whose greatness gets a free access,
Whose fair bodily gifts are framed most lovely to each eye.
Virtue you have, of virtue you have left proofs to the whole
world,
And virtue is grateful with beauty and richess adorned,
Neither doubt you a whit, time will your passion utter.
Hardly remains fire hid where skill is bent to the hiding,
But in a mind that would his flames should not be repressed, 60
Nature worketh enough with a small help for the revealing.
Give therefore to the muse great praise in whose very likeness
You do approach to the fruit your only desires be to gather.

Cleophila. First shall fertile grounds not yield increase of a good
seed;
First the rivers shall cease to repay their floods to the ocean;
First may a trusty greyhound transform himself to a tiger;
First shall virtue be vice, and beauty be counted a blemish,
Ere that I leave with song of praise her praise to solemnize,
Her praise, whence to the world all praise had his only
beginning:
But yet well I do find each man most wise in his own case. 70
None can speak of a wound with skill, if he have not a wound
felt.°
Great to thee my estate seems, thy estate is blest by my
judgement:
And yet neither of us great or blest deemeth his own self.
For yet (weigh this, alas!) great is not great to a greater.
What judge you doth a hillock show by the lofty Olympus?

Such this small greatness doth seem compared to the greatest.
When cedars to the ground be oppressed by the weight of an
    emmet,°
Or when a rich ruby's just price be the worth of a walnut,
Or to the sun for wonders seem small sparks of a candle:
Then by my high cedar, rich ruby, and only shining sun,   80
Virtue, richess, beauties of mine shall great be reputed.
O no, no, hardy shepherd, worth can never enter a title,
Where proofs justly do teach, thus matched, such worth to be
    naught worth.
Let not a puppet abuse thy sprite, kings' crowns do not help
    them
From the cruel headache, nor shoes of gold do the gout heal,
And precious couches full oft are shaked with a fever.
If then a bodily evil in a bodily gloss be not hidden,
Shall such morning dews be an ease to the heat of a love's
    fire?

Dorus. O glitt'ring miseries of man, if this be the fortune
Of those fortune lulls, so small rest rests in a kingdom.   90
What marvel though a prince transform himself to a pastor?
Come from marble bowers, many times the gay harbour of
    anguish,
Unto a silly cabin, though weak, yet stronger against woes.
Now by thy words I begin, most famous lady, to gather
Comfort into my soul. I do find, I do find, what a blessing
Is chanced to my life, that from such muddy abundance
Of carking agonies (to estates which still be adherent)
Destiny keeps me aloof. For if all thy estate to thy virtue
Joined, by thy beauty adorned, be no means these griefs to
    abolish;
If neither by that help, thou canst climb up to thy fancy,   100
Nor yet, fancy so dressed, do receive more plausible hearing;
Then do I think, indeed, that better it is to be private
In sorrow's torments than, tied to the pomps of a palace,
Nurse inward maladies, which have not scope to be breathed
    out,
But perforce digest all bitter juices of horror
In silence, from a man's own self with company robbed.
Better yet do I live, that though by my thoughts I be plunged
Into my life's bondage, yet may disburden a passion

(Oppressed with ruinous conceits) by the help of an outcry:

Not limited to a whisp'ring note, the lament of a courtier,   110

But sometimes to the woods, sometimes to the heavens, do
  decipher,

With bold clamour unheard, unmarked, what I seek, what I
  suffer:

And when I meet these trees,° in the earth's fair livery
  clothed,

Ease I do feel (such ease as falls to one wholly diseased)

For that I find in them part of my estate represented.

   A   B

Laurel shows what I seek, by the myrrh is showed   A Victory
  how I seek it,   B Lamenta-
                                                            tion
   C   C Quietness
                                                          D Love
Olive paints me the peace that I must aspire to by   E Refusal
  conquest:
                                                          F Death
   D

Myrtle makes my request, my request is crowned with
      E

  a willow.
  F

Cypress promiseth help, but a help where comes no
  recomfort.

Sweet juniper saith this, though I burn, yet I burn in a sweet   120
  fire.

Yew doth make me bethink what kind of bow the boy holdeth

Which shoots strongly without any noise and deadly without
  smart.

Fir trees great and green, fixed on a high hill but a barren,

Like to my noble thoughts, still new, well placed, to me
  fruitless.

Fig that yields most pleasant fruit, his shadow is hurtful,

Thus be her gifts most sweet, thus more danger to be near
  her,

But in a palm when I mark how he doth rise under a burden,

And may I not (say I then) get up though griefs be so
  weighty?

Pine is a mast to a ship, to my ship shall hope for a mast
  serve?

Pine is high, hope is as high; sharp-leaved, sharp yet be my   130
  hope's buds.

Elm embraced by a vine, embracing fancy reviveth.
Poplar changeth his hue from a rising sun to a setting:
Thus to my sun do I yield, such looks her beams do afford
  me.
Old aged oak cut down, of new works serves to the building:
So my desires, by my fear cut down, be the frames of her
  honour.
Ash makes spears which shields do resist, her force no
  repulse takes:
Palms do rejoice to be joined by the match of a male to a
  female,
And shall sensive things be so senseless as to resist sense?
Thus be my thoughts dispersed, thus thinking nurseth a
  thinking,
Thus both trees and each thing else be the books of a fancy.   140
But to the cedar, queen of woods, when I lift my beteared
  eyes,
Then do I shape to myself that form which reigns so within
  me,
And think there she do dwell and hear what plaints I do utter:
When that noble top doth nod, I believe she salutes me;
When by the wind it maketh a noise, I do think she doth
  answer.
Then kneeling to the ground, oft thus do I speak to that
  image:
'Only jewel, O only jewel, which only deservest
That men's hearts be thy seat and endless fame be thy
  servant,
O descend for a while from this great height to behold me,
But naught else do behold (else is naught worth the   150
  beholding)
Save what a work by thyself is wrought: and since I am
  altered
Thus by thy work, disdain not that which is by thyself done.
In mean caves oft treasure abides, to an hostry° a king comes.
And so behind foul clouds full oft fair stars do lie hidden.'

Cleophila. Hardy shepherd, such as thy merits, such may be her
  insight
Justly to grant thy reward, such envy I bear to thy fortune.
But to myself what wish can I make for a salve to my sorrows,

Whom both nature seems to debar from means to be helped,
And if a mean were found, fortune th'whole course of it
hinders.
Thus plagued how can I frame to my sore any hope of   160
amendment?
Whence may I show to my mind any light of a possible
escape?
Bound, and bound by so noble bands as loath to be unbound,
Gaoler I am to myself, prison and prisoner to mine own self.
Yet be my hopes thus placed, here fixed lives my recomfort,
That that dear diamond, where wisdom holdeth a sure seat,
Whose force had such force so to transform, nay to reform
me,
Will at length perceive these flames by her beams to be
kindled,
And will pity the wound festered so strangely within me.
O be it so, grant such an event, O gods, that event give.
And for a sure sacrifice I do daily oblation offer   170
Of my own heart, where thoughts be the temple, sight is an
altar.
But cease, worthy shepherd, now cease we to weary the
hearers
With moanful melodies, for enough our griefs be revealed,
If by the parties meant our meanings rightly be marked,
And sorrows do require some respite unto the senses.

What exclaiming praises Basilius gave first to Cleophila's song, and
now to this eclogue, any man may guess that knows love is better than a
pair of spectacles to make everything seem greater which is seen through
it; and then is it never tongue-tied where fit commendation (whereof
womankind is so lickerous) is offered unto it. But the wasting of the
torches served as a watch unto them to make them see the time's waste.
And therefore the duke, though unwilling, rase from his seat (which he
thought excellently settled of the one side), and considering Cleophila's
late hurt, persuaded her to take that far spent night's rest. And so of all
sides they went to recommend themselves to the elder brother of Death.

Here ends the first eclogues of the
Countess of Pembroke's Arcadia.

THE SECOND ECLOGUES

THE rude tumult of the Phagonians gave occasion to the honest shepherds to begin their pastorals this day with a dance which they called the skirmish betwixt Reason and Passion. For seven shepherds, which were named the reasonable shepherds, joined themselves, four of them making a square and the other two going a little wide of either side, like wings for the main battle, and the seventh man foremost, like the forlorn hope,° to begin the skirmish. In like order came out the seven appassionate shepherds, all keeping the pace of their foot by their voice and sundry consorted instruments they held in their arms. And first the foremost of the reasonable side began to sing:

> Thou rebel vile, come, to thy master yield.

And the other that met with him answered:

> No tyrant, no; mine, mine shall be the field.

Reason. Can Reason then a tyrant counted be?
Passion. If Reason will that Passions be not free.
R.   But Reason will that Reason govern most.
P.   And Passion will that Passion rule the roast.
R.   Your will is will; but Reason reason is.
P.   Will hath his will when Reason's will doth miss.
R.   Whom Passion leads unto his death is bent.
P.   And let him die, so that he die content.   10
R.   By nature you to Reason faith have sworn.
P.   Not so, but fellowlike together born.
R.   Who Passion doth ensue lives in annoy.
P.   Who Passion doth forsake lives void of joy.
R.   Passion is blind, and treads an unknown trace.
P.   Reason hath eyes to see his own ill case.

Then, as they approached nearer, the two of Reason's side, as if they shot at the other, thus sang:

R.   Dare Passions then abide in Reason's light?
P.   And is not Reason dimmed with Passion's might?
R.   O foolish thing which glory dost destroy!
P.   O glorious title of a foolish toy!   20
R.   Weakness you are, dare you with our strength fight?
P.   Because our weakness weak'neth all your might.
R.   O sacred Reason, help our virtuous toils!

P.   O Passion, pass on feeble Reason's spoils!
R.   We with ourselves abide a daily strife.
P.   We gladly use the sweetness of our life.
R.   But yet our strife sure peace in end doth breed.
P.   We now have peace, your peace we do not need.

Then did the two square battles meet and, instead of fighting, embrace
one another, singing thus:

R.   We are too strong; but Reason seeks not blood.
P.   Who be too weak do feign they be too good.   30
R.   Though we cannot o'ercome, our cause is just.
P.   Let us o'ercome, and let us be unjust.
R.   Yet Passion, yield at length to Reason's stroke.
P.   What shall we win by taking Reason's yoke?
R.   The joys you have shall be made permanent.
P.   But so we shall with grief learn to repent.
R.   Repent indeed, but that shall be your bliss.
P.   How know we that, since present joys we miss?
R.   You know it not; of Reason therefore know it.
P.   No Reason yet had ever skill to show it.   40
R.P. Then let us both to heav'nly rules give place,
        Which Passions kill, and Reason do deface.

Then embraced they one another, and came to the duke who framed his
praises of them according to Cleophila's liking, that sat at that time
betwixt the duke and duchess, as if she had had her choice of drowning or
burning. But her two unrestrained parts, the mind and eye, had their free
convoy to the delicate Philoclea, whose look was not short in well
requiting it; although she knew it was a hateful sight to the marking eye of
her jealous mother. But Dicus, that had in this time taken a great liking of
Dorus for the good parts he found above his age in him, had a delight to
taste the fruits of his wit—though in a subject which he himself most
of all other despised; and so entered into speech with him in the manner
of this following eclogue:

Dicus   Dorus

Dicus. Dorus, tell me,° where is thy wonted motion
        To make these woods resound thy lamentation?
        Thy saint is dead, or dead is thy devotion.
    For who doth hold his love in estimation,
        To witness that he thinks his thoughts delicious,
        Seeks to make each thing badge of his sweet passion.

Dorus. But what doth make thee, Dicus, so suspicious
    Of my due faith, which needs must be immutable?
    Who others' virtue doubt, themselves are vicious.
  Not so; although my metal were most mutable,   10
    Her beams have wrought therein most sure impression:
    To such a force soon change were nothing suitable.

Dicus. The heart well set doth never shun confession:
    If noble be thy bands, make them notorious:
    Silence doth seem the mask of base oppression.
  Who glories in his love doth make love glorious:
    But who doth fear, or bideth muett° wilfully,
    Shows guilty heart doth deem his state opprobrious.
  Thou, then, that fram'st both words and voice most skilfully,
    Yield to our ears a sweet and sound relation,   20
    If love took thee by force, or caught thee guilefully.

Dorus. If sunny beams shame heav'nly habitation;
    If three-leaved grass seem to the sheep unsavoury,
    Then base and sour is love's most high vocation.
  Or if sheep's cries can help the sun's own bravery,
    Then may I hope my pipe may have ability
    To help her praise, who decks me in her slavery.
  No, no; no words ennoble self-nobility.
    As for your doubts, her voice was it deceived me,
    Her eyes the force beyond my possibility.   30

Dicus. Thy words well voiced, well graced, had almost heaved
    me
    Quite from myself to love love's contemplation;
    Till of these thoughts thy sudden end bereaved me.
  Go on, therefore, and tell us by what fashion
    In thy own proof he gets so strange possession;
    And how possessed, he strengthens his invasion?

Dorus. Sight is his root, in thought is his progression,
    His childhood wonder, prenticeship attention,
    His youth delight, his age the soul's oppression;
  Doubt is his sleep, he waketh in invention;   40
    Fancy his food, his clothing is of carefulness;
    Beauty his book, his play lovers' dissension;
  His eyes are curious search, but veiled with warefulness;
    His wings desire oft clipped with desperation;

Largess his hands could never skill of sparefulness.
But how he doth by might or by persuasion
    To conquer, and his conquest how to ratify,
    Experience doubts, and schools hold disputation.

Dicus. But so thy sheep may thy good wishes satisfy
    With large increase, and wool of fine perfection,   50
    So she thy love, her eyes thy eyes may gratify,
As thou wilt give our souls a dear refection,
    By telling how she was, how now she framed is
    To help or hurt in thee her own infection.

Dorus. Blest be the name wherewith my mistress named is;
    Whose wounds are salves, whose yokes please more than
        pleasure doth:
    Her stains are beams, virtue the fault she blamed is.
The heart, eye, ear here only find his treasure doth:
    All numb'ring arts her endless graces number not:
    Time, place, life, wit scarcely her rare gifts measure doth.   60
Is she in rage? So is the sun in summer hot,
    Yet harvest brings. Doth she, alas, absent herself?
    The sun is hid; his kindly shadows cumber not.
But when to give some grace she doth content herself,
    O then it shines; then are the heav'ns distributed,
    And Venus seems, to make up her, she spent herself.
Thus then (I say) my mischiefs have contributed
    A greater good by her divine reflection;
    My harms to me, my bliss to her attributed.
Thus she is framed: her eyes are my direction;   70
    Her love my life; her anger my instruction;
    Lastly, what so she be, that's my protection.

Dicus. Thy safety sure is wrapped in destruction;
    For that construction° thy own words do bear.
    A man to fear a woman's moody eye,
Or reason lie a slave to servile sense,
    There seek defence where weakness is the force,
    Is late remorse in folly dearly bought.

Dorus. If I had thought to hear blasphemous words,
    My breast to swords, my soul to hell have sold   80
    I sooner would than thus my ears defile
With words so vile, which viler breath doth breed.

O herds, take heed! for I a wolf have found
Who, hunting round the strongest for to kill,
His breast doth fill with earth of others' woe,
And loaden so, pulls down; pulled down, destroys.
O shepherd boys, eschew these tongues of venom
Which do envenom both the soul and senses!
Our best defences are to fly these adders.
O tongues, right ladders made to climb dishonour,   90
Who judge that honour which hath scope to slander!

Dicus. Dorus, you wander far in great reproaches,
    So love encroaches on your charmed reason;
    But it is season for to end our singing,
    Such anger bringing; as for me, my fancy
In sick man's franzy rather takes compassion
    Than rage for rage: rather my wish I send to thee,
    Thou soon may have some help or change of passion.
She oft her looks, the stars her favour, bend to thee:
    Fortune store, Nature health, Love grant persuasion.   100
A quiet mind none but thyself can lend to thee,
    Thus I commend to thee all our former love.

Dorus. Well do I prove error lies oft in zeal;
    Yet is it seal (though error) of true heart.
    Naught could impart such heats to friendly mind.
    But for to find thy words did her disgrace,
    Whose only face the little heaven is,
Which who doth miss his eyes are but delusions,
    Barred from their chiefest object of delightfulness,
    Thrown on this earth the chaos of confusions.   110
As for thy wish to my enraged spitefulness,
    The lovely blow with rare reward, my prayer is
    Thou mayst love her that I may see thy sightfulness.
The quiet mind (whereof myself impairer is,
    As thou dost think) should most of all disquiet me
    Without her love than any mind who fairer is.
Her only cure from surfeit woes can diet me:
    She holds the balance of my contentation:
    Her cleared looks (naught else) in storms can quiet me.
Nay, rather than my ease discontentation   120
    Should breed to her, let me for ay dejected be
    From any joy which might her grief occasion.

With so sweet plagues my happy harms infected be:
  Pain wills me die, yet will of death I mortify;
  For though life irks, in life my loves protected be.
Thus for each change my changeless heart I fortify.

When they had ended to the good pleasing of the assistants,° especially
of Cleophila who never forgat to give due commendation to her friend
Dorus, the more to advance him in his pursuit (although therein he had
brought his matters to a more wished conclusion than yet she knew of),
out starts a jolly younker (his name was Nico) whose tongue had borne a
very itching silence all this while; and having spied one Pas (a mate of his
as mad as himself—both indeed lads to climb any tree in the world), he
bestowed this manner of salutation upon him, and was with like reverence requited:

Nico   Pas   Dicus°

Nico. And are you there, old Pas? In truth I ever thought
  Among us all we should find out some thing of naught.

Pas. And I am here the same, so mote I thrive and thee,
  Despaired in all this flock to find a knave but thee.

Nico. Ah, now I see why thou art in thyself so blind;
  Thy grey hood hides the thing that thou despair'st to find.

Pas. My grey hood is mine own, all be it be but grey,
  Not as the scrip thou stal'st while Dorcas sleeping lay.

Nico. Mine was the scrip; but thou, that seeming rayed° with
    love,
  Didst snatch from Cosma's hand her green ywroughten glove.   10

Pas. Ah fool, so courtiers do. But who did lively skip
  When for a treen-dish stol'n thy father did thee whip?

Nico. Indeed the witch thy dam her crouch° from shoulder
    spread,
  For pilf'ring Lalus' lamb, with crouch to bless thy head.

Pas. My voice the lamb did win, Menalcas was our judge
  Of singing match we made, whence he with shame did
    trudge.

Nico. Couldst thou make Lalus fly? so nightingales avoid
  When with the cawing crows their music is annoyed.

Pas. Nay, like to nightingales the other birds give ear,
  My pipe and song made him both song and pipe forswear.   20

Nico. I think it well; such voice would make one music hate:
   But if I had been there, th'hadst met another mate.

Pas. Another sure, as is a gander from a goose;
   But still when thou dost sing methinks a colt is loose.

Nico. Well aimed, by my hat;° for as thou sangst last day
   The neighbours all did cry, 'Alas, what ass doth bray?'

Pas. But here is Dicus old; let him then speak the word
   To whether with best cause the nymphs fair flow'rs afford.

Nico. Content; but I will lay a wager hereunto,
   That profit may ensue to him that best can do.   30
   I have (and long shall have) a white great nimble cat,
   A king upon a mouse, a strong foe to a rat;
   Fine ears, long tail he hath, with lion's curbed° claw
   Which oft he lifteth up, and stays his lifted paw,
   Deep musing to himself, which after-mewing shows,
   Till with licked beard his eye of fire espy his foes.
   If thou (alas, poor if!) do win, then win thou this;
   And if I better sing, let me thy Cosma kiss.

Pas. Kiss her? Now mayst thou kiss. I have a fitter match:
   A pretty cur it is; his name iwis is Catch,   40
   No ear nor tail he hath, lest they should him disgrace,
   A ruddy hair his coat, with fine long speckled face:
   He never musing stands, but with himself will play,
   Leaping at every fly, and angry with a flea:
   He eft would kill a mouse, but he disdains the fight,
   And makes our home good sport with dancing bolt upright.
   This is my pawn; the prize let Dicus' judgement show:
   Such odds I willing lay; for him and you I know.

Dicus. Sing then my lads, but sing with better vein than yet,
   Or else who singeth worse, my skill will hardly hit.   50

Nico. Who doubts but Pas' fine pipe again will bring
   The ancient praise to Arcad shepherds' skill?
   Pan is not dead since Pas begins to sing.

Pas. Who evermore will love Apollo's quill,
   Since Nico doth to sing so widely gape?
   Nico his place far better furnish will.

Nico. Was this not he who, for Syringa's scape
   Raging in woes, first pastors taught to plain?
   Do you not hear his voice, and see his shape?

Pas. This is not he that failed her to gain,   60
   Which made a bay, made bay a holy tree;
   But this is one that doth his music stain.

Nico. O fauns, O fairies all and do you see
   And suffer such a wrong? A wrong, I trow,
   That Nico must with Pas compared be.

Pas. O nymphs, I tell you news, for Pas you know;
   While I was warbling out your wonted praise,
   Nico would needs with Pas his bagpipe blow.

Nico. If never I did fail your holydays,
   With dances, carols, or with barleybreak,°   70
   Let Pas now know how Nico maketh lays.

Pas. If each day hath been holy for your sake
   Unto my pipe, O nymphs, now help my pipe,
   For Pas well knows what lays can Nico make.

Nico. Alas, how oft I look on cherries ripe
   Methinks I see the lips my Leuca hath,
   And wanting her, my weeping eyes I wipe.

Pas. Alas, when I in spring meet roses rathe,°
   And think from Cosma's sweet red lips I live,
   I leave mine eyes unwiped, my cheeks to bathe.   80

Nico. As I of late near bushes used my sieve,
   I spied a thrush·where she did make her nest;
   That will I take, and to my Leuca give.

Pas. But long have I a sparrow gaily dressed,
   As white as milk, and coming to the call,
   To put it with my hand in Cosma's breast.

Nico. I oft do sue, and Leuca saith I shall;
   But when I did come near with heat and hope,
   She ran away and threw at me a ball.

Pas. Cosma once said she left the wicket ope   90
   For me to come; and so she did. I came,
   But in the place found nothing but a rope.

Nico. When Leuca doth appear the sun for shame
   Doth hide himself; for to himself he says,
   If Leuca live, she darken will my fame.

Pas. When Cosma doth come forth the sun displays
   His utmost light; for well his wit doth know
   Cosma's fair beams emblemish much his rays.

Nico. Leuca to me did yestermorning show
   In perfect light, which could not me deceive,   100
   Her naked leg, more white than whitest snow.

Pas. But yesternight by light I did receive
   From Cosma's eyes, which full in darkness shine,
   I saw her arm where purest lillies cleave.

Nico. She once stark nak'd did bathe a little tine;°
   But still (methought), with beauties from her fell,°
   She did the water wash, and make more fine.

Pas. She once, to cool herself, stood in a well;
   But ever since that well is well besought,
   And for rose-water sold of rarest smell.   110

Nico. To river's bank, being a-walking brought,
   She bid me spy her baby in the brook.
   Alas (said I) this babe doth nurse my thought.

Pas. As in a glass I held she once did look,
   I said my hands well paid her for mine eyes,
   Since in my hands self goodly sight she took.

Nico. O if I had a ladder for the skies,
   I would climb up, and bring a pretty star
   To wear upon her neck that open lies.

Pas. O if I had Apollo's golden car,   120
   I would come down and yield to her my place,
   That (shining now) she then might shine more far.

Nico. Nothing, O Leuca, shall thy fame deface,
   While shepherds' tunes be heard, or rhymes be read,
   Or while that shepherds love a lovely face.

Pas. Thy name, O Cosma, shall with praise be spread
   As far as any shepherds piping be,
   As far as love possesseth any head.

Nico. Thy monument is laid in many a tree,
   With name engraved; so though thy body die.
   The after-folks shall wonder still at thee.   130

Pas. So oft these woods have heard me 'Cosma' cry,
   That after death to heav'n in woods' resound,
   With echo's help, shall 'Cosma, Cosma' fly.

Nico. Peace, peace, good Pas, thou weariest e'en the ground
   With sluttish song; I pray thee learn to blea,
   For good thou mayst yet prove in sheepish sound.

Pas. My father hath at home a pretty jay,
   Go win of him (for chatt'ring) praise or shame;
   For so yet of a conquest speak thou may.   140

Nico. Tell me (and be my Pan) the monster's name
   That hath four legs, and with two only goes;
   That hath four eyes, and only two can frame.

Pas. Tell this (and Phoebus be): what monster grows
   With so strong lives that body cannot rest
   In ease until that body life forgoes?°

Dicus. Enough, enough; so ill hath done the best
   That, since the having them to neither due,
   Let cat and dog fight which shall have both you.

Some speech there straight grew among the hearers what they should mean by the riddles of the two monsters. But Cleophila, whose heart better delighted in wailful ditties as more according to her fortune, she desired Histor he would repeat the lamentation some days before he told them that he had heard of a stranger made to the wise Boulon—indeed Cleophila desirous to hear of Plangus's love, whose valour she had well seen (though against herself) in the combat of the six princes. Basilius, as soon as he understood Cleophila's pleasure, commanded Histor upon pain of his life (as though everything were a matter of life and death that pertained to his mistress's service) immediately to sing it; who, with great cunning varying his voice according to the diversity of the persons, thus performed his pleasure:

Histor

   As I behind a bush did sit
   I silent heard more words of wit
   Than erst I knew; but first did plain
   The one, which tother would refrain.

Plangus   Boulon

Plangus. Alas, how long this pilgrimage doth last?
   What greater ills have now the heav'ns in store

   To couple coming harms with sorrows past?
Long since my voice is hoarse, and throat is sore,
   With cries to skies, and curses to the ground;
   But more I plain, I feel my woes the more.   10
Ah where was first that cruel cunning found
   To frame of earth a vessel of the mind,
   Where it should be to self-destruction bound?
What needed so high sprites such mansions blind?
   Or wrapped in flesh what do they here obtain,
   But glorious name of wretched human-kind?
Balls to the stars, and thralls to Fortune's reign;
   Turned from themselves, infected with their cage,
   Where death is feared, and life is held with pain.
Like players placed to fill a filthy stage,   20
   Where change of thoughts one fool to other shows,
   And all but jests, save only sorrow's rage.
The child feels that; the man that feeling knows,
   With cries first born,° the presage of his life,
   Where wit but serves to have true taste of woes.
A shop of shame, a book where blots be rife
   This body is; this body so composed
   As in itself to nourish mortal strife.
So diverse be the elements disposed
   In this weak work that it can never be   30
   Made uniform to any state reposed.
Grief only makes his wretched state to see
   (E'en like a top which naught but whipping moves)
   This man, this talking beast, this walking tree.
Grief is the stone which finest judgement proves;
   For who grieves not hath but a blockish brain,
   Since cause of grief no cause from life removes.

Boulon. How long wilt thou with moanful music stain
   The cheerful notes these pleasant places yield,
   Where all good haps a perfect state maintain?   40

Plangus. Cursed be good haps, and cursed be they that build
   Their hopes on haps, and do not make despair
   For all these certain blows the surest shield.
Shall I that saw Erona's shining hair
   Torn with her hands, and those same hands of snow
   With loss of purest blood themselves to tear,

Shall I that saw those breasts where beauties flow,
　　Swelling with sighs, made pale with mind's disease,
　　And saw those eyes (those suns) such show'rs to show,
Shall I whose ears her mournful words did seize   50
　　(Her words in syrup laid of sweetest breath),
　　Relent those thoughts which then did so displease?
No, no; despair my daily lesson saith,
　　And saith, although I seek my life to fly,
　　Plangus must live to see Erona's death.
Plangus must live some help for her to try
　　Though in despair, for love so forceth me;
　　Plangus doth live, and shall Erona die?
Erona die? O heav'n (if heav'n there be)
　　Hath all thy whirling course so small effect?   60
　　Serve all thy starry eyes this shame to see?
Let dolts in haste some altars fair erect
　　To those high pow'rs which idly sit above,
　　And virtue do in greatest need neglect.

Boulon. O man, take heed how thou the gods do move
　　To causeful wrath which thou canst not resist.
　　Blasphemous words the speaker vain do prove.
Alas, while we are wrapped in foggy mist
　　Of our self-love (so passions do deceive)
　　We think they hurt when most they do assist.   70
To harm us worms should that high justice leave
　　His nature? nay, himself? for so it is.
　　What glory from our loss can he receive?
But still our dazzled eyes their way do miss,
　　While that we do at his sweet scourge repine,
　　The kindly way to beat us on to bliss.
If she must die, then hath she passed the line
　　Of loathsome days, whose loss how canst thou moan,
　　That dost so well their miseries define?
But such we are, with inward tempest blown   80
　　Of winds quite contrary in waves of will:
　　We moan that lost, which had we did bemoan.

Plangus. And shall she die, shall cruel fire spill
　　Those beams that set so many hearts on fire?
　　Hath she not force e'en death with love to kill?
Nay, e'en cold death inflamed with hot desire

Her to enjoy (where joy itself is thrall)
Will spoil the earth of his most rich attire.
Thus death becomes a rival to us all,
   And hopes with foul embracements her to get, 90
   In whose decay virtue's fair shrine must fall.
O virtue weak, shall death his triumph set
   Upon thy spoils, which never should lie waste?
   Let death first die; be thou his worthy let.
By what eclipse shall that sun be defaced?
   What mine hath erst thrown down so fair a tower?
   What sacrilege hath such a saint disgraced?
The world the garden is, she is the flower
   That sweetens all the place; she is the guest
   Of rarest price, both heav'n and earth her bower. 100
And shall (O me) all this in ashes rest?
   Alas, if you a phoenix new will have
   Burnt by the sun, she first must build her nest.
But well you know the gentle sun would save
   Such beams so like his own, which might have might
   In him, the thoughts of Phaethon's dam° to grave.
Therefore, alas, you use vile Vulcan's spite,
   Which nothing spares, to melt that virgin wax
   Which while it is, it is all Asia's light.
O Mars, for what doth serve thy armed axe? 110
   To let that witold° beast consume in flames
   Thy Venus' child, whose beauty Venus lacks?
O Venus (if her praise no envy frames
   In thy high mind) get her thy husband's grace.
   Sweet speaking oft a currish heart reclaims.
O eyes of mine where once she saw her face
   (Her face which was more lively in my heart),
   O brain where thought of her hath only place,
O hand, which touched her hand when we did part;
   O lips, that kissed that hand with my tears sprent; 120
   O tongue, then dumb, not daring tell my smart;
O soul, whose love in her is only spent,
   What e'er you see, think, touch, kiss, speak, or love,
   Let all for her, and unto her be bent.

Boulon. Thy wailing words do much my spirits move,
   They uttered are in such a feeling fashion

That sorrow's work against my will I prove.
Methinks I am partaker of thy passion,
    And in thy case do glass mine own debility—
    Self-guilty folk most prone to feel compassion.   130
Yet reason saith, reason should have ability
    To hold these wordly things in such proportion
    As let them come or go with e'en facility.
But our desire's tyrannical extortion
    Doth force us there to set our chief delightfulness
    Where but a baiting place° is all our portion.
But still, although we fail of perfect rightfulnesss,
    Seek we to tame these childish superfluities?
    Let us not wink though void of purest sightfulness;
For what can breed more peevish incongruities   140
    Than man to yield to female lamentations?
    Let us some grammar learn of more congruities.

Plangus. If through mine ears pierce any consolations
    By wise discourse, sweet tunes, or poet's fiction;
    If aught I cease these hideous exclamations,
While that my soul, she, she lives in affliction;
    Then let my life long time° on earth maintained be,
    To wretched me the last worst malediction.
Can I, that know her sacred parts, restrained be
    From any joy; know fortune's vile displacing her,   150
    In moral rules let raging woes contained be?
Can I forget, when they in prison placing her,
    With swelling heart in spite and due disdainfulness
    She lay for dead, till I helped with unlacing her?
Can I forget from how much mourning plainfulness
    With diamond in window glass she graved,
    'Erona die, and end this ugly painfulness'?
Can I forget in how strange phrase she craved
    That quickly they would her burn, drown, or smother,
    As if by death she only might be saved?   160
Then let me eke forget one hand from other;
    Let me forget that Plangus I am called;
    Let me forget I am son to my mother;
But if if my memory thus must be thralled
    To that strange stroke which conquered all my senses,
    Can thoughts still thinking so rest unappalled?

Boulon. Who still doth seek against himself offences,
    What pardon can avail? Or who employs him
    To hurt himself, what shields can be defences?
Woe to poor man: each outward thing annoys him   170
    In diverse kinds; yet as he were not filled,
    He heaps in inward grief that most destroys him.
Thus is our thought with pain for thistles tilled:
    Thus be our noblest parts dried up with sorrow:
    Thus is our mind with too much minding spilled.
One day lays up stuff of grief for the morrow;
    And whose good hap doth leave him unprovided,
    Condoling cause of friendship he will borrow.
Betwixt the good and shade of good divided,
    We pity deem that which but weakness is;   180
    So are we from our high creation slided.
But Plangus, lest I may your sickness miss
    Or rubbing, hurt the sore, I here do end.
    The ass did hurt° when he did think to kiss.

Histor. Thus did they say, and then away did wend;
    High time for me, for scattered were my sheep
    While I their speech in my rude rhyming penned.
Yet for that night my cabin did them keep
    While Plangus did a story strange declare;
    But hoarse and dry, my pipes I now must spare.   190

So well did Histor's voice express the passion of Plangus that all the princely beholders were stricken into a silent consideration of it; indeed everyone making that he heard of another the balance of his own troubles. Pamela was the first that commanded her thoughts to give place to some necessary words; and so, remembering herself what Histor had said the other time of the pastorals touching Musidorus (which as then she regarded not), she now desired him, if he did bear it in memory, that he would tell what strange adventure it was that had led away the two Greek princes from Erona, after they had slain Otanes and settled her in her kingdom. And when she had asked thus much, having had nothing but vehement desire to her counsel, her sweet body did even tremble for fear lest she had done amiss. But glad was her shepherd, not to have his doings spoken of, but because any question of him proceeded out of that mouth. Histor made answer that Plangus indeed had before his departure towards Thessalia and Macedon, at his importunate desire, made a brief declaration unto him thereof, but always with protestation that such things they were as many particularities of them had been full works to excellent historiographers; and that the first adventure was a man of monstrous bigness and force (and therefore commonly called a giant) who had wasted all the whole country of Paphlagonia by the help of a strong castle in the top of a high rock, where he kept a most terrible dragon which he had with such art from youth trained up that it was much more at his commandment than the best reclaimed hawk; so that it would fly abroad and do incredible damage, and ever duly return again to the castle where the giant kept no living man but himself. This, besides his own force, forced the miserable people to come to what composition he would: which was that monthly they should send him° two maids not above sixteen years old, and two boys or young men under nineteen. The women he used at his beastly pleasure, and kept them imprisoned in his castle; the young men he was wont to sacrifice to an idol. This being come to the ears of those valiant young princes who (the harder a thing were the more their hearts rase unto it) went to the desolate people, and there (after many horrible complaints of parents whose children by public force were taken from them) they offered themselves to pay the next month's wages, if better they could not do. Their beauty made all the people pity them, but in the end self-respect prevailed over the pity, and the time being come, they armed themselves secretly under their long garments, and carrying short swords under their arms, were in that sort brought unto him by a man appointed to deliver them, for more the giant would not suffer to enter; who, when he saw their faces, was a proud man of so goodly a sacrifice. But they were no sooner in but that, drawing out their swords, they made him look to his own life. Which he did, running to a horse-load of a mast° he always used, and so weaponed (for armed he ever went) he let loose his trusty dragon. And so matched that ill-favoured couple with the matchless princes, who (having an excellent strength, and courage to make that strength awake) had within small space dispatched the world of those monsters, Pyrocles having killed the dragon and Musidorus the giant. What honours were done unto them by that people (which they continually observe as towards their savers) were superfluous to tell.

But thence were they led by the fame of a great war betwixt two brethren, where the younger had rebelled against the elder (being king of Syria), forced thereunto because he had taken away from him the principality of Damascus which their father in partage° had bestowed upon him. There did they show as much their wisdom as their valour; for the one putting himself of the one side, and the other of the other, they so behaved themselves that either part thought they had the bravest champion in the world, insomuch as both were content to let the matter be tried by them to save the blood of so many which of both sides were but one people. But they (having the matter without exception put into their hands) instead of fighting fell to arbitrage, and making the brothers see the shamefulness of their fault so to sever themselves whom nature in their very beginning had so nearly knit, and yet remembering that whosoever hath thoroughly offended a prince can never think himself in perfect safety under him, they did determine that the king, giving in riches to his brother as much as his principality came unto, should enjoy Damascus; and they, finding the younger a prince of great worthiness, did so much by their credit with the Paphlagonians that they married him to the inheritrix of that goodly province—leaving in this sort a perpetual monument of wit, liberality, and courage.

But after this the next notable chance fell unto them (for many hundred of their valiant acts Plangus said he neither could tell, nor much time would serve for the repeating) was by the great lady of Palestina's means (called Andromana) who, hearing of their singular valour, sent to beseech their aid against a young prince of Arabia who had promised her marriage, and upon that having gotten a child of her, had now left her. They, though they knew she should have done well to have been sure of the church before he had been sure of the bed, yet pitying womanhood and desiring to know what answer the Arabian could make for himself, they went to offer themselves unto her. But they had not been there a while, and made her see their activity in jousts and their valour in particular combats, but that she had quite forgotten her old fancy that had cost her so dear, and was grown into the miserablest and strangest passion of love that can be imagined; for she loved them both with equal ardency. The only odds was that when she saw Pyrocles she thought she most desired him, and when she looked on Musidorus then was Pyrocles overweighed. At these words a man might have seen the eyes both of Pamela and Philoclea cast upon their servants to see whether they had committed any trespass or no. But Histor proceeded on in declaring her divided desire. When she looked on Musidorus then thought she a sweet brownness to be the most delightful beauty; but when she marked Pyrocles' pure white and red (for such difference Plangus said was betwixt them) then roses and lilies were the fairest flowers. Musidorus as the elder and stronger, Pyrocles as the younger and more delicate, contented her. In fine, she would wish sometimes Musidorus to be Pyrocles, another time Pyrocles to be Musidorus; but still she would have both hers. But those two princes (that seemed to love anything better than love) did so utterly discomfort her that she was forced to fly to force and put them both (by a sleight she played) in prison, where what allurements she used indifferently were long to tell. But at length they obstinately so much more refusing her (as their courages disdained to be compelled to anything), they had been like enough to have tarried there a good number of days but that the Arabian prince (hearing of their imprisonment) grew proud of his strength, and entered into Palestina with hope to conquer it. Which the people feeling (whether the lady would or no), delivered the prisoners, who having likewise by their good conduct delivered them of the Arabians, they themselves went into Egypt, as well to fly such a heart-burning woman (who shortly after, as Plangus said, had likewise forgotten them and, after divers changes, at last married herself to an apple-monger) as because they heard great fame of the king of Egypt's court, to be by reason of his magnificence full of valiant knights, as also his country well policied with good laws and customs, worthy to be learned.

But many notable accidents met with them as they passed the desert way betwixt Palestina and Egypt, worthy to have whole books written of them. But Plangus's appassionate mind could not brook long discourses, and therefore hasted himself to let me know the generality of their doings, which certainly were such as made me greatly delighted to hear them.

'But did he tell you no further', said the sweetest Philoclea, 'of those princes?'

'Yes', answered Histor, 'of a strange chance fell to them in Egypt, and that was this: riding together about six miles from the great city of Memphis they heard a pitiful cry as of one that either extreme grief or present fear had made his voice his best instrument of defence. They went the next way they thought should guide them to the party, and there found they a young man, well apparelled and handsomely proportioned, in the hands of four murdering villains who were ready to slay him, having stayed for nothing but that he told them he knew a place where a great treasure was hid. The covetousness of that made them delay the killing of him till one of the four, weary to follow him any longer, was ready to have given his mortal wound, at which he cried. But the other three stopped their fellow, when (in good time for him) came in these two princes who (seeing, how justly soever he had deserved death, that the manner was unjust by which they sought to lay it upon him) came in among them with threatenings if they did not let him loose. But the four (better knowing their own number than the others' valour) scorned their commandment, till by the death of three of them the fourth was taught with running away to leave the prisoner to their discretion; who (falling on his knees unto them as to the bestowers of a life upon him) told them the ground of his mischance, to this purpose: that he was a servant and of nearest credit to Amasis, son and heir to Sesostris, king of Egypt, and being of one age was also so like him as hardly (but by the great difference of their outward estates) the one could be known from the other; that the king Sesostris, after the death of Amasis's mother, had married a young woman who had turned the ordinary course of stepmother's hate to so unbridled a love towards her husband's son Amasis that neither the name of a father in him, of a husband in her, nor of a mother and son between themselves, could keep her back from disorderly seeking that of Amasis which is a wickedness to accept. But he (besides his duty to virtue) having his heart already pledged to Artaxia, queen of Persia, the more she loved him, the more detested her; which finding her hot spirits to work upon, shame, disdain, and lust converted all her affection to a most revengeful hatred, insomuch that all her study was for some naughty policy to overthrow him, whereof in the end this young man offered her occasion. For considering the resemblance he bare to his master, she began to make the poor youth believe she did extremely affect him in respect of that likeness; which he, privy to all his master's counsels, well knew she immoderately loved. Thermuthis (for so the young man was called) thought himself advanced to the stars when he saw so fair a queen bend her goodwill towards him, which she (so far was she become a slave to sin) sealed unto him with the fruition of her unchaste body. When she thus had angled Thermuthis then began she to accuse Amasis to his father as having sought to defile his bed; which opinion being something gotten in, though not fully imprinted in Sesostris's head, she caused Thermuthis (who was fully at her devotion) to come one night in his master's apparel he had that day worn to her chamber with his sword ready to kill the king as he slept, for so had she persuaded him to do. But as soon as he entered into the chamber she awaked the king, and making him see him he took to be his son (being deceived by candle-light and his raiment) in that order coming to kill him, the poor Thermuthis astonished and running away, she sent those four trusty servants after him, to whom she had before hand given charge to have eye of him, and as soon as he should fly out of the chamber to follow him (under colour to help him by her commandment) till they trained him into some secret place, and there murder him. And thus much one of them appointed to kill him (who was the man the queen of Egypt most trusted) had revealed unto him, thinking his speedy death should keep it from being opened. "And", said Thermuthis, "by this time I fear the king hath done some hurt to my dear master, whom thus miserably I have ruined."

And indeed so the king meant to have done, and presently to have killed him, whom she caused to be brought by force out of his lodging, as though thither he had fled to shift himself, and so escape—the poor prince newly being come out of his sleep, and with his amazedness rather condemning himself than otherwise. But the king (neither taking pains to examine the matter to the uttermost, nor so much as to hear what Amasis could say in a matter by many circumstances easy enough to have been refelled),° he presently caused him to be carried to the Red Sea, there to be put in a ship without any man but himself in it, and so to be left to the wind's discretion. But the two princes, having understood the beginning of this matter by Thermuthis, taking him with them, they entered into Memphis as the poor prince was some few miles already carried out towards his ship of death. Which they understanding, and fearing they should not have leisure to tell the king and save him, they first pursued after him and by force of arms, joined with the help of some of the country who were willing to help their prince, they rescued him out of their hands and, bringing him back to the king, made him understand the whole circumstances by Thermuthis's confession; whose pardon they got, considering what a fault the king himself had done to run so hastily in the condemning his only son in a cause might both by Thermuthis's absence and many other ways have been proved contrary. As for his wife, she was past either pardoning or punishing; for when she heard the matter was revealed, she killed herself. "Thence," Plangus said, "having left the father and son in unity, and Amasis acknowledging his life of them with great love (which notwithstanding he could not have done if he had known how Artaxia hated them), they returned, as it was thought, to Greece-ward; whom he had still followed, and by many misfortunes could never find. And now his last hope is in one of their countries, being nevertheless in great doubt that they are already perished by sea."'

Thus did Histor epitomise the worthy acts of those two worthies, making (though unknown) their own ears witnesses of their glory; which in no respect rejoiced them so much as that their beloved ladies heard it, of whose esteeming them they had tenderest regard, and chiefly desired they might know it was no dishonour they sought unto them whose honour they held in more precious reckoning than their own lives. But indeed unmeasurable was the contentment of the two ladies who, besides love had taught them to trust, might find by the circumstance of these things that these could be no other than their lovers, although either's heart was so deeply plunged in her own that she never pained herself to call in question her sister's case; so that neither Pamela ever took conceit of the Amazon, nor Philoclea of the shepherd. As for Gynecia, such an inward lordship Cleophila held in her that she saw only her, she heard nobody but her, and thought of nothing but of her; so that Histor's narration passed through her ears without any marking, judging (as commonly they do that are full of thoughts) by the beginning that it should nothing appertain to the party upon whom she knit all her imagining power. The duke would divers times very fain have broken off Histor's speech but that, finding Cleophila yield him acceptable audience, he was in doubt to displease her. But well afraid he was lest the great praises he gave to the famous Pyrocles might kindle Cleophila's heart unto him; for comparing their worthiness he was forced to confess in himself there would prove a noble match between them, which made him fear that Cleophila's young mind might be stirred that way. Therefore, as soon, or rather before, Histor had ended, lest he might renew again some mention of those two princes, he called to Philisides who (according to his custom) sat so melancholy as though his mind were banished from the place he loved to be, imprisoned in his body; and desired him he would begin some eclogue with some other of the shepherds according to the accustomed guise. Philisides (though very unwilling) at the duke's commandment offered to sing with Lalus; but Lalus directly refused him, saying she should within few days be married to the fair Kala and since he had gotten his desire, he would sing no more. Then the duke willed Philisides to declare the discourse of his own fortunes, unknown to them as being a stranger in that country. But he prayed the duke to pardon him, the time being far too joyful to suffer the rehearsal of his miseries. But to satisfy Basilius some way, he began an eclogue betwixt himself and the echo, framing his voice so in those desert places as what words he would have the echo reply unto, those he would sing higher than the rest, and so kindly framed a disputation betwixt himself and it; which, with these hexameters in the following order, he uttered:

Philisides	*Echo*

- - - ◡ ◡ - - - ◡ ◡ - ◡ ◡ - -

Fair rocks, goodly rivers, sweet woods, when shall I see
    peace?   Peace.
Peace? What bars me my tongue? Who is it that comes me
    so nigh?   I.
Oh! I do know what guest I have met; it is echo.   'Tis echo.

Well met, echo, approach; then tell me thy will too.   I will too.
  Echo, what do I get yielding my sprite to my griefs?   Griefs.
What medicine may I find for a pain that draws me to
    death?   Death.
O poisonous medicine! What worse to me can be than it?   It.
In what state was I then, when I took this deadly
    disease?   Ease.
And what manner a mind which had to that humour a vein?   Vain.
10 Hath not reason enough vehemence the desire to reprove?   Prove.
Oft prove I; but what salve when reason seeks to be gone?   One.
Oh! What is it? What is it that may be a salve to my love?   Love.
What do lovers seek for, long seeking for to enjoy?   Joy.
What be the joys for which to enjoy they went to the pains?   Pains.
Then to an earnest love what doth best victory lend?   End.
End? But I can never end; love will not give me the leave.   Leave.
How be the minds disposed that cannot taste thy physic?   Sick.
Yet say again thy advice for th'ills that I told thee.   I told thee.
Doth th'infected wretch of his ill th'extremity know?   No.
20 But if he know not his harms what guides hath he whilst he
    be blind?   Blind.
What blind guides can he have that leans to a fancy?   A fancy.
Can fancies want eyes, or he fall that steppeth aloft?   Oft.
What causes first made these torments on me to light?   Light.
Can then a cause be so light that forceth a man to go die?   Aye.
Yet tell what light thing I had in me to draw me to die?   Eye.
Eyesight made me to yield, but what first pierced to mine
    eyes?   Eyes.
Eyes' hurters, eyes' hurt, but what from them to me falls?   Falls.
But when I first did fall, what brought most fall to my
    heart?   Art.
Art? What can be that art which thou dost mean by thy
    speech?   Speech.
30 What be the fruits of speaking art? What grows by the
    words?   Words.
O much more than words: those words served more to me
    bless.   Less.
O when shall I be known where most to be known I do
    long?   Long.
Long be thy woes for such news, but how recks she my
    thoughts?   Oughts.
Then, then what do I gain, since unto her will I do wind?   Wind.

Wind, tempests, and storms; yet in end what gives she
    desire?   Ire.
Silly reward! Yet among women hath she of virtue the
    most.   Most.
What great name may I give to so heav'nly a woman?   A woe-man.
Woe, but seems to me joy that agrees to my thought so.   I thought so.
Think so, for of my desired bliss it is only the course. Curse.
Cursed be thyself for cursing that which leads me to joys. Toys.   40
What be the sweet creatures° where lowly demands be not
    heard?   Hard.
Hard to be got, but got constant, to be held like steels. Eels.
How can they be unkind? Speak for th'hast narrowly pried. Pride.
Whence can pride come there, since springs of beauty be
    thence?   Thence.
Horrible is this blasphemy unto the most holy.   O lie.
Thou li'st false echo, their minds as virtue be just.   Just.
Mock'st thou those diamonds which only be matched by
    the gods?   Odds.
Odds? What an odds is there since them to the heav'ns I
    prefer?   Err.
Tell yet again me the names of these fair formed to do
    ev'ls.   Dev'ls.
Dev'ls? If in hell such dev'ls do abide, to the hells I do go. Go.   50

    Philisides was commended for the placing of his echo, but little did he
regard their praises; who had set the foundation of his honour there
where he was most despised. And therefore returning again to the train
of his desolate pensiveness, Cleophila seeing nobody offer to fill the
stage, as if her long-restrained conceits did now burst out of prison, she
thus (desiring her voice should be accorded to nothing but to Philoclea's
ears) threw down the burden of her mind in Anacreon's kind of verses:°

                      ⏑–⏑–⏑––

          My muse what ails this ardour
          To blaze my only secrets?
          Alas, it is no glory
          To sing my own decayed state.
          Alas, it is no comfort
          To speak without an answer.
          Alas, it is no wisdom
          To show the wound without cure,

My muse what ails this ardour?
My eyes be dim, my limbs shake,   10
My voice is hoarse, my throat scorched,
My tongue to this my roof cleaves,
My fancy amazed, my thoughts dulled,
My heart doth ache, my life faints,
My soul begins to take leave.
So great a passion all feel,
To think a sore so deadly
I should so rashly rip up.

My muse what ails this ardour?
If that to sing thou art bent,   20
Go sing the fall of old Thebes,
The wars of ugly centaurs,
The life, the death of Hector,
So may thy song be famous;
Or if to love thou art bent,
Recount the rape of Europe,
Adonis' end, Venus' net,
The sleepy kiss the moon stale;°
So may thy song be pleasant.

My muse what ails this ardour   30
To blaze my only secrets?
Wherein do only flourish
The sorry fruits of anguish,
The song thereof a last will,
The tunes be cries, the words plaints,
The singer is the song's theme
Wherein no ear can have joy,
Nor eye receives due object,
Ne pleasure here, ne fame got.

My muse what ails this ardour?   40
'Alas', she saith, 'I am thine,
So are thy pains my pains too.
Thy heated heart my seat is
Wherein I burn, thy breath is
My voice, too hot to keep in.
Besides, lo here the author

Of all thy harms; lo here she
That only can redress thee,
Of her I will demand help.'

My muse, I yield, my muse sing,   50
But all thy song herein knit:
The life we lead is all love,
The love we hold is all death,
Nor aught I crave to feed life,
Nor aught I seek to shun death,
But only that my goddess
My life, my death, do count hers.

Basilius, when she had fully ended her song, fell prostrate upon the
ground, and thanked the gods they had preserved his life so long as to
hear the very music they themselves used in an earthly body. And then
with like grace to Cleophila, never left entreating her till she had (taking a
lyra Basilius held for her) sung these phaleuciacs:°

— — — ∪ ∪ — ∪ — ∪ — ∪

Reason, tell me thy mind, if here be reason
In this strange violence, to make resistance.
Where sweet graces erect the stately banner
Of virtue's regiment, shining in harness
Of fortune's diadems, by beauty mustered.
Say then, Reason, I say what is thy counsel?

Her loose hair be the shot, the breasts the pikes be,
Scouts each motion is, the hands the horsemen,
Her lips are the riches the wars to maintain,
Where well couched abides a coffer of pearl,   10
Her legs carriage is of all the sweet camp.
Say then, Reason, I say what is thy counsel?

Her cannons be her eyes, mine eyes the walls be,
Which at first volley gave too open entry,
Nor rampire did abide; my brain was up blown,
Undermined with a speech, the piercer of thoughts.
Thus weakened by myself, no help remaineth.
Say then, Reason, I say what is thy counsel?

And now fame, the herald of her true honour,
Doth proclaim (with a sound made all by men's mouths)   20

That nature, sovereign of earthly dwellers,
Commands all creatures to yield obeisance
Under this, this her own, her only darling.
Say then, Reason, I say what is thy counsel?

Reason sighs, but in end he thus doth answer:
'Naught can reason avail in heav'nly matters.'
Thus nature's diamond, receive thy conquest,
Thus pure pearl, I do yield my senses and soul.
Thus sweet pain, I do yield what e'er I can yield.
Reason look to thyself, I serve a goddess.   30

Dorus had long, he thought, kept silence from saying somewhat which
might tend to the glory of her in whom all glory (to his seeming) was
included. But now he brake it, singing these verses, called asclepiadics:°

-- -- ∪ ∪ -- -- ∪ ∪ -- ∪ ∪

O sweet woods, the delight of solitariness!
O how much I do like your solitariness!
Where man's mind hath a freed consideration
Of goodness to receive lovely direction;
Where senses do behold th'order of heav'nly host,
And wise thoughts do behold what the creator is.
Contemplation here holdeth his only seat,
Bounded with no limits, borne with a wing of hope,
Climbs even unto the stars; nature is under it.
Naught disturbs thy quiet, all to thy service yield,   10
Each sight draws on a thought (thought mother of science),
Sweet birds kindly do grant harmony unto thee,
Fair trees' shade is enough fortification,
Nor danger to thyself, if be not in thyself.

O sweet woods, the delight of solitariness!
O how much I do like your solitariness!
Here no treason is hid, veiled in innocence,
Nor envy's snaky eye finds any harbour here,
Nor flatterers' venomous insinuations,
Nor cunning humorists'° puddled opinions,   20
Nor courteous ruin of proffered usury,
Nor time prattled away, cradle of ignorance,
Nor causeless duty, nor cumber of arrogance,
Nor trifling title of vanity dazzleth us,

Nor golden manacles stand for a paradise,
Here wrong's name is unheard; slander a monster is.
Keep thy sprite from abuse, here no abuse doth haunt.
What man grafts in a tree dissimulation?

O sweet woods, the delight of solitariness!
O how well I do like your solitariness! 30
Yet dear soil, if a soul closed in a mansion
As sweet as violets, fair as a lily is,
Straight as cedar, a voice stains the canary birds,
Whose shade safety doth hold, danger avoideth her:
Such wisdom that in her lives speculation:
Such goodness that in her simplicity triumphs:
Where envy's snaky eye winketh or else dieth,
Slander wants a pretext, flattery gone beyond:
Oh! If such a one have bent to a lonely life,
Her steps glad we receive, glad we receive her eyes. 40
    And think not she doth hurt our solitariness,
    For such company decks such solitariness.

The other shepherds were offering themselves to have continued the
sports, but the night had so quietly spent most part of herself among
them that the duke, for that time, licensed them; and so bringing
Cleophila to her lodging (who would much rather have done the same for
Philoclea), of all sides they went to counterfeit a sleep in their beds, for a
true one their agonies could not afford them. Yet there they lay (for so
might they be most solitary for the food of their thoughts) till it was near
noon the next day. After which Basilius was to continue his Apollo
devotions, and the others to meditate upon their private desires.

Here ends the second eclogues.

THE THIRD ECLOGUES

LALUS, not with many painted words, nor false-hearted promises, had
won the consent of his beloved Kala, but with a true and simple making
her know he loved her; not forcing himself beyond his reach to buy her
affection, but giving her such pretty presents as neither could weary him
with the giving nor shame her for the taking. Thus the first strawberries
he could find were ever in a clean washed dish sent to Kala. Thus posies
of the spring flowers were wrapped up in a little green silk and dedicated

to Kala's breasts. Thus sometimes his sweetest cream, sometimes the best cake-bread his mother made, were reserved for Kala's taste. Neither would he stick to kill a lamb when she would be content to come over the way unto him. But then lo, how the house was swept, and rather no fire than any smoke left to trouble her. Then love songs were not dainty, when she would hear them, and as much mannerly silence when she would not. In going to church, great worship to Kala, so that all the parish said never a maid they knew so well waited on; and when dancing was about the maypole, nobody taken out but she, and he after a leap or two to show her his own activity, would frame all the rest of his dancing only to grace her. As for her father's sheep, he had no less care of them than his own; so that she might play her as she would, warranted with honest Lalus's carefulness. But if he spied Kala favoured any one of the flock more than his fellows, then that was cherished, shearing him so (when shorn he must be) as might most become him; but while the wool was on, wrapping within it some verses (wherein Lalus had a special gift), and making the innocent beast his unwitting messenger. Thus constantly continuing, though he were none of the fairest, at length he wan Kala's heart, the honestest wench in all those quarters. And so, with consent of both parents (without which neither Lalus would ask nor Kala grant), their marriage day was appointed; which, because it fell out in this time, I think it shall not be impertinent to remember a little our shepherds while the other greater persons are either sleeping or otherwise occupied. Lalus's marriage time once known, there needed no inviting of the neighbours in that valley; for so well was Lalus beloved that they were all ready to do him credit. Neither yet came they like harpies to devour him, but one brought a fat pig, the other a tender kid, a third a great goose; as for cheese, milk and butter were the gossips' presents. Thither came of stranger shepherds only the melancholy Philisides; for the virtuous Coredens° had long since left off all joyful solemnities, and as for Strephon and Klaius, they had lost their mistress, which put them into such extreme sorrows as they could scarcely abide the light of the day, much less the eyes of men. But of the Arcadian-born shepherds, thither came good old Geron, young Histor (though unwilling), and upright Dicus, merry Pas, and jolly Nico; as for Dametas, they durst not presume, his pride was such, to invite him; and Dorus they found might not be spared. And there under a bower was made of boughs (for Lalus's house was not able to receive them), they were entertained with hearty welcome, and every one placed according to his age. The women (for such was the manner of that country) kept together to make good cheer among themselves, from which otherwise a certain painful modesty

restrains them. And there might the sadder matrons give good counsel to
Kala who, poor soul, wept for fear of that she desired. But among the
shepherds was all honest liberty; no fear of dangerous telltales (who hunt
greater preys), nor indeed minds in them to give telltales any occasion,
but one questioning with another of the manuring his ground, and
governing his flock. The highest point they reached to was to talk of the
holiness of marriage; to which purpose, as soon as their sober dinner was
ended, Dicus instead of thanks sang this song with a clear voice and
cheerful countenance:

> Let mother earth° now deck herself in flowers,
> To see her offspring seek a good increase,
> Where justest love doth vanquish Cupid's powers
> And war of thoughts is swallowed up in peace
>   Which never may decrease,
>   But like the turtles fair
>   Live one in two, a well united pair,
>   Which, that no chance may stain,
>   O Hymen long their coupled joys maintain.
>
> O heav'n awake, show forth thy stately face;   10
> Let not these slumb'ring clouds thy beauties hide,
> But with thy cheerful presence help to grace
> The honest bridegroom and the bashful bride,
>   Whose loves may ever bide,
>   Like to the elm and vine,
>   With mutual embracements them to twine;
>   In which delightful pain,
>   O Hymen long their coupled joys maintain.
>
> Ye muses all which chaste affects allow,
> And have to Lalus showed your secret skill,   20
> To this chaste love your sacred favours bow,
> And so to him and her your gifts distil,
>   That they all vice may kill;
>   And like to lilies pure
>   Do please all eyes, and spotless do endure;
>   Where, that all bliss may reign,
>   O Hymen long their coupled joys maintain.
>
> Ye nymphs which in the waters empire have,
> Since Lalus' music oft doth yield you praise,
> Grant to the thing which we for Lalus crave: 30

Let one time (but long first) close up their days,
    One grave their bodies seize,
    And like two rivers sweet
    When they, though diverse, do together meet,
    One stream both streams contain;
    O Hymen long their coupled joys maintain.

Pan, father Pan, the god of silly sheep,
Whose care is cause that they in number grow,
Have much more care of them that them do keep,
Since from these good the others' good doth flow,   40
    And make their issue show
    In number like the herd
    Of younglings which thyself with love hast reared,
    Or like the drops of rain;
    O Hymen long their coupled joys maintain.

Virtue, if not a god, yet God's chief part,
Be thou the knot of this their open vow:
That still he be her head, she be his heart,
He lean to her, she unto him do bow;
    Each other still allow,   50
    Like oak and mistletoe,
    Her strength from him, his praise from her do grow.
    In which most lovely train,
    O Hymen long their coupled joys maintain.

But thou foul Cupid, sire to lawless lust,
Be thou far hence with thy empoisoned dart
Which, though of glitt'ring gold, shall here take rust
Where simple love, which chasteness doth impart,
    Avoids thy hurtful art,
    Not needing charming skill   60
    Such minds with sweet affections for to fill,
    Which being pure and plain,
    O Hymen long their coupled joys maintain.

All churlish words, shrewd answers, crabbed looks,
All privateness, self-seeking, inward spite,
All waywardness which nothing kindly brooks,
All strife for toys, and claiming master's right,
    Be hence ay put to flight;
    All stirring husband's hate

Gainst neighbours good for womanish debate   70
Be fled as things most vain,
O Hymen long their coupled joys maintain.

All peacock pride, and fruits of peacock's pride,
Longing to be with loss of substance gay
With recklessness what may thy house betide,
So that you may on higher slippers stay,
    For ever hence away.
    Yet let not sluttery,
    The sink of filth, be counted housewifery;
But keeping wholesome mean,   80
    O Hymen long their coupled joys maintain.

But above all, away vile jealousy,
The ill of ills, just cause to be unjust,
(How can he love, suspecting treachery?
How can she love where love cannot win trust?)
    Go snake, hide thee in dust,
    Ne dare once show thy face
    Where open hearts do hold so constant place;
That they thy sting restrain,
    O Hymen long their coupled joys maintain.   90

The earth is decked with flow'rs, the heav'ns displayed,
Muses grant gifts, nymphs long and joined life,
Pan store of babes, virtue their thoughts well stayed,
Cupid's lust gone, and gone is bitter strife,
    Happy man, happy wife.
    No pride shall them oppress,
    Nor yet shall yield to loathsome sluttishness,
    And jealousy is slain;
    For Hymen will their coupled joys maintain.

'Truly Dicus,' said Nico, 'although thou didst not grant me the prize the last day, when undoubtedly I wan it, yet must I needs say thou for thy part hast sung well and thriftily.'

Pas straight desired all the company they would bear witness that Nico had once in his life spoken wisely: 'For', said he, 'I will tell it to his father, who will be a glad man when he hears such news.'

'Very true,' said Nico, 'but, indeed, so would not thine in like case, for he would look thou shouldst live but one hour longer, that a discreet word wandered out of thy mouth.'

'And I pray thee,' said Pas, 'gentle Nico, tell me what mischance it was that brought thee to taste so fine a meat?'

'Marry, goodman blockhead,' said Nico, 'because he speaks against jealousy, the filthy traitor to true affection, and yet disguising itself in the raiment of love.'

'Sentences, sentences,'° cried Pas, 'alas, how ripe-witted these young folks be nowadays! But well counselled shall that husband be when this man comes to exhort him not to be jealous.'

'And so shall he,' answered Nico, 'for I have seen a fresh example, though it be not very fit to be known.'

'Come, come,' said Pas, 'be not so squeamish. I know thou longest more to tell it than we to hear it.'

But for all his words Nico would not bestow his voice till he was generally entreated of the rest; and then with a merry marriage look he sang this following discourse—for with a better grace he could sing than tell:

> A neighbour mine° not long ago there was
> (But nameless he, for blameless he shall be)
> That married had a trick and bonny lass
> As in a summer day a man might see;
>   But he himself a foul unhandsome groom,
>   And far unfit to hold so good a room.
>
> Now whether moved with self-unworthiness,
> Or with her beauty, fit to make a prey,
> Fell jealousy did so his brain oppress
> That if he absent were but half a day,   10
>   He guessed the worst (you wot what is the worst)
>   And in himself new doubting causes nursed.
>
> While thus he feared the silly innocent,
> Who yet was good, because she knew none ill,
> Unto his house a jolly shepherd went,
> To whom our prince did bear a great goodwill,
>   Because in wrestling and in pastoral
>   He far did pass the rest of shepherds all.
>
> And therefore he a courtier was benamed,
> And as a courtier was with cheer received   20
> (For they have tongues to make a poor man blamed
> If he to them his duty misconceived);
>   And for this courtier should well like his table,
>   The goodman bad his wife be serviceable.

And so she was, and all with good intent,
But few days passed while she good manner used,
But that her husband thought her service bent
To such an end as he might be abused.
   Yet, like a coward fearing stranger's pride,
   He made the simple wench his wrath abide.   30

With chumpish° looks, hard words, and secret nips,
Grumbling at her when she his kindness sought,
Asking her how she tasted courtier's lips,
He forced her think that which she never thought.
   In fine, it made her guess there was some sweet
   In that which he so feared that she should meet.

When once this entered was in woman's heart,
And that it had inflamed a new desire,
There rested then to play a woman's part,
Fuel to seek and not to quench the fire;   40
   But (for his jealous eye she well did find)
   She studied cunning how the same to blind.

And thus she did: one day to him she came
And (though against his will) on him she leaned,
And out gan cry, 'ah wellaway, for shame,
If you help not our wedlock will be stained!'
   The goodman starting, asked what did her move?
   She sighed, and said the bad guest sought her love.

He little looking that she should complain
Of that whereto he feared she was inclined,   50
Bussing her oft, and in his heart full fain,
He did demand what remedy to find;
   How they might get that guest from them to wend,
   And yet the prince (that loved him) not offend.

'Husband', quoth she, 'go to him by and by,
And tell him that you find I do him love,
And therefore pray him that of courtesy
He will absent himself, lest he should move
   A young girl's heart to that were shame for both,
   Whereto you know his honest heart were loath.   60

Thus shall you show that him you do not doubt,
And as for me, sweet husband, I must bear.'

Glad was the man when he had heard her out;
And did the same, although with mickle fear.
  For fear he did lest he the young man might
  In choler put, with whom he would not fight.

The courtly shepherd much aghast at this,
Not seeing erst such token in the wife,
Though full of scorn, would not his duty miss,
Knowing that ill becomes a household strife,   70
  Did go his way, but sojourned near thereby,
  That yet the ground hereof he might espy.

The wife thus having settled husband's brain
(Who would have sworn his spouse Diana was),
Watched when she a further point might gain;
Which little time did fitly bring to pass.
  For to the court her man was called by name,
  Whither he needs must go for fear of blame.

Three days before that he must sure depart,
She written had (but in a hand disguised)   80
A letter such which might from either part
Seem to proceed, so well it was devised.
  She sealed it first, then she the sealing brake,
  And to her jealous husband did it take.

With weeping eyes (her eyes she taught to weep)
She told him that the courtier had it sent:
'Alas', quoth she, 'thus women's shame doth creep.'
The goodman read on both sides the content;
  It title had: *Unto my only love.*
  Subscription was: *Yours most, if you will prove.*   90

The pistle° self, such kind of words it had:
'My sweetest joy, the comfort of my sprite,
So may thy flocks increase, thy dear heart glad,
So may each thing e'en as thou wishest light,
  As thou wilt deign to read, and gently read,
  This mourning ink in which my heart doth bleed.

Long have I loved (alas, thou worthy art),
Long have I loved (alas, love craveth love),
Long have I loved thyself; alas, my heart
Doth break now tongue unto thy name doth move;   100

And think not that thy answer answer is,
But that it is my doom of bale or bliss.

The jealous wretch must now to court be gone;
Ne can he fail, for prince hath for him sent;
Now is the time we may be here alone,
And give a long desire a sweet content.
　　Thus shall you both reward a lover true,
　　And eke revenge his wrong suspecting you.'

And this was all, and this the husband read
With chafe enough, till she him pacified,   110
Desiring that no grief in him he bred
Now that he had her words so truly tried;
　　But that he would to him the letter show,
　　That with his fault he might her goodness know.

That straight was done, with many a boistrous threat
That to the duke he would his sin declare;
But now the courtier gan to smell the feat,
And with some words which showed little care,
　　He stayed until the goodman was departed,
　　Then gave he him the blow which never smarted.   120

Thus may you see the jealous wretch was made
The pander of the thing he most did fear.
Take heed, therefore, how you ensue that trade,
Lest that some marks of jealousy you bear;
　　For sure no jealousy can that prevent
　　Whereto two parties once be full content.

'Behold,' said Pas, 'a whole dicker° of wit! He hath picked out such a
tale, with intention to keep a husband from jealousy, which were enough
to make a sanctified husband jealous, to see subtleties so much in the
feminine gender. But, said he, 'I will strike Nico dead with the wise
words shall flow out of my gorge'; and without further entreaty thus sang:

　　Who doth desire that chaste his wife should be,
　　First be he true, for truth doth truth deserve.
　　Then such be he, as she his worth may see;
　　And one man still, credit with her preserve.

　　Not toying kind, nor causelessly unkind,
　　Not stirring thoughts, nor yet denying right,

Not spying faults, nor in plain errors blind;
Never hard hand, nor ever reins too light.

As far from want, as far from vain expense
(The one doth force, the latter doth entice);   10
Allow good company, but keep from thence
All filthy mouths that glory in their vice.

This done, thou hast no more, but leave the rest
To virtue, fortune, time, and woman's breast.

'Well concluded', said Nico, 'when he hath done all, he leaves the matter to his wife's discretion. Now whensoever thou marriest, let her discretion deck thy head with Actaeon's ornament!'°

Pas was so angry with his wish (being indeed towards marriage) that they might perchance have fallen to buffets, but that Dicus (who knew it more wisdom to let a fray than part a fray) desired Philisides (who as a stranger sat among them, revolving in his mind all the tempests of evil fortunes he had passed) that he would do so much grace to the company as to sing one of his country songs. Philisides knew it no good manners to be squeamish of his cunning, having put himself in their company, and yet loath either in time of marriage to sing his sorrows, more fit for funerals, or by any outward matter to be drawn to such mirth as to betray (as it were) that passion to which he had given over himself, he took a mean way betwixt both and sang this song he had learned before he had ever subjected his thoughts to acknowledge no master but a mistress:

As I my little flock on Ister bank°
(A little flock, but well my pipe they couthe°)
Did piping lead, the sun already sank
Beyond our world, and ere I gat my booth
Each thing with mantle black the night did soothe,
    Saving the glow-worm, which would courteous be
    Of that small light oft watching shepherds see.

The welkin had full niggardly enclosed
In coffer of dim clouds his silver groats,
Ycleped stars; each thing to rest disposed: 10
The caves were full, the mountains void of goats;
The birds' eyes closed, closed their chirping notes.
    As for the nightingale, wood-music's king,
    It August was, he deigned not then to sing.

Amid my sheep, though I saw naught to fear,
Yet (for I nothing saw) I feared sore;
Then found I which thing is a charge to bear,
For for my sheep I dreaded mickle more
Than ever for myself since I was bore.
    I sat me down, for see to go ne could,   20
    And sang unto my sheep lest stray they should.

The song I sang old Languet had me taught,
Languet, the shepherd best swift Ister knew,
For clerkly rede, and hating what is naught,°
For faithful heart, clean hands, and mouth as true.
With his sweet skill my skill-less youth he drew
    To have a feeling taste of him that sits
    Beyond the heav'n, far more beyond our wits.

He said the music best thilk° powers pleased
Was jump° concord between our wit and will,   30
Where highest notes to godliness are raised,
And lowest sink not down to jot of ill.
With old true tales° he wont mine ears to fill:
    How shepherds did of yore, how now, they thrive,
    Spoiling their flock, or while twixt them they strive.

He liked me, but pitied lustful youth.
His good strong staff my slipp'ry years upbore.
He still hoped well, because I loved truth;
Till forced to part, with heart and eyes e'en sore,
To worthy Coredens° he gave me o'er.   40
    But thus in oak's true shade recounted he
    Which now in night's deep shade sheep heard of me.

Such manner time there was° (what time I not)°
When all this earth, this dam or mould of ours,
Was only woned° with such a beasts begot;
Unknown as then were they that builden towers.
The cattle, wild or tame, in nature's bowers
    Might freely roam or rest, as seemed them;
    Man was not man their dwellings in to hem.

The beasts had sure some beastly policy;   50
For nothing can endure where order nis.°
For once the lion by the lamb did lie;
The fearful hind the leopard did kiss;

Hurtless was tiger's paw and serpent's hiss.
    This think I well: the beasts with courage clad
    Like senators a harmless empire had.

At which, whether the others did repine
(For envy harb'reth most in feeblest hearts),°
Or that they all to changing did incline
(As e'en in beasts their dams leave changing parts),   60
The multitude to Jove a suit imparts,
    With neighing, blaying, braying, and barking,
    Roaring, and howling, for to have a king.

A king in language theirs they said they would
(For then their language was a perfect speech).
The birds likewise with chirps and pewing° could,
Cackling and chatt'ring, that of Jove beseech.
Only the owl still warned them not to seech°
    So hastily that which they would repent;
    But saw they would, and he to deserts went.   70

Jove wisely said (for wisdom wisely says):
'O beasts, take heed what you of me desire.
Rulers will think all things made them to please,
And soon forget the swink due to their hire.°
But since you will, part of my heav'nly fire
    I will you lend; the rest yourselves must give,
    That it both seen and felt may with you live.'

Full glad they were, and took the naked sprite,
Which straight the earth yclothed in his clay.
The lion, heart; the ounce° gave active might;   80
The horse, good shape; the sparrow, lust to play;
Nightingale, voice, enticing songs to say.
    Elephant gave a perfect memory;
    And parrot, ready tongue, that to apply.

The fox gave craft; the dog gave flattery;
Ass, patience; the mole, a working thought;
Eagle, high look; wolf, secret cruelty;
Monkey, sweet breath; the cow, her fair eyes brought;
The ermine, whitest skin spotted with naught;
    The sheep, mild-seeming face; climbing, the bear;   90
    The stag did give the harm-eschewing fear.

The hare her sleights; the cat his melancholy;
Ant, industry; and cony, skill to build;
Cranes, order; storks, to be appearing holy;
Chameleon, ease to change; duck, ease to yield;
Crocodile, tears which might be falsely spilled.
    Ape great thing gave, though he did mowing stand:
    The instrument of instruments, the hand.

Each other beast likewise his present brings;
And (but they drad their prince they oft should want)   100
They all consented were to give him wings.
And ay more awe towards him for to plant,
To their own work this privilege they grant:
    That from thenceforth to all eternity
    No beast should freely speak, but only he.

Thus man was made; thus man their lord became;
Who at the first, wanting or hiding pride,
He did to beasts' best use his cunning frame,
With water drink, herbs meat, and naked hide,
And fellow-like let his dominion slide,   110
    Not in his sayings saying 'I', but 'we';
    As if he meant his lordship common be.

But when his seat so rooted he had found
That they now skilled not how from him to wend,
Then gan in guiltless earth full many a wound,
Iron to seek, which gainst itself should bend
To tear the bowels that good corn should send.
    But yet the common dam none did bemoan,
    Because (though hurt) they never heard her groan.

Then gan he factions in the beasts to breed;   120
Where helping weaker sort, the nobler beasts
(As tigers, leopards, bears, and lions' seed)
Disdained with this, in deserts sought their rests;
Where famine ravin taught their hungry chests,
    That craftily he forced them to do ill;
    Which being done, he afterwards would kill

For murder done, which never erst was seen,
By those great beasts. As for the weakers' good,
He chose themselves his guarders for to been

Gainst those of might of whom in fear they stood,   130
As horse and dog; not great, but gentle blood.
  Blithe were the commons, cattle of the field,
  Tho when they saw their foen° of greatness killed.

But they, or spent, or made of slender might,
Then quickly did the meaner cattle find,
The great beams gone, the house on shoulders light;
For by and by the horse fair bits did bind;
The dog was in a collar taught his kind.
  As for the gentle birds, like case might rue
  When falcon they, and goshawk, saw in mew.   140

Worst fell to smallest birds, and meanest herd,
Who now his own, full like his own he used.
Yet first but wool, or feathers, off he teared;
And when they were well used to be abused,
For hungry throat their flesh with teeth he bruised;
  At length for glutton taste he did them kill;
  At last for sport their silly lives did spill.

But yet, O man, rage not beyond thy need;°
Deem it no gloire° to swell in tyranny.
Thou art of blood; joy not to make things bleed.   150
Thou fearest death; think they are loath to die.
A plaint of guiltless hurt doth pierce the sky.
  And you, poor beasts, in patience bide your hell,
  Or know your strengths,° and then you shall do well.

Thus did I sing and pipe eight sullen hours
To sheep whom love, not knowledge, made to hear;
Now fancy's fits, now fortune's baleful stours.
But then I homeward called my lambkins dear;
For to my dimmed eyes began t'appear
  The night grown old, her black head waxen grey,   160
  Sure shepherd's sign that morn would soon fetch day.

According to the nature of diverse ears, diverse judgements straight followed: some praising his voice; others the words, fit to frame a pastoral style; others the strangeness of the tale, and scanning what he should mean by it. But old Geron (who had borne him a grudge ever since, in one of their eclogues, he had taken him up over-bitterly) took hold of this occasion to make his revenge and said he never saw thing worse proportioned than to bring in a tale of he knew not what beasts at such a banquet when rather some song of love, or matter for joyful melody, was to be brought forth. 'But', said he, 'this is the right conceit of young men who think then they speak wiseliest when they cannot understand themselves.' Then invited he Histor to answer him in eclogue-wise; who, indeed, having been long in love with the fair bride Kala, and now prevented, was grown into a detestation of marriage. But thus it was:

Geron   Histor

Geron. In faith, good Histor, long is your delay
    From holy marriage, sweet and surest mean
    Our foolish lusts in honest rules to stay.
I pray thee do to Lalus' sample lean.
    Thou seest how frisk and jolly now he is
    That last day seemed he could not chaw a bean.
Believe me, man, there is no greater bliss
    Than is the quiet joy of loving wife,
    Which whoso wants, half of himself doth miss.
Friend without change, playfellow without strife,   10
    Food without fullness, counsel without pride,
    Is this sweet doubling of our single life.

Histor. No doubt to whom so good chance did betide
    As for to find a pasture strowed with gold,
    He were a fool if there he did not bide.
Who would not have a phoenix if he could?
    The humming wasp, if it had not a sting,
    Before all flies the wasp accept I would.
But this bad world few golden fields doth bring;
    Phoenix but one, of crows we millions have;   20
    The wasp seems gay, but is a cumbrous thing.
If many Kalas our Arcadia gave,
    Lalus' example I would soon ensue;
    And think I did myself from sorrow save.
But of such wives we find a slender crew;
    Shrewdness so stirs, pride so puffs up their heart,
    They seldom ponder what to them is due.
With meagre looks, as if they still did smart,
    Puling and whimp'ring, or else scolding flat,
    Make home more pain than following of the cart.   30
Either dull silence, or eternal chat;

Still contrary to what her husband says:
    If he do praise the dog, she likes the cat.
Austere she is, when he would honest plays;
    And gamesome then, when he thinks on his sheep;
    She bids him go, and yet from journey stays.
She war doth ever with his kinsfolk keep,
    And makes them fremd who friends by nature are,
    Envying shallow toys with malice deep.
And if, forsooth, there come some new-found ware,   40
    The little coin his sweating brows have got
    Must go for that, if for her lours he care;
Or else: 'Nay, faith, mine is the lucklest lot
    That ever fell to honest woman yet;
    No wife but I hath such a man, God wot.'
Such is their speech who be of sober wit;
    But who do let their tongues show well their rage,
    Lord, what by-words they speak, what spite they spit!
The house is made a very loathsome cage,
    Wherein the bird doth never sing, but cry   50
    With such a will that nothing can assuage.
Dearly the servants do their wages buy,
    Reviled for each small fault, sometimes for none;
    They better live that in a gaol do lie.
Let other fouler spots away be blown,
    For I seek not their shame; but still, methinks,
    A better life it is to lie alone.

Geron. Who for each fickle fear from virtue shrinks
    Shall in this life embrace no worthy thing;
    No mortal man the cup of surety drinks.   60
The heav'ns do not good haps in handfuls bring,
    But let us pick our good from out much bad;
    That still our little world may know his king.
But certainly so long we may be glad
    While that we do what nature doth require,
    And for th'event we never ought be sad.
Man oft is plagued with air, is burnt with fire,
    In water drowned, in earth his burial is;
    And shall we not therefore their use desire?
Nature above all things requireth this: 70
    That we our kind do labour to maintain;

Which drawn-out line doth hold all human bliss.
Thy father justly may of thee complain,°
    If thou do not repay his deeds for thee,
    In granting unto him a grandsire's gain.
Thy commonwealth may rightly grieved be,
    Which must by this immortal be preserved,
    If thus thou murder thy posterity.
His very being he hath not deserved
    Who for a self-conceit will that forbear   80
    Whereby that being ay must be conserved.
And God forbid women such cattle were
    As you paint them; but well in you I find,
    No man doth speak aright who speaks in fear.
Who only sees the ill is worse than blind.
    These fifty winters married I have been;
    And yet find no such faults in womankind.
I have a wife worthy to be a queen,
    So well she can command, and yet obey;
    In ruling of a house so well she's seen.   90
And yet in all this time betwixt us tway,
    We bear our double yoke with such consent,
    There never passed foul word, I dare well say.
But these be your love-toys which still are spent
    In lawless games, and love not as you should,
    But with much study learn late to repent.
How well last day before our prince you could
    Blind Cupid's works with wonder testify!
    Yet now the root of him abase you would.
Go to, go to, and Cupid now apply   100
    To that where thou thy Cupid mayst avow,
    And thou shalt find in women virtues lie.
Sweet supple minds which soon to wisdom bow,
    Where they by wisdom's rules directed are,
    And are not forced fond thraldom to allow.
As we to get are framed, so they to spare;
    We made for pains, our pains they made to cherish;
    We care abroad, and they of home have care.
O Histor, seek within thyself to flourish;
    Thy house by thee must live, or else be gone,   110
    And then who shall the name of Histor nourish?
Riches of children pass a prince's throne;

> Which touch the father's heart with secret joy
> When without shame he saith: 'these be mine own.'
> Marry therefore; for marriage will destroy
>> Those passions which to youthful head do climb,
>> Mothers and nurses of all vain annoy.

Histor. Perchance I will, but now methinks it time
>> We go unto the bride, and use this day
>> To speak with her, while freely speak we may.   120

He spake these last words with such affection as a curious eye might easily have perceived he liked Lalus's fortune better than he loved his person. But then, indeed, did all arise, and went to the women; where spending all the day and good part of the night in dancing, carolling, and wassailing, lastly they left Lalus where he long desired to be left, and with many unfeigned thanks returned every man to his home. But some of them, having to cross the way of the two lodges, might see a lady° making doleful lamentations over a body seemed dead unto them.

But methinks Dametas cries unto me, if I come not the sooner to comfort him, he will leave off his golden work hath already cost him so much labour and longing.

Here end the third eclogues.

THE FOURTH ECLOGUES

THE shepherds, finding no place for them in these garboils, to which their quiet hearts (whose highest ambition was in keeping themselves up in goodness) had at all no aptness, retired themselves from among the clamorous multitude, and (as sorrow refuseth not sorrowful company) went up together to the western side of a hill whose prospect extended it so far as they might well discern many of Arcadia's beauties. And there, looking upon the sun's as then declining race, the poor men sat pensive of their present miseries, as if they found a wearisomeness of their woeful words; till at last good old Geron (who as he had longest tasted the benefits of Basilius's government so seemed to have a special feeling of the present loss), wiping his eyes and long white beard bedewed with great drops of tears, began in this sort to complain:

'Alas, poor sheep', said he, 'which hitherto have enjoyed your fruitful pasture in such quietness as your wool, among other things, hath made this country famous, your best days are now passed. Now must you become the victual of an army, and perchance an army of foreign enemies. You are now not only to fear home wolves but alien lions; now, I say, now that Basilius, our right Basilius is deceased. Alas, sweet pastures, shall soldiers that know not how to use you possess you? Shall they that cannot speak Arcadian language be lords over your shepherds? For, alas, with good cause may we look for any evil, since Basilius our only strength is taken from us.'

To that all the other shepherds present uttered pitiful voices, especially the very born Arcadians. For, as for the other, though humanity moved them to pity human cases, especially of a prince under whom they had found a refuge of their miseries and justice equally administered, yet they could not so naturally feel the lively touch of sorrow, but rather used this occasion to record their own private sorrows which they thought would not have agreed with a joyful time. Among them the principals were Strephon, Klaius, and Philisides. Strephon and Klaius would require a whole book° to recount their sorrows and the strange causes of their sorrows—another place perchance will serve for the declaring of them. But in short two gentlemen they were both in love with one maid of that country named Urania, thought a shepherd's daughter, but indeed of far greater birth. For her sake they had both taken this trade of life, each knowing other's love, but yet of so high a quality their friendship was that they never so much as brake company one from the other, but continued their pursuit, like two true runners both employing their best speed, but one not hindering the other. But after many marvellous adventures, Urania never yielding better than hate for their love, upon a strange occasion had left the country, giving withal strait commandment to those two by writing that they should tarry in Arcadia until they heard from her. And now some months were passed that they had no news of her; but yet rather meaning to break their hearts than break her commandment, they bare it out as well as such evil might be until now that the general complaints of all men called in like question their particular griefs, which eclogue-wise they specified in this double sestine:

Strephon   Klaius

Strephon. Ye goat-herd gods, that love the grassy mountains,
  Ye nymphs, which haunt the springs in pleasant valleys,
  Ye satyrs, joyed with free and quiet forests,
  Vouchsafe your silent ears to plaining music
  Which to my woes gives still an early morning,
  And draws the dolour on till weary evening.

Klaius. O Mercury, foregoer to the evening,
  O heav'nly huntress of the savage mountains,
  O lovely star, entitled of the morning,
  While that my voice doth fill these woeful valleys,   10
  Vouchsafe your silent ears to plaining music,
  Which oft hath Echo tired in secret forests.

Strephon. I that was once free burgess of the forests,
  Where shade from sun, and sport I sought in evening,
  I that was once esteemed for pleasant music,
  Am banished now among the monstrous mountains
  Of huge despair, and foul affliction's valleys,
  Am grown a screech-owl to myself each morning.

Klaius. I that was once delighted every morning,
  Hunting the wild inhabiters of forests,   20
  I that was once the music of these valleys,
  So darkened am that all my day is evening,
  Heart-broken so, that molehills seem high mountains,
  And fill the vales with cries instead of music.

Strephon. Long since, alas, my deadly swannish music
  Hath made itself a crier of the morning,
  And hath with wailing strength climbed highest mountains;
  Long since my thoughts more desert be than forests;
  Long since I see my joys come to their evening,
  And state thrown down to over-trodden valleys.   30

Klaius. Long since the happy dwellers of these valleys
  Have prayed me leave my strange exclaiming music,
  Which troubles their day's work, and joys of evening;
  Long since I hate the night, more hate the morning;
  Long since my thoughts chase me like beasts in forests,
  And make me wish myself laid under mountains.

Strephon. Meseems I see the high and stately mountains
  Transform themselves to low dejected valleys;
  Meseems I hear in these ill-changed forests
  The nightingales do learn of owls their music;   40
  Meseems I feel the comfort of the morning
  Turned to the mortal serene° of an evening.

Klaius. Meseems I see a filthy cloudy evening
  As soon as sun begins to climb the mountains;

Meseems I feel a noisome scent the morning
When I do smell the flowers of these valleys;
Meseems I hear (when I do hear sweet music)
The dreadful cries of murdered men in forests.

Strephon. I wish to fire the trees of all these forests;
　I give the sun a last farewell each evening;   50
　I curse the fiddling finders-out of music;
　With envy I do hate the lofty mountains,
　And with despite despise the humble valleys;
　I do detest night, evening, day, and morning.

Klaius. Curse to myself my prayer is, the morning;
　My fire is more than can be made with forests;
　My state more base than are the basest valleys;
　I wish no evenings more to see, each evening;
　Shamed, I hate myself in sight of mountains,
　And stop mine ears lest I grow mad with music.   60

Strephon. For she, whose parts maintained a perfect music,
　Whose beauties shined more than the blushing morning,
　Who much did pass in state the stately mountains,
　In straightness passed the cedars of the forests,
　Hath cast me, wretch, into eternal evening,
　By taking her two suns from these dark valleys.

Klaius. For she, with whom compared the Alps are valleys,°
　She, whose least word brings from the spheres their music,
　At whose approach the sun rase in the evening,
　Who, where she went, bare in her forehead morning,   70
　Is gone, is gone from these our spoiled forests,
　Turning to deserts our best pastured mountains.

Strephon. These mountains witness shall, so shall these valleys,

Klaius. These forests eke, made wretched by our music,
　Our morning hymn this is, and song at evening.

But, as though all this had been but the taking of a taste to their
wailings, Strephon again began this dizain, which was answered unto
him in that kind of verse which is called the crown:°

Strephon. I joy in grief, and do detest all joys;
　Despise delight, am tired with thought of ease.
　I turn my mind to all forms of annoys,

And with the change of them my fancy please.
I study that which most may me displease,
And in despite of that displeasure's might
Embrace that most that most my soul destroys;
Blinded with beams, fell darkness is my sight;
Dwell in my ruins, feed with sucking smart,
I think from me, not from my woes, to part.   10

Klaius. I think from me, not from my woes, to part,
And loathe this time called life, nay think that life
Nature to me for torment did impart;
Think my hard haps have blunted death's sharp knife,
Not sparing me in whom his works be rife;
And thinking this, think nature, life, and death
Place sorrow's triumph on my conquered heart.
Whereto I yield, and seek no other breath
But from the scent of some infectious grave;
Nor of my fortune aught but mischief crave.   20

Strephon. Nor of my fortune aught but mischief crave,
And seek to nourish that which now contains
All what I am. If I myself will save,
Then must I save what in me chiefly reigns,
Which is the hateful web of sorrow's pains.
Sorrow then cherish me, for I am sorrow;
No being now but sorrow I can have;
Then deck me as thine own; thy help I borrow,
Since thou my riches art, and that thou hast
Enough to make a fertile mind lie waste.   30

Klaius. Enough to make a fertile mind lie waste
Is that huge storm which pours itself on me.
Hailstones of tears, of sighs a monstrous blast,
Thunders of cries; lightnings my wild looks be,
The darkened heav'n my soul which naught can see;
The flying sprites which trees by roots up tear
Be those despairs which have my hopes quite waste.
The difference is: all folks those storms forbear,
But I cannot; who then myself should fly,
So close unto myself my wracks do lie.   40

Strephon. So close unto myself my wracks do lie;
Both cause, effect, beginning, and the end

Are all in me: what help then can I try?
My ship, myself, whose course to love doth bend,
Sore beaten doth her mast of comfort spend;
Her cable, reason, breaks from anchor, hope;
Fancy, her tackling, torn away doth fly;
Ruin, the wind, hath blown her from her scope;
Bruised with waves of care, but broken is
On rock, despair, the burial of my bliss.   50

Klaius. On rock, despair, the burial of my bliss,
    I long do plough with plough of deep desire;
    The seed fast-meaning is, no truth to miss;
    I harrow it with thoughts, which all conspire
    Favour to make my chief and only hire.
    But, woe is me, the year is gone about,
    And now I fain would reap, I reap but this,
    Hate fully grown, absence new sprongen out.
    So that I see, although my sight impair,
    Vain is their pain who labour in despair.   60

Strephon. Vain is their pain who labour in despair.
    For so did I, when with my angle, will.
    I sought to catch the fish torpedo fair.°
    E'en then despair did hope already kill;
    Yet fancy would perforce employ his skill,
    And this hath got: the catcher now is caught,
    Lamed with the angle which itself did bear,
    And unto death, quite drowned in dolours, brought
    To death, as then disguised in her fair face.
    Thus, thus alas, I had my loss in chase.   70

Klaius. Thus, thus alas, I had my loss in chase
    When first that crowned basilisk° I knew,
    Whose footsteps I with kisses oft did trace,
    Till by such hap as I must ever rue
    Mine eyes did light upon her shining hue,
    And hers on me, astonished with that sight.
    Since then my heart did lose his wonted place,
    Infected so with her sweet poison's might
    That, leaving me for dead, to her it went.
    But ah, her flight hath my dead relics spent.°   80

Strephon. But ah, her flight hath my dead relics spent,
  Her flight from me, from me, though dead to me,
  Yet living still in her, while her beams lent
  Such vital spark that her mine eyes might see.
  But now those living lights absented be,
  Full dead before, I now to dust should fall,
  But that eternal pains my soul have hent,
  And keep it still within this body thrall;
  That thus I must, while in this death I dwell,
  In earthly fetters feel a lasting hell.   90

Klaius. In earthly fetters feel a lasting hell
  Alas I do; from which to find release,
  I would the earth, I would the heavens sell.
  But vain it is to think those pains should cease,
  Where life is death, and death cannot breed peace.
  O fair, O only fair, from thee, alas,
  These foul, most foul, disasters to me fell;
  Since thou from me (O me) O sun didst pass.
  Therefore esteeming all good blessings toys,
  I joy in grief, and do detest all joys.   100

Strephon. I joy in grief, and do detest all joys.
  But now an end, O Klaius, now an end,
  For e'en the herbs our hateful music stroys,°
  And from our burning breath the trees do bend.

When they had ended, with earnest entreaty they obtained of Philisides that he would impart some part of the sorrow his countenance so
well witnessed unto them. And he (who by no entreaty of the duke would
be brought unto it) in this doleful time was content thus to manifest
himself:

'The name of Samothea° is so famous that, telling you I am of that, I
shall not need to extend myself further in telling you what that country is.
But there I was born, of such parentage as neither left me so great that I
was a mark for envy nor so base that I was subject to contempt, brought
up from my cradle age with such care as parents are wont to bestow upon
their children whom they mean to make the maintainers of their name.
And as soon as my memory grew strong enough to receive what might be
delivered unto it by my senses, they offered learning unto me, especially
that kind that teacheth what in truth and not in opinion is to be embraced,
and what to be eschewed. Neither was I barred from seeking the natural
knowledge of things so far as the narrow sight of man hath pierced into

it. And because the mind's commandment is vain without the body be enabled to obey it, my strength was exercised with horsemanship, weapons, and suchlike other qualities as, besides the practice, carried in themselves some serviceable use; wherein I so profited that, as I was not excellent, so I was accompanable.° After that by my years, or perchance by a sooner privilege than years commonly grant, I was thought able to be mine own master, I was suffered to spend some time in travel, that by the comparison of many things I might ripen my judgement; since greatness, power, riches, and suchlike standing in relation to another, who doth know none but his own, doth not know his own. Then being home returned, and thought of good hope (for the world rarely bestows a better title upon youth), I continued to use the benefits of a quiet mind; in truth (I call him to witness that knoweth hearts) even in the secret of my soul bent to honesty—thus far you see, as no pompous spectacle, so an untroubled tenor of a well guided life. But alas, what should I make pathetical exclamations to a most true event? So it happened that love (which what it is, your own feeling can best tell you) diverted this course of tranquillity; which, though I did with so much covering hide that I was thought void of it as any man, yet my wound which smarted to myself brought me in fine to this change, much in state but more in mind. But how love first took me I did once, using the liberty of versifying, set down in a song, in a dream indeed it was; and thus did I poetically describe my dream:

Now was our heav'nly vault deprived of the light
With sun's depart; and now the darkness of the night
Did light those beamy stars which greater light did dark.
Now each thing which enjoyed that fiery quickning spark
Which life is called were moved their spirits to repose,
And wanting use of eyes, their eyes began to close.
A silence sweet each where with one concent embraced
(A music sweet to one in careful musing placed);
And mother earth, now clad in mourning weeds, did breathe
A dull desire to kiss the image of our death;   10
When I, disgraced wretch, not wretched then, did give
My senses such release as they which quiet live,
Whose brains boil not in woes, nor breasts with beatings ache,
With nature's praise are wont in safest home to take.
Far from my thoughts was aught whereto their minds aspire
Who under courtly pomps do hatch a base desire.
Free all my powers were from those captiving snares
Which heav'nly purest gifts defile in muddy cares.

Ne could my soul itself accuse of such a fault
As tender conscience might with furious pangs assault.   20
But like the feeble flow'r (whose stalk cannot sustain
His weighty top) his top doth downward drooping lean;
Or as the silly bird in well acquainted nest
Doth hide his head with cares but only how to rest,
So I in simple course, and unentangled mind,
Did suffer drowsy lids mine eyes then clear to blind;
And laying down my head, did nature's rule observe,
Which senses up doth shut the senses to preserve.
They first their use forgot, then fancies lost their force,
Till deadly sleep at length possessed my living corse.   30
A living corse I lay; but ah, my wakeful mind
(Which made of heav'nly stuff no mortal change doth bind)
Flew up with freer wings of fleshy bondage free;
And having placed my thoughts, my thoughts thus placed me:
Methought, nay sure I was, I was in fairest wood
Of Samothea land; a land which whilom stood
An honour to the world, while honour was their end,
And while their line of years they did in virtue spend.
But there I was, and there my calmy thoughts I fed
On nature's sweet repast, as healthful senses led.   40
Her gifts my study was, her beauties were my sport;
My work her works to know, her dwelling my resort.
Those lamps of heav'nly fire to fixed motion bound,
The ever turning spheres, the never moving ground;
What essence dest'ny hath; if fortune be or no;
Whence our immortal souls to mortal earth do flow;
What life it is, and how that all these lives do gather,
With outward maker's force, or like an inward father.
Such thoughts, methought, I thought, and strained my single
     mind
Then void of nearer cares, the depth of things to find.   50
When lo, with hugest noise (such noise a tower makes
When it blown up with mine a fall of ruin takes;
Or such a noise it was as highest thunders send,
Or cannons thunder-like, all shot together, lend),
The moon asunder rent (O gods, O pardon me,
That forced with grief reveals what grieved eyes did see),
The moon asunder rent; whereat with sudden fall
(More swift than falcon's stoop to feeding falconer's call)

There came a chariot fair by doves and sparrows guided,
Whose storm-like course stayed not till hard by me it bided.   60
I, wretch, astonished was, and thought the deathful doom
Of heav'n, of earth, of hell, of time and place was come.
But straight there issued forth two ladies (ladies sure
They seemed to me) on whom did wait a virgin pure;
Strange were the ladies' weeds, yet more unfit than strange.
The first with clothes tucked up, as nymphs in woods do range,
Tucked up e'en with the knees, with bow and arrows prest;
Her right arm naked was, discovered was her breast.
But heavy was her pace, and such a meagre cheer°
As little hunting mind (God knows) did there appear.   70
The other had with art (more than our women know,
As stuff meant for the sale set out to glaring show)
A wanton woman's face, and with curled knots had twined
Her hair which, by the help of painter's cunning, shined.
When I such guests did see come out of such a house,
The mountains great with child I thought brought forth a
    mouse.
But walking forth, the first thus to the second said:
'Venus, come on.' Said she: 'Diane, you are obeyed.'
Those names abashed me much, when those great names I
    heard;
Although their fame (meseemed) from truth had greatly jarred.°   80
As I thus musing stood, Diana called to her
Her waiting nymph, a nymph that did excel as far
All things that erst I saw, as orient pearls exceed
That which their mother hight, or else their silly seed;
Indeed a perfect hue, indeed a sweet concent
Of all those graces' gifts the heav'ns have ever lent.
And so she was attired, as one that did not prize
Too much her peerless parts, nor yet could them despise.
But called, she came apace; a pace wherein did move
The band of beauties all, the little world of love.   90
And bending humbled eyes (O eyes, the sun of sight)
She waited mistress' will, who thus disclosed her sprite:
'Sweet Mira mine', quoth she, 'the pleasure of my mind,
In whom of all my rules the perfect proof I find,
To only thee thou seest we grant this special grace
Us to attend, in this most private time and place.
Be silent therefore now, and so be silent still

Of what thou seest; close up in secret knot thy will.'
She answered was with look, and well performed behest.
And Mira I admired; her shape sank in my breast.   100
But thus with ireful eyes, and face that shook with spite,
Diana did begin: 'What moved me to invite
Your presence, sister dear, first to my moony sphere,
And hither now, vouchsafe to take with willing ear.
I know full well you know what discord long hath reigned
Betwixt us two; how much that discord foul hath stained
Both our estates, while each the other did deprave,
Proof speaks too much to us that feeling trial have.
Our names are quite forgot, our temples are defaced;
Our off'rings spoiled, our priests from priesthood are displaced. 110
Is this thy fruit, O strife? those thousand churches high,
Those thousand altars fair now in the dust to lie?
In mortal minds our minds but planets' names preserve;
No knee once bowed, forsooth, for them they say we serve.
Are we their servants grown? no doubt a noble stay;
Celestial pow'rs to worms, Jove's children serve to clay.
But such they say we be; this praise our discord bred,
While we for mutual spite a striving passion fed.
But let us wiser be; and what foul discord brake,
So much more strong again let fastest concord make.   120
Our years do it require; you see we both do feel
The weak'ning work of time's for ever whirling wheel.
Although we be divine, our grandsire Saturn is
With age's force decayed, yet once the heav'n was his.
And now before we seek by wise Apollo's skill
Our young years to renew (for so he saith he will)
Let us a perfect peace betwixt us two resolve;
Which, lest the ruinous want of government dissolve,
Let one the princess be, to her the other yield;
For vain equality is but contention's field.   130
And let her have the gifts that should in both remain;
In her let beauty both and chasteness fully reign;
So as, if I prevail, you give your gifts to me;
If you, on you I lay what in my office be.
Now resteth only this: which of us two is she
To whom precedence shall of both accorded be.
For that (so that you like) hereby doth lie a youth
(She beckoned unto me), as yet of spotless truth,

Who may this doubt discern; for better wit than lot
Becometh us; in us fortune determines not.   140
This crown of amber fair° (an amber crown she held)
To worthiest let him give when both he hath beheld;
And be it as he saith.' Venus was glad to hear
Such proffer made, which she well showed with smiling cheer;
As though she were the same as when by Paris' doom
She had chief goddesses in beauty overcome.
And smirkly° thus gan say: 'I never sought debate,
Diana dear, my mind to love and not to hate
Was ever apt; but you my pastimes did despise.
I never spited you, but thought you over wise.   150
Now kindness proffered is, none kinder is than I;
And so most ready am this mean of peace to try.
And let him be our judge; the lad doth please me well.'
Thus both did come to me, and both began to tell
(For both together spake, each loath to be behind)
That they by solemn oath their deities would bind
To stand unto my will; their will they made me know.
If that was first aghast, when first I saw their show,
Now bolder waxed, waxed proud that I such sway might bear;
For near acquaintance doth diminish reverent fear.   160
And having bound them fast by Styx they should obey
To all what I decreed, did thus my verdict say:
'How ill both you can rule, well hath your discord taught;
Ne yet, for what I see, your beauties merit aught.
To yonder nymph therefore (to Mira I did point)
The crown above you both for ever I appoint.'
I would have spoken out, but out they both did cry:
'Fie, fie, what have we done? ungodly rebel, fie!
But now we must needs yield to what our oaths require.'
'Yet thou shalt not go free,' quoth Venus, 'such a fire   170
Her beauty kindle shall within thy foolish mind
That thou full oft shalt wish thy judging eyes were blind.'
'Nay then,' Diana, said, 'the chasteness I will give
In ashes of despair, though burnt, shall make thee live.'
'Nay thou', said both, 'shalt see such beams shine in her face
That thou shalt never dare seek help of wretched case.'
And with that cursed curse away to heav'n they fled,
First having all their gifts upon fair Mira spread.
The rest I cannot tell, for therewithal I waked

And found with deadly fear that all my sinews shaked.   180
Was it a dream? O dream, how hast thou wrought in me
That I things erst unseen should first in dreaming see?
And thou, O traitor sleep, made for to be our rest,
How hast thou framed the pain wherewith I am oppressed?
O coward Cupid, thus dost thou thy honour keep,
Unarmed, alas unwarned, to take a man asleep?

In such, or suchlike, sort in a dream was offered unto me the sight of
her in whose respect all things afterwards seemed but blind darkness
unto me. For so it fell out that her I saw, I say that sweet and
incomparable Mira (so like her which in that rather vision than dream of
mine I had seen), that I began to persuade myself in my nativity I was
allotted unto her; to her, I say, whom even Coredens° made the upshot of
all his despairing desires, and so, alas, from all other exercises of my
mind bent myself only to the pursuit of her favour. But having spent some
part of my youth in following of her, sometimes with some measure of
favour, sometimes with unkind interpretations of my most kind thoughts,
in the end having attempted all means to establish my blissful estate, and
having been not only refused all comfort but new quarrels picked against
me, I did resolve by perpetual absence to choke mine own ill fortunes.
Yet before I departed these following elegiacs I sent unto her:

                    – ◡ ◡ – – – – – – – – ◡ ◡ – –
                    – – – ◡ ◡ – – ◡ ◡ – ◡ ◡ –

Unto the caitiff wretch whom long affliction holdeth,
    and now fully believes help to be quite perished,
Grant yet, grant yet a look, to the last monument of his anguish.
    O you (alas so I find) cause of his only ruin.
Dread not a whit (O goodly cruel) that pity may enter
    Into thy heart by the sight of this epistle I send;
And so refuse to behold of these strange wounds the recital,
    Lest it might thee allure home to thyself to return
(Unto thyself I do mean, those graces dwell so within thee,
    gratefulness, sweetness, holy love, hearty regard).   10
Such thing cannot I seek (despair hath giv'n me my answer,
    despair most tragical clause to a deadly request);
Such thing cannot he hope that knows thy determinate
        hardness;
    hard like a rich marble; hard, but a fair diamond.

Can those eyes, that of eyes drowned in most hearty flowing
    tears
  (tears, and tears of a man) had no return to remorse;
Can those eyes now yield to the kind conceit of a sorrow,
  which ink only relates, but ne laments, ne replies?
Ah, that, that do I not conceive, though that to me lief were
  more than Nestor's years, more than a king's diadem.   20
Ah, that, that do I not conceive; to the heaven when a mouse
    climbs
  then may I hope t'achieve grace of a heavenly tiger.
But, but alas, like a man condemned doth crave to be heard
    speak,
  not that he hopes for amends of the disaster he feels,
But finding th'approach of death with an inly relenting,
  gives an adieu to the world, as to his only delight;
Right so my boiling heart, inflamed with fire of a fair eye,
  bubbling out doth breathe signs of his hugy dolours,
Now that he finds to what end his life and love be reserved,
  and that he thence must part where to live only I lived.   30
O fair, O fairest, are such the triumphs to thy fairness?
  can death beauty become? must I be such a monument?
Must I be only the mark shall prove that virtue is angry?
  shall prove that fierceness can with a white dove abide?
Shall to the world appear that faith and love be rewarded
  with mortal disdain, bent to unendly revenge?
Unto revenge? O sweet, on a wretch wilt thou be revenged?
  shall such high planets tend to the loss of a worm?
And to revenge who do bend would in that kind be revenged,
  as th'offence was done, and go beyond if he can.   40
All my 'offence was love; with love then must I be chastened,
  and with more by the laws that to revenge do belong.
If that love be a fault, more fault in you to be lovely;
  love never had me oppressed, but that I saw to be loved.
You be the cause that I love; what reason blameth a shadow
  that with a body't goes, since by a body it is?
If the love hate you did, you should your beauty have hidden;
  you should those fair eyes have with a veil covered.
But fool, fool that I am, those eyes would shine from a dark
    cave;
  what veils then do prevail, but to a more miracle?   50
Or those golden locks (those locks which lock me to bondage)

torn you should disperse unto the blasts of a wind.
But fool, fool that I am, though I had but a hair of her head
    found,
    ee'n as I am, so I should unto that hair be a thrall.
Or with a fair hand's nails (O hand which nails me to this
    death)
    you should have your face (since love is ill) blemished.
O wretch, what do I say? should that fair face be defaced?
    should my too much sight cause so true a sun to be lost?
First let Cimmerian darkness be my onl'habitation,
    first be mine eyes pulled out, first be my brain perished,   60
Ere that I should consent to do such excessive a damage
    unto the earth by the hurt of this her heavenly jewel.
O not but such love you say you could have afforded,
    as might learn temp'rance void of a rage's events.
O sweet simplicity, from whence should love be so learned?
    unto Cupid that boy shall a pedant be found?
Well, but faulty I was; reason to my passion yielded,
    passion unto my rage, rage to a hasty revenge.
But what's this for a fault, for which such faith be abolished,
    such faith, so stainless, inviolate, violent?   70
Shall I not? O may I not thus yet refresh the remembrance
    what sweet joys I had once, and what a place I did hold?
Shall I not once object that you, you granted a favour
    unto the man whom now such miseries you award?
Bend your thoughts to the dear sweet words which then to me
    giv'n were;
    think what a world is now, think who hath altered her heart.
What? was I then worthy such good, now worthy so much evil?
    now fled, then cherished? then so nigh, now so remote?
Did not a rosed breath, from lips more rosy proceeding,
    say that I well should find in what a care I was had?   80
With much more: now what do I find but care to abhor me,
    care that I sink in grief, care that I live banished?
And banished do I live, nor now will seek a recov'ry,
    since so she will, whose will is to me more than a law.
If then a man in most ill case may give you a farewell;
    farewell, long farewell,° all my woe, all my delight.

Philisides would have gone on in telling the rest of his unhappy
adventures, and by what desperate works of fortune he was become a
shepherd; but the shepherd Dicus desired him he would for that time

leave particular passions, and join in bewailing this general loss of that country which had been a nurse to strangers as well as a mother to Arcadians. And so, having purchased silence, Agelastus° rather cried out than sang this following lamentation:

Since that to death is gone the shepherd high
  Who most the silly shepherd's pipe did prize,
  Your doleful tunes sweet muses now apply.
And you, O trees (if any life there lies
  In trees) now through your porous barks receive
  The strange resound of these my causeful cries;
And let my breath upon your branches cleave,
  My breath distinguished into words of woe,
  That so I may signs of my sorrows leave.
But if among yourselves some one tree grow   10
  That aptest is to figure misery,
  Let it ambassade bear your griefs to show.
The weeping myrrh I think will not deny
  Her help to this, this justest cause of plaint.
  Your doleful tunes sweet muses now apply.

And thou, poor earth, whom fortune doth attaint
  In nature's name to suffer such a harm
  As for to lose thy gem, our earthly saint,
Upon thy face let coaly ravens swarm;
  Let all the sea thy tears accounted be;   20
  Thy bowels with all killing metals arm.
Let gold now rust, let diamonds waste in thee;
  Let pearls be wan with woe their dam doth bear;
  Thyself henceforth the light do never see.
And you, O flow'rs, which sometimes princes were,
  Till these strange alt'rings you did hap to try,
  Of prince's loss yourselves for tokens rear.
Lily in mourning black thy whiteness dye.
  O hyacinth let ai° be on thee still.
  Your doleful tunes sweet muses now apply.   30

O echo, all these woods with roaring fill,
  And do not only mark the accents last
  But all, for all reach not my wailful will;
One echo to another echo cast
  Sound of my griefs, and let it never end
  Till that it hath all woods and waters passed.

Nay, to the heav'ns your just complainings send,
   And stay the stars' inconstant constant race
   Till that they do unto our dolours bend;
And ask the reason of that special grace   40
   That they, which have no lives, should live so long,
   And virtuous souls so soon should lose their place?
Ask if in great men good men so do throng
   That he for want of elbow-room must die?
   Or if that they be scant, if this be wrong?
Did wisdom this our wretched time espy
   In one true chest to rob all virtue's treasure?
   Your doleful tunes sweet muses now apply.

And if that any counsel you to measure
   Your doleful tunes, to them still plaining say   50
   To well felt grief, plaint is the only pleasure.
O light of sun, which is entitled day,
   O well thou dost that thou no longer bidest;
   For mourning night her black weeds may display.
O Phoebus with good cause thy face thou hidest
   Rather than have thy all-beholding eye
   Fouled with this sight while thou thy chariot guidest.
And well (methinks) becomes this vaulty sky
   A stately tomb to cover him deceased. .
   Your doleful tunes sweet muses now apply.   60

O Philomela° with thy breast oppressed
   By shame and grief, help, help me to lament
   Such cursed harms as cannot be redressed.
Or if thy mourning notes be fully spent,
   Then give a quiet ear unto my plaining;
   For I to teach the world complaint am bent.
Ye dimmy clouds, which well employ your staining
   This cheerful air with your obscured cheer,
   Witness your woeful tears with daily raining.

And if, O sun, thou ever didst appear   70
   In shape which by man's eye might be perceived,
   Virtue is dead, now set thy triumph here.
Now set thy triumph in this world, bereaved
   Of what was good, where now no good doth lie;
   And by thy pomp our loss will be conceived.

O notes of mine, yourselves together tie;
    With too much grief methinks you are dissolved.
    Your doleful tunes sweet muses now apply.

Time ever old and young is still revolved
    Within itself, and never taketh end;   80
    But mankind is for ay to naught resolved.
The filthy snake her aged coat can mend,
    And getting youth again, in youth doth flourish;
    But unto man, age ever death doth send.
The very trees with grafting we can cherish,
    So that we can long time produce° their time;
    But man which helpeth them, helpless must perish.
Thus, thus, the minds which over all do climb,
    When they by years' experience get best graces,
    Must finish then by death's detested crime.   90
We last short while, and build long-lasting places.
    Ah, let us all against foul nature cry;
    We nature's works do help, she us defaces.
For how can nature unto this reply:
    That she her child, I say, her best child killeth?
    Your doleful tunes sweet muses now apply.

Alas, methinks my weakened voice but spilleth
    The vehement course of this just lamentation;
    Methinks my sound no place with sorrow filleth.
I know not I, but once in detestation   100
    I have myself, and all what life containeth,
    Since death on virtue's fort hath made invasion.
One word of woe another after traineth;
    Ne do I care how rude be my invention,
    So it be seen what sorrow in me reigneth.
O elements, by whose (they say) contention
    Our bodies be in living pow'r maintained,
    Was this man's death the fruit of your dissension?
O physic's power, which (some say) hath refrained
    Approach of death, alas thou helpest meagrely   110
    When once one is for Atropos° distrained.
Great be physicians' brags, but aid is beggarly;
    When rooted moisture fails, or groweth dry,
    They leave off all, and say death comes too eagerly.
They are but words therefore which men do buy

Of any since god Aesculapius° ceased.
Your doleful tunes sweet muses now apply.

Justice, justice is now, alas, oppressed;
    Bountifulness hath made his last conclusion;
    Goodness for best attire in dust is dressed.   120
Shepherds bewail your uttermost confusion;
    And see by this picture to you presented,
    Death is our home, life is but a delusion.
For see, alas, who is from you absented.
    Absented? nay, I say for ever banished
    From such as were to die for him contented.
Out of our sight in turn of hand° is vanished
    Shepherd of shepherds, whose well settled order
    Private with wealth, public with quiet, garnished.
While he did live, far, far was all disorder;   130
    Example more prevailing than direction,
    Far was home-strife, and far was foe from border.
His life a law, his look a full correction;
    As in his health we healthful were preserved,
    So in his sickness grew our sure infection;
His death our death. But ah, my muse hath swarved
    From such deep plaint as should such woes descry,
    Which he of us for ever hath deserved.
The style of heavy heart can never fly
    So high as should make such a pain notorious.   140
    Cease muse, therefore; thy dart, O death, apply;
And farewell prince, whom goodness hath made glorious.

Agelastus, when he had ended his song, thus maintained the lamentation in this rhyming sestine, having the doleful tune of the other
shepherds' pipes joined unto him:

    Farewell O sun,° Arcadia's clearest light;
    Farewell O pearl, the poor man's plenteous treasure;
    Farewell O golden staff, the weak man's might;
    Farewell O joy, the woeful's only pleasure.
    Wisdom farewell, the skill-less man's direction;
    Farewell with thee, farewell all our affection.

    For what place now is left for our affection,
    Now that of purest lamp is queint° the light
    Which to our darkened minds was best direction;

Now that the mine is lost of all our treasure,   10
Now death hath swallowed up our worldly pleasure,
We orphans left, void of all public might?

Orphans indeed, deprived of father's might;
For he our father was in all affection,
In our well doing placing all his pleasure,
Still studying how to us to be a light.
As well he was in peace a safest treasure;
In war his wit and word was our direction.

Whence, whence alas, shall we seek our direction
When that we fear our hateful neighbours' might,   20
Who long have gaped to get Arcadians' treasure?
Shall we now find a guide of such affection,
Who for our sakes will think all travail light,
And make his pain to keep us safe his pleasure?

No, no, for ever gone is all our pleasure;
For ever wand'ring from all good direction;
For ever blinded of our clearest light;
For ever lamed of our surest might;
For ever banished from well placed affection;
For ever robbed of our royal treasure.   30

Let tears for him therefore be all our treasure,
And in our wailful naming him our pleasure.
Let hating of ourselves be our affection,
And unto death bend still our thoughts' direction.
Let us against ourselves employ our might,
And putting out our eyes seek we our light.

Farewell our light, farewell our spoiled treasure;
Farewell our might, farewell our daunted pleasure;
Farewell direction, farewell all affection.

The night began to cast her dark canopy over them; and they, even wearied with their woes, bended homewards, hoping by a sleep, forgetting themselves, to ease their present dolours, when they were met with a troop of twenty horsemen. The chief of which asking them for the duke, and understanding the hard news, did thereupon stay among them, and send away with speed to Philanax. But since the night is an ease of all things, it shall at this present ease my memory, tired with these troublesome matters.

Here end the fourth eclogues.

'What tongue can her perfections tell'

What tongue can her perfections tell
In whose each part all pens may dwell?
Her hair fine threads of finest gold
In curled knots man's thought to hold;
But that her forehead says, 'in me
A whiter beauty you may see.'
Whiter indeed; more white than snow
Which on cold winter's face doth grow.

  That doth present those even brows,
Whose equal lines their angles bows,   10
Like to the moon when after change
Her horned head abroad doth range;
And arches be to heav'nly lids,
Whose wink each bold attempt forbids.

  For the black stars those spheres contain,
Their matchless praise,° e'en praise doth stain.
No lamp whose light by art is got,
No sun which shines, and seeth not,
Can liken them without all peer,
Save one as much as other clear;   20
Which only thus unhappy be
Because themselves they cannot see.

  Her cheeks with kindly claret spread,
Aurora-like new out of bed,
Or like the fresh queen-apple's° side,
Blushing at sight of Phoebus' pride.
Her nose, her chin, pure ivory wears,
No purer than the pretty ears,
Save that therein appears some blood,
Like wine and milk that mingled stood.   30
In whose incirclets if you gaze
Your eyes may tread a lover's maze,
But with such turns the voice to stray,
No talk untaught can find the way.
The tip no jewel needs to wear;
The tip is jewel of the ear.

  But who those ruddy lips can miss,
Which blessed still themselves do kiss?
Rubies, cherries, and roses new,

In worth, in taste, in perfect hue,   40
Which never part but that they show
Of precious pearl the double row,
The second sweetly-fenced ward
Her heav'nly-dewed tongue to guard,
Whence never word in vain did flow.
   Fair under these doth stately grow
The handle of this pleasant work,
The neck, in which strange graces lurk.
Such be, I think, the sumptuous towers
Which skill doth make in princes' bowers.   50
   So good a say° invites the eye
A little downward to espy
The lovely clusters of her breasts,
Of Venus' babe the wanton nests,
Like pommels round of marble clear,
Where azured veins well mixed appear,
With dearest tops of porphyry.°
   Betwixt these two a way doth lie,
A way more worthy beauty's fame
Than that which bears the milken name.   60
This leads unto the joyous field
Which only still doth lilies yield;
But lilies such whose native smell
The Indian odours doth excel.
Waist it is called, for it doth waste
Men's lives until it be embraced.
   There may one see, and yet not see,
Her ribs in white well armed be,
More white than Neptune's foamy face
When struggling rocks he would embrace.   70
   In these delights the wand'ring thought
Might of each side astray be brought,
But that her navel doth unite
In curious circle busy sight,
A dainty seal of virgin wax
Where nothing but impression lacks.
   Her belly there glad sight doth fill,
Justly entitled Cupid's hill;
A hill most fit for such a master,
A spotless mine of alabaster,   80

Like alabaster fair and sleek,
But soft and supple, satin-like,
In that sweet seat the boy doth sport.
Loath, I must leave his chief resort;
For such an use the world hath gotten,
The best things still must be forgotten.

Yet never shall my song omit
Those thighs (for Ovid's song more fit)
Which, flanked with two sugared flanks,
Lift up their stately swelling banks   90
That Albion cliffs in whiteness pass,
With haunches smooth as looking glass.

But bow all knees, now of her knees
My tongue doth tell what fancy sees:
The knots of joy, the gems of love,
Whose motion makes all graces move;
Whose bought incaved° doth yield such sight,
Like cunning painter° shadowing white.
The gart'ring place° with childlike sign
Shows easy print in metal fine.   100

But there again the flesh doth rise
In her brave calves like crystal skies,
Whose Atlas° is a smallest small,
More white than whitest bone of whale.

There oft steals out that round clean foot,
This noble cedar's precious root;
In show and scent pale violets,
Whose step on earth all beauty sets.

But back unto her back, my muse,
Where Leda's swan his feathers mews,°   110
Along whose ridge such bones are met,
Like comfits round in marchpane set.

Her shoulders be like two white doves,
Perching within square royal rooves,
Which leaded are with silver skin,
Passing the hate-spot ermelin.°

And thence those arms derived are;
The phoenix' wings be not so rare
For faultless length and stainless hue.

Ah, woe is me, my woes renew!   120
Now course doth lead me to her hand,

Of my first love the fatal band,
Where whiteness doth for ever sit;
Nature herself enamelled it.
For there with strange compact doth lie
Warm snow, moist pearl, soft ivory.
There fall those sapphire-coloured brooks,
Which conduit-like, with curious crooks,
Sweet islands make in that sweet land.
As for the fingers of the hand,   130
The bloody shafts of Cupid's war,
With amethysts they headed are.
  Thus hath each part his beauty's part;
But how the Graces do impart
To all her limbs a special grace,
Becoming every time and place,
Which doth e'en beauty beautify,
And most bewitch the wretched eye!
How all this is but a fair inn
Of fairer guest which dwells within,   140
Of whose high praise, and praiseful bliss,
Goodness the pen, heav'n paper is;
The ink immortal fame doth lend.

As I began, so must I end:
  No tongue can her perfections tell,
  In whose each part all pens may dwell.

'Since nature's works be good'

Since nature's works be good, and death doth serve
As nature's work, why should we fear to die?
Since fear is vain but when it may preserve,
Why should we fear that which we cannot fly?

Fear is more pain than is the pain it fears,
Disarming human minds of native might;
While each conceit an ugly figure bears,
Which were not ill, well viewed in reason's light.

Our owly eyes, which dimmed with passions be,
And scarce discern the dawn of coming day,   10
Let them be cleared, and now begin to see
Our life is but a step in dusty way.
    Then let us hold the bliss of peaceful mind,
    Since this we feel, great loss we cannot find.

LAMON'S TALE

A shepherd's tale no height of style desires
To raise in words what in effect is low;
A plaining song plain-singing° voice requires,
For warbling notes from inward cheering flow,
I then, whose burdened breast but thus aspires
Of shepherds two the silly case to show
  Need not the stately Muses' help invoke
  For creeping rhymes, which often sighings choke.
But you, O you, that think not tears too dear
To spend for harms, although they touch you not,   10
And deign to deem your neighbours' mischief near
Although they be of meaner parents got: ,
You I invite with easy ears to hear
The poor-clad truth of love's wrong-ordered lot.
  Who may be glad, be glad you be not such;
  Who share in woe, weigh others have as much.
There was (O seldom blessed word of was!)
A pair of friends, or rather one called two,
Trained in the life which on short-bitten grass
In shine or storm must set the clouted shoe:°   20
He that the other did in some years pass,
And in those gifts that years distribute do
  Was Klaius called (ah Klaius, woeful wight!)
  The later born, yet too soon, Strephon hight.
Epirus° high was honest Klaius' nest;
To Strephon Aeol's land first breathing lent;
But East and West were joined by friendship's hest,
As Strephon's ear and heart to Klaius bent,
So Klaius' soul did in his Strephon rest.
Still both their flocks flocking together went,   30
  As if they would of owners' humour be;
  And eke their pipes did well, as friends, agree.
Klaius for skill of herbs,° and shepherds' art,
Among the wisest was accounted wise;
Yet not so wise, as of unstained heart;
Strephon was young, yet marked with humble eyes
How elder ruled their flocks, and cured their smart,

So that the grave did not his words despise.
   Both free of mind; both did clear-dealing love;
   And both had skill in verse their voice to move.   40
Their cheerful minds, till poisoned was their cheer,
The honest sports of earthy lodging prove;
Now for a clod-like hare in form° they peer;
Now bolt and cudgel squirrels' leap do move;
Now the ambitious lark with mirror clear
They catch, while he (fool!) to himself makes love.
   And now at keels° they try a harmless chance;
   And now their cur they teach to fetch and dance.
When merry May first early calls the morn
With merry maids a-Maying they do go;   50
Then do they pull from sharp and niggard thorn
The plenteous sweets (can sweets so sharply grow?);
Then some green gowns° are by the lasses worn
In chastest plays, till home they walk a-row;
   While dance about the may-pole is begun;
   When, if need were, they could at quintain° run.
While thus they ran a low, but levelled, race,
While thus they lived (this was indeed a life!)
With nature pleased, content with present case,
Free of proud fears, brave beggary, smiling strife   60
Of climb-fall court, the envy-hatching place;
While those restless desires in great men rife
   To visit so low folks did much disdain;
   This while, though poor, they in themselves did reign.°
One day (O day, that shined to make them dark!)
While they did ward sun-beams with shady bay,
And Klaius, taking for his younglings cark°
(Lest greedy eyes to them might challenge lay)
Busy with ochre did their shoulders mark
(His mark a pillar was devoid of stay:°   70
   As bragging that, free of all passions' moan,
   Well might he others bear, but lean to none):
Strephon with leavy twigs of laurel tree°
A garland made on temples for to wear,
For he then chosen was the dignity
Of village-lord, that Whitsuntide, to bear;
And full, poor fool, of boyish bravery
With triumph's shows would show he naught did fear.

But fore-accounting oft makes builders miss;
  They found, they felt, they had no lease of bliss.   80
For ere that either had his purpose done,
Behold (beholding well it doth deserve)
They saw a maid, who thitherward did run
To catch her sparrow, which from her did swerve,
As she a black silk cap on him begun
To set, for foil of his milk-white° to serve.
  She chirping ran; he peeping flew away;
  Till hard by them both he and she did stay.
Well for to see they kept themselves unseen,
And saw this fairest maid, of fairer mind,   90
By fortune mean, in nature born a queen,
How well apaid she was her bird to find;
How tenderly her tender hands between
In ivory cage she did the micher bind;
  How rosy moistened lips about his beak
  Moving, she seemed at once to kiss and speak.
Chastened but thus, and thus his lesson taught,
The happy wretch she put into her breast
Which to their eyes the bowls of Venus brought,
For they seemed made even of sky-metal best,   100
And that the bias of her blood was wrought.
Betwixt them two the peeper took his nest,
  Where, snugging° well, he well appeared content
  So to have done amiss, so to be shent.
This done, but done with captive-killing grace,
Each motion seeming shot from beauty's bow,
With length laid down she decked the lonely place.
Proud grew the grass that under her did grow;
The trees spread out their arms to shade her face;
But she, on elbow leaned,° with sighs did show   110
  No grass, no trees, nor yet her sparrow might
  To long-perplexed mind breed long delight.
She troubled was (alas that it mought be!)
With tedious brawlings of her parents dear,
Who would have her in will and word agree
To wed Antaxius, their neighbour near.
A herdman rich of much account was he,
In whom no ill did reign, nor good appear.°
  In some such one she liked not his desire;

Fain would be free; but dreadeth parents' ire.   120
Kindly, sweet soul, she did unkindness take
That bagged baggage of a miser's mud
Should price of her, as in a market, make.
But gold can gild a rotten piece of wood;
To yield she found her noble heart did ache;
To strive she feared how it with virtue stood.
   These doubting clouds o'er-casting heavenly brain,
    At length in rows of kiss-cheek tears they rain.
Cupid, the wag, that lately conquered had
Wise counsellors, stout captains, puissant kings,   130
And tied them fast to lead his triumph bad,°
Glutted with them, now plays with meanest things.
So oft in feasts with costly changes clad
To crammed maws a sprat new stomach brings;
   So lords, with sport of stag and heron full,
    Sometimes we see small birds from nests do pull.
So now for prey these shepherds two he took,
Whose metal stiff he knew he could not bend
With hearsay, pictures, or a window-look,
With one good dance, or letter finely penned,   140
That were in court a well proportioned hook,
Where piercing wits do quickly apprehend:
   Their senses rude plain objects only move,
    And so must see great cause before they love.
Therefore love armed in her now takes the field,
Making her beams his bravery and might;
Her hands, which pierced the soul's seven-double shield,
Were now his darts, leaving his wonted fight.
Brave crest to him her scorn-gold hair did yield;
His complete harness was her purest white.   150
   But fearing lest all white might seem too good,
    In cheeks and lips the tyrant threatens blood.°
Besides this force, within her eyes he kept
A fire, to burn the prisoners he gains,
Whose boiling heat increased as she wept:
For even in forge cold water fire maintains,
Thus proud and fierce unto the hearts he stepped
Of them, poor souls; and cutting reason's reins,
   Made them his own before they had it wist.
    But if they had, could sheephooks this resist?   160

Klaius straight felt, and groaned at the blow,
And called, now wounded, purpose to his aid:
Strephon, fond boy, delighted, did not know
That it was love that shined in shining maid;
But lickerous, poisoned, fain to her would go,
If him new-learned manners had not stayed.
   For then Urania homeward did arise,
   Leaving in pain their well-fed hungry eyes.
She went; they stayed; or, rightly for to say,
She stayed in them, they went in thought with her;   170
Klaius indeed would fain have pulled away
This mote from out his eye, this inward burr.
And now, proud rebel, gan for to gainsay
The lesson which but late he learned too fur:°
   Meaning with absence to refresh the thought
   To which her presence such a fever brought.
Strephon did leap with joy and jollity,
Thinking it just more therein to delight
Than in good dog, fair field, or shading tree;
So have I seen trim books in velvet dight   180
With golden leaves, and painted babery,°
Of silly boys please unacquainted sight;
   But when the rod began to play his part
   Fain would, but could not, fly from golden smart.
He quickly learned Urania was her name,
And straight, for failing, graved it in his heart;
He knew her haunt, and haunted in the same,
And taught his sheep her sheep in food to thwart;
Which soon as it did bateful question frame
He might on knees confess his faulty part,   190
   And yield himself unto her punishment,
   While nought but game the self-hurt wanton meant.
Nay, even unto her home he oft would go,
Where bold and hurtless many plays he tries,
Her parents liking well it should be so,
For simple goodness shined in his eyes.
There did he make her laugh, in spite of woe,
So as good thoughts of him in all arise,
   While into none doubt of his love did sink,
   For not himself to be in love did think.   200
But glad Desire, his late embosomed guest,

Yet but a babe,° with milk of sight he nursed;
Desire, the more he sucked, more sought the breast,
Like dropsy folk still drink to be a thirst;
Till one fair even an hour e'er sun did rest,
Who then in Lion's cave° did enter first,
 By neighbours prayed, she went abroad thereby,
 At barley-break° her sweet swift foot to try.
Never the earth on his round shoulders bare
A maid trained up from high or low degree   210
That in her doings better could compare
Mirth with respect, few words with courtesy,
A careless comeliness with comely care,
Self-'gard° with mildness, sport with majesty:
 Which made her yield to deck this shepherds' band;
 And still, believe me, Strephon was at hand.
A-field they go, where many lookers be,
And thou, seek-sorrow Klaius, them among;
Indeed, thou said'st it was thy friend to see,
Strephon, whose absence seemed unto thee long, 220
While most with her, he less did keep with thee,
No, no; it was in spite of wisdom's song,
 Which absence wished; love played a victor's part;
 The heaven-love loadstone drew thy iron heart.
Then couples three be straight allotted there;
They of both ends the middle two do fly,
The two that in mid place, Hell called were,
Must strive with waiting foot and watching eye
To catch off them, and them to hell to bear,
That they, as well, as they, Hell may supply: 230
 Like some which seek to salve their blotted name
 With others' bolt, till all do taste of shame.
There may you see, soon as the middle two
Do coupled towards either couple make,
They, false and fearful, do their hands undo,
Brother his brother, friend doth friend forsake,
Heeding himself, cares not how fellow do,
But of a stranger mutual help doth take:
 As perjured cowards in adversity
 With sight of fear from friends to frembed° do fly. 240
These sports shepherds devised such faults to show.
Geron, though old, yet gamesome, kept one end,

With Cosma, for whose love Pas passed in woe;
Fair Nous with Pas the lot to Hell did send;
Pas thought it hell, while he was Cosma fro.
At other end Uran did Strephon lend
  Her happy-making hand, of whom one look
  From Nous and Cosma all their beauty took.
The play began: Pas durst not Cosma chase,
But did intend next bout with her to meet;   250
So he, with Nous to Geron turned their race,
With whom to join fast ran Urania sweet;
But light-legged Pas had got the middle space,
Geron strave hard, but aged were his feet,
  And therefore finding force now faint to be
  He thought grey hairs afforded subtlety.
And so when Pas hand-reached him to take,
The fox on knees and elbows tumbled down;
Pas could not stay, but over him did rake,
And crowned the earth with his first touching crown;   260
His heels, grown proud, did seem at heaven to shake;
But Nous, that slipped from Pas, did catch the clown.
  So laughing all, yet Pas to ease somedel,°
  Geron with Uran were condemned to hell.
Cosma this while to Strephon safely came,
And all to second barley-break are bent.
The two in Hell did toward Cosma frame,
Who should to Pas, but they would her prevent.
Pas, mad with fall, and madder with the shame,
Most mad with beams which he thought Cosma sent,   270
  With such mad haste he did to Cosma go
  That to her breast he gave a noisome blow.
She, quick, and proud, and who did Pas despise,
Up with her fist, and took him on the face.
'Another time', quoth she, 'become more wise'.
Thus Pas did kiss her hand with little grace,
And each way luckless, yet in humble guise,
Did hold her fast, for fear of more disgrace;
  While Strephon might with pretty Nous have met;
  But all this while another course he fet.   280
For as Urania after Cosma ran,
He, ravished with sight how gracefully
She moved her limbs, and drew the aged man,

Left Nous to coast the loved beauty nigh.
Nous cried, and chafed, but he no other can;
Till Uran, seeing Pas to Cosma fly,
   And Strephon single, turned after him.
   Strephon so chased did seem in milk to swim.
He ran, but ran with eye o'er shoulder cast,
More marking her, than how himself did go,   290
Like Numid lions° by the hunters chased,
Though they do fly, yet backwardly do glow
With proud aspect, disdaining greater haste;
What rage in them, that love in him did show:
   But God gives them instinct the man to shun,
   And he by law of barley-break must run.
But as his heat with running did augment,
Much more his sight increased his hot desire:
So is in her the best of nature spent;
The air her sweet race moved doth blow the fire.   300
Her feet be pursuivants from Cupid sent,
With whose fine steps all loves and joys conspire.
   The hidden beauties seemed in wait to lie
   To down proud hearts that would not willing die.
Thus fast he fled from her he followed sore,
Still shunning Nous to lengthen pleasing race:
Till that he spied old Geron could no more,
Then did he slack his love-instructed pace;
So that Uran, whose arm old Geron bore,
Laid hold on him with most lay-holding grace.   310
   So caught, him seemed he caught of joys the bell.
   And thought it heaven so to be drawn to hell.
To hell he goes, and Nous with him must dwell.°
Nous sware it was no right, for his default.
Who would be caught, that she should go to Hell;
But so she must. And now the third assault
Of barley-break among the six befell.
Pas Cosma matched, yet angry with his fault;
   The other end Geron with Uran guard;
   I think you think Strephon bent thitherward.   320
Nous counselled Strephon Geron to pursue,
For he was old, and eas'ly would be caught;
But he drew her as love his fancy drew,
And so to take the gem Urania sought,

While Geron old came safe to Cosma true,
Though him to meet at all she stirred nought.
  For Pas, whether it were for fear or love,
  Moved not himself, nor suffered her to move.
So they three did together idly stay,
While dear Uran, whose course was Pas to meet,   330
(He staying thus), was fain abroad to stray
With larger round, to shun the following feet.
Strephon, whose eyes on her back parts did play,
With love drawn on, so fast with pace unmeet
  Drew dainty Nous, that she not able so
  To run, brake from his hands, and let him go.
He single thus, hoped soon with her to be
Who nothing earthly, but of fire and air,
Though with soft legs, did run as fast as he.
He thrice reached, thrice deceived, when her to bear   340
He hopes, with dainty turns she him doth flee.
So on the downs we see, near Wilton fair,°
  A hasty hare from greedy greyhound go,
  And past all hope his chaps to frustrate so.
But this strange race more strange conceits did yield:
Who victor seemed was to his ruin brought;
Who seemed o'erthrown was mistress of the field.
She fled, and took: he followed, and was caught.
So have I heard to pierce pursuing shield
By parents trained, the Tartars wild are taught,   350
  With shafts shot out from their back-turned bow.
  But ah! Her darts did far more deeply go.
As Venus' bird, the white, swift, lovely dove
(O happy dove, that art compared to her!)
Doth on her wings her utmost swiftness prove,
Finding the gripe of falcon fierce not fur:
So did Uran the narr the swifter move
(Yet beauty still as fast as she did stir)
  Till with long race dear she° was breathless brought,
  And then the Phoenix feared to be caught.   360
Among the rest that there did take delight
To see the sports of double-shining day,
And did the tribute of their wondering sight
To nature's heir, the fair Urania, pay,
I told you Klaius was the hapless wight

Who earnest found what they accounted play.
    He did not there do homage of his eyes,
    But on his eyes his heart did sacrifice.
With gazing looks, short sighs, unsettled feet,
He stood, but turned as girosol° to sun: 370
His fancies still did her in half way meet,
His soul did fly as she was seen to run.
In sum, proud Boreas never ruled fleet
(Who Neptune's web on danger's distaff spun)
    With greater power, than she did make them wend.
    Each way, as she, that age's praise, did bend.
Till spying well she well nigh weary was,
And surely taught by his love-open eye,
His eye, that even did mark her trodden grass,
That she would fain the catch of Strephon fly,   380
Giving his reason passport for to pass
Whither it would, so it would let him die.
    He that before shunned her to shun such harms
    Now runs, and takes her in his clipping arms.
For with pretence from Strephon her to guard
He met her full; but full of warefulness,
With inbowed bosom well for her prepared;
When Strephon, cursing his own backwardness.
Came to her back, and so with double ward
Imprison her, who both them did possess   390
    As heart-bound slaves; and happy then embrace
    Virtue's proof, fortune's victor, beauty's place.
Her race did not her beauty's beams augment.
For they were ever in the best degree;
But yet a setting forth it some way lent,
As rubies' lustre when they rubbed be.
The dainty dew on face and body went
As on sweet flowers when morning drops we see;
    Her breath, then short, seemed loath from home to pass,
    Which more it moved, the more it sweeter was.   400
Happy, O happy, if they so might bide
To see her eyes, with how true humbleness
They looked down to triumph over pride!
With how sweet saws she blamed their sauciness:
To feel the panting heart, which through her side
Did beat their hands, which durst so near to press;

To see, to feel, to hear, to taste, to know
   More than, besides her, all the earth could show.
But never did Medea's golden weed
On Creon's child° his poison sooner throw   410
Than those delights through all their sinews breed
A creeping, serpent-like, of mortal woe:
Till she brake from their arms (although indeed
Going from them, from them she could not go)
   And fare-welling the flock, did homeward wend,
   And so that even the barley-break did end.

It ended, but the others' woe began:
Began, at least, to be conceived as woe,
For then wise Klaius found no absence can
Help him, who can no more her sight forego.   420
He found man's virtue is but part of man,
And part must follow where whole man doth go;
   He found that Reason's self now reasons found
   To fasten knots, which fancy first had bound.

So doth he yield; so takes he on his yoke.
Not knowing who did draw with him therein;
Strephon, poor youth, because he saw no smoke,
Did not conceive what fire he had within:
But after this to greater rage it broke,
Till of his life it did full conquest win,   430
   First killing mirth, then banishing all rest,
   Filling his eyes with tears, with sighs his breast.

Then sports grew pains; all talking tedious;
On thoughts he feeds; his looks their figure change;
The day seems long, but night is odious:
No sleeps but dreams; no dreams, but visions strange,
Till finding still his evil increasing thus
One day he with his flock abroad did range,
   And coming where he hoped to be alone
   Thus, on a hillock set, he made his moan: 440
'Alas! What weights are these that load my heart!
I am as dull as winter-starved sheep,
Tired as a jade° in overloaden cart;
Yet thoughts do fly, though I can scarcely creep;
All visions seem, at every bush I start;
Drowsy am I, and yet can rarely sleep.
   Sure I bewitched am, it is even that;

Late near a cross I met an ugly cat.°
'For, but by charms, how fall these things on me
That from those eyes where heavenly apples been,   450
Those eyes, which nothing like themselves can see,
Of fair Urania, fairer than a green
Proudly bedecked in April's livery,
A shot unheard gave me a wound unseen?
 He was invisible that hurt me so;
 And none invisible but sprites can go.
'When I see her my sinews shake for fear;
And yet, dear soul, I know she hurteth none;
Amid my flock with woe my voice I tear,
And, but bewitched, who to his flock would moan?   460
Her cherry lips, milk hands and golden hair
I still do see, though I be still alone.
 Now make me think that there is not a fiend
 Who, hid in angel's shape, my life would end.
'The sports wherein I wonted to do well
Come she, and sweet the air with open breast,
Then so I fail, when most I would do well,
That at me so amazed my fellows jest.
Sometimes to her news of myself to tell
I go about, but then is all my best   470
 Wry words, and stammering, or else doltish dumb;
 Say then, can this but of enchantment come?
'Nay, each thing is bewitched to know my case:
The nightingales for woe their songs refrain;
In river as I looked my pining face,
As pined a face as mine I saw again.
The courteous mountains, grieved at my disgrace,
Their snowy hair tear off in melting pain.
 And now the dropping trees do weep for me,
 And now fair evenings blush my shame to see.   480
'But you, my pipe, whilom my chief delight,
Till strange delight, delight to nothing ware;
And you, my flock, care of my careful sight,
While I was I, and so had cause to care;
And thou, my dog, whose truth and valiant might
Made wolves (not inward wolves) my ewes to spare:
 Go you not from your master in his woe:
 Let it suffice that he himself forego.

'For though, like wax, this magic makes me waste.
Or like a lamb whose dam away is fet   490
(Stol'n from her young by thieves' unchoosing haste)
He treble baas for help, but none can get;
Though thus, and worse, though now I am at last,
Of all the games that here e'er now I met:
   Do you remember still you once were mine,
   Till my eyes had their curse from blessed thine.
'Be you with me while I unheard do cry;
While I do score my losses on the wind;
While I in heart my will write e'er I die,
In which by will my will and wits I bind   500
Still to be hers, about her aye to fly,
As this same sprite about my fancies blind
   Doth daily haunt: but so, that mine become
   As much more loving, as less cumbersome.
'Alas! A cloud hath overcast mine eyes,
And yet I see her shine amid the cloud.
Alas! Of ghosts I hear the ghastly cries,
Yet there, me seems, I hear her singing loud.
This song she sings in most commanding wise:
"Come, shepherd's boy, let now thy heart be bowed   510
   To make itself to my least look a slave:
   Leave sheep, leave all, I will no piecing° have."
'I will, I will, alas, alas, I will!
Wilt thou have more? More have, if more I be.
Away, ragg'd rams, care I what murrain° kill?
Out, shrieking pipe, made of some witched tree;
Go, bawling cur, thy hungry maw go fill
On yond foul flock belonging not to me.'
   With that, his dog he henced,° his flock he cursed;
   With that (yet kissed first) his pipe he burst.   520
This said, this done, he rase, even tired with rest,
With heart as careful, as with careless grace;
With shrinking legs, but with a swelling breast;
With eyes which threatened they would drown his face;
Fearing the worst, not knowing what were best,
And giving to his sight a wand'ring race,
   He saw behind a bush where Klaius sat:
   His well known friend, but yet his unknown mate,
Klaius the wretch, who lately yelden was

To bear the bonds which time nor wit could break   530
(With blushing soul at sight of judgement's glass,
While guilty thoughts accused his Reason weak)
This morn alone to lonely walk did pass
Within himself of her dear self to speak,
   Till Strephon's plaining voice him nearer drew,
   Where by his words his self-like cause he knew.
For hearing him so oft with words of woe
Urania name, whose force he knew so well,
He quickly knew what witchcraft gave the blow
Which made his Strephon think himself in hell;   540
Which when he did in perfect image show,
To his own wit, thought upon thought did swell,
   Breeding huge storms within his inward part,
   Which thus breathed out° with earthquake of his heart:

ASTROPHIL AND STELLA

1°

Loving in truth, and fain in verse my love to show,
That she (dear she) might take some pleasure of my pain;
Pleasure might cause her read, reading might make her know;
Knowledge might pity win, and pity grace obtain;
  I sought fit words to paint the blackest face of woe,
Studying inventions fine, her wits to entertain;
Oft turning others' leaves, to see if thence would flow
Some fresh and fruitful showers upon my sunburnt brain.
  But words came halting forth, wanting invention's stay;
Invention, nature's child, fled step-dame study's blows;   10
And others' feet still seemed but strangers in my way.
Thus great with child to speak, and helpless in my throes,
  Biting my truant pen, beating myself for spite,
  'Fool,' said my muse to me; 'look in thy heart, and write.'

2

Not at first sight, nor with a dribbed° shot,
  Love gave the wound which while I breathe will bleed:
  But known worth° did in mine of time proceed,
Till by degrees it had full conquest got.
I saw, and liked; I liked, but loved not;
  I loved, but straight did not what love decreed:
  At length to love's decrees I, forced, agreed,
Yet with repining at so partial lot.
  Now even that footstep of lost liberty
Is gone, and now like slave-born Muscovite°   10
I call it praise to suffer tyranny;
And now employ the remnant of my wit
  To make myself believe that all is well,
  While with a feeling skill I paint° my hell.

3

Let dainty wits cry on the sisters nine,
That bravely masked, their fancies may be told:

Or Pindar's apes, flaunt they in phrases fine,
Enam'lling with pied flowers their thoughts of gold:
   Or else let them in statelier glory shine,
Ennobling new-found tropes with problems old:
Or with strange similes enrich each line,
Of herbs or beasts, which Ind or Afric hold.°
   For me, in sooth, no muse but one I know;
   Phrases and problems from my reach do grow,   10
And strange things cost too dear for my poor sprites.
   How then? Even thus: in Stella's face I read
   What love and beauty be; then all my deed
But copying is, what in her nature writes.

4

Virtue, alas, now let me take some rest:
Thou sett'st a bate between my will and wit.
If vain love have my simple soul oppressed,
Leave what thou lik'st not, deal not thou with it.
   Thy sceptre use in some old Cato's breast;°
Churches or schools are for thy seat more fit.
I do confess—pardon a fault confessed—
My mouth too tender is for thy hard bit.°
   But if that needs thou wilt usurping be
   The little reason that is left in me,   10
And still the effect of thy persuasions prove:
   I swear, my heart such one shall show to thee
   That shrines in flesh so true a deity,
That, virtue, thou thy self shalt be in love.

5

It is most true, that eyes are formed to serve
The inward light; and that the heavenly part
Ought to be king, from whose rules who do swerve,
Rebels to Nature, strive for their own smart.
   It is most true, what we call Cupid's dart,
An image is, which for ourselves we carve;
And, fools, adore in temple of our heart,
Till that good god make church and churchmen starve.
   True, that true beauty virtue is indeed,
Whereof this beauty can be but a shade,   10

Which elements with mortal mixture breed;°
True, that on earth we are but pilgrims made,
    And should in soul up to our country° move;
True; and yet true, that I must Stella love.

6°

Some lovers speak, when they their muses entertain,
Of hopes begot by fear, of wot not what desires,
Of force of heavenly beams, infusing hellish pain,
Of living deaths, dear wounds, fair storms and freezing fires.°
   Some one his song in Jove, and Jove's strange tales, attires,
Broidered with bulls and swans, powdered with golden rain.°
Another, humbler, wit to shepherd's pipe retires,
Yet hiding royal blood full oft in rural vein.°
   To some a sweetest plaint a sweetest style affords,
   While tears pour out his ink, and sighs breathe out his words,   10
His paper, pale despair, and pain his pen doth move.°
   I can speak what I feel,° and feel as much as they,
   But think that all the map of my state I display,
When trembling voice brings forth, that I do Stella love.

7°

When nature made her chief work, Stella's eyes,
In colour black why wrapped she beams so bright?
Would she in beamy black, like painter wise,
Frame daintiest lustre, mixed of shades and light?
   Or did she else that sober hue devise
In object best to knit and strength° our sight,
Lest, if no veil those brave gleams did disguise,
They, sun-like, should more dazzle than delight?
   Or would she her miraculous power show,
   That, whereas black seems beauty's contrary,   10
She even in black doth make all beauties flow?
Both so, and thus: she minding love should be
   Placed ever there, gave him this mourning weed
   To honour all their deaths, who for her bleed.

8

Love, born in Greece, of late fled from his native place,
   Forced by a tedious proof, that Turkish hardened heart°

Is no fit mark to pierce with his fine pointed dart;
And pleased with our soft peace, stayed here his flying race.
But finding these North climes too coldly him embrace,
  Not used to frozen clips, he strave to find some part
  Where with most ease and warmth he might employ his art.
At length he perched himself in Stella's joyful face,
  Whose fair skin, beamy eyes, like morning sun on snow,
Deceived the quaking boy, who thought from so pure light   10
Effects of lively heat must needs in nature grow.
But she, most fair, most cold, made him thence take his flight
  To my close heart, where, while some firebrands he did lay,
  He burnt unwares his wings, and cannot fly away.

9

Queen Virtue's court, which some call Stella's face,
  Prepared by Nature's chiefest furniture,
  Hath his front built of alablaster pure;
Gold is the covering of that stately place.
The door, by which sometimes comes forth her grace,
  Red porphyr is, which lock of pearl makes sure;
  Whose porches rich (which name of 'cheeks' endure)
Marble, mixed red and white, do interlace.
  The windows now through which this heavenly guest
Looks o'er the world, and can find nothing such   10
Which dare claim from those lights the name of 'best',
Of touch they are that without touch doth touch,
  Which Cupid's self from Beauty's mine did draw:
  Of touch they are, and poor I am their straw.°

10

Reason, in faith thou art well served, that still
Would'st brabbling° be with sense and love in me.
I rather wished thee climb the muses' hill,
Or reach the fruit of nature's choicest tree,
  Or seek heaven's course, or heaven's inside, to see.
Why should'st thou toil our thorny soil to till?
Leave sense, and those which sense's objects be:
Deal thou with powers of thoughts, leave love to will.
  But thou would'st needs fight both with love and sense,
With sword of wit giving wounds of dispraise,   10
Till downright blows did foil thy cunning fence:

For soon as they strake thee with Stella's rays,
   Reason, thou kneeled'st, and offered'st straight to prove
   By reason good, good reason her to love.

11

In truth, O Love, with what a boyish kind
   Thou dost proceed in thy most serious ways:
   That when the heaven to thee his best displays
Yet of that best thou leav'st the best behind.
For like a child, that some fair book doth find,
   With gilded leaves or coloured vellum plays,
   Or at the most, on some fine picture stays,
But never heeds the fruit of writer's mind:
   So when thou saw'st, in nature's cabinet,
Stella, thou straight look'st babies in her eyes,   10
In her cheek's pit thou did'st thy pit-fold° set,
And in her breast bo-peep or couching lies,
   Playing and shining in each outward part:
   But, fool, seek'st not to get into her heart.

12

Cupid, because thou shin'st in Stella's eyes,
   That from her locks, thy day-nets,° none 'scapes free,
   That those lips swell, so full of thee they be,
That her sweet breath makes oft thy flames to rise,
That in her breast thy pap well sugared lies,
   That her grace gracious makes thy wrongs, that she,
   What words so e'er she speaks, persuades for thee,
That her clear voice lifts thy fame to the skies;
   Thou countest Stella thine, like those whose powers,
Having got up a breach° by fighting well,   10
Cry, 'Victory, this fair day all is ours!'
O no, her heart is such a citadel,
   So fortified with wit, stored with disdain,
   That to win it, is all the skill and pain.

13

Phoebus was judge between Jove, Mars, and Love,
   Of those three gods, whose arms the fairest were.
   Jove's golden shield did eagle sables° bear,

Whose talents° held young Ganymede above:
But in vert field° Mars bare a golden spear
   Which through a bleeding heart his point did shove.
   Each had his crest: Mars carried Venus' glove,
Jove on his helm the thunderbolt did rear.
Cupid then smiles, for on his crest there lies
   Stella's fair hair, her face he makes his shield,   10
   Where roses gules are borne in silver field.°
Phoebus drew wide the curtains of the skies
   To blaze° these last, and sware devoutly then,
   The first, thus matched, were scarcely gentlemen.

14

Alas, have I not pain enough, my friend,
   Upon whose breast a fiercer gripe doth tire
   Than did on him who first stale down the fire,°
While Love on me doth all his quiver spend,
But with your rhubarb° words you must contend
   To grieve me worse, in saying that desire
   Doth plunge my well-formed soul even in the mire
Of sinful thoughts, which do in ruin end?
   If that be sin, which doth the manners frame,
Well stayed with truth in word, and faith of deed,   10
Ready of wit, and fearing nought but shame:
   If that be sin, which in fixed hearts doth breed
   A loathing of all loose unchastity:
   Then love is sin, and let me sinful be.

15

You that do search for every purling spring
   Which from the ribs of old Parnassus flows;
   And every flower, not sweet perhaps, which grows
Near thereabouts, into your poesy wring;°
You that do dictionary's method bring
   Into your rhymes, running in rattling rows;°
   You that poor Petrarch's long-deceased woes
With new-born sighs and denizened° wit do sing:°
   You take wrong ways, those far-fet helps be such
   As do bewray a want of inward touch: 10
And sure at length stol'n goods do come to light.

But if (both for your love and skill) your name
  You seek to nurse at fullest breasts of fame,
Stella behold, and then begin to endite.

16

In nature apt to like, when I did see,
  Beauties, which were of many carats fine,
  My boiling sprites did thither soon incline,
And, love, I thought that I was full of thee.
But finding not those restless flames in me
  Which others said did make their souls to pine,
  I thought those babes of some pin's hurt did whine,
By my love judging what love's pain might be.
  But while I thus with this young lion played,°
Mine eyes (shall I say cursed or blessed?) beheld   10
Stella: now she is named, need more be said?
In her sight I a lesson new have spelled;
  I now have learned love right, and learned even so
  As who by being poisoned doth poison know.

17

His mother dear Cupid offended late,
  Because that Mars, grown slacker in her love,
  With pricking shot he did not throughly move,
To keep the pace of their first loving state.
The boy refused, for fear of Mars's hate,
  Who threatened stripes if he his wrath did prove.°
  But she in chafe him from her lap did shove,
Brake bow, brake shafts, while Cupid weeping sate:
  Till that his grandame, Nature, pitying it,
Of Stella's brows made him two better bows,   10
And in her eyes of arrows infinite.
O how for joy he leaps, O how he crows,
  And straight therewith, like wags new got to play,
  Falls to shrewd° turns; and I was in his way.

18

With what sharp checks I in myself am shent°
  When into reason's audit I do go,
  And by just counts myself a bankrupt know
Of all those goods, which heaven to me hath lent,

Unable quit to pay even nature's rent,°
  Which unto it by birthright I do owe:
  And which is worse, no good excuse can show,
But that my wealth I have most idly spent.
  My youth doth waste, my knowledge brings forth toys,
My wit doth strive those passions to defend°   10
Which for reward spoil it with vain annoys.
I see my course to lose myself doth bend:
  I see, and yet no greater sorrow take
  Than that I lose no more for Stella's sake.

19

On Cupid's bow how are my heart-strings bent,
  That see my wrack, and yet embrace the same!
  When most I glory, then I feel most shame:
I willing run, yet while I run, repent.
My best wits still their own disgrace invent;
  My very ink turns straight to Stella's name;
  And yet my words, as them my pen doth frame,
Avise themselves that they are vainly spent.
  For though she pass all things, yet what is all
That unto me, who fare like him that both   10
Looks to the skies, and in a ditch doth fall?°
O let me prop my mind, yet in his growth,
  And not in nature for best fruits unfit.
  'Scholar,' saith Love, 'bend hitherward your wit.'

20

Fly, fly, my friends, I have my death wound, fly;
See there that boy, that murth'ring boy I say,
Who like a thief hid in dark bush doth lie,
Till bloody bullet get him wrongful prey.
  So tyrant he no fitter place could spy,
Nor so fair level° in so secret stay
As that sweet black° which veils the heav'nly eye;
There himself with his shot he close doth lay.
  Poor passenger, pass now thereby I did,
And stayed, pleased with the prospect of the place,   10
While that black hue from me the bad guest hid:
But straight I saw motions of lightning grace,

And then descried the glist'ring of his dart:
But ere I could fly thence, it pierced my heart.

21

Your words, my friend, right healthful caustics,° blame
  My young mind marred, whom love doth windlass° so
  That mine own writings like bad servants show,
My wits, quick in vain thoughts, in virtue lame;
That Plato I read for nought, but if he tame
  Such coltish gyres;° that to my birth I owe
  Nobler desires, lest else that friendly foe,
Great expectation, wear a train of shame.
  For since mad March great promise made of me,°
If now the May of my years much decline,   10
What can be hoped my harvest time will be?
Sure you say well; your wisdom's golden mine
  Dig deep with learning's spade; now tell me this,
  Hath this world aught so fair as Stella is?

22

In highest way of heaven the sun did ride,
  Progressing then from fair twins' golden place,°
  Having no scarf of clouds before his face,
But shining forth of heat in his chief pride,
When some fair ladies, by hard promise tied,°
  On horseback met him in his furious race;
  Yet each prepared, with fan's well-shading grace,
From that foe's wounds their tender skins to hide.
Stella alone with face unarmed marched,
  Either to do like him, which open shone,   10
  Or careless of the wealth because her own;
Yet were the hid and meaner beauties parched,
  Her daintiest bare went free. The cause was this:
  The sun, which others burned, did her but kiss.

23

The curious wits, seeing dull pensiveness
  Bewray itself in my long settled eyes,
  Whence these same fumes of melancholy rise
With idle pains, and missing aim, do guess.

Some, that know how my spring I did address,°
  Deem that my muse some fruit of knowledge plies;
  Others, because the prince my service tries,°
Think that I think state errors to redress.
  But harder judges judge ambition's rage,°
Scourge of itself, still climbing slippery place,   10
Holds my young brain captived in golden cage.
O fools, or over-wise: alas, the race
  Of all my thoughts hath neither stop nor start
  But only Stella's eyes and Stella's heart.

24°

Rich fools there be, whose base and filthy heart
Lies hatching still the goods wherein they flow;
And damning their own selves to Tantal's smart,
Wealth breeding want, more blessed, more wretched grow.
  Yet to those fools heaven such wit doth impart
As what their hands do hold, their heads do know,
And knowing, love, and loving, lay apart,
As sacred things, far from all danger's show.
  But that rich fool, who by blind fortune's lot
The richest gem of love and life enjoys,   10
And can with foul abuse such beauties blot,
Let him, deprived of sweet but unfelt joys,
  Exiled for aye from those high treasures which
  He knows not, grow in only folly rich.

25

The wisest scholar of the wight most wise,
  By Phoebus' doom, with sugared sentence says,
  That virtue, if it once met with our eyes,
Strange flames of love it in our souls would raise;°
  But for that man with pain this truth descries,
While he each thing in sense's balance weighs,
And so nor will, nor can, behold those skies
Which inward sun to heroic mind displays:
  Virtue of late, with virtuous care to stir
Love of herself, takes Stella's shape, that she   10
To mortal eyes might sweetly shine in her.
It is most true, for since I her did see,
  Virtue's great beauty in that face I prove,
  And find the effect, for I do burn in love.

26°

Though dusty wits dare scorn astrology,
And fools can think those lamps of purest light,
Whose numbers, ways, greatness, eternity,
Promising wonders, wonder to invite,
　To have for no cause birthright in the sky,
But for to spangle the black weeds of night;
Or for some brawl, which in that chamber high
They should still dance, to please a gazer's sight:
　For me, I do Nature unidle know,
And know great causes great effects procure,　　　　10
And know those bodies high reign on the low.
And if these rules did fail, proof makes me sure,
　　Who oft fore-judge my after-following race
　　By only those two eyes in Stella's face.

27

Because I oft, in dark abstracted guise,
　Seem most alone in greatest company,
　With dearth of words, or answers quite awry,
To them that would make speech of speech arise,
They deem, and of that doom the rumour flies,
　That poison foul of bubbling pride doth lie
　So in my swelling breast, that only I
Fawn on myself, and others do despise.
　Yet pride, I think, doth not my soul possess,°
Which looks too oft in his unflatt'ring glass;　　　　10
But one worse fault, ambition, I confess,
That makes me oft my best friends overpass,°
　　Unseen, unheard, while thought to highest place
　　Bends all his powers, even unto Stella's grace.

28°

You that with allegory's curious frame
　Of others' children changelings use to make,
　With me those pains, for God's sake, do not take;
I list not dig so deep for brazen fame.
When I say 'Stella', I do mean the same
　Princess of beauty, for whose only sake
　The reins of love I love, though never slake,

And joy therein, though nations count it shame.
   I beg no subject to use eloquence,
Nor in hid ways to guide philosophy.   10
Look at my hands for no such quintessence,
But know that I, in pure simplicity,
   Breathe out the flames which burn within my heart,
   Love only reading unto me this art.

29°

Like some weak lords, neighboured by mighty kings,
   To keep themselves and their chief cities free,
   Do easily yield, that all their coasts may be
Ready to store their camps of needful things:
So Stella's heart, finding what power love brings,
   To keep itself in life and liberty,
   Doth willing grant, that in the frontiers he
Use all to help his other conquerings.
And thus her heart escapes; but thus her eyes
   Serve him with shot, her lips his heralds are,   10
   Her breasts his tents, legs his triumphal car,
Her flesh his food, her skin his armour brave;
And I, but for because my prospect lies
Upon that coast, am giv'n up for a slave.

30°

Whether the Turkish new moon minded be
   To fill his horns this year on Christian coast;°
   How Pole's right king means, without leave of host,
To warm with ill-made fire cold Muscovy;°
If French can yet three parts in one agree;°
   What now the Dutch in their full diets boast;°
   How Holland hearts, now so good towns be lost,
Trust in the pleasing shade of Orange tree;°
   How Ulster likes of that same golden bit
Wherewith my father once made it half tame;°   10
If in the Scottish court be welt'ring yet;°
These questions busy wits to me do frame.
   I, cumbered with good manners, answer do,
   But know not how, for still I think of you.

31

With how sad steps, O moon, thou climb'st the skies;
  How silently, and with how wan a face.
  What, may it be that even in heav'nly place
That busy archer his sharp arrows tries?
Sure, if that long-with-love-acquainted eyes
  Can judge of love, thou feel'st a lover's case;
  I read it in thy looks; thy languished grace
To me, that feel the like, thy state descries.
  Then even of fellowship, O moon, tell me,
Is constant love deemed there but want of wit?   10
Are beauties there as proud as here they be?
Do they above love to be loved, and yet
  Those lovers scorn whom that love doth possess?
  Do they call virtue there ungratefulness?°

32

Morpheus, the lively son of deadly sleep,
  Witness of life to them that living die;°
  A prophet oft, and oft an history,°
A poet eke, as humours fly or creep;
Since thou in me so sure a power dost keep
  That never I with closed-up sense do lie
  But by thy work my Stella I descry
Teaching blind eyes both how to smile and weep,
  Vouchsafe of all acquaintance° this to tell:
Whence hast thou ivory, rubies, pearl and gold   10
To show her skin, lips, teeth and head so well?
'Fool,' answers he; 'no Ind's such treasures hold,
  But from thy heart, while my sire charmeth thee,
  Sweet Stella's image I do steal to me.'

33°

I might (unhappy word), O me, I might,
And then would not, or could not, see my bliss:
Till now, wrapped in a most infernal night,
I find how heavenly day, wretch, I did miss.
  Heart, rend thyself, thou dost thyself but right;
No lovely Paris made thy Helen his;
No force, no fraud, robbed thee of thy delight;

Nor Fortune of thy fortune author is;
   But to myself myself did give the blow,
   While too much wit (forsooth) so troubled me   10
That I respects for both our sakes must show:
And yet could not by rising morn foresee
   How fair a day was near. O punished eyes,
   That I had been more foolish, or more wise!

34°

Come, let me write. 'And to what end?' To ease
   A burdened heart. 'How can words ease, which are
   The glasses of thy daily vexing care?'
Oft cruel fights well pictured forth do please.°
'Art not ashamed to publish thy disease?'
   Nay, that may breed my fame, it is so rare.
   'But will not wise men think thy words fond ware?'°
Then be they close,° and so none shall displease.
   'What idler thing, than speak and not be heard?'
What harder thing than smart, and not to speak?   10
Peace, foolish wit; with wit my wit is marred.
Thus write I while I doubt to write, and wreak
   My harms on ink's poor loss; perhaps some find
   Stella's great powers, that so confuse my mind.

35

What may words say, or what may words not say,
Where truth itself must speak like flattery?
Within what bounds can one his liking stay,
Where nature doth with infinite agree?°
   What Nestor's counsels° can my flames allay,
Since reason's self doth blow the coal in me?
And ah, what hope that hope should once see day,
Where Cupid is sworn page to chastity?
Honour is honoured, that thou dost possess
   Him as thy slave; and now long needy fame   10
   Doth even grow rich, naming my Stella's name.
Wit learns in thee perfection to express;
   Not thou by praise, but praise in thee is raised;
   It is a praise to praise, when thou art praised.

36

Stella, whence doth this new assault arise,
A conquered, yelden,° ransacked heart to win?
Whereto long since, through my long battered eyes,
Whole armies of thy beauties entered in;
  And there, long since, love, thy lieutenant lies;
My forces razed, thy banners raised within.
Of conquest do not these effects suffice,
But wilt new war upon thine own begin?
  With so sweet voice, and by sweet nature so,
In sweetest strength, so sweetly skilled withal,   10
In all sweet stratagems sweet art can show,
That not my soul, which at thy foot did fall,
  Long since forced by thy beams, but stone nor tree,
  By sense's privilege, can 'scape from thee.°

37°

My mouth doth water, and my breast doth swell,
  My tongue doth itch, my thoughts in labour be;
  Listen then, lordings, with good ear to me,
For of my life I must a riddle tell.
Towards Aurora's court a nymph doth dwell,
  Rich in all beauties which man's eye can see;
  Beauties so far from reach of words, that we
Abase her praise, saying she doth excel;
  Rich in the treasure of deserved renown;
Rich in the riches of a royal heart;   10
Rich in those gifts which give the eternal crown;
Who though most rich in these, and every part
  Which make the patents of true worldly bliss,
  Hath no misfortune, but that Rich she is.

38

This night, while sleep begins with heavy wings
  To hatch° mine eyes, and that unbitted° thought
  Doth fall to stray, and my chief powers are brought
To leave the sceptre of all subject things,
The first that straight my fancy's error° brings
  Unto my mind, is Stella's image, wrought
  By love's own self; but with so curious draught°

That she, methinks, not only shines, but sings.°
  I start, look, hark; but what in closed-up sense
Was held, in opened sense it flies away,   10
Leaving me nought but wailing eloquence.
I, seeing better sights in sight's decay,
    Called it anew, and wooed sleep again:
    But him, her host, that unkind guest had slain.°

39

Come sleep, O sleep, the certain knot of peace,
The baiting place° of wit, the balm of woe,
The poor man's wealth, the prisoner's release,
The indifferent judge between the high and low;
    With shield of proof shield me from out the press°
Of those fierce darts despair at me doth throw:
O make in me those civil wars to cease;
I will good tribute pay, if thou do so.
    Take thou of me smooth pillows, sweetest bed,
A chamber deaf to noise, and blind to light;   10
A rosy garland, and a weary head;°
And if these things, as being thine by right,
    Move not thy heavy grace, thou shalt in me,
    Livelier than elsewhere, Stella's image see.

40

As good to write, as for to lie and groan.
    O Stella dear, how much thy power hath wrought,
    That hast my mind, none of the basest, brought
My still kept course, while others sleep, to moan.
Alas, if from the height of virtue's throne
    Thou canst vouchsafe the influence of a thought
    Upon a wretch, that long thy grace hath sought;
Weigh then how I by thee am overthrown:
    And then, think thus: although thy beauty be
    Made manifest by such a victory,   10
Yet noblest conquerors do wrecks avoid.
    Since then thou hast so far subdued me,
    That in my heart I offer still to thee,
O, do not let thy temple° be destroyed.

41°

Having this day my horse, my hand, my lance,
　Guided so well, that I obtained the prize,
　Both by the judgement of the English eyes
And of some sent from that sweet enemy, France;
Horsemen my skill in horsemanship advance;
　Town-folks my strength; a daintier° judge applies
　His praise to sleight, which from good use doth rise;°
Some lucky wits impute it but to chance;
　Others, because of both sides I do take
My blood from them, who did excel in this,　　　　　　10
Think nature me a man of arms did make.°
How far they shoot awry! The true cause is,
　Stella looked on, and from her heavenly face
　Sent forth the beams, which made so fair my race.

42

O eyes, which do the spheres of beauty move,
Whose beams be joys, whose joys all virtues be,
Who, while they make love conquer, conquer love;
The schools where Venus hath learned chastity;
　O eyes, where humble looks most glorious prove,
Only loved tyrants, just in cruelty;
Do not, O do not, from poor me remove;
Keep still my zenith, ever shine on me.
　For though I never see them, but straight ways
My life forgets to nourish languished sprites;　　　　　　10
Yet still on me, O eyes, dart down your rays;
And if from majesty of sacred lights,
　Oppressing mortal sense, my death proceed,
　Wracks triumphs be, which love (high set) doth breed.°

43

Fair eyes, sweet lips, dear heart, that foolish I
Could hope by Cupid's help on you to prey;
Since to himself he doth your gifts apply.
And his main force, choice sport, and easeful stay.
　For when he will see who dare him gainsay,
Then with those eyes he looks; lo, by and by
Each soul doth at love's feet his weapons lay,

Glad if for her he give them leave to die.
  When he will play, then in her lips he is,
Where, blushing red, that love's self doth them love,   10
With either lip he doth the other kiss
But when he will for quiet's sake remove
  From all the world, her heart is then his room,
  Where well he knows, no man to him can come.

44

My words, I know, do well set forth my mind;
  My mind bemoans his sense of inward smart;
  Such smart may pity claim of any heart;
Her heart (sweet heart) is of no tiger's kind:
And yet she hears, yet I no pity find,
  But more I cry, less grace she doth impart.
  Alas, what cause is there so overthwart,°
That nobleness itself makes thus unkind?
  I much do guess, yet find no truth save this:
That when the breath of my complaints doth touch   10
Those dainty doors unto the court of bliss,
The heavenly nature of that place is such
  That once come there, the sobs of mine annoys
  Are metamorphosed straight to tunes of joys.

45

Stella oft sees the very face of woe
  Painted in my beclouded stormy face;
  But cannot skill° to pity my disgrace,
Not though thereof the cause herself she know;
Yet hearing late a fable, which did show
  Of lovers never known a grievous case,
  Pity thereof gat in her breast such place
That, from that sea derived, tears' spring did flow.
  Alas, if fancy drawn by imaged things,
Though false, yet with free scope more grace doth breed   10
Than servant's wrack, where new doubts honour brings;
Then think, my dear, that you in me do read
  Of lover's ruin some sad tragedy:
  I am not I, pity the tale of me.°

46

I cursed thee oft; I pity now thy case,
  Blind-hitting boy, since she that thee and me
  Rules with a beck, so tyrannizeth thee,
That thou must want or food, or dwelling-place.
For she protests to banish thee her face—
  Her face? O love, a rogue thou then should'st be,
  If love learn not alone to love and see,
Without desire to feed of further grace.
  Alas poor wag, that now a scholar art
To such a school-mistress, whose lessons new   10
Thou needs must miss, and so thou needs must smart.
Yet dear, let me this pardon get of you,
  So long (though he from book mich to desire)
  Till without fuel you can make hot fire.

47

What, have I thus betrayed my liberty?
  Can those black beams such burning marks° engrave
  In my free side? or am I born a slave,
Whose neck becomes such yoke of tyranny?
Or want I sense to feel my misery?
  Or spirit, disdain of such disdain to have,
  Who for long faith, though daily help I crave,
May get no alms, but scorn of beggary?
  Virtue, awake: beauty but beauty is;
I may, I must, I can, I will, I do   10
Leave following that, which it is gain to miss.
Let her go. Soft, but here she comes. Go to,
  Unkind, I love you not—: O me, that eye
  Doth make my heart give to my tongue the lie.

48

Soul's joy, bend not those morning stars from me,
  Where virtue is made strong by beauty's might,
  Where love is chasteness, pain doth learn delight,
And humbleness grows one with majesty.
Whatever may ensue, O let me be
  Co-partner of the riches of that sight;

Let not mine eyes be hell-driven from that light;
O look, O shine, O let me die, and see.
   For though I oft my self of them bemoan,
   That through my heart their beamy darts be gone,   10
Whose cureless wounds even now most freshly bleed;
   Yet since my death-wound is already got,
   Dear killer, spare not thy sweet cruel shot:
A kind of grace it is to slay with speed.°

49°

I on my horse, and love on me, doth try
   Our horsemanships, while by strange work I prove
   A horseman to my horse, a horse to love;
And now man's wrongs in me, poor beast, descry.
The reins wherewith my rider doth me tie
   Are humbled thoughts, which bit of reverence move,
   Curbed in with fear, but with gilt boss° above
Of hope, which makes it seem fair to the eye.
   The wand is will; thou, fancy, saddle art,
Girt fast by memory; and while I spur   10
My horse, he spurs with sharp desire my heart;
He sits me fast, however I do stir;
   And now hath made me to his hand so right
   That in the manage° myself takes delight.

50°

Stella, the fullness of my thoughts of thee
Cannot be stayed within my panting breast,
But they do swell and struggle forth of me,
Till that in words thy figure be expressed.
   And yet, as soon as they so formed be,
According to my lord love's own behest,
With sad eyes I their weak proportion see,
To portrait° that which in this world is best;
   So that I cannot choose but write my mind,
And cannot choose but put out what I write,   10
While those poor babes° their death in birth do find:
And now my pen these lines had dashed quite,
   But that they stopped his fury from the same,
   Because their forefront bare sweet Stella's name.

51°

Pardon, mine ears, both I and they do pray,
  So may your tongue still fluently proceed,
  To them that do such entertainment need,
So may you still have somewhat new to say.
On silly° me do not the burden lay
  Of all the grave conceits your brain doth breed;
  But find some Hercules to bear, in steed°
Of Atlas tired, your wisdom's heavenly sway.
  For me, while you discourse of courtly tides,
Of cunning'st fishers in most troubled streams,°   10
Of straying ways, when valiant error guides;
Meanwhile my heart confers with Stella's beams,
  And is even irked that so sweet comedy
  By such unsuited speech should hindered be.

52°

A strife is grown between virtue and love,
  While each pretends that Stella must be his.
  Her eyes, her lips, her all, saith love, do this,
Since they do wear his badge, most firmly prove.
But virtue thus that title doth disprove:
  That Stella (O dear name) that Stella is
  That virtuous soul, sure heir of heavenly bliss,
Not this fair outside, which our hearts doth move;
  And therefore, though her beauty and her grace
Be love's indeed, in Stella's self he may   10
By no pretence claim any manner place.
Well, love, since this demur our suit doth stay,
  Let virtue have that Stella's self; yet thus,
  That virtue but that body grant to us.

53°

In martial sports I had my cunning tried,
  And yet to break more staves° did me address,
  While with the people's shouts, I must confess,
Youth, luck and praise even filled my veins with pride;
When Cupid, having me, his slave, descried
  In Mars's livery, prancing in the press:
  'What now, sir fool,' said he; 'I would no less,

Look here, I say.' I looked, and Stella spied,
  Who hard by made a window send forth light.
My heart then quaked, then dazzled were mine eyes,   10
One hand forgot to rule,° th'other to fight;
Nor trumpet's sound° I heard, nor friendly cries;
  My foe came on, and beat the air for me,
  Till that her blush taught me my shame to see.

54

Because I breathe not love to every one,
  Nor do not use set colours for to wear,
  Nor nourish special locks of vowed hair,
Nor give each speech a full point of a groan,
The courtly nymphs, acquainted with the moan
  Of them, who in their lips love's standard bear:
  'What, he?' say they of me, 'now I dare swear,
He cannot love; no, no, let him alone.'
  And think so still, so Stella know my mind.
Profess indeed I do not Cupid's art;   10
But you fair maids, at length this true shall find,
That his right badge is but worn in the heart;
  Dumb swans, not chattering pies, do lovers prove;°
  They love indeed, who quake to say they love.

55

Muses, I oft invoked your holy aid,
  With choicest flowers my speech to engarland so
  That it, despised in true but naked show,
Might win some grace in your sweet skill arrayed;
And oft whole troops of saddest words I stayed,
  Striving abroad a-foraging to go,
  Until by your inspiring I might know
How their black banner might be best displayed.°
  But now I mean no more your help to try,
Nor other sugaring of my speech to prove,   10
But on her name incessantly to cry:
For let me but name her, whom I do love,
  So sweet sounds straight mine ear and heart do hit
  That I well find no eloquence like it.

56

Fie, school of patience, fie; your lesson is
  Far, far too long to learn it without book:
  What, a whole week without one piece of look,°
And think I should not your large precepts miss?
When I might read those letters fair of bliss,
  Which in her face teach virtue, I could brook
  Somewhat thy leaden counsels, which I took
As of a friend that meant not much amiss:
  But now that I, alas, do want her sight,
What, dost thou think that I can ever take   10
In thy cold stuff a phlegmatique° delight?
No, patience; if thou wilt my good, then make
  Her come, and hear with patience my desire,
  And then with patience bid me bear my fire.

57°

Woe, having made with many fights his own
  Each sense of mine, each gift, each power of mind,
  Grown now his slaves, he forced them out to find
The thorough'st words, fit for woe's self to groan,
Hoping that when they might find Stella alone,
  Before she could prepare to be unkind,
  Her soul, armed but with such a dainty rind,
Should soon be pierced with sharpness of the moan.
  She heard my plaints, and did not only hear,
But them (so sweet she is) most sweetly sing,   10
With that fair breast making woe's darkness clear.°
A pretty case! I hoped her to bring
  To feel my griefs, and she with face and voice
  So sweets my pains, that my pains me rejoice.

58

Doubt there hath been, when with his golden chain
  The orator so far men's hearts doth bind
  That no pace else their guided steps can find
But as he them more short or slack doth rein
Whether with words this sovereignty he gain,
  Clothed with fine tropes, with strongest reasons lined,
  Or else pronouncing grace, wherewith his mind

Prints his own lively form in rudest brain.°
  Now judge by this: in piercing phrases late
  The anatomy of all my woes I wrate,   10
Stella's sweet breath the same to me did read.
  O voice, O face, maugre my speech's might,
  Which wooed woe, most ravishing delight
Even those sad words even in sad me did breed.

59

Dear, why make you more of a dog than me?
  If he do love, I burn, I burn in love;
  If he wait well, I never thence would move;
If he be fair, yet but a dog can be.
Little he is, so little worth is he;
  He barks, my songs thy own voice oft doth prove;
  Bidden, perhaps he fetcheth thee a glove;
But I unbid fetch even my soul to thee.
  Yet while I languish, him that bosom clips,
That lap doth lap, nay lets, in spite of spite,   10
This sour-breathed mate taste of those sugared lips.
Alas, if you grant only such delight
  To witless things, then love, I hope (since wit
  Becomes a clog) will soon ease me of it.

60

When my good angel° guides me to the place
  Where all my good I do in Stella see,
  That heaven of joys throws only down on me
Thundered disdains, and lightnings of disgrace;
But when the rugged'st step of fortune's race
  Makes me fall from her sight, then sweetly she
  With words, wherein the muses' treasures be,
Shows love and pity to my absent case.
  Now I, wit-beaten long by hardest fate,
So dull am, that I cannot look into   10
The ground of this fierce love and lovely hate,
Then some good body tell me how I do,
  Whose presence absence, absence presence is;
  Blessed in my curse, and cursed in my bliss.

61

Oft with true sighs, oft with uncalled tears,
Now with slow words, now with dumb eloquence,
I Stella's eyes assail, invade her ears;
But this at last is her sweet-breathed defence:
    That who indeed infelt affection bears,
So captives to his saint both soul and sense
That wholly hers, all selfness° he forbears;
Thence his desires he learns, his life's course thence.
    Now since her chaste mind hates this love in me,
    With chastened mind I straight must show that she   10
Shall quickly me from what she hates remove.
    O doctor Cupid, thou for me reply;
    Driven else to grant, by angel's sophistry,
That I love not, without I leave to love.

62

Late tired with woe, even ready for to pine
With rage of love, I called my love unkind;
She in whose eyes love, though unfelt, doth shine,
Sweet said that I true love in her should find.
    I joyed, but straight thus watered was my wine,°
That love she did, but loved a love not blind,°
Which would not let me, whom she loved, decline
From nobler course, fit for my birth and mind:
    And therefore, by her love's authority,
    Willed me these tempests of vain love to fly,   10
And anchor fast myself on virtue's shore.
    Alas, if this the only metal be
    Of love, new-coined to help my beggary,
Dear, love me not, that you may love me more.

63

O grammar rules, O now your virtues show:
    So children still read you with awful eyes,
    As my young dove° may in your precepts wise,
Her grant to me, by her own virtue, know.
For late, with heart most high, with eyes most low,
    I craved the thing, which ever she denies:
    She, lightning love, displaying Venus' skies,

Lest once should not be heard, twice said, 'No, no.'
　　Sing then, my muse, now Io Paean sing;
　　Heavens, envy not at my high triumphing,   10
But grammar's force with sweet success confirm.
　　For grammar says (O this, dear Stella, weigh),
　　For grammar says (to grammar who says nay?)
That in one speech two negatives affirm.°

First song

Doubt you to whom my muse these songs intendeth,
Which now my breast, o'ercharged, to music lendeth?
To you, to you, all song of praise is due;
Only in you my song begins and endeth.

Who hath the eyes which marry state with pleasure,
Who keeps the key of nature's chiefest treasure?
To you, to you, all song of praise is due;
Only for you the heaven forgat all measure.

Who hath the lips, where wit in fairness reigneth,
Who womankind at once both decks and staineth?   10
To you, to you, all song of praise is due;
Only by you Cupid his crown maintaineth.

Who hath the feet, whose step all sweetness planteth,
Who else for whom fame worthy trumpets wanteth?
To you, to you, all song of praise is due;
Only to you her sceptre Venus granteth.

Who hath the breast, whose milk doth passions nourish,
Whose grace is such, that when it chides doth cherish?
To you, to you, all song of praise is due;
Only through you the tree of life doth flourish.   20

Who hath the hand which without stroke subdueth,
Who long-dead beauty with increase reneweth?°
To you, to you, all song of praise is due;
Only at you all envy hopeless rueth.

Who hath the hair which loosest, fastest, tieth?
Who makes a man live then glad, when he dieth?
To you, to you, all song of praise is due;
Only of you the flatterer never lieth.

Who hath the voice which soul from senses sunders?
Whose force but yours the bolts of beauty thunders?   30
To you, to you, all song of praise is due;
Only with you not miracles are wonders.°

Doubt you to whom my muse these notes intendeth,
Which now my breast, o'ercharged, to music lendeth?
To you, to you, all song of praise is due;
Only in you my song begins and endeth.

64

No more, my dear, no more these counsels try;°
  O give my passions leave to run their race.
  Let fortune lay on me her worst disgrace,
Let folk o'ercharged with brain against me cry,
Let clouds bedim my face, break in mine eye,
  Let me no steps but of lost labour trace,
  Let all the earth with scorn recount my case,
But do not will me from my love to fly.
  I do not envy Aristotle's wit,
Nor do aspire to Caesar's bleeding fame,   10
Nor aught do care, though some above me sit,
Nor hope, nor wish, another course to frame,
  But that which once may win thy cruel heart.
  Thou art my wit, and thou my virtue art.

65

Love, by sure proof I may call thee unkind,
That giv'st no better ear to my just cries;
Thou whom to me such my good turns should bind,
As I may well recount, but none can prize.
  For when, nak'd boy, thou could'st no harbour find
In this old world, grown now so too too wise,
I lodged thee in my heart; and being blind
By nature born, I gave to thee mine eyes.°
  Mine eyes, my light, my heart, my life, alas,
If so great services may scorned be,   10
Yet let this thought thy tigerish courage pass,
That I, perhaps, am somewhat kin to thee:
  Since in thine arms, if learn'd fame truth hath spread,
  Thou bear'st the arrow, I the arrow head.°

66

And do I see some cause a hope to feed,
Or doth the tedious burden of long woe
In weakened minds, quick apprehending breed,
Of every image, which may comfort show?
  I cannot brag of word, much less of deed;
Fortune wheels still with me in one sort slow;
My wealth no more, and no whit less my need;
Desire still on the stilts° of fear doth go.
  And yet amid all fears, a hope there is
Stol'n to my heart, since last fair night, nay day: 10
Stella's eyes sent to me the beams of bliss,
Looking on me, while I looked other way;
    But when mine eyes back to their heaven did move,
    They fled with blush, which guilty seemed of love.

67

Hope, art thou true, or dost thou flatter me?
  Doth Stella now begin with piteous eye
  The ruins of her conquest to espy;
Will she take time, before all wracked be?
Her eyes' speech is translated thus by thee:
  But fail'st thou not, in phrase so heavenly-high?
  Look on again, the fair text better try;
What blushing notes dost thou in margin see?°
  What sighs stol'n out, or killed before full born?
Hast thou found such, and such-like arguments?   10
Or art thou else to comfort me forsworn?
Well, how so thou interpret the contents,
    I am resolved thy error to maintain,
    Rather than by more truth to get more pain.

68

Stella, the only planet of my light,
  Light of my life, and life of my desire,
  Chief good whereto my hope doth only aspire,
World of my wealth, and heaven of my delight;
Why dost thou spend the treasures of thy sprite
  With voice more fit to wed Amphion's lyre,°
  Seeking to quench in me the noble fire

Fed by thy worth, and kindled by thy sight?
  And all in vain, for while thy breath most sweet
With choicest words, thy words with reasons rare,   10
Thy reasons firmly set on virtue's feet,
Labour to kill in me this killing care:
    O think I then, what paradise of joy
    It is, so fair a virtue to enjoy.°

69

O joy too high for my low style to show;
  O bliss, fit for a nobler state than me;
  Envy, put out thine eyes, lest thou do see
What oceans of delight in me do flow.
My friend, that oft saw through all masks my woe,
  Come, come, and let me pour myself on thee;
  Gone is the winter of my misery,
My spring appears;° O see what here doth grow!
  For Stella hath, with words where faith doth shine,
Of her high heart giv'n me the monarchy;   10
I, I, O I may say, that she is mine.
And though she give but thus conditionally
    This realm of bliss, while virtuous course I take,
    No kings be crowned, but they some covenants make.

70

My muse may well grudge at my heavenly joy,
If still I force her in sad rhymes to creep;
She oft hath drunk my tears, now hopes to enjoy
Nectar of mirth, since I Jove's cup do keep.°
  Sonnets be not bound prentice to annoy;
Trebles sing high, as well as basses deep;
Grief but love's winter livery is; the boy
Hath cheeks to smile, as well as eyes to weep.
  Come then my muse, show thou height of delight
In well raised notes; my pen the best it may   10
Shall paint out joy, though but in black and white.
Cease, eager muse; peace pen, for my sake stay;
    I give you here my hand for truth of this:
    Wise silence is best music unto bliss.

71

Who will in fairest book of nature know
 How virtue may best lodged in beauty be,
 Let him but learn of love to read in thee,
Stella, those fair lines which true goodness show.
There shall he find all vices' overthrow,
 Not by rude force, but sweetest sovereignty
 Of reason, from whose light those night-birds° fly,
That inward sun in thine eyes shineth so.
 And not content to be perfection's heir
Thy self, dost strive all minds that way to move,   10
Who mark in thee what is in thee most fair;
So while thy beauty draws the heart to love,
 As fast thy virtue bends that love to good.
 But ah, desire still cries: 'Give me some food.'°

72

Desire, though thou my old companion art,
 And oft so clings to my pure love, that I
 One from the other scarcely can descry,
While each doth blow the fire of my heart;
Now from thy fellowship I needs must part;
 Venus is taught with Dian's wings to fly;
 I must no more in thy sweet passions lie;
Virtue's gold now must head my Cupid's dart.°
 Service and honour, wonder with delight,
Fear to offend, will worthy to appear,   10
Care shining in mine eyes, faith in my sprite;
These things are left me by my only dear.
 But thou, desire, because thou would'st have all,
 Now banished art—but yet, alas, how shall?

Second song°

Have I caught my heavenly jewel
Teaching sleep most fair to be?
Now will I teach her that she,
When she wakes, is too too cruel.

Since sweet sleep her eyes hath charmed,
The two only darts of love:
Now will I with that boy prove
Some play, while he is disarmed.

Her tongue waking still refuseth,
Giving frankly niggard° 'no';   10
Now will I attempt to know
What 'no' her tongue sleeping useth.

See, the hand which, waking, guardeth,
Sleeping, grants a free resort;
Now will I invade the fort;
Cowards love with loss rewardeth.°

But, O fool, think of the danger
Of her just and high disdain;
Now will I, alas, refrain;
Love fears nothing else but anger.   20

Yet those lips so sweetly swelling
Do invite a stealing kiss:
Now will I but venture this;
Who will read, must first learn spelling.

O sweet kiss—but ah, she is waking,
Louring° beauty chastens me;
Now will I away hence flee;
Fool, more fool, for no more taking.

73

Love still a boy, and oft a wanton is,
Schooled only by his mother's tender eye;
What wonder then if he his lesson miss,
When for so soft a rod° dear play he try?
   And yet my Star, because a sugared kiss
In sport I sucked, while she asleep did lie,
Doth lour, nay chide; nay, threat, for only this.
Sweet, it was saucy love, not humble I.
   But no 'scuse serves, she makes her wrath appear
   In beauty's throne; see now, who dares come near   10
Those scarlet judges, threatening bloody pain?°
   O heavenly fool, thy most kiss-worthy face

Anger invests with such a lovely grace
That anger's self I needs must kiss again.

74

I never drank of Aganippe well,°
Nor ever did in shade of Tempe° sit;
And muses scorn with vulgar brains to dwell;
Poor layman I, for sacred rites unfit.
    Some do I hear of poet's fury tell,
But (God wot) wot not what they mean by it;°
And this I swear, by blackest brook of hell,°
I am no pick-purse of another's wit.
    How falls it then, that with so smooth an ease
My thoughts I speak, and what I speak doth flow   10
In verse, and that my verse best wits doth please?°
Guess we the cause: 'What, is it thus?' Fie, no;
    'Or so?' Much less. 'How then?' Sure, thus it is:
    My lips are sweet, inspired with Stella's kiss.

75°

Of all the kings that ever here did reign,
Edward, named fourth, as first in praise I name;
Not for his fair outside, nor well lined brain,
Although less gifts imp° feathers oft on fame;
    Nor that he could, young-wise, wise-valiant, frame
His sire's revenge, joined with a kingdom's gain;
And gained by Mars, could yet mad Mars so tame,
That balance weighed what sword did late obtain;°
    Nor that he made the flower-de-luce so 'fraid,
Though strongly hedged of bloody lion's paws,   10
That witty Lewis to him a tribute paid;°
Nor this, nor that, nor any such small cause;
    But only for this worthy knight durst prove
    To lose his crown, rather than fail his love.°

76°

She comes, and straight therewith her shining twins do move
  Their rays to me, who in her tedious absence lay
  Benighted in cold woe; but now appears my day,
The only light of joy, the only warmth of love.
She comes, with light and warmth, which like Aurora prove

Of gentle force, so that mine eyes dare gladly play
  With such a rosy morn, whose beams most freshly gay
Scorch not, but only do dark chilling sprites remove.
  But lo, while I do speak, it groweth noon with me;
Her flamy glistering lights increase with time and place;   10
My heart cries, 'Ah, it burns;' mine eyes now dazzled be;
No wind, no shade, can cool; what help then in my case,
  But with short breath, long looks, staid feet and walking° head,
  Pray that my sun go down with meeker beams to bed.

77°

Those looks, whose beams be joy, whose motion is delight;
That face, whose lecture° shows what perfect beauty is;
That presence, which doth give dark hearts a living light;
That grace, which Venus weeps that she herself doth miss;
  That hand, which without touch holds more than Atlas' might;
Those lips, which make death's pay a mean price for a kiss;
That skin, whose pass-praise hue scorns this poor term of 'white';
Those words, which do sublime° the quintessence of bliss;
  That voice, which makes the soul plant himself in the ears;
That conversation sweet, where such high comforts be,   10
As construed in true speech, the name of heaven it bears,
Makes me in my best thoughts and quiet'st judgement see
  That in no more but these I might be fully blessed:
  Yet ah, my maiden muse doth blush to tell the rest.

78°

O how the pleasant airs of true love be
    Infected by those vapours which arise
    From out that noisome gulf, which gaping lies
Between the jaws of hellish jealousy:
A monster, others' harm, self-misery,
    Beauty's plague, virtue's scourge, succour of lies;
    Who his own joy to his own hurt applies,
And only cherish doth with injury;
    Who, since he hath, by nature's special grace,
    So piercing paws, as spoil when they embrace;   10
So nimble feet, as stir still, though on thorns;
    So many eyes, aye seeking their own woe;
    So ample ears, as never good news know:
Is it not ill that such a devil wants horns?

79

Sweet kiss, thy sweets I fain would sweetly endite,
  Which even of sweetness sweetest sweetener art:°
  Pleasing'st consort, where each sense holds a part;
Which, coupling doves, guides Venus' chariot right;
Best charge, and bravest retreat in Cupid's fight;
  A double key, which opens to the heart,
  Most rich, when most his riches it impart;
Nest of young joys, schoolmaster of delight,
  Teaching the mean at once to take and give;
The friendly fray, where blows both wound and heal;   10
The pretty death, while each in other live;
Poor hope's first wealth, hostage of promised weal,
  Breakfast of love—but lo, lo, where she is:
  Cease we to praise, now pray we for a kiss.

80

Sweet swelling lip, well may'st thou swell in pride,
  Since best wits think it wit thee to admire;
  Nature's praise, virtue's stall, Cupid's cold fire,
Whence words, not words, but heavenly graces slide;
The new Parnassus, where the muses bide;
  Sweetener of music, wisdom's beautifier;
  Breather of life, and fastener of desire,
Where beauty's blush in honour's grain° is dyed.
  Thus much my heart compelled my mouth to say:
  But now, spite of my heart, my mouth will stay,   10
Loathing all lies, doubting this flattery is,
  And no spur can his resty° race renew,
  Without how far this praise is short of you,
Sweet lip, you teach my mouth with one sweet kiss.

81

O kiss, which dost those ruddy gems impart,
Or gems, or fruits of new-found paradise,
Breathing all bliss, and sweetening to the heart,
Teaching dumb lips a nobler exercise;
  O kiss, which souls, even souls together ties
By links of love, and only nature's art;
How fain would I paint thee to all men's eyes,

Or of thy gifts at least shade out some part.
  But she forbids; with blushing words, she says
  She builds her fame on higher seated praise;   10
But my heart burns, I cannot silent be.
  Then since (dear life) you fain would have me peace,
  And I, mad with delight, want wit to cease,
Stop you my mouth with still still kissing me.

82

Nymph of the garden° where all beauties be;
  Beauties, which do in excellency pass
  His who till death looked in a watery glass,°
Or hers whom naked the Trojan boy did see:°
Sweet garden nymph, which keeps the cherry tree,
  Whose fruit doth far th'Hesperian taste surpass;
  Most sweet-fair, most fair-sweet, do not, alas,
From coming near those cherries banish me.
  For though, full of desire, empty of wit,
  Admitted late by your best-graced grace,   10
I caught at one of them a hungry bit;
  Pardon that fault, once more grant me the place,
  And I do swear, even by the same delight,
  I will but kiss, I never more will bite.

83

Good brother Philip,° I have borne you long;
  I was content you should in favour creep,
  While craftily you seemed your cut to keep,°
As though that fair soft hand did you great wrong.
I bare (with envy) yet I bare your song,
  When in her neck you did love-ditties peep;
  Nay, more fool I, oft suffered you to sleep
In lilies' nest, where love's self lies along.
  What, doth high place ambitious thoughts augment?
Is sauciness reward of courtesy?   10
Cannot such grace your silly self content,
But you must needs with those lips billing be,
  And through those lips drink nectar from that tongue?
  Leave that, sir Phip,° lest off your neck be wrung.

Third song

If Orpheus' voice had force to breathe such music's love
Through pores of senseless trees, as it could make them move;
If stones good measure danced, the Theban walls to build,
To cadence of the tunes, which Amphion's lyre did yield;°
More cause a like effect at leastwise bringeth:
O stones, O trees, learn hearing: Stella singeth.

If love might sweeten so a boy of shepherd brood,
To make a lizard dull to taste love's dainty food;
If eagle fierce could so in Grecian maid delight,
As his light was her eyes, her death his endless night;°   10
Earth gave that love, Heaven I trow love refineth:
O birds, O beasts, look, love: lo, Stella shineth.

The birds, beasts, stones, and trees feel this, and feeling, love;
And if the trees, nor stones, stir not, the same to prove,
Nor beasts nor birds do come unto this blessed gaze,
Know, that small love is quick, and great love doth amaze:
They are amazed, but you with reason armed:
O eyes, O ears of men, how are you charmed!

84°

Highway, since you my chief Parnassus be,
    And that my muse, to some ears not unsweet,°
    Tempers her words to trampling horse's feet
More oft than to a chamber melody;°
Now blessed you, bear onward blessed me
    To her, where I my heart safeliest shall meet.
    My muse and I must you of duty greet,
With thanks and wishes, wishing thankfully.
    Be you still fair, honoured by public heed,
By no encroachment wronged, nor time forgot;   10
Nor blamed for blood, nor shamed for sinful deed.
    And that you know, I envy you no lot
    Of highest wish, I wish you so much bliss,
    Hundreds of years you Stella's feet may kiss.

85

I see the house; my heart, thy self contain;
    Beware full sails drown not thy tottering barge,

Lest joy, by nature apt sprites to enlarge,
Thee to thy wrack beyond thy limits strain;°
Nor do like lords, whose weak confused brain,
  Not pointing to fit folks each undercharge,°
  While every office themselves will discharge,
With doing all, leave nothing done but pain.
  But give apt servants their due place; let eyes
See beauty's total sum summed in her face;   10
Let ears hear speech, which wit to wonder ties;
Let breath suck up those sweets; let arms embrace
  The globe of weal; lips love's indentures make;
  Thou but of all the kingly tribute take.

Fourth song

Only joy, now here you are,
Fit to hear and ease my care;
Let my whispering voice obtain
Sweet reward for sharpest pain:
Take me to thee and thee to me.
'No, no, no, no, my dear, let be.'

Night hath closed all in her cloak,
Twinkling stars love-thoughts provoke;
Danger hence good care doth keep;
Jealousy itself doth sleep: 10
Take me to thee and thee to me.
'No, no, no, no, my dear, let be.'

Better place no wit can find
Cupid's yoke to loose or bind;
These sweet flowers on fine bed too°
Us in their best language woo:
Take me to thee and thee to me.
'No, no, no, no, my dear, let be.'

This small light the moon bestows
Serves thy beams but to disclose,   20
So to raise my hap more high;
Fear not else, none can us spy:
Take me to thee and thee to me.
'No, no, no, no, my dear, let be.'

That you heard was but a mouse;
Dumb sleep holdeth all the house;
Yet asleep, methinks, they say,
Young folks, take time while you may:
Take me to thee and thee to me.
'No, no, no, no, my dear, let be.'   30

Niggard time threats, if we miss
This large offer of our bliss
Long stay ere he grant the same;
Sweet then, while each thing doth frame:
Take me to thee and thee to me.
'No, no, no, no, my dear, let be.'

Your fair mother is abed,°
Candles out, and curtains spread;
She thinks you do letters write;°
Write, but first let me endite: 40
Take me to thee and thee to me.
'No, no, no, no, my dear, let be.'

Sweet, alas, why strive you thus?
Concord better fitteth us.
Leave to Mars the force of hands,
Your power in your beauty stands:
Take me to thee and thee to me.
'No, no, no, no, my dear, let be.'

Woe to me, and do you swear
Me to hate, but I forbear?   50
Cursed be my destinies all,
That brought me so high, to fall;
Soon with my death I will please thee.
'No, no, no, no, my dear, let be.'

86

Alas, whence came this change of looks? If I
    Have changed desert, let mine own conscience be
    A still felt plague, to self condemning me:
Let woe gripe on my heart, shame load mine eye.
But if all faith, like spotless ermine,° lie
    Safe in my soul, which only doth to thee
    (As his sole object of felicity)

With wings of love in air of wonder fly,
  O ease your hand, treat not so hard your slave;
In justice pains come not till faults do call;   10
Or if I needs, sweet judge, must torments have,
Use something else to chasten me withal
  Than those blessed eyes, where all my hopes do dwell.
  No doom should make one's heaven become his hell.

Fifth song°

While favour fed my hope, delight with hope was brought;
Thought waited on delight, and speech did follow thought;
Then grew my tongue and pen records unto thy glory;
I thought all words were lost, that were not spent of thee;
I thought each place was dark but where thy lights would be,
And all ears worse than deaf, that heard not out thy story.

I said thou wert most fair, and so indeed thou art;
I said thou wert most sweet, sweet poison to my heart;
I said my soul was thine—O that I then had lied!
I said thine eyes were stars, thy breasts the milken way,   10
Thy fingers Cupid's shafts, thy voice the angels' lay,
And all I said so well, as no man it denied.

But now that hope is lost, unkindness kills delight,
Yet thought and speech do live, though metamorphosed quite;
For rage now rules the reins, which guided were by pleasure.
I think now of thy faults, who late thought of thy praise;
That speech falls now to blame, which did thy honour raise;
The same key open can, which can lock up a treasure.

Thou then, whom partial heavens conspired in one to frame,
The proof of beauty's worth, th'inheritrix of fame,   20
The mansion seat of bliss, and just excuse of lovers;
See now those feathers plucked, wherewith thou flew'st most high;
See what clouds of reproach shall dark thy honour's sky;
Whose own fault casts him down, hardly high seat recovers.

And O my muse, though oft you lulled her in your lap,
And then, a heavenly child, gave her ambrosian pap,
And to that brain of hers your hidd'nest gifts infused;
Since she, disdaining me, doth you in me disdain,

Suffer her not to laugh, while we both suffer pain;
Princes in subjects wronged, must deem themselves abused.   30

Your client poor my self, shall Stella handle so?°
Revenge, revenge, my muse; defiance' trumpet blow;
Threaten what may be done, yet do more than you threaten.
Ah, my suit granted is; I feel my breast to swell;
Now child, a lesson new you shall begin to spell:
Sweet babes must babies have,° but shrewd° girls must be beaten.

Think now no more to hear of warm fine-odoured snow,
Nor blushing lilies, nor pearls' ruby-hidden row,
Nor of that golden sea, whose waves in curls are broken:
But of thy soul, so fraught with such ungratefulness,   40
As where thou soon might'st help, most faith doth most oppress;
Ungrateful who is called, the worst of evils is spoken.°

Yet worse than worst, I say thou art a thief. A thief?
No God forbid. A thief, and of worst thieves the chief;
Thieves steal for need, and steal but goods, which pain recovers,
But thou, rich in all joys,° dost rob my joys from me,
Which cannot be restored by time nor industry.
Of foes the spoil is evil, far worse of constant lovers.

Yet gentle English thieves do rob, but will not slay;
Thou, English murdering thief, wilt have hearts for thy prey;   50
The name of 'murderer' now on thy fair forehead sitteth;
And even while I do speak, my death wounds bleeding be,
Which, I protest, proceed from only cruel thee.
Who may, and will not, save, murder in truth committeth.

But murder, private fault, seems but a toy to thee;
I lay then to thy charge, unjustest tyranny,
If rule by force without all claim a tyrant showeth.
For thou dost lord my heart, who am not born thy slave;
And which is worse, makes me, most guiltless, torments have;
A rightful prince by unright deeds a tyrant groweth.   60

Lo, you grow proud with this, for tyrants make folk bow.
Of foul rebellion then I do appeach thee now;
Rebel by nature's law, rebel by law of reason.
Thou, sweetest subject, wert born in the realm of love,
And yet against thy prince thy force dost daily prove;
No virtue merits praise, once touched with blot of treason.

But valiant rebels oft in fools' mouths purchase fame;
I now then stain thy white with vagabonding shame,
Both rebel to the son, and vagrant from the mother:
For wearing Venus' badge in every part of thee   70
Unto Diana's train thou, runaway, did'st flee:
Who faileth one, is false, though trusty to another.

What, is not this enough? Nay, far worse cometh here:
A witch I say thou art, though thou so fair appear;
For I protest, my sight never thy face enjoyeth,
But I in me am changed; I am alive and dead;
My feet are turned to roots; my heart becometh lead.
No witchcraft is so evil, as which man's mind destroyeth.

Yet witches may repent; thou art far worse than they;
Alas, that I am forced such evil of thee to say!   80
I say thou art a devil, though clothed in angel's shining;
For thy face tempts my soul to leave the heaven for thee,
And thy words of refuse do pour even hell on me.
Who tempt, and tempted plague, are devils in true defining.

You then, ungrateful thief; you murdering tyrant, you;
You rebel runaway, to lord and lady untrue;
You witch, you devil, alas—you still of me beloved;
You see what I can say; mend yet your froward mind,
And such skill in my muse you, reconciled, shall find,
That all these cruel words your praises shall be proved.°   90

Sixth song°

O you that hear this voice,
O you that see this face,
Say whether of the choice
Deserves the former° place:
Fear not to judge this bate,
For it is void of hate.

This side doth beauty take;
For that, doth music speak;
Fit orators to make
The strongest judgements weak: 10
The bar to plead their right
Is only true delight.

Thus doth the voice and face,
These gentle lawyers, wage,
Like loving brothers' case
For father's heritage,
That each, while each contends,
Itself to other lends.

For beauty beautifies
With heavenly hue and grace   20
The heavenly harmonies;
And in this faultless face
The perfect beauties be
A perfect harmony.

Music more lofty swells
In speeches nobly placed;
Beauty as far excels
In action aptly graced;
A friend each party draws
To countenance his cause.   30

Love more affected seems
To beauty's lovely light,
And wonder more esteems
Of music's wondrous might;
But both to both so bent
As both in both are spent.

Music doth witness call
The ear, his truth to try;
Beauty brings to the hall
The judgement of the eye: 40
Both in their objects such,
As no exceptions touch.

The common sense,° which might
Be arbiter of this,
To be, forsooth, upright,
To both sides partial is:
He lays on this chief praise,
Chief praise on that he lays.

Then reason, princess high,
Whose throne is in the mind,   50

Which music can in sky
And hidden beauties find:
Say whether thou wilt crown
With limitless renown.

Seventh song°

Whose senses in so ill consort their stepdame nature lays,
That ravishing delight in them most sweet tunes do not raise;
Or if they do delight therein, yet are so cloyed with wit,
As with sententious lips to set a title vain on it;
O let them hear these sacred tunes, and learn in wonder's
    schools
To be, in things past bounds of wit, fools, if they be not fools.

Who have so leaden eyes, as not to see sweet beauty's show;
Or seeing, have so wooden wits, as not that worth to know;
Or knowing, have so muddy minds, as not to be in love;
Or loving, have so frothy thoughts as eas'ly thence to move: 10
O, let them see these heavenly beams, and in fair letters read
A lesson fit, both sight and skill, love and firm love to breed.

Hear then, but then with wonder hear; see, but adoring see;
No mortal gifts, no earthly fruits, now here descended be;
See; do you see this face? A face? Nay, image of the skies,
Of which the two life-giving lights are figured in her eyes.
Hear you this soul-invading voice, and count it but a voice?
The very essence of their tunes, when angels do rejoice.

Eighth song°

In a grove most rich of shade,°
Where birds wanton music made,
May then young his pied weeds showing,
New perfumed with flowers fresh growing,

Astrophil with Stella sweet
Did for mutual comfort meet;
Both within themselves oppressed,
But each in the other blessed.

Him great harms had taught much care:
Her fair neck a foul yoke bare: 10
But her sight his cares did banish,
In his sight her yoke did vanish.

Wept they had, alas the while;
But now tears themselves did smile,
While their eyes, by love directed,
Interchangeably reflected.

Sigh they did; but now betwixt
Sighs of woes were glad sighs mixed,
With arms crossed,° yet testifying
Restless rest, and living dying.   20

Their ears hungry of each word,
Which the dear tongue would afford,
But their tongues restrained from walking,
Till their hearts had ended talking.

But when their tongues could not speak
Love itself did silence break;
Love did set his lips asunder,
Thus to speak in love and wonder:

'Stella, sovereign of my joy,
Fair triumpher of annoy,   30
Stella, star of heavenly fire,
Stella, lodestar of desire;

'Stella, in whose shining eyes
Are the lights of Cupid's skies;
Whose beams, where they once are darted,
Love therewith is straight imparted;

'Stella, whose voice when it speaks
Senses all asunder breaks;
Stella, whose voice when it singeth
Angels to acquaintance bringeth;   40

'Stella, in whose body is
Writ each character of bliss;
Whose face all, all beauty passeth,
Save thy mind, which yet surpasseth:

'Grant, O grant—but speech, alas,
Fails me, fearing on to pass;
Grant—O me, what am I saying?
But no fault there is in praying:

'Grant, O dear, on knees I pray'—
(Knees on ground he then did stay)   50
'That not I, but since I love you,
Time and place for me may move you.

'Never season was more fit,
Never room more apt for it;
Smiling air allows my reason;
These birds sing, "Now use the season";

'This small wind, which so sweet is,
See how it the leaves doth kiss,
Each tree in his best attiring
Sense of love to love inspiring.   60

'Love makes earth the water drink,
Love to earth makes water sink;
And if dumb things be so witty,
Shall a heavenly grace want pity?'

There his hands in their speech fain
Would have made tongue's language plain:
But her hands, his hands repelling,
Gave repulse, all grace excelling.

Then she spake; her speech was such
As not ears, but heart did touch;   70
While such wise she love denied,
As yet love she signified.

'Astrophil,' said she, 'my love
Cease in these effects to prove:
Now be still; yet still believe me,
Thy grief more than death would grieve me.

'If that any thought in me
Can taste comfort but of thee,
Let me, fed with hellish anguish,
Joyless, hopeless, endless languish.   80

'If those eyes you praised be
Half so dear as you to me,
Let me home return, stark blinded
Of those eyes, and blinder minded.

'If to secret of my heart
I do any wish impart
Where thou art not foremost placed,
Be both wish and I defaced.

'If more may be said, I say:
All my bliss in thee I lay;　　　　　　　　90
If thou love, my love content thee,
For all love, all faith is meant thee.

'Trust me, while I thee deny,
In my self the smart I try;
Tyrant honour thus doth use thee;
Stella's self might not refuse thee.

'Therefore, dear, this no more move,
Lest, though I leave not thy love,
Which too deep in me is framed,
I should blush when thou art named.'　　　100

Therewithal away she went,
Leaving him so passion-rent
With what she had done and spoken,
That therewith my song is broken.°

Ninth song°

Go, my flock, go get you hence,
Seek a better place of feeding,
Where you may have some defence
From the storms in my breast breeding,
And showers from my eyes proceeding.

Leave a wretch, in whom all woe
Can abide to keep no measure;
Merry flock, such one forego,
Unto whom mirth is displeasure,
Only rich in mischief's treasure.　　　　　　10

Yet, alas, before you go,
Hear your woeful master's story,
Which to stones I else would show:
Sorrow only then hath glory,
When 'tis excellently sorry.

Stella, fiercest shepherdess,
Fiercest, but yet fairest ever;
Stella, whom, O heavens, do bless,
Though against me she persevere,
Though I bliss inherit never;   20

Stella hath refused me,
Stella, who more love hath proved
In this caitiff° heart to be
Than can in good ewes be moved
Toward lambkins best beloved.

Stella hath refused me;
Astrophil, that so well served,
In this pleasant spring must see,
While in pride flowers be preserved,   30
Himself only winter-starved.

Why, alas, doth she then swear
That she loveth me so dearly,
Seeing me so long to bear
Coals of love, that burn so clearly,
And yet leave me helpless merely?

Is that love? Forsooth, I trow,
If I saw my good dog grieved,
And a help for him did know,   40
My love should not be believed
But he were by me relieved.

No, she hates me, wellaway,
Faining love somewhat, to please me;
For she knows, if she display
All her hate, death soon would seize me,
And of hideous torments ease me.

Then adieu, dear flock, adieu:
But alas, if in your straying
Heavenly Stella meet with you,
Tell her, in your piteous blaying,
Her poor slave's unjust decaying.   50

87

When I was forced from Stella, ever dear,
Stella, food of my thoughts, heart of my heart,
Stella, whose eyes make all my tempests clear,
By iron laws of duty° to depart;
   Alas, I found that she with me did smart,°
I saw that tears did in her eyes appear;
I saw that sighs her sweetest lips did part,
And her sad words my sadded sense did hear.
   For me, I wept, to see pearls scattered so;
   I sighed her sighs, and wailed for her woe,   10
Yet swam in joy, such love in her was seen.
   Thus while th'effect most bitter was to me,
   And nothing than the cause more sweet could be,
I had been vexed, if vexed I had not been.

88°

Out, traitor absence; darest thou counsel me
From my dear captainess to run away,
Because in brave array here marcheth she
That to win me, oft shows a present pay?
   Is faith so weak? Or is such force in thee?
When sun° is hid, can stars such beams display?
Cannot heaven's food, once felt, keep stomachs free
From base desire on earthly cates° to prey?
   Tush, absence; while thy mists eclipse that light,
   My orphan sense flies to the inward sight,   10
Where memory sets forth the beams of love;
   That where before heart loved and eyes did see,
   In heart both sight and love now coupled be;
United powers make each the stronger be.

89°

Now that of absence the most irksome night
  With darkest shade doth overcome my day;
  Since Stella's eyes, wont to give me my day,
Leaving my hemisphere, leave me in night;
Each day seems long, and longs for long-stayed night;
  The night as tedious, woos the approach of day;
  Tired with the dusty toils of busy day,
Languished with horrors of the silent night,
Suffering the ills both of the day and night,
  While no night is more dark than is my day,   10
Nor no day hath less quiet than my night;
  With such bad mixture of my night and day,
That living thus in blackest winter night,
  I feel the flames of hottest summer day.

90°

Stella, think not that I by verse seek fame;
  Who seek, who hope, who love, who live, but thee:
  Thine eyes my pride, thy lips my history;
If thou praise not, all other praise is shame.
Nor so ambitious am I, as to frame
  A nest for my young praise in laurel tree;
  In truth I swear, I wish not there should be
Graved in mine epitaph a poet's name:
  Ne if I would, could I just title make,
That any laud° to me thereof should grow,   10
Without my plumes from others' wings I take.
For nothing from my wit or will doth flow,
  Since all my words thy beauty doth endite,
  And love doth hold my hand, and makes me write.

91

Stella, while now, by honour's cruel might,°
  I am from you, light of my life, misled,
  And that fair you, my sun, thus overspread
With absence' veil, I live in sorrow's night;
If this dark place yet show, like candle light,
  Some beauty's piece, as amber-coloured head,

  Milk hands, rose cheeks, or lips more sweet, more red,
Or seeing jets, black, but in blackness bright:
  They please, I do confess, they please mine eyes.
But why? Because of you they models be,   10
Models such be wood-globes of glistering skies.°
Dear, therefore be not jealous over me;
  If you hear that they seem my heart to move,
  Not them, O no, but you in them I love.

92

Be your words made, good sir, of Indian ware,°
  That you allow me them by so small rate?
  Or do you cutted Spartans° imitate?
Or do you mean my tender ears to spare,
That to my questions you so total° are?
  When I demand of Phoenix Stella's state,
  You say, forsooth, you left her well of late.
O God, think you that satisfies my care?
  I would know whether she did sit or walk,
How clothed, how waited on? Sighed she or smiled?   10
Whereof, with whom, how often did she talk?
With what pastime time's journey she beguiled?
  If her lips deigned to sweeten my poor name?
  Say all, and all well said, still say the same.

Tenth song°

  O dear life, when shall it be
    That mine eyes thine eyes may see,
    And in them my mind discover,
    Whether absence have had force
    Thy remembrance to divorce
    From the image of thy lover?

  O if I myself find not
    After parting aught forgot,
    Nor debarred from beauty's treasure,
    Let no tongue aspire to tell   10
    In what high joys I shall dwell;
    Only thought aims at the pleasure.

Thought, therefore, I will send thee
  To take up the place for me
  Long I will not after tarry.
  There unseen thou may'st be bold
  Those fair wonders to behold,
  Which in them my hopes do carry.

Thought, see thou no place forbear;
  Enter bravely everywhere,
  Seize on all to her belonging;
  But if thou would'st guarded be,
  Fearing her beams, take with thee
  Strength of liking, rage of longing.

Think of that most grateful time
  When my leaping heart will climb
  In my lips to have his biding,
  There those roses for to kiss
  Which do breathe a sugared bliss,
  Opening rubies, pearls dividing.

Think of my most princely power,
  When I, blessed, shall devour
  With my greedy lickerous senses,
  Beauty, music, sweetness, love,
  While she doth against me prove
  Her strong darts but weak defences.

Think, think of those dallyings,
  When with dove-like murmurings,
  With glad moaning passed anguish,
  We change eyes, and heart for heart
  Each to other do impart,
  Joying, till joy make us languish.

O my thought, my thoughts surcease;
  Thy delights my woes increase,
  My life melts with too much thinking.
  Think no more, but die in me,
  Till thou shalt revived be
  At her lips my nectar drinking.

20

30

40

93

O fate, O fault, O curse, child of my bliss;
    What sobs can give words grace my grief to show?
    What ink is black enough to paint my woe?
Through me, wretch me, even Stella vexed is.
Yet truth—if caitiff's breath might call thee—this
    Witness with me, that my foul stumbling so
    From carelessness did in no manner grow;
But wit, confused with too much care, did miss.°
    And do I then myself this vain 'scuse give?
I have (live I, and know this?) harmed thee;   10
Though worlds 'quit me, shall I myself forgive?
Only with pains my pains thus eased be,
    That all my hurts in my heart's wrack I read;
    I cry thy sighs; my dear, thy tears I bleed.

94

Grief, find the words; for thou hast made my brain
    So dark with misty vapours, which arise
    From out thy heavy mould, that inbent eyes
Can scarce discern the shape of mine own pain.
Do thou then (for thou canst), do thou complain,
    For my poor soul, which now that sickness tries
    Which even to sense, sense of itself denies,
Though harbingers of death lodge there his train.
    Or if thy love of plaint yet mine forbears,
As of a caitiff, worthy so to die;   10
Yet wail thyself, and wail with causeful tears,
That though in wretchedness thy life doth lie,
Yet grow'st more wretched than thy nature bears,
By being placed in such a wretch as I.

95

Yet sighs, dear sighs, indeed true friends you are,
    That do not leave your least friend at the worst;
    But as you with my breast I oft have nursed,
So grateful now you wait upon my care.
Faint coward joy no longer tarry dare,
    Seeing hope yield when this woe strake him first;
    Delight protests he is not for the accursed,

Though oft himself my mate-in-arms he sware.
  Nay, sorrow comes with such main rage, that he
Kills his own children, tears, finding that they   10
By love were made apt to consort with me.
Only true sighs, you do not go away:
    Thank may you have for such a thankful part,
    Thank-worthiest yet, when you shall break my heart.

96

Thought, with good cause thou lik'st so well the night,
    Since kind or chance gives both one livery:
    Both sadly black, both blackly darkened be,
Night barred from sun, thou from thy own sun's light.
Silence in both displays his sullen might;
    Slow heaviness in both holds one degree,
    That full of doubts, thou of perplexity;
Thy tears express night's native moisture right.
    In both a mazeful° solitariness:
In night, of sprites the ghastly powers stir,   10
In thee, or sprites, or sprited ghastliness,
But, but, alas, night's side the odds hath, far,
    For that at length yet doth invite some rest,
    Thou, though still tired, yet still dost it detest.

97°

Dian, that fain would cheer her friend, the night,
    Shows her oft at the full her fairest face,
    Bringing with her those starry nymphs, whose chase
From heavenly standing° hits each mortal wight.
But ah, poor night, in love with Phoebus' light,
    And endlessly despairing of his grace,
    Herself (to show no other joy hath place)
Silent and sad, in mourning weeds doth dight:°
    Even so, alas, a lady, Dian's peer,
With choice delights and rarest company   10
Would fain drive clouds from out my heavy cheer.
But woe is me, though joy itself were she,
    She could not show my blind brain ways of joy,
    While I despair my sun's sight to enjoy.

98°

Ah bed, the field where joy's peace some do see,
 The field where all my thoughts to war be trained,
 How is thy grace by my strange fortune stained!
How thy lee shores° by my sighs stormed be!
With sweet soft shades thou oft invitest me
 To steal some rest; but, wretch, I am constrained
 (Spurred with love's spur, though galled and shortly reined
With care's hard hand) to turn and toss in thee,
 While the black horrors of the silent night
 Paint woe's black face so lively to my sight   10
That tedious leisure marks each wrinkled line.
 But when Aurora leads out Phoebus' dance,°
 Mine eyes then only wink,° for spite, perchance,
That worms should have their sun, and I want mine.

99

When far spent night persuades each mortal eye,
 To whom nor art nor nature granteth light,
 To lay his then mark-wanting shafts° of sight,
Closed with their quivers, in sleep's armoury;
With windows ope then most my mind doth lie,
 Viewing the shape of darkness and delight,
 Takes in that sad hue, which with the inward night
Of his mazed powers keeps perfect harmony.
 But when birds charm,° and that sweet air, which is
Morn's messenger, with rose-enamelled skies,   10
Calls each wight to salute the flower of bliss:
In tomb of lids then buried are mine eyes,
 Forced by their lord, who is ashamed to find
 Such light in sense, with such a darkened mind.

100

O tears, no tears, but rain from beauty's skies,°
 Making those lilies and those roses grow
 Which aye most fair, now more than most fair show,
While graceful pity beauty beautifies:
O honeyed sighs, which from that breast do rise
 Whose pants do make unspilling cream to flow,
 Winged with whose breath so pleasing zephyrs blow,

As can refresh the hell where my soul fries:
  O plaints, conserved in such a sugared phrase°
  That eloquence itself envies your praise,   10
While sobbed-out words a perfect music give:
  Such tears, sighs, plaints, no sorrow is, but joy;
  Or if such heavenly signs must prove annoy,
All mirth farewell, let me in sorrow live.

101

Stella is sick, and in that sick-bed lies
Sweetness, that breathes and pants as oft as she;
And grace, sick too, such fine conclusions tries
That sickness brags itself best graced to be.
  Beauty is sick, but sick in so fair guise
That in that paleness beauty's white we see;
And joy, which is inseparate from these eyes,
Stella now learns (strange case!) to weep in thee.
  Love moves thy pain, and like a faithful page,
As thy looks stir, runs up and down, to make   10
All folks prest° at thy will thy pain to assuage;
Nature with care sweats for her darling's sake,
  Knowing worlds pass, ere she enough can find
  Of such heaven stuff,° to clothe so heavenly mind.

102°

Where be those roses gone, which sweetened so our eyes?
  Where those red cheeks, which oft with fair increase did frame
  The height of honour in the kindly badge of shame?
Who hath the crimson weeds stol'n from my morning skies?
How doth the colour vade° of those vermilion dyes,
  Which nature's self did make, and self engrained the same?
  I would know by what right this paleness overcame
That hue, whose force my heart still unto thraldom ties?
  Galen's adoptive sons,° who by a beaten way
  Their judgements hackney on,° the fault on sickness lay;   10
But feeling proof makes me say they mistake it far:
  It is but love, which makes his paper perfect white
  To write therein more fresh the story of delight,
While beauty's reddest ink Venus for him doth stir.

103

O happy Thames, that didst my Stella bear!
I saw thyself, with many a smiling line°
Upon thy cheerful face, joy's livery wear,
While those fair planets on thy streams did shine.
 The boat for joy could not to dance forbear,
While wanton winds, with beauties so divine
Ravished, stayed not, till in her golden hair
They did themselves (O sweetest prison!) twine.
 And fain those Aeol's youths° there would their stay
Have made; but forced by nature still to fly,   10
First did with puffing kiss those locks display.
She, so dishevelled, blushed; from window I
 With sight thereof cried out, 'O fair disgrace;
 Let honour's self to thee grant highest place.'

104

Envious wits, what hath been mine offence,
 That with such poisonous care my looks you mark,
 That to each word, nay, sigh, of mine you hark,
As grudging me my sorrow's eloquence?
Ah, is it not enough, that I am thence,
Thence, so far thence, that scarcely any spark
 Of comfort dare come to this dungeon dark,
Where rigorous exile locks up all my sense?
 But if I by a happy window pass;
If I but stars upon my armour bear;°   10
Sick, thirsty, glad, though but of empty glass;
Your moral notes straight my hid meaning tear
 From out my ribs, and puffing prove that I
 Do Stella love. Fools, who doth it deny?

Eleventh song

'Who is it that this dark night
Underneath my window plaineth?'
It is one that from thy sight
Being, ah, exiled, disdaineth
Every other vulgar light.

'Why, alas, and are you he?
Be not yet those fancies changed?'
Dear, when you find change in me,
Though from me you be estranged,
Let my change to ruin be.　　　　　　　10

'Well, in absence this will die;
Leave to see, and leave to wonder.'
Absence sure will help, if I
Can learn, how myself to sunder
From what in my heart doth lie.

'But time will these thoughts remove;
Time doth work what no man knoweth.'
Time doth as the subject prove;
With time still the affection groweth
In the faithful turtle dove.　　　　　　20

'What if you new beauties see,
Will they not stir new affection?'
I will think they pictures be,
Image-like of saint's perfection,
Poorly counterfeiting thee.

'But your reason's purest light
Bids you leave such minds° to nourish.'
Dear, do reason no such spite;
Never doth thy beauty flourish
More than in my reason's sight.　　　　30

'But the wrongs love bears, will make
Love at length leave undertaking.'
No, the more fools do it shake
In a ground of so firm making
Deeper still they drive the stake.

'Peace, I think that some give ear;
Come no more, lest I get anger.'
Bliss, I will my bliss forbear,
Fearing, sweet, you to endanger,
But my soul shall harbour there.　　　　40

'Well, be gone, be gone, I say,
Lest that Argus' eyes° perceive you.'
O, unjust is fortune's sway,
Which can make me thus to leave you,
And from louts to run away.

105°

Unhappy sight, and hath she vanished by,
  So near, in so good time, so free a place?
  Dead glass, dost thou thy object so embrace
As what my heart still sees, thou canst not spy?
I swear by her I love and lack, that I
  Was not in fault, who bent thy dazzling race
  Only unto the heaven of Stella's face,
Counting but dust what in the way did lie.
  But cease, mine eyes, your tears do witness well
That you, guiltless thereof, your nectar missed.   10
Cursed be the page from whom the bad torch fell,
Cursed be the night which did your strife resist,
  Cursed be the coachman, which did drive so fast,
  With no worse curse than absence makes me taste.

106

O absent presence, Stella is not here;
  False flattering hope, that with so fair a face
  Bare me in hand,° that in this orphan place
Stella, I say my Stella, should appear.
What say'st thou now? Where is that dainty cheer°
  Thou told'st mine eyes should help their famished case?
  But thou art gone, now that self-felt disgrace
Doth make me most to wish thy comfort near.
  But here I do store of fair ladies meet,
  Who may with charm of conversation sweet°   10
Make in my heavy mould new thoughts to grow:
  Sure they prevail as much with me, as he
  That bade his friend, but then new maimed, to be
Merry with him, and not think of his woe.

107

Stella, since thou so right a princess art
  Of all the powers which life bestows on me,
  That ere by them aught undertaken be
They first resort unto that sovereign part;
Sweet, for a while give respite to my heart,
  Which pants as though it still should leap to thee;
  And on my thoughts give thy lieutenancy
To this great cause,° which needs both use and art;
  And as a queen, who from her presence sends
Whom she employs, dismiss from thee my wit,   10
Till it have wrought what thy own will attends.
On servants' shame oft master's blame doth sit;
  O, let not fools in me thy works reprove,
  And scorning say, 'See, what it is to love!'

108°

When sorrow, using mine own fire's might,
  Melts down his lead into my boiling breast,
  Through that dark furnace to my heart oppressed
There shines a joy from thee, my only light;
But soon as thought of thee breeds my delight,
  And my young soul flutters to thee, his nest;
  Most rude despair, my daily unbidden guest,
Clips straight my wings, straight wraps me in his night,
  And makes me then bow down my head, and say:
'Ah, what doth Phoebus' gold° that wretch avail   10
Whom iron doors do keep from use of day?'
So strangely, alas, thy works in me prevail,
  That in my woes for thee thou art my joy,
  And in my joys for thee my only annoy.

THE DEFENCE OF POESY

WHEN the right virtuous Edward Wotton and I were at the Emperor's
court together,° we gave ourselves to learn horsemanship of John Pietro
Pugliano, one that with great commendation had the place of an esquire
in his stable.° And he, according to the fertileness of the Italian wit, did
not only afford us the demonstration of his practice, but sought to enrich
our minds with the contemplations therein, which he thought most
precious. But with none I remember mine ears were at that time more
laden, than when (either angered with slow payment, or moved with our
learner-like admiration) he exercised his speech in the praise of his
10 faculty.° He said soldiers were the noblest estate of mankind, and
horsemen the noblest of soldiers. He said they were the masters of war
and ornaments of peace, speedy goers and strong abiders, triumphers
both in camps and courts. Nay, to so unbelieved a point he proceeded as
that no earthly thing bred such wonder to a prince as to be a good
horseman—skill of government was but a *pedanteria*° in comparison.
Then would he add certain praises, by telling what a peerless beast the
horse was, the only serviceable courtier without flattery, the beast of most
beauty, faithfulness, courage, and such more, that if I had not been a
piece of a logician° before I came to him, I think he would have
20 persuaded me to have wished myself a horse. But thus much at least with
his no few words he drave into me, that self-love is better than any gilding
to make that seem gorgeous wherein ourselves be parties. Wherein, if
Pugliano's strong affection and weak arguments will not satisfy you, I will
give you a nearer example of myself, who (I know not by what mischance)
in these my not old years and idlest times having slipped into the title of a
poet,° am provoked to say something unto you in the defence of that my
unelected vocation, which if I handle with more good will than good
reasons, bear with me, since the scholar is to be pardoned that followeth
the steps of his master. And yet I must say that, as I have more just cause
30 to make a pitiful defence of poor poetry, which from almost the highest
estimation of learning is fallen to be the laughing-stock of children,° so
have I need to bring some more available proofs: since the former is by no
man barred of his deserved credit, the silly latter hath had even the names
of philosophers used to the defacing of it, with great danger of civil war
among the Muses.

And first, truly, to all them that, professing learning, inveigh against
poetry, may justly be objected that they go very near to ungratefulness, to

seek to deface that which, in the noblest nations and languages that are known, hath been the first light-giver to ignorance, and first nurse, whose milk by little and little enabled them to feed afterwards of tougher 40 knowledges. And will they now play the hedgehog that, being received into the den, drave out his host?° Or rather the vipers, that with their birth kill their parents?°

Let learned Greece in any of his manifold sciences be able to show me one book before Musaeus, Homer, and Hesiod, all three nothing else but poets.° Nay, let any history be brought that can say any writers were there before them, if they were not men of the same skill, as Orpheus, Linus,° and some other are named, who, having been the first of that country that made pens deliverers of their knowledge to the posterity, may justly challenge to be called their fathers in learning: for not only in time they 50 had this priority (although in itself antiquity be venerable) but went before them, as causes to draw with their charming sweetness the wild untamed wits to an admiration of knowledge. So, as Amphion was said to move stones with his poetry to build Thebes,° and Orpheus to be listened to by beasts, indeed, stony and beastly people;° so among the Romans were Livius Andronicus and Ennius.° So in the Italian language the first that made it aspire to be a treasure-house of science were the poets Dante, Boccaccio, and Petrarch. So in our English were Gower and Chaucer,° after whom, encouraged and delighted with their excellent fore-going, others have followed, to beautify our mother tongue, as well 60 in the same kind as in other arts.

This did so notably show itself, that the philosophers of Greece durst not a long time appear to the world but under the masks of poets. So Thales, Empedocles, and Parmenides sang their natural philosophy in verses; so did Pythagoras and Phocylides their moral counsels; so did Tyrtaeus in war matters, and Solon° in matters of policy: or rather they, being poets, did exercise their delightful vein in those points of highest knowledge, which before them lay hid to the world. For that wise Solon was directly a poet it is manifest, having written in verse the notable fable of the Atlantic Island, which was continued by Plato. And truly even Plato whosoever well considereth shall find that in the body of his work, though 70 the inside and strength were philosophy, the skin, as it were, and beauty depended most of poetry: for all standeth upon dialogues, wherein he feigneth many honest burgesses of Athens to speak of such matters, that, if they had been set on the rack, they would never have confessed them, besides his poetical describing the circumstances of their meetings, as the well ordering of a banquet, the delicacy of a walk, with interlacing mere tales, as Gyges' ring° and others, which who knoweth not to be flowers of poetry did never walk into Apollo's garden.

And even historiographers° (although their lips sound of things done, and verity be written in their foreheads) have been glad to borrow both fashion and, perchance, weight of the poets. So Herodotus entitled his History by the name of the nine Muses;° and both he and all the rest that followed him either stale or usurped of poetry their passionate describing of passions, the many particularities of battles, which no man could affirm; or, if that be denied me, long orations put in the mouths of great kings and captains, which it is certain they never pronounced.

So that truly neither philosopher nor historiographer could at the first have entered into the gates of popular judgements, if they had not taken a great passport of poetry, which in all nations at this day where learning flourisheth not, is plain to be seen; in all which they have some feeling of poetry.

In Turkey,° besides their law-giving divines, they have no other writers but poets. In our neighbour country Ireland, where truly learning goeth very bare, yet are their poets held in a devout reverence.° Even among the most barbarous and simple Indians where no writing is, yet have they their poets who make and sing songs, which they call *areytos*,° both of their ancestors' deeds and praises of their gods: a sufficient probability that, if ever learning come among them, it must be by having their hard dull wits softened and sharpened with the sweet delights of poetry—for until they find a pleasure in the exercises of the mind, great promises of much knowledge will little persuade them that know not the fruits of knowledge. In Wales, the true remnant of the ancient Britons, as there are good authorities to show the long time they had poets, which they called bards, so through all the conquests of Romans, Saxons, Danes, and Normans, some of whom did seek to ruin all memory of learning from among them, yet do their poets even to this day last; so as it is not more notable in soon beginning than in long continuing.°

But since the authors of most of our sciences were the Romans, and before them the Greeks, let us a little stand upon their authorities, but even so far as to see what names they have given unto this now scorned skill.

Among the Romans a poet was called *vates*, which is as much as a diviner, foreseer, or prophet, as by his conjoined words *vaticinium* and *vaticinari* is manifest: so heavenly a title did that excellent people bestow upon this heart-ravishing knowledge. And so far were they carried into the admiration thereof, that they thought in the chanceable hitting upon any such verses great foretokens of their following fortunes were placed.

Whereupon grew the word of *Sortes Virgilianae*, when by sudden opening
Virgil's book they lighted upon any verse of his making, whereof the
histories of the emperors' lives are full: as of Albinus, the governor of our 120
island, who in his childhood met with this verse

> Arma amens capio nec sat rationis in armis

and in his age performed it.° Which, although it were a very vain and
godless superstition, as also it was to think spirits were commanded by
such verses—whereupon this word charms, derived of *carmina*, cometh
—so yet serveth it to show the great reverence those wits were held in;
and altogether not without ground, since both the oracles of Delphos and
Sibylla's prophecies were wholly delivered in verses.° For that same
exquisite observing of number and measure in the words, and that high
flying liberty of conceit proper to the poet, did seem to have some divine 130
force in it.

And may not I presume a little further, to show the reasonableness of
this word *vates*, and say that the holy David's Psalms are a divine poem? If
I do, I shall not do it without the testimony of great learned men, both
ancient and modern. But even the name of Psalms will speak for me,
which being interpreted, is nothing but songs; then that it is fully written
in metre, as all learned Hebricians agree, although the rules be not yet
fully found;° lastly and principally, his handling his prophecy, which is
merely poetical: for what else is the awaking his musical instruments, the
often and free changing of persons, his notable *prosopopoeias*,° when he 140
maketh you, as it were, see God coming in His majesty, his telling of the
beasts' joyfulness and hills leaping,° but a heavenly poesy, wherein
almost he showeth himself a passionate lover of that unspeakable and
everlasting beauty to be seen by the eyes of the mind, only cleared by
faith? But truly now having named him, I fear me I seem to profane that
holy name, applying it to poetry, which is among us thrown down to so
ridiculous an estimation. But they that with quiet judgements will look a
little deeper into it, shall find the end and working of it such as, being
rightly applied, deserveth not to be scourged out of the Church of God.

But now let us see how the Greeks named it, and how they deemed of 150
it. The Greeks called him a 'poet', which name hath, as the most
excellent, gone through other languages. It cometh of this word *poiein*,
which is, to make: wherein, I know not whether by luck or wisdom, we
Englishmen have met with the Greeks in calling him a maker:° which
name, how high and incomparable a title it is, I had rather were known by
marking the scope of other sciences than by any partial allegation.

There is no art delivered to mankind that hath not the works of nature

for his principal object, without which they could not consist, and on
which they so depend, as they become actors and players, as it were, of
160 what nature will have set forth. So doth the astronomer look upon the
stars, and, by that he seeth, set down what order nature hath taken
therein. So doth the geometrician and arithmetician in their diverse sorts
of quantities. So doth the musician in times tell you which by nature
agree, which not. The natural philosopher thereon hath his name, and
the moral philosopher standeth upon the natural virtues, vices, or
passions of man; and follow nature (saith he) therein, and thou shalt not
err. The lawyer saith what men have determined; the historian what men
have done. The grammarian speaketh only of the rules of speech; and the
rhetorician and logician, considering what in nature will soonest prove
170 and persuade, thereon give artificial rules, which still are compassed
within the circle of a question according to the proposed matter. The
physician weigheth the nature of man's body, and the nature of things
helpful or hurtful unto it. And the metaphysic, though it be in the second
and abstract notions, and therefore be counted supernatural, yet doth he
indeed build upon the depth of nature. Only the poet, disdaining to be
tied to any such subjection, lifted up with the vigour of his own invention,
doth grow in effect another nature, in making things either better than
nature bringeth forth, or, quite anew, forms such as never were in nature,
as the Heroes, Demigods, Cyclops, Chimeras, Furies,° and such like: so
180 as he goeth hand in hand with nature, not enclosed within the narrow
warrant of her gifts, but freely ranging only within the zodiac of his own
wit. Nature never set forth the earth in so rich tapestry as divers poets
have done; neither with so pleasant rivers, fruitful trees, sweet-smelling
flowers, nor whatsoever else may make the too much loved earth more
lovely. Her world is brazen, the poets only deliver a golden.

But let those things alone, and go to man—for whom as the other
things are, so it seemeth in him her uttermost cunning is employed—and
know whether she have brought forth so true a lover as Theagenes, so
constant a friend as Pylades, so valiant a man as Orlando, so right a prince
190 as Xenophon's Cyrus, so excellent a man every way as Virgil's Aeneas.°
Neither let this be jestingly conceived, because the works of the one be
essential, the other in imitation or fiction; for any understanding knoweth
the skill of each artificer standeth in that *idea* or fore-conceit° of the work,
and not in the work itself. And that the poet hath that *idea* is manifest, by
delivering them forth in such excellency as he had imagined them.
Which delivering forth also is not wholly imaginative,° as we are wont to
say by them that build castles in the air; but so far substantially it worketh,
not only to make a Cyrus,° which had been but a particular excellency as

nature might have done, but to bestow a Cyrus upon the world to make many Cyruses, if they will learn aright why and how that maker made 200 him.

Neither let it be deemed too saucy a comparison to balance the highest point of man's wit with the efficacy of nature; but rather give right honour to the heavenly Maker of that maker, who having made man to His own likeness, set him beyond and over all the works of that second nature: which in nothing he showeth so much as in poetry, when with the force of a divine breath he bringeth things forth surpassing her doings—with no small arguments to the incredulous of that first accursed fall of Adam, since our erected wit maketh us know what perfection is, and yet our infected will keepeth us from reaching unto it. But these arguments will 210 by few be understood, and by fewer granted. This much (I hope) will be given me, that the Greeks with some probability of reason gave him the name above all names of learning.

Now let us go to a more ordinary opening of him, that the truth may be the more palpable: and so I hope, though we get not so unmatched a praise as the etymology of his names will grant, yet his very description, which no man will deny, shall not justly be barred from a principal commendation.

Poesy therefore is an art of imitation, for so Aristotle termeth it in the word *mimesis*—that is to say, a representing, counterfeiting, or figuring 220 forth—to speak metaphorically, a speaking picture°—with this end, to teach and delight.

Of this have been three general kinds. The chief, both in antiquity and excellency, were they that did imitate the unconceivable excellencies of God. Such were David in his Psalms; Solomon in his Song of Songs, in his Ecclesiastes, and Proverbs; Moses and Deborah in their Hymns; and the writer of Job: which, beside other, the learned Emanuel Tremellius and Franciscus Junius° do entitle the poetical part of the Scripture. Against these none will speak that hath the Holy Ghost in due holy reverence. (In this kind, though in a full wrong divinity, were Orpheus, 230 Amphion, Homer in his Hymns, and many other, both Greeks and Romans.) And this poesy must be used by whosoever will follow St James's counsel in singing psalms when they are merry, and I know is used with the fruit of comfort by some, when, in sorrowful pangs of their death-bringing sins, they find the consolation of the never-leaving goodness.

The second kind is of them that deal with matters philosophical, either moral, as Tyrtaeus, Phocylides, Cato, or natural, as Lucretius and Virgil's *Georgics*; or astronomical, as Manilius and Pontanus; or historical,

240   as Lucan:° which who mislike, the fault is in their judgement quite
      out of taste, and not in the sweet food of sweetly uttered knowledge.
          But because this second sort is wrapped within the fold of the
      proposed subject, and takes not the course of his own invention, whether
      they properly be poets or no let grammarians dispute, and go to the third,
      indeed right poets, of whom chiefly this question° ariseth: betwixt whom
      and these second is such a kind of difference as betwixt the meaner sort
      of painters, who counterfeit only such faces as are set before them, and
      the more excellent, who having no law but wit, bestow that in colours
      upon you which is fittest for the eye to see: as the constant though
250   lamenting look of Lucretia,° when she punished in herself another's
      fault, wherein he painteth not Lucretia whom he never saw, but painteth
      the outward beauty of such a virtue. For these third be they which most
      properly do imitate to teach and delight, and to imitate borrow nothing of
      what is, hath been, or shall be; but range, only reined with learned
      discretion, into the divine consideration of what may be and should be.
      These be they that, as the first and most noble sort may justly be termed
      vates, so these are waited on in the excellentest languages and best
      understandings with the fore-described name of poets.° For these
      indeed do merely make to imitate, and imitate both to delight and teach;
260   and delight, to move men to take that goodness in hand, which without
      delight they would fly as from a stranger; and teach, to make them know
      that goodness whereunto they are moved—which being the noblest
      scope to which ever any learning was directed, yet want there not idle
      tongues to bark at them.
          These be subdivided into sundry more special denominations. The
      most notable be the heroic, lyric, tragic, comic, satiric, iambic, elegiac,
      pastoral,° and certain others, some of these being termed according to
      the matter they deal with, some by the sorts of verses they liked best to
      write in; for indeed the greatest part of poets have apparelled their
270   poetical inventions in that numbrous° kind of writing which is called
      verse—indeed but apparelled, verse being but an ornament and no cause
      to poetry, since there have been many most excellent poets that never
      versified, and now swarm many versifiers that need never answer to the
      name of poets. For Xenophon, who did imitate so excellently as to give us
      effigiem iusti imperii, the portraiture of a just empire, under the name of
      Cyrus, (as Cicero saith of him)° made therein an absolute heroical poem.
      So did Heliodorus in his sugared invention of that picture of love in
      Theagenes and Chariclea;° and yet both these wrote in prose: which I
      speak to show that it is not rhyming and versing that maketh a poet—no
280   more than a long gown maketh an advocate, who though he pleaded in

armour should be an advocate and no soldier. But it is that feigning notable images of virtues, vices, or what else, with that delightful teaching, which must be the right describing note to know a poet by; although indeed the senate of poets hath chosen verse as their fittest raiment, meaning, as in matter they passed all in all, so in manner to go beyond them: not speaking (table-talk fashion or like men in a dream) words as they chanceably fall from the mouth, but peising each syllable of each word by just proportion according to the dignity of the subject.

Now therefore it shall not be amiss first to weigh this latter sort of poetry by his works, and then by his parts; and if in neither of these 290 anatomies he be condemnable, I hope we shall obtain a more favourable sentence.

This purifying of wit—this enriching of memory, enabling of judgement, and enlarging of conceit—which commonly we call learning, under what name soever it come forth, or to what immediate end soever it be directed, the final end is to lead and draw us to as high a perfection as our degenerate souls, made worse by their clayey lodgings, can be capable of.

This, according to the inclination of the man, bred many-formed impressions. For some that thought this felicity principally to be gotten 300 by knowledge, and no knowledge to be so high or heavenly as acquaintance with the stars, gave themselves to astronomy; others, persuading themselves to be demigods if they knew the causes of things, became natural and supernatural philosophers; some an admirable delight drew to music; and some the certainty of demonstration to the mathematics. But all, one and other, having this scope: to know, and by knowledge to lift up the mind from the dungeon of the body to the enjoying his own divine essence.

But when by the balance of experience it was found that the astronomer, looking to the stars, might fall in a ditch,° that the inquiring 310 philosopher might be blind in himself, and the mathematician might draw forth a straight line with a crooked heart, then lo, did proof, the overruler of opinions, make manifest that all these are but serving sciences, which, as they have each a private end in themselves, so yet are they all directed to the highest end of the mistress-knowledge, by the Greeks called *architektonikê*°, which stands (as I think) in the knowledge of a man's self, in the ethic and politic consideration, with the end of well-doing and not of well-knowing only—even as the saddler's next end is to make a good saddle, but his further end to serve a nobler faculty, which is horsemanship, so the horseman's to soldiery, and the soldier not 320 only to have the skill, but to perform the practice of a soldier. So that, the ending end of all earthly learning being virtuous action, those skills that most serve to bring forth that have a most just title to be princes over all the rest.

Wherein, if we can, show we the poet's nobleness, by setting him before his other competitors. Among whom as principal challengers step forth the moral philosophers,° whom, me thinketh, I see coming towards me with a sullen gravity, as though they could not abide vice by daylight, rudely clothed for to witness outwardly their contempt of outward things,

330 with books in their hands against glory, whereto they set their names, sophistically speaking against subtlety, and angry with any man in whom they see the foul fault of anger. These men casting largesse as they go, of definitions, divisions, and distinctions, with a scornful interrogative do soberly ask whether it be possible to find any path so ready to lead a man to virtue as that which teacheth what virtue is; and teach it not only by delivering forth his very being, his causes and effects, but also by making known his enemy, vice, which must be destroyed, and his cumbersome servant, passion, which must be mastered; by showing the generalities that containeth it, and the specialities that are derived from it; lastly, by

340 plain setting down how it extendeth itself out of the limits of a man's own little world to the government of families and maintaining of public societies.

The historian scarcely giveth leisure to the moralist to say so much, but that he, laden with old mouse-eaten records, authorizing himself (for the most part) upon other histories, whose greatest authorities are built upon the notable foundation of hearsay; having much ado to accord differing writers and to pick truth out of their partiality; better acquainted with a thousand years ago than with the present age, and yet better knowing how this world goeth than how his own wit runneth; curious for

350 antiquities and inquisitive of novelties; a wonder to young folks and a tyrant in table talk, denieth, in a great chafe, that any man for teaching of virtue, and virtuous actions is comparable to him. 'I am *testis temporum, lux veritatis, vita memoriae, magistra vitae, nuntia vetustatis.*° The philosopher', saith he, 'teacheth a disputative virtue, but I do an active. His virtue is excellent in the dangerless Academy of Plato, but mine showeth forth her honourable face in the battles of Marathon, Pharsalia, Poitiers, and Agincourt.° He teacheth virtue by certain abstract considerations, but I only bid you follow the footing of them that have gone before you. Old-aged experience goeth beyond the fine-witted philosopher, but I

360 give the experience of many ages. Lastly, if he make the songbook, I put the learner's hand to the lute; and if he be the guide, I am the light.' Then would he allege you innumerable examples, confirming story by stories,

how much the wisest senators and princes have been directed by the credit of history, as Brutus, Alphonsus of Aragon,° and who not, if need be? At length the long line of their disputation maketh a point in this, that the one giveth the precept, and the other the example.

Now whom shall we find (since the question standeth for the highest form in the school of learning) to be moderator?° Truly, as me seemeth, the poet; and if not a moderator, even the man that ought to carry the title from them both, and much more from all other serving sciences. 370 Therefore compare we the poet with the historian and with the moral philosopher; and if he go beyond them both, no other human skill can match him. For as for the divine, with all reverence it is ever to be excepted, not only for having his scope as far beyond any of these as eternity exceedeth a moment, but even for passing each of these in themselves. And for the lawyer, though *Ius* be the daughter of Justice, and justice the chief of virtues, yet because he seeketh to make men good rather *formidine poenae* than *virtutis amore;*° or, to say righter, doth not endeavour to make men good, but that their evil hurt not others; having no care, so he be a good citizen, how bad a man he be: therefore as our 380 wickedness maketh him necessary, and necessity maketh him honourable, so is he not in the deepest truth to stand in rank with these who all endeavour to take naughtiness away and plant goodness even in the secretest cabinet of our souls. And these four are all that any way deal in that consideration of men's manners, which being the supreme knowledge, they that best breed it deserve the best commendation.

The philosopher, therefore, and the historian are they which would win the goal, the one by precept, the other by example. But both, not having both, do both halt.° For the philosopher, setting down with thorny arguments the bare rule, is so hard of utterance and so misty to be 390 conceived, that one that hath no other guide but him shall wade in him till he be old before he shall find sufficient cause to be honest. For his knowledge standeth so upon the abstract and general, that happy is that man who may understand him, and more happy that can apply what he doth understand. On the other side, the historian, wanting the precept, is so tied, not to what should be but to what is, to the particular truth of things and not to the general reason of things, that his example draweth no necessary consequence, and therefore a less fruitful doctrine.

Now doth the peerless poet perform both: for whatsoever the philosopher saith should be done, he giveth a perfect picture of it in someone 400 by whom he presupposeth it was done, so as he coupleth the general notion with the particular example. A perfect picture I say, for he yieldeth to the powers of the mind an image of that whereof the philosopher bestoweth but a wordish description, which doth neither strike, pierce, nor possess the sight of the soul so much as that other doth. For as in outward things, to a man that had never seen an elephant or a rhinoceros,° who should tell him most exquisitely all their shapes, colour, bigness, and particular marks, or of a gorgeous palace the architecture,° with declaring the full beauties, might well make the hearer able to 410 repeat, as it were by rote, all he had heard, yet should never satisfy his inward conceit with being witness to itself of a true lively knowledge; but the same man, as soon as he might see those beasts well painted, or that house well in model, should straightways grow, without need of any description, to a judicial comprehending of them: so no doubt the philosopher with his learned definitions—be it of virtue, vices, matters of public policy or private government—replenisheth the memory with many infallible grounds of wisdom, which, notwithstanding, lie dark before the imaginative and judging power, if they be not illuminated or figured forth by the speaking picture of poesy.

420   Tully taketh much pains, and many times not without poetical helps, to make us know the force love of our country hath in us.° Let us but hear old Anchises speaking in the midst of Troy's flames,° or see Ulysses in the fulness of all Calypso's delights bewail his absence from barren and beggarly Ithaca.° Anger, the Stoics said, was a short madness:° let but Sophocles bring you Ajax on a stage,° killing or whipping sheep and oxen, thinking them the army of Greeks, with their chieftains Agamemnon and Menelaus, and tell me if you have not a more familiar insight into anger than finding in the schoolmen° his *genus* and differ-ence. See whether wisdom and temperance in Ulysses and Diomedes, 430 valour in Achilles, friendship in Nisus and Euryalus,° even to an ignorant man carry not an apparent shining; and, contrarily, the remorse of conscience in Oedipus, the soon repenting pride in Agamemnon, the self-devouring cruelty in his father Atreus, the violence of ambition in the two Theban brothers, the sour-sweetness of revenge in Medea;° and, to fall lower, the Terentian Gnatho° and our Chaucer's Pandar° so expressed that we now use their names to signify their trades: and finally, all virtues, vices, and passions so in their own natural seats laid to the view, that we seem not to hear of them, but clearly to see through them.

But even in the most excellent determination of goodness, what 440 philosopher's counsel can so readily direct a prince, as the feigned Cyrus in Xenophon; or a virtuous man in all fortunes, as Aeneas in Virgil; or a whole commonwealth, as the way of Sir Thomas More's *Utopia*?° I say the way, because where Sir Thomas More erred, it was the fault of the man and not of the poet, for that way of patterning a commonwealth was most absolute,° though he perchance hath not so absolutely performed it. For the question is, whether the feigned image of poetry or the regular instruction of philosophy hath the more force in teaching: wherein if the philosophers have more rightly showed themselves philosophers than the poets have attained to the high top of their profession, as in truth

Mediocribus esse poetis,
Non dii, non homines, non concessere columnae;°   450

it is, I say again, not the fault of the art, but that by few men that art can be accomplished.

Certainly, even our Saviour Christ could as well have given the moral commonplaces of uncharitableness and humbleness as the divine narration of Dives and Lazarus;° or of disobedience and mercy, as that heavenly discourse of the lost child and the gracious father;° but that His through-searching wisdom knew the estate of Dives burning in hell, and of Lazarus in Abraham's bosom, would more constantly (as it were) inhabit both the memory and judgement. Truly, for myself, meseems I   460 see before mine eyes the lost child's disdainful prodigality, turned to envy a swine's dinner: which by the learned divines are thought not historical acts, but instructing parables.

For conclusion, I say the philosopher teacheth, but he teacheth obscurely, so as the learned only can understand him, that is to say, he teacheth them that are already taught; but the poet is the food for the tenderest stomachs, the poet is indeed the right popular philosopher, whereof Aesop's tales give good proof: whose pretty allegories, stealing under the formal tales of beasts, make many, more beastly than beasts, begin to hear the sound of virtue from these dumb speakers.   470

But now may it be alleged that if this imagining of matters be so fit for the imagination, then must the historian needs surpass, who bringeth you images of true matters, such as indeed were done, and not such as fantastically or falsely may be suggested to have been done. Truly, Aristotle himself, in his discourse of poesy,° plainly determineth this question, saying that poetry is *philosophoteron* and *spoudaioteron*, that is to say, it is more philosophical and more studiously serious than history. His reason is, because poesy dealeth with *katholou*, that is to say, with the universal consideration, and the history with *kathekaston*, the particular: now, saith he, the universal weighs what is fit to be said or done, either in   480 likelihood or necessity (which the poesy considereth in his imposed names), and the particular only marks whether Alcibiades did, or suffered, this or that. Thus far Aristotle: which reason of his (as all his) is most full of reason. For indeed, if the question were whether it were

better to have a particular act truly or falsely set down, there is no doubt
which is to be chosen, no more than whether you had rather have
Vespasian's picture right as he was,° or, at the painter's pleasure, nothing
resembling. But if the question be for your own use and learning,
whether it be better to have it set down as it should be, or as it was,
then certainly is more doctrinable the feigned Cyrus in Xenophon
than the true Cyrus in Justin,° and the feigned Aeneas in Virgil
than the right Aeneas in Dares Phrygius:° as to a lady that desired
to fashion her countenance to the best grace, a painter should more
benefit her to portrait a most sweet face, writing Canidia upon it,
than to paint Canidia as she was, who, Horace sweareth, was full ill-
favoured.°

If the poet do his part aright, he will show you in Tantalus, Atreus, and
such like, nothing that is not to be shunned; in Cyrus, Aeneas, Ulysses,
each thing to be followed; where the historian, bound to tell things as
things were, cannot be liberal (without he will be poetical) of a perfect
pattern, but, as in Alexander or Scipio himself,° show doings, some to be
liked, some to be misliked. And then how will you discern what to follow
but by your own discretion, which you had without reading Quintus
Curtius? And whereas a man may say, though in universal consideration
of doctrine° the poet prevaileth, yet that the history,° in his saying such a
thing was done, doth warrant a man more in that he shall follow—the
answer is manifest: that, if he stand upon that was (as if he should argue,
because it rained yesterday, therefore it should rain today), then indeed
hath it some advantage to a gross conceit;° but if he know an example only
informs a conjectured likelihood, and so go by reason, the poet doth so
far exceed him as he is to frame his example to that which is most
reasonable (be it in warlike, politic, or private matters), where the
historian in his bare 'was' hath many times that which we call fortune to
overrule the best wisdom. Many times he must tell events whereof he can
yield no cause; or, if he do, it must be poetically.

For that a feigned example hath as much force to teach as a true
example (for as for to move, it is clear, since the feigned may be tuned to
the highest key of passion), let us take one example wherein an historian
and a poet did concur. Herodotus and Justin do both testify that Zopyrus,
King Darius' faithful servant, seeing his master long resisted by the
rebellious Babylonians, feigned himself in extreme disgrace of his king:
for verifying of which, he caused his own nose and ears to be cut off, and
so flying to the Babylonians, was received, and for his known valour so
sure credited, that he did find means to deliver them over to Darius.°
Much like matter doth Livy record of Tarquinius and his son.°

Xenophon excellently feigneth such another stratagem performed by Abradatas in Cyrus' behalf.° Now would I fain know, if occasion be presented unto you to serve your prince by such an honest dissimulation, why you do not as well learn it of Xenophon's fiction as of the other's verity; and truly so much the better, as you shall save your nose by the bargain: for Abradatas did not counterfeit so far. So then the best of the historian is subject to the poet; for whatsoever action, or faction, whatsoever counsel, policy, or war stratagem the historian is bound to recite, that may the poet (if he list) with his imitation make his own, beautifying it both for further teaching, and more delighting, as it please him: having all, from Dante's heaven to his hell,° under the authority of his pen. Which if I be asked what poets have done so, as I might well name some, so yet say I, and say again, I speak of the art, and not of the artificer.

Now, to that which commonly is attributed to the praise of history, in respect of the notable learning is got by marking the success, as though therein a man should see virtue exalted and vice punished—truly that commendation is particular to poetry, and far off from history. For indeed poetry ever sets virtue so out in her best colours, making Fortune her well-waiting handmaid, that one must needs be enamoured of her. Well may you see Ulysses in a storm, and in other hard plights;° but they are but exercises of patience and magnanimity, to make them shine the more in the near-following prosperity. And of the contrary part, if evil men come to the stage, they ever go out (as the tragedy writer° answered to one that misliked the show of such persons) so manacled as they little animate folks to follow them. But the history, being captived to the truth of a foolish world, is many times a terror from well-doing, and an encouragement to unbridled wickedness. For see we not valiant Miltiades rot in his fetters?° The just Phocion and the accomplished Socrates put to death like traitors?° The cruel Severus live prosperously?° The excellent Severus miserably murdered?° Sulla and Marius dying in their beds?° Pompey and Cicero slain then when they would have thought exile a happiness?° See we not virtuous Cato driven to kill himself, and rebel Caesar so advanced that his name yet, after 1600 years, lasteth in the highest honour?° And mark but even Caesar's own words° of the aforenamed Sulla (who in that only did honestly, to put down his dishonest tyranny), *literas nescivit*, as if want of learning caused him to do well. He meant it not by poetry, which, not content with earthly plagues, deviseth new punishments in hell for tyrants, nor yet by philosophy, which teacheth *occidendos esse*; but no doubt by skill in history, for that indeed can afford you Cypselus, Periander, Phalaris,

Dionysius, and I know not how many more of the same kennel, that
speed well enough in their abominable injustice of usurpation.°

I conclude, therefore, that he excelleth history, not only in furnishing
the mind with knowledge, but in setting it forward to that which
570 deserveth to be called and accounted good: which setting forward, and
moving to well-doing, indeed setteth the laurel crown upon the poets as
victorious, not only of the historian, but over the philosopher, howsoever
in teaching it may be questionable.

For suppose it be granted (that which I suppose with great reason may
be denied) that the philosopher, in respect of his methodical proceeding,
doth teach more perfectly than the poet, yet do I think that no man is so
much *philophilosophos*° as to compare the philosopher in moving with the
poet. And that moving is of a higher degree than teaching, it may by this
appear, that it is well nigh both the cause and effect of teaching. For who
580 will be taught, if he be not moved with desire to be taught? And what so
much good doth that teaching bring forth (I speak still of moral doctrine)
as that it moveth one to do that which it doth teach? For, as Aristotle saith,
it is not *gnosis* but *praxis*° must be the fruit. And how *praxis* can be, without
being moved to practise, it is no hard matter to consider.

The philosopher showeth you the way, he informeth you of the
particularities, as well of the tediousness of the way, as of the pleasant
lodging you shall have when your journey is ended, as of the many
by-turnings that may divert you from your way. But this is to no man but
to him that will read him, and read him with attentive studious painful-
590 ness; which constant desire whosoever hath in him, hath already passed
half the hardness of the way, and therefore is beholding to the philosopher but for the other half. Nay truly, learned men have learnedly
thought that where once reason hath so much overmastered passion as
that the mind hath a free desire to do well, the inward light each mind
hath in itself is as good as a philosopher's book; since in nature we know it
is well to do well, and what is well, and what is evil, although not in the
words of art which philosophers bestow upon us; for out of natural
conceit° the philosophers drew it. But to be moved to do that which we
know, or to be moved with desire to know: *hoc opus, hic labor est.*°
600   Now therein of all sciences (I speak still of human,° and according to
the human conceit) is our poet the monarch. For he doth not only show
the way, but giveth so sweet a prospect into the way, as will entice any
man to enter into it. Nay, he doth, as if your journey should lie through a
fair vineyard, at the first give you a cluster of grapes, that full of that taste,
you may long to pass further. He beginneth not with obscure definitions,
which must blur the margin with interpretations, and load the memory

with doubtfulness; but he cometh to you with words set in delightful proportion, either accompanied with, or prepared for, the well enchanting skill of music; and with a tale forsooth he cometh unto you, with a tale which holdeth children from play, and old men from the chimney corner. 610 And, pretending no more, doth intend the winning of the mind from wickedness to virtue—even as the child is often brought to take most wholesome things by hiding them in such other as have a pleasant taste, which, if one should begin to tell them the nature of aloes or rhubarbum° they should receive, would sooner take their physic at their ears than at their mouth. So is it in men (most of which are childish in the best things, till they be cradled in their graves): glad will they be to hear the tales of Hercules, Achilles, Cyrus, Aeneas; and, hearing them, must needs hear the right description of wisdom, valour, and justice; which, if they had been barely, that is to say philosophically, set out, they would swear they 620 be brought to school again.

That imitation whereof poetry is, hath the most conveniency to nature of all other, insomuch that, as Aristotle saith, those things which in themselves are horrible, as cruel battles, unnatural monsters, are made in poetical imitation delightful.° Truly, I have known men that even with reading *Amadis de Gaule*° (which God knoweth wanteth much of a perfect poesy) have found their hearts moved to the exercise of courtesy, liberality, and especially courage. Who readeth Aeneas carrying old Anchises on his back,° that wisheth not it were his fortune to perform so excellent an act? Whom doth not these words of Turnus move, the tale of 630 Turnus having planted his image in the imagination,

> Fugientem haec terra videbit?
> Usque adeone mori miserum est?°

Where the philosophers, as they scorn to delight, so much they be content little to move—saving wrangling whether *virtus* be the chief or the only good, whether the contemplative or the active life do excel —which Plato and Boethius well knew, and therefore made mistress Philosophy very often borrow the masking raiment of poesy.° For even those hard-hearted evil men who think virtue a school name, and know no other good but *indulgere genio*,° and therefore despise the austere 640 admonitions of the philosopher, and feel not the inward reason they stand upon, yet will be content to be delighted—which is all the good-fellow poet seemeth to promise—and so steal to see the form of goodness (which seen they cannot but love) ere themselves be aware, as if they took a medicine of cherries.

Infinite proofs of the strange effects of this poetical invention might be

alleged; only two shall serve, which are so often remembered as I think all
men know them. The one of Menenius Agrippa,° who, when the whole
people of Rome had resolutely divided themselves from the senate, with
650 apparent show of utter ruin, though he were (for that time) an excellent
orator, came not among them upon trust of figurative speeches or
cunning insinuations, and much less with far-fet maxims of philosophy,
which (especially if they were Platonic) they must have learned geometry
before they could well have conceived;° but forsooth he behaves himself
like a homely and familiar poet. He telleth them a tale, that there was a
time when all the parts of the body made a mutinous conspiracy against
the belly, which they thought devoured the fruits of each other's labour;
they concluded they would let so unprofitable a spender starve. In the
end, to be short (for the tale is notorious, and as notorious that it was a
660 tale), with punishing the belly they plagued themselves. This applied by
him wrought such effect in the people, as I never read that only words°
brought forth but then so sudden and so good an alteration; for upon
reasonable conditions a perfect reconcilement ensued. The other is of
Nathan the prophet,° who, when the holy David had so far forsaken God
as to confirm adultery with murder, when he was to do the tenderest
office of a friend in laying his own shame before his eyes, sent by God to
call again so chosen a servant, how doth he it but by telling of a man
whose beloved lamb was ungratefully taken from his bosom? The
application most divinely true, but the discourse itself feigned; which
670 made David (I speak of the second and instrumental cause) as in a glass
see his own filthiness, as that heavenly psalm of mercy° well testifieth.

By these, therefore, examples and reasons, I think it may be manifest
that the poet, with that same hand of delight, doth draw the mind more
effectually than any other art doth. And so a conclusion not unfitly
ensueth: that, as virtue is the most excellent resting place for all worldly
learning to make his end° of, so poetry, being the most familiar to teach
it, and most princely to move towards it, in the most excellent work is
the most excellent workman.

But I am content not only to decipher him by his works (although
680 works, in commendation or dispraise, must ever hold a high authority),
but more narrowly will examine his parts; so that (as in a man) though all
together may carry a presence full of majesty and beauty, perchance in
some one defectuous piece we may find blemish.

Now in his parts, kinds, or species (as you list to term them), it is to be
noted that some poesies have coupled together two or three kinds, as the
tragical and comical, whereupon is risen the tragi-comical. Some, in the
manner, have mingled prose and verse, as Sannazaro and Boethius.°

Some have mingled matters heroical and pastoral.° But that cometh all to one in this question, for, if severed they be good, the conjunction cannot be hurtful. Therefore, perchance forgetting some and leaving some as 690 needless to be remembered, it shall not be amiss in a word to cite the special kinds, to see what faults may be found in the right use of them.

Is it then the Pastoral poem which is misliked? (For perchance where the hedge is lowest they will soonest leap over.) Is the poor pipe disdained, which sometime out of Meliboeus'° mouth can show the misery of people under hard lords or ravening soldiers? And again, by Tityrus,° what blessedness is derived to them that lie lowest from the goodness of them that sit highest; sometimes, under the pretty tales of wolves and sheep, can include the whole considerations of wrong-doing and patience;° sometimes show that contentions for trifles can get but a 700 trifling victory:° where perchance a man may see that even Alexander and Darius, when they strave who should be cock of this world's dunghill,° the benefit they got was that the after-livers may say

> Haec memini et victum frustra contendere Thyrsin:
> Ex illo Corydon, Corydon est tempore nobis.°

Or is it the lamenting Elegiac; which in a kind heart would move rather pity than blame; who bewails with the great philosopher Heraclitus,° the weakness of mankind and the wretchedness of the world; who surely is to be praised, either for compassionate accompanying just causes of lamentations, or for rightly painting out how weak be the passions of 710 woefulness? Is it the bitter but wholesome Iambic,° who rubs the galled mind, in making shame the trumpet of villainy, with bold and open crying out against naughtiness? Or the Satiric, who

> Omne vafer vitium ridenti tangit amico;°

who sportingly never leaveth till he make a man laugh at folly, and at length ashamed, to laugh at himself, which he cannot avoid without avoiding the folly; who, while

> circum praecordia ludit,°

giveth us to feel how many headaches a passionate life bringeth us to; how, when all is done,   720

> Est Ulubris, animus si nos non deficit aequus?°

No, perchance it is the Comic, whom naughty play-makers and stage-keepers have justly made odious.° To the arguments of abuse I will answer after. Only this much now is to be said, that the comedy is an

imitation of the common errors of our life, which he representeth in the most ridiculous and scornful sort that may be, so as it is impossible that any beholder can be content to be such a one. Now, as in geometry the oblique must be known as well as the right, and in arithmetic the odd as well as the even, so in the actions of our life who seeth not the filthiness of
730 evil wanteth a great foil to perceive the beauty of virtue. This doth the comedy handle so in our private and domestical matters as with hearing it we get as it were an experience what is to be looked for of a niggardly Demea, of a crafty Davus, of a flattering Gnatho, of a vainglorious Thraso;° and not only to know what effects are to be expected, but to know who be such, by the signifying badge given them by the comedian.° And little reason hath any man to say that men learn the evil by seeing it so set out, since, as I said before, there is no man living but, by the force truth hath in nature, no sooner seeth these men play their parts, but wisheth them *in pistrinum*;° although perchance the sack of his own faults
740 lie so hidden behind his back that he seeth not himself dance the same measure; whereto yet nothing can more open his eyes than to find his own actions contemptibly set forth.

So that the right use of comedy will (I think) by nobody be blamed; and much less of the high and excellent Tragedy, that openeth the greatest wounds, and showeth forth the ulcers that are covered with tissue;° that maketh kings fear to be tyrants, and tyrants manifest their tyrannical humours; that, with stirring the affects of admiration and commiseration,° teacheth the uncertainty of this world, and upon how weak foundations gilden roofs are builded; that maketh us know

750   Qui sceptra saevus duro imperio regit
             Timet timentes; metus in auctorem redit.°

But how much it can move, Plutarch yieldeth a notable testimony of the abominable tyrant Alexander Pheraeus,° from whose eyes a tragedy, well made and represented, drew abundance of tears, who without all pity had murdered infinite numbers, and some of his own blood: so as he, that was not ashamed to make matters for tragedies, yet could not resist the sweet violence of a tragedy. And if it wrought no further good in him, it was that he, in despite of himself, withdrew himself from hearkening to that which might mollify his hardened heart. But it is not the tragedy they do
760 mislike; for it were too absurd to cast out so excellent a representation of whatsoever is most worthy to be learned.

Is it the Lyric° that most displeaseth, who with his tuned lyre and well-accorded voice, giveth praise, the reward of virtue, to virtuous acts; who gives moral precepts, and natural problems; who sometimes raiseth up his voice to the height of the heavens, in singing the lauds of the immortal God? Certainly, I must confess my own barbarousness, I never heard the old song of Percy and Douglas° that I found not my heart moved more than with a trumpet; and yet is it sung but by some blind crowder,° with no rougher voice than rude style; which, being so evil apparelled in the dust and cobwebs of that uncivil age, what would it work 770 trimmed in the gorgeous eloquence of Pindar?° In Hungary° I have seen it the manner at all feasts, and other such meetings, to have songs of their ancestors' valour, which that right soldierlike nation think one of the chiefest kindlers of brave courage. The incomparable Lacedemonians° did not only carry that kind of music ever with them to the field, but even at home, as such songs were made, so were they all content to be singers of them—when the lusty men were to tell what they did, the old men what they had done, and the young what they would do. And where a man may say that Pindar many times praiseth highly victories of small moment, matters rather of sport than virtue; as it may be answered, it was 780 the fault of the poet, and not of the poetry, so indeed the chief fault was in the time and custom of the Greeks, who set those toys at so high a price that Philip of Macedon reckoned a horserace won at Olympus among his three fearful felicities.° But as the unimitable Pindar often did, so is that kind most capable and most fit to awake the thoughts from the sleep of idleness to embrace honourable enterprises.

There rests the Heroical—whose very name (I think) should daunt all backbiters: for by what conceit can a tongue be directed to speak evil of that which draweth with him no less champions than Achilles, Cyrus, Aeneas, Turnus, Tydeus,° and Rinaldo?°—who doth not only teach and 790 move to a truth, but teacheth and moveth to the most high and excellent truth; who maketh magnanimity and justice shine through all misty fearfulness and foggy desires; who, if the saying of Plato and Tully° be true, that who could see virtue would be wonderfully ravished with the love of her beauty—this man sets her out to make her more lovely in her holiday apparel, to the eye of any that will deign not to disdain until they understand. But if anything be already said in the defence of sweet poetry, all concurreth to the maintaining the heroical, which is not only a kind, but the best and most accomplished kind of poetry. For as the image of each action stirreth and instructeth the mind, so the lofty image 800 of such worthies most inflameth the mind with desire to be worthy, and informs with counsel how to be worthy. Only let Aeneas be worn in the tablet of your memory, how he governeth himself in the ruin of his country; in the preserving his old father, and carrying away his religious ceremonies; in obeying God's commandment to leave Dido, though not only all passionate kindness, but even the human consideration of virtuous gratefulness, would have craved other of him; how in storms, how in sports, how in war, how in peace, how a fugitive, how victorious, how besieged, how besieging, how to strangers, how to allies, how to enemies, how to his own; lastly, how in his inward self, and how in his outward government—and I think, in a mind not prejudiced with a prejudicating humour, he will be found in excellency fruitful, yea, even as Horace saith,

> melius Chrysippo et Crantore.°

But truly I imagine it falleth out with these poet-whippers, as with some good women, who often are sick, but in faith they cannot tell where; so the name of poetry is odious to them, but neither his cause nor effects, neither the sum that contains him, nor the particularities descending from him, give any fast handle to their carping dispraise.

Since then poetry is of all human learning the most ancient and of most fatherly antiquity, as from whence other learnings have taken their beginnings; since it is so universal that no learned nation doth despise it, nor barbarous nation is without it; since both Roman and Greek gave such divine names unto it, the one of prophesying, the other of making,° and that indeed that name of making is fit for him, considering that where all other arts retain themselves within their subject, and receive, as it were, their being from it, the poet only bringeth his own stuff, and doth not learn a conceit out of a matter, but maketh matter for a conceit; since neither his description nor end containing any evil, the thing described cannot be evil; since his effects be so good as to teach goodness and to delight the learners; since therein (namely in moral doctrine, the chief of all knowledges) he doth not only far pass the historian, but, for instructing, is well nigh comparable to the philosopher, for moving leaves him behind him; since the Holy Scripture (wherein there is no uncleanness) hath whole parts in it poetical, and that even our Saviour Christ vouchsafed to use the flowers of it;° since all his kinds are not only in their united forms but in their severed dissections fully commendable; I think (and think I think rightly) the laurel crown appointed for triumphant captains doth worthily (of all other learnings) honour the poet's triumph.

But because we have ears as well as tongues, and that the lightest reasons that may be will seem to weigh greatly, if nothing be put in the counterbalance, let us hear, and, as well as we can, ponder what objections be made against this art, which may be worthy either of yielding or answering.

First, truly I note not only in these *misomousoi*, poet-haters, but in all that kind of people who seek a praise by dispraising others, that they do prodigally spend a great many wandering words in quips and scoffs, carping and taunting at each thing which, by stirring the spleen,° may stay the brain from a through-beholding the worthiness of the subject. Those kind of objections, as they are full of a very idle easiness, since there is 850 nothing of so sacred a majesty but that an itching tongue may rub itself upon it, so deserve they no other answer, but, instead of laughing at the jest, to laugh at the jester. We know a playing wit can praise the discretion of an ass, the comfortableness of being in debt, and the jolly commodities of being sick of the plague.° So of the contrary side, if we will turn Ovid's verse

Ut lateat virtus proximitate mali,°

that good lie hid in nearness of the evil, Agrippa will be as merry in showing the vanity of science as Erasmus was in the commending of folly.° Neither shall any man or matter escape some touch of these 860 smiling railers. But for Erasmus and Agrippa, they had another foundation than the superficial part would promise.° Marry, these other pleasant faultfinders, who will correct the verb before they understand the noun, and confute others' knowledge before they confirm their own—I would have them only remember that scoffing cometh not of wisdom.° So as the best title in true English they get with their merriments is to be called good fools; for so have our grave forefathers ever termed that humorous kind of jesters.

But that which giveth greatest scope to their scorning humour is rhyming and versing. It is already said (and, as I think, truly said), it is not 870 rhyming and versing that maketh poesy. One may be a poet without versing, and a versifier without poetry. But yet, presuppose it were inseparable (as indeed it seemeth Scaliger judgeth),° truly it were an inseparable commendation. For if *oratio* next to *ratio*, speech next to reason, be the greatest gift bestowed upon mortality,° that cannot be praiseless which doth most polish that blessing of speech; which considers each word, not only (as a man may say) by his most forcible quality, but by his best measured quantity, carrying even in themselves a harmony—without,° perchance, number, measure, order, proportion be in our time grown odious. But lay aside the just praise it hath, by being 880 the only fit speech for music (music, I say, the most divine striker of the senses), thus much is undoubtedly true, that if reading be foolish without remembering, memory being the only treasure of knowledge,° those words which are fittest for memory are likewise most convenient for knowledge. Now, that verse far exceedeth prose in the knitting up of memory, the reason is manifest: the words (besides their delight, which hath a great affinity to memory) being so set as one cannot be lost but the whole work fails; which accusing itself, calleth the remembrance back to itself, and so most strongly confirmeth it. Besides, one word so, as it 890 were, begetting another, as, be it in rhyme or measured verse, by the former a man shall have a near guess to the follower. Lastly, even they that have taught the art of memory have showed nothing so apt for it as a certain room divided into many places well and thoroughly known.° Now, that hath the verse in effect perfectly, every word having his natural seat, which seat must needs make the word remembered. But what needeth more in a thing so known to all men? Who is it that ever was a scholar that doth not carry away some verses of Virgil, Horace, or Cato, which in his youth he learned, and even to his old age serve him for hourly lessons? But the fitness it hath for memory is notably proved by all 900 delivery of arts: wherein for the most part, from grammar to logic, mathematics, physic, and the rest, the rules chiefly necessary to be borne away are compiled in verses. So that, verse being in itself sweet and orderly, and being best for memory, the only handle of knowledge, it must be in jest that any man can speak against it.

Now then go we to the most important imputations laid to the poor poets. For aught I can yet learn, they are these. First, that there being many other more fruitful knowledges, a man might better spend his time in them than in this. Secondly, that it is the mother of lies. Thirdly, that it is the nurse of abuse, infecting us with many pestilent desires; with a 910 siren's sweetness drawing the mind to the serpent's tail of sinful fancies (and herein, especially, comedies give the largest field to ear, as Chaucer saith);° how, both in other nations and in ours, before poets did soften us, we were full of courage, given to martial exercises, the pillars of manlike liberty, and not lulled asleep in shady idleness with poets' pastimes. And lastly, and chiefly, they cry out with open mouth as if they had overshot Robin Hood,° that Plato banished them out of his commonwealth.° Truly, this is much, if there be much truth in it.

First, to the first. That a man might better spend his time, is a reason indeed; but it doth (as they say) but *petere principium*.° For if it be as I 920 affirm, that no learning is so good as that which teacheth and moveth to virtue; and that none can both teach and move thereto so much as poetry: then is the conclusion manifest that ink and paper cannot be to a more profitable purpose employed. And certainly, though a man should grant their first assumption, it should follow (methinks) very unwillingly, that good is not good, because better is better. But I still and utterly deny that there is sprong out of earth a more fruitful knowledge.

To the second, therefore, that they should be the principal liars, I will answer paradoxically, but truly, I think truly, that of all writers under the sun the poet is the least liar, and, though he would, as a poet can scarcely be a liar. The astronomer, with his cousin the geometrician, can hardly escape, when they take upon them to measure the height of the stars. How often, think you, do the physicians lie, when they aver things good for sicknesses, which afterwards send Charon° a great number of souls drowned in a potion before they come to his ferry? And no less of the rest, which take upon them to affirm. Now, for the poet, he nothing affirms, and therefore never lieth. For, as I take it, to lie is to affirm that to be true which is false. So as the other artists,° and especially the historian, affirming many things, can, in the cloudy knowledge of mankind, hardly escape from many lies. But the poet (as I said before) never affirmeth. The poet never maketh any circles° about your imagination, to conjure you to believe for true what he writes. He citeth not authorities of other histories, but even for his entry calleth the sweet Muses to inspire into him a good invention; in truth, not labouring to tell you what is or is not, but what should or should not be. And therefore, though he recount things not true, yet because he telleth them not for true, he lieth not—without we will say that Nathan lied in his speech before-alleged to David; which as a wicked man durst scarce say, so think I none so simple would say that Aesop lied in the tales of his beasts; for who thinks that Aesop wrote it for actually true were well worthy to have his name chronicled among the beasts he writeth of. What child is there, that, coming to a play, and seeing *Thebes* written in great letters upon an old door, doth believe that it is Thebes? If then a man can arrive to that child's age to know that the poets' persons and doings are but pictures what should be, and not stories what have been, they will never give the lie to things not affirmatively but allegorically and figuratively written. And therefore, as in history, looking for truth, they may go away full fraught with falsehood, so in poesy, looking but for fiction, they shall use the narration but as an imaginative ground-plot of a profitable invention. But hereto is replied, that the poets give names to men they write of, which argueth a conceit of an actual truth, and so, not being true, proves a falsehood. And doth the lawyer lie then, when under the names of *John-a-stiles* and *John-a-nokes*° he puts his case? But that is easily answered. Their naming of men is but to make their picture the more lively, and not to build any history: painting men, they cannot leave men nameless. We see we cannot play at chess but that we must give names to our chessmen; and yet, methinks, he were a very partial champion of truth that would say we lied for giving a piece of wood the reverend title of a bishop. The poet nameth Cyrus or Aeneas no other way than to show what men of their fames, fortunes, and estates should do.

970   Their third is, how much it abuseth men's wit, training it to wanton sinfulness and lustful love: for indeed that is the principal, if not only, abuse I can hear alleged.° They say, the comedies rather teach than reprehend amorous conceits. They say the lyric is larded with passionate sonnets; the elegiac weeps the want of his mistress; and that even to the heroical, Cupid hath ambitiously climbed.° Alas, Love, I would thou couldst as well defend thyself as thou canst offend others. I would those on whom thou dost attend could either put thee away, or yield good reason why they keep thee. But grant love of beauty to be a beastly fault (although it be very hard, since only man, and no beast, hath that gift to 980 discern beauty); grant that lovely name of Love to deserve all hateful reproaches (although even some of my masters the philosophers spent a good deal of their lamp-oil in setting forth the excellency of it);° grant, I say, whatsoever they will have granted, that not only love, but lust, but vanity, but (if they list) scurrility, possesseth many leaves of the poets' books; yet think I, when this is granted, they will find their sentence may with good manners put the last words foremost, and not say that poetry abuseth man's wit, but that man's wit abuseth poetry.

For I will not deny but that man's wit may make poesy, which should be *eikastiké* (which some learned have defined: figuring forth good things), 990 to be *phantastiké*° (which doth, contrariwise, infect the fancy with unworthy objects), as the painter, that should give to the eye either some excellent perspective, or some fine picture, fit for building or fortification, or containing in it some notable example (as Abraham sacrificing his son Isaac, Judith killing Holofernes, David fighting with Goliath), may leave those, and please an ill-pleased eye with wanton shows of better hidden matters. But what, shall the abuse of a thing make the right use odious? Nay truly, though I yield that poesy may not only be abused, but that being abused, by the reason of his sweet charming force, it can do more hurt than any other army of words: yet shall it be so far from 1000 concluding that the abuse should give reproach to the abused, that, contrariwise, it is a good reason that whatsoever, being abused, doth most harm, being rightly used (and upon the right use each thing conceiveth his title), doth most good. Do we not see the skill of physic, the best rampire to our often-assaulted bodies, being abused, teach poison, the most violent destroyer? Doth not knowledge of law, whose end is to even and right all things, being abused, grow the crooked fosterer of horrible injuries? Doth not (to go to the highest) God's word abused breed heresy, and His name abused become blasphemy? Truly, a needle cannot do much hurt, and as truly (with leave of ladies be it spoken) it cannot do much good: with a sword thou may'st kill thy father, 1010 and with a sword thou may'st defend thy prince and country. So that, as in their calling poets fathers of lies they said nothing, so in this their argument of abuse they prove the commendation.

They allege herewith, that before poets began to be in price our nation had set their hearts' delight upon action, and not imagination: rather doing things worthy to be written, than writing things fit to be done. What that before-time was, I think scarcely Sphinx can tell, since no memory is so ancient that hath not the precedent of poetry. And certain it is that, in our plainest homeliness, yet never was the Albion nation without poetry.° Marry, this argument, though it be levelled against poetry, yet is it indeed 1020 a chainshot° against all learning, or bookishness as they commonly term it. Of such mind were certain Goths,° of whom it is written that, having in the spoil of a famous city taken a fair library, one hangman° (belike fit to execute the fruits of their wits) who had murdered a great number of bodies, would have set fire in it: no, said another very gravely, take heed what you do, for while they are busy about these toys, we shall with more leisure conquer their countries. This indeed is the ordinary doctrine of ignorance, and many words sometimes I have heard spent in it. But because this reason is generally against all learning as well as poetry, or rather, all learning but poetry; because it were too large a digression to 1030 handle it, or at least too superfluous (since it is manifest that all government of action is to be gotten by knowledge, and knowledge best by gathering many knowledges, which is reading), I only, with Horace, to him that is of that opinion

> jubeo stultum esse libenter;°

for as for poetry itself, it is the freest from this objection.

For poetry is the companion of camps. I dare undertake, Orlando Furioso, or honest King Arthur, will never displease a soldier; but the quiddity of *ens* and *prima materia*° will hardly agree with a corslet;° and therefore, as I said in the beginning, even Turks and Tartars are 1040 delighted with poets. Homer, a Greek, flourished before Greece flourished. And if to a slight conjecture a conjecture may be opposed, truly it may seem, that as by him their learned men took almost their first light of knowledge, so their active men received their first motions of courage. Only Alexander's example may serve, who by Plutarch is accounted of such virtue, that Fortune was not his guide but his footstool; whose acts speak for him, though Plutarch did not: indeed the phoenix of warlike princes. This Alexander left his schoolmaster, living

Aristotle, behind him, but took dead Homer with him.° He put the
philosopher Callisthenes to death for his seeming philosophical, indeed
mutinous, stubbornness, but the chief thing he was ever heard to wish for
was that Homer had been alive. He well found he received more bravery
of mind by the pattern of Achilles than by hearing the definition of
fortitude. And therefore, if Cato misliked Fulvius for carrying Ennius
with him to the field, it may be answered that, if Cato misliked it, the
noble Fulvius liked it, or else he had not done it; for it was not the
excellent Cato Uticensis (whose authority I would much more have
reverenced), but it was the former,° in truth a bitter punisher of faults
(but else a man that had never well sacrificed to the Graces: he misliked
and cried out against all Greek learning, and yet, being eighty years old,
began to learn it, belike fearing that Pluto understood not Latin). Indeed,
the Roman laws allowed no person to be carried to the wars but he that
was in the soldier's roll; and therefore, though Cato misliked his
unmustered° person, he misliked not his work. And if he had, Scipio
Nasica, judged by common consent the best Roman, loved him. Both the
other Scipio brothers, who had by their virtues no less surnames than of
Asia and Afric, so loved him that they caused his body to be buried in
their sepulture.° So as Cato's authority, being but against his person, and
that answered with so far greater than himself, is herein of no validity.

But now indeed my burden is great; now Plato's name is laid upon me,
whom, I must confess, of all philosophers I have ever esteemed most
worthy of reverence, and with good reason: since of all philosophers he is
the most poetical. Yet if he will defile the fountain out of which his
flowing streams have proceeded, let us boldly examine with what reasons
he did it. First, truly, a man might maliciously object that Plato, being a
philosopher, was a natural enemy of poets. For indeed, after the
philosophers had picked out of the sweet mysteries of poetry the right
discerning true points of knowledge, they forthwith putting it in method,
and making a school-art of that which the poets did only teach by a divine
delightfulness, beginning to spurn at their guides, like ungrateful
prentices, were not content to set up shops for themselves, but sought by
all means to discredit their masters; which by the force of delight being
barred them, the less they could overthrow them, the more they hated
them. For indeed, they found for Homer seven cities strave who should
have him for their citizen; where many cities banished philosophers as
not fit members to live among them.° For only repeating certain of
Euripides' verses, many Athenians had their lives saved of the Syracusans, where the Athenians themselves thought many philosophers
unworthy to live.° Certain poets, as Simonides and Pindar, had so

prevailed with Hiero the First, that of a tyrant they made him a just king;° 1090
where Plato could do so little with Dionysius, that he himself of a
philosopher was made a slave.° But who should do thus, I confess, should
requite the objections made against poets with like cavillations against
philosophers; as likewise one should do that should bid one read
Phaedrus or *Symposium* in Plato, or the discourse of love in Plutarch, and
see whether any poet do authorize abominable filthiness, as they do.°
Again, a man might ask out of what commonwealth Plato did banish
them: in sooth, thence where he himself alloweth community of women°
—so as belike this banishment grew not for effeminate wantonness,
since little should poetical sonnets be hurtful when a man might have 1100
what woman he listed. But I honour philosophical instructions, and bless
the wits which bred them: so as they be not abused, which is likewise
stretched to poetry.

St Paul himself (who yet, for the credit of poets, twice citeth poets, and
one of them by the name of 'their prophet')° setteth a watchword upon
philosophy—indeed upon the abuse. So doth Plato upon the abuse, not
upon poetry. Plato found fault that the poets of his time filled the world
with wrong opinions of the gods, making light tales of that unspotted
essence, and therefore would not have the youth depraved with such
opinions. Herein may much be said. Let this suffice: the poets did not 1110
induce such opinions, but did imitate those opinions already induced.
For all the Greek stories can well testify that the very religion of that time
stood upon many and many-fashioned gods, not taught so by the poets,
but followed according to their nature of imitation. Who list may read in
Plutarch the discourses of Isis and Osiris, of the cause why oracles
ceased, of the divine providence,° and see whether the theology of that
nation stood not upon such dreams which the poets indeed superstitiously observed—and truly (since they had not the light of Christ) did
much better in it than the philosophers, who, shaking off superstition,
brought in atheism. Plato therefore (whose authority I had much rather 1120
justly construe than unjustly resist) meant not in general of poets, in
those words of which Julius Scaliger saith *Qua authoritate barbari quidam
atque hispidi abuti velint ad poetas e republica exigendos;*° but only meant to
drive out those wrong opinions of the Deity (whereof now, without
further law, Christianity hath taken away all the hurtful belief) perchance
(as he thought) nourished by the then esteemed poets. And a man need
go no further than to Plato himself to know his meaning: who, in his
dialogue called *Ion*, giveth high and rightly divine commendation unto
poetry.° So as Plato, banishing the abuse, not the thing, not banishing it,
but giving due honour unto it, shall be our patron, and not our adversary. 1130

For indeed I had much rather (since truly I may do it) show their mistaking of Plato (under whose lion's skin they would make an ass-like braying against poesy)° than go about to overthrow his authority; whom, the wiser a man is, the more just cause he shall find to have in admiration; especially since he attributeth unto poesy more than myself do,° namely, to be a very inspiring of a divine force, far above man's wit, as in the forenamed dialogue is apparent.

Of the other side, who would show the honours have been by the best sort of judgements granted them, a whole sea of examples would present themselves: Alexanders, Caesars, Scipios, all favourers of poets; Laelius, called the Roman Socrates, himself a poet, so as part of *Heautontimoru-menos* in Terence was supposed to be made by him;° and even the Greek Socrates, whom Apollo confirmed to be the only wise man, is said to have spent part of his old time in putting Aesop's fables into verses.° And therefore, full evil should it become his scholar Plato to put such words in his master's mouth against poets. But what need more? Aristotle writes the Art of Poesy; and why, if it should not be written? Plutarch teacheth the use to be gathered of them; and how, if they should not be read? And who reads Plutarch's either history or philosophy, shall find he trimmeth both their garments with guards° of poesy. But I list not to defend poesy with the help of his underling historiography. Let it suffice to have showed it is a fit soil for praise to dwell upon; and what dispraise may be set upon it, is either easily overcome, or transformed into just commendation.

So that, since the excellencies of it may be so easily and so justly confirmed, and the low-creeping objections so soon trodden down: it not being an art of lies, but of true doctrine; not of effeminateness, but of notable stirring of courage; not of abusing man's wit, but of strengthening man's wit; not banished, but honoured by Plato: let us rather plant more laurels for to engarland the poets' heads (which honour of being laureate, whereas besides them only triumphant captains were, is a sufficient authority to show the price they ought to be held in) than suffer the ill-savoured breath of such wrong-speakers once to blow upon the clear springs of poesy.

But since I have run so long a career° in this matter, methinks, before I give my pen a full stop, it shall be but a little more lost time to inquire why England, the mother of excellent minds, should be grown so hard a stepmother to poets, who certainly in wit ought to pass all other, since all only proceedeth from their wit, being indeed makers of themselves, not takers of others. How can I but exclaim

Musa, mihi causas memora, quo numine laeso?°

Sweet poesy, that hath anciently had kings, emperors, senators, great captains, such as, besides a thousand others, David, Adrian, Sophocles, Germanicus, not only to favour poets, but to be poets;° and of our nearer times can present for her patrons a Robert, king of Sicily, the great King Francis of France, King James of Scotland;° such cardinals as Bembus and Bibbiena;° such famous preachers and teachers as Beza and Melanchthon;° so learned philosophers as Fracastorius° and Scaliger; so great orators as Pontanus and Muretus;° so piercing wits as George Buchanan;° so grave counsellors as, beside many, but before all, that 1180 Hôpital of France,° than whom (I think) that realm never brought forth a more accomplished judgement, more firmly builded upon virtue: I say these, with numbers of others, not only to read others' poesies, but to poetize for others' reading—that poesy, thus embraced in all other places, should only find in our time a hard welcome in England, I think the very earth lamenteth it, and therefore decketh our soil with fewer laurels than it was accustomed. For heretofore poets have in England also flourished, and, which is to be noted, even in those times when the trumpet of Mars did sound loudest.° And now that an overfaint quietness should seem to strew the house° for poets, they are almost in as good 1190 reputation as the mountebanks at Venice.° Truly even that, as of the one side it giveth great praise to poesy, which like Venus (but to better purpose) had rather be troubled in the net with Mars than enjoy the homely quiet of Vulcan: so serves it for a piece of a reason why they are less grateful to idle England, which now can scarce endure the pain of a pen.

Upon this necessarily followeth, that base men with servile wits° undertake it, who think it enough if they can be rewarded of the printer. And so as Epaminondas is said with the honour of his virtue to have made an office, by his exercising it, which before was contemptible, to become 1200 highly respected;° so these men, no more but setting their names to it, by their own disgracefulness disgrace the most graceful poesy. For now, as if all the Muses were got with child to bring forth bastard poets, without any commission° they do post over the banks of Helicon, till they make the readers more weary than post-horses; while, in the meantime, they

Queis meliore luto finxit praecordia Titan°

are better content to suppress the outflowings of their wit, than, by publishing them, to be accounted knights of the same order.° But I that, before ever I durst aspire unto the dignity, am admitted into the company of the paper-blurrers, do find the very true cause of our wanting 1210

estimation is want of desert—taking upon us to be poets in despite of
Pallas.

Now, wherein we want desert were a thankworthy labour to express;
but if I knew, I should have mended myself. But I, as I never desired the
title, so have I neglected the means to come by it. Only, overmastered by
some thoughts, I yielded an inky tribute unto them. Marry, they that
delight in poesy itself should seek to know what they do, and how they do;
and especially look themselves in an unflattering glass of reason, if they
be inclinable unto it. For poesy must not be drawn by the ears; it must be
1220 gently led, or rather it must lead—which was partly the cause that made
the ancient-learned affirm it was a divine gift, and no human skill: since
all other knowledges lie ready for any that hath strength of wit. A poet no
industry can make, if his own genius be not carried into it; and therefore
it is an old proverb, *orator fit, poeta nascitur.*°

Yet confess I always that as the fertilest ground must be manured,
so must the highest-flying wit have a Daedalus° to guide him. That
Daedalus, they say, both in this and in other, hath three wings to bear
itself up into the air of due commendation: that is, art, imitation, and
exercise. But these, neither artificial rules nor imitative patterns, we°
1230 much cumber ourselves withal. Exercise indeed we do, but that very
fore-backwardly:° for where we should exercise to know, we exercise as
having known; and so is our brain delivered of much matter which never
was begotten by knowledge. For there being two principal parts, matter
to be expressed by words and words to express the matter, in neither we
use art or imitation rightly. Our matter is *quodlibet*° indeed, though
wrongly performing Ovid's verse,

Quicquid conabor dicere, versus erit;°

never marshalling it into any assured rank, that almost the readers cannot
tell where to find themselves.

1240   Chaucer, undoubtedly, did excellently in his *Troilus and Criseyde*; of
whom, truly, I know not whether to marvel more, either that he in that
misty time could see so clearly, or that we in this clear age go so
stumblingly after him.° Yet had he great wants, fit to be forgiven in so
reverent an antiquity. I account the *Mirror of Magistrates* meetly furnished
of beautiful parts,° and in the Earl of Surrey's lyrics many things tasting
of a noble birth, and worthy of a noble mind.° The *Shepheardes Calender*
hath much poetry in his eclogues, indeed worthy the reading, if I be not
deceived.° (That same framing of his style to an old rustic language I dare
not allow,° since neither Theocritus in Greek, Virgil in Latin, nor
1250 Sannazaro in Italian did affect it.) Besides these I do not remember to

have seen but few (to speak boldly) printed that have poetical sinews in them; for proof whereof, let but most of the verses be put in prose, and then ask the meaning, and it will be found that one verse did but beget another, without ordering at the first what should be at the last; which becomes a confused mass of words, with a tingling sound of rhyme, barely accompanied with reason.

Our tragedies and comedies (not without cause cried out against), observing rules neither of honest civility nor skilful poetry—excepting *Gorboduc* (again, I say, of these that I have seen), which notwithstanding as it is full of stately speeches and well-sounding phrases, climbing to the 1260 height of Seneca's style, and as full of notable morality, which it doth most delightfully teach, and so obtain the very end of poesy, yet in truth it is very defectuous in the circumstances, which grieveth me, because it might not remain as an exact model of all tragedies.° For it is faulty both in place and time, the two necessary companions of all corporal actions. For where the stage should always represent but one place, and the uttermost time presupposed in it should be, both by Aristotle's precept and common reason, but one day, there is both many days, and many places, inartificially° imagined.

But if it be so in *Gorboduc*, how much more in all the rest, where you 1270 shall have Asia of the one side, and Afric of the other, and so many other under-kingdoms, that the player, when he cometh in, must ever begin with telling where he is, or else the tale will not be conceived? Now you shall have three ladies walk to gather flowers: and then we must believe the stage to be a garden. By and by we hear news of shipwreck in the same place: and then we are to blame if we accept it not for a rock. Upon the back of that comes out a hideous monster with fire and smoke: and then the miserable beholders are bound to take it for a cave. While in the meantime two armies fly in, represented with four swords and bucklers: and then what hard heart will not receive it for a pitched field? 1280

Now, of time they are much more liberal: for ordinary it is that two young princes fall in love; after many traverses,° she is got with child, delivered of a fair boy; he is lost, groweth a man, falls in love, and is ready to get another child; and all this in two hours' space: which, how absurd it is in sense, even sense may imagine, and art hath taught, and all ancient examples justified—and at this day, the ordinary players in Italy° will not err in. Yet will some bring in an example of *Eunuchus* in Terence, that containeth matter of two days, yet far short of twenty years.° True it is, and so was it to be played in two days, and so fitted to the time it set forth. And though Plautus have in one place done amiss,° let us hit with him, 1290 and not miss with him.

But they will say: How then shall we set forth a story which containeth both many places and many times? And do they not know that a tragedy is tied to the laws of poesy, and not of history; not bound to follow the story, but having liberty either to feign a quite new matter or to frame the history to the most tragical conveniency? Again, many things may be told which cannot be showed, if they know the difference betwixt reporting and representing. As, for example, I may speak (though I am here) of Peru, and in speech digress from that to the description of Calicut;° but in action I cannot represent it without Pacolet's horse;° and so was the manner the ancients took, by some *Nuntius*° to recount things done in former time or other place. Lastly, if they will represent a history, they must not (as Horace saith) begin *ab ovo*,° but they must come to the principal point of that one action which they will represent.

By example this will be best expressed. I have a story of young Polydorus, delivered for safety's sake, with great riches, by his father Priam to Polymnestor, king of Thrace, in the Trojan war time; he, after some years, hearing the overthrow of Priam, for to make the treasure his own, murdereth the child; the body of the child is taken up by Hecuba; she, the same day, findeth a sleight to be revenged most cruelly of the tyrant. Where now would one of our tragedy writers begin, but with the delivery of the child? Then should he sail over into Thrace, and so spend I know not how many years, and travel numbers of places. But where doth Euripides?° Even with the finding of the body, leaving the rest to be told by the spirit of Polydorus. This need no further to be enlarged; the dullest wit may conceive it.

But besides these gross absurdities, how all their plays be neither right tragedies, nor right comedies, mingling kings and clowns, not because the matter so carrieth it, but thrust in the clown by head and shoulders to play a part in majestical matters with neither decency nor discretion, so as neither the admiration and commiseration, nor the right sportfulness, is by their mongrel tragi-comedy obtained. I know Apuleius did somewhat so,° but that is a thing recounted with space of time, not represented in one moment; and I know the ancients have one or two examples of tragi-comedies, as Plautus hath *Amphitryo*;° but, if we mark them well, we shall find that they never, or very daintily,° match hornpipes and funerals. So falleth it out that, having indeed no right comedy, in that comical part of our tragedy, we have nothing but scurrility, unworthy of any chaste ears, or some extreme show of doltishness, indeed fit to lift up a loud laughter, and nothing else: where the whole tract of a comedy should be full of delight, as the tragedy should be still maintained in a well-raised admiration.

But our comedians think there is no delight without laughter; which is very wrong, for though laughter may come with delight, yet cometh it not of delight, as though delight should be the cause of laughter; but well may one thing breed both together. Nay, rather in themselves they have, as it were, a kind of contrariety: for delight we scarcely do but in things that have a conveniency to ourselves or to the general nature; laughter almost ever cometh of things most disproportioned to ourselves and nature. Delight hath a joy in it, either permanent or present. Laughter hath only 1340 a scornful tickling.°

For example, we are ravished with delight to see a fair woman, and yet are far from being moved to laughter; we laugh at deformed creatures, wherein certainly we cannot delight. We delight in good chances, we laugh at mischances: we delight to hear the happiness of our friends, or country, at which he were worthy to be laughed at that would laugh; we shall, contrarily, laugh sometimes to find a matter quite mistaken and go down the hill against the bias° in the mouth of some such men—as for the respect of them one shall be heartily sorry, he cannot choose but laugh, and so is rather pained than delighted with laughter. 1350

Yet deny I not but that they may go well together. For as in Alexander's picture well set out° we delight without laughter, and in twenty mad antics° we laugh without delight; so in Hercules, painted with his great beard and furious countenance, in a woman's attire, spinning at Omphale's commandment,° it breedeth both delight and laughter: for the representing of so strange a power in love procureth delight, and the scornfulness of the action stirreth laughter. But I speak to this purpose that all the end of the comical part be not upon such scornful matters as stir laughter only, but, mixed with it, that delightful teaching which is the end of poesy. And the great fault even in that point of laughter, and 1360 forbidden plainly by Aristotle, is that they stir laughter in sinful things, which are rather execrable than ridiculous, or in miserable, which are rather to be pitied than scorned. For what is it to make folks gape at a wretched beggar and a beggarly clown; or, against law of hospitality, to jest at strangers, because they speak not English so well as we do? What do we learn, since it is certain

> Nil habet infelix paupertas durius in se,
> Quam quod ridiculos homines facit?°

But rather, a busy loving courtier and a heartless threatening Thraso;° a self-wise-seeming schoolmaster;° an awry-transformed traveller. 1370 These, if we saw walk in stage names, which we play naturally, therein

were delightful laughter, and teaching delightfulness—as in the other,°
the tragedies of Buchanan do justly bring forth a divine admiration.

But I have lavished out too many words of this play matter. I do it
because, as they are excelling parts of poesy, so is there none so much
used in England, and none can be more pitifully abused; which, like an
unmannerly daughter showing a bad education, causeth her mother
Poesy's honesty to be called in question.

Other sort of poetry almost have we none, but that lyrical kind of songs
1380 and sonnets: which, Lord, if He gave us so good minds, how well it might
be employed, and with how heavenly fruit, both private and public, in
singing the praises of the immortal beauty: the immortal goodness of that
God who giveth us hands to write and wits to conceive; of which we might
well want words, but never matter; of which we could turn our eyes to
nothing, but we should ever have new-budding occasions. But truly
many of such writings as come under the banner of unresistible love, if I
were a mistress, would never persuade me they were in love: so coldly
they apply fiery speeches,° as men that had rather read lovers' writings
—and so caught up certain swelling phrases which hang together, like a
1390 man that once told my father that the wind was at north-west and by
south, because he would be sure to name winds enough—than that in
truth they feel those passions, which easily (as I think) may be bewrayed
by that same forcibleness or *energia*° (as the Greeks call it) of the writer.
But let this be a sufficient though short note, that we miss the right use of
the material point of poesy.

Now, for the outside of it, which is words, or (as I may term it) diction,
it is even well worse. So is that honey-flowing matron Eloquence
apparelled, or rather disguised, in a courtesan-like painted affectation:
one time, with so far-fet words that may seem monsters but must seem
1400 strangers to any poor Englishman; another time, with coursing of a letter,
as if they were bound to follow the method of a dictionary; another time,
with figures and flowers, extremely winter-starved.° But I would this
fault were only peculiar to versifiers, and had not as large possession
among prose-printers; and (which is to be marvelled) among many
scholars; and (which is to be pitied) among some preachers. Truly I
could wish, if at least I might be so bold to wish a thing beyond the reach
of my capacity, the diligent imitators of Tully and Demosthenes (most
worthy to be imitated) did not so much keep Nizolian paper-books of
their figures and phrases, as by attentive translation (as it were) devour
1410 them whole, and make them wholly theirs:° for now they cast sugar and
spice upon every dish that is served to the table—like those Indians, not
content to wear earrings at the fit and natural place of the ears, but they

will thrust jewels through their nose and lips, because they will be sure to be fine. Tully, when he was to drive out Catiline, as it were with a thunderbolt of eloquence, often used the figure of repetition, as *Vivit. Vivit? Imo in senatum venit, &c.*° Indeed, inflamed with a well-grounded rage, he would have his words (as it were) double out of his mouth, and so do that artificially which we see men in choler do naturally. And we, having noted the grace of those words, hale them in sometimes to a familiar epistle, when it were too too much choler to be choleric.° How well store of *similiter cadences*° doth sound with the gravity of the pulpit, I would but invoke Demosthenes' soul to tell, who with a rare daintiness° useth them. Truly they have made me think of the sophister that with too much subtlety would prove two eggs three, and though he might be counted a sophister, had none for his labour.° So these men bringing in such a kind of eloquence, well may they obtain an opinion of a seeming finesse, but persuade few—which should be the end of their finesse. Now for similitudes, in certain printed discourses,° I think all herbarists, all stories of beasts, fowls, and fishes are rifled up, that they come in multitudes to wait upon any of our conceits; which certainly is as absurd a surfeit to the ears as is possible. For the force of a similitude not being to prove anything to a contrary disputer, but only to explain to a willing hearer, when that is done, the rest is a most tedious prattling, rather over-swaying the memory from the purpose whereto they were applied, than any whit informing the judgement, already either satisfied, or by similitudes not to be satisfied. For my part, I do not doubt, when Antonius and Crassus, the great forefathers of Cicero in eloquence, the one (as Cicero testifieth of them) pretended not to know art, the other not to set by it, because with a plain sensibleness they might win credit of popular ears (which credit is the nearest step to persuasion, which persuasion is the chief mark of oratory), I do not doubt (I say) but that they used these knacks very sparingly;° which who doth generally use, any man may see doth dance to his own music, and so be noted by the audience more careful to speak curiously° than to speak truly. Undoubtedly (at least to my opinion undoubtedly), I have found in divers smally learned courtiers a more sound style than in some professors of learning; of which I can guess no other cause, but that the courtier, following that which by practice he findeth fittest to nature, therein (though he know it not) doth according to art, though not by art: where the other, using art to show art, and not to hide art° (as in these cases he should do), flieth from nature, and indeed abuseth art.

But what? Methinks I deserve to be pounded° for straying from poetry or oratory. But both have such an affinity in the wordish consideration,°

1420

1430

1440

1450

that I think this digression will make my meaning receive the fuller understanding: which is not to take upon me to teach poets how they should do, but only, finding myself sick among the rest, to show some one or two spots of the common infection grown among the most part of writers, that, acknowledging ourselves somewhat awry, we may bend to the right use both of matter and manner: whereto our language giveth us
1460 great occasion, being indeed capable of any excellent exercising of it. I know some will say it is a mingled language.° And why not so much the better, taking the best of both the other? Another will say it wanteth grammar. Nay truly, it hath that praise, that it wants not grammar: for grammar it might have, but it needs it not, being so easy in itself, and so void of those cumbersome differences of cases, genders, moods, and tenses, which I think was a piece of the Tower of Babylon's curse,° that a man should be put to school to learn his mother-tongue. But for the uttering sweetly and properly the conceits of the mind (which is the end of speech), that hath it equally with any other tongue in the world; and is
1470 particularly happy in compositions of two or three words together, near the Greek, far beyond the Latin, which is one of the greatest beauties can be in a language.°

Now of versifying there are two sorts,° the one ancient, the other modern: the ancient marked the quantity of each syllable, and according to that framed his verse; the modern, observing only number (with some regard of the accent), the chief life of it standeth in that like sounding of the words, which we call rhyme. Whether of these be the more excellent, would bear many speeches: the ancient (no doubt) more fit for music, both words and time observing quantity, and more fit lively to express
1480 diverse passions, by the low or lofty sound of the well-weighed syllable; the latter likewise, with his rhyme, striketh a certain music to the ear, and, in fine, since it doth delight, though by another way, it obtains the same purpose: there being in either sweetness, and wanting in neither majesty. Truly the English, before any vulgar° language I know, is fit for both sorts. For, for the ancient,° the Italian is so full of vowels that it must ever be cumbered with elisions; the Dutch° so, of the other side, with consonants, that they cannot yield the sweet sliding, fit for a verse; the French in his whole language hath not one word that hath his accent in the last syllable saving two, called *antepenultima*; and little more hath the
1490 Spanish, and therefore very gracelessly may they use dactyls.° The English is subject to none of these defects. Now for the rhyme, though we do not observe quantity, yet we observe the accent very precisely, which other languages either cannot do, or will not do so absolutely. That *caesura*, or breathing place in the midst of the verse, neither Italian nor

Spanish have, the French and we never almost fail of. Lastly, even the
very rhyme itself, the Italian cannot put it in the last syllable, by the
French named the masculine rhyme, but still in the next to the last, which
the French call the female, or the next before that, which the Italian term
sdrucciola.° The example of the former is *buono: suono,* of the *sdrucciola* is
femina: semina. The French, of the other side, hath both the male, as *bon:* 1500
son, and the female, as *plaise: taise,* but the *sdrucciola* he hath not: where
the English hath all three, as *due: true, father: rather, motion: potion*—with
much more which might be said, but that already I find the triflingness of
this discourse is much too much enlarged.

So that since the ever-praiseworthy Poesy is full of virtue-breeding
delightfulness, and void of no gift that ought to be in the noble name of
learning; since the blames laid against it are either false or feeble; since
the cause why it is not esteemed in England is the fault of poet-apes°, not
poets; since, lastly, our tongue is most fit to honour poesy, and to be
honoured by poesy; I conjure you all that have had the evil luck to read 1510
this ink-wasting toy of mine, even in the name of the nine Muses, no
more to scorn the sacred mysteries of poesy; no more to laugh at the
name of poets, as though they were next inheritors to fools; no more to
jest at the reverent title of a rhymer; but to believe, with Aristotle,° that
they were the ancient treasurers of the Grecians' divinity; to believe, with
Bembus, that they were first bringers-in of all civility; to believe, with
Scaliger,° that no philosopher's precepts can sooner make you an honest
man than the reading of Virgil; to believe, with Clauserus, the translator
of Cornutus, that it pleased the heavenly Deity, by Hesiod and Homer,
under the veil of fables, to give us all knowledge, logic, rhetoric, 1520
philosophy natural and moral, and *quid non?;*° to believe, with me, that
there are many mysteries contained in poetry, which of purpose were
written darkly, lest by profane wits it should be abused; to believe, with
Landino,° that they are so beloved of the gods that whatsoever they write
proceeds of a divine fury; lastly, to believe themselves, when they tell you
they will make you immortal by their verses. Thus doing, your name shall
flourish in the printers' shops; thus doing, you shall be of kin to many a
poetical preface; thus doing, you shall be most fair, most rich, most wise,
most all, you shall dwell upon superlatives; thus doing, though you be
libertino patre natus, you shall suddenly grow *Herculea proles,*°   1530

> Si quid mea carmina possunt;°

thus doing, your soul shall be placed with Dante's Beatrice, or Virgil's
Anchises. But if (fie of such a but) you be born so near the dull-making

cataract of Nilus° that you cannot hear the planet-like music of poetry; if you have so earth-creeping a mind that it cannot lift itself up to look to the sky of poetry, or rather, by a certain rustical disdain, will become such a mome as to be a Momus° of poetry; then, though I will not wish unto you the ass's ears of Midas,° nor to be driven by a poet's verses, as Bubonax° was, to hang himself, nor to be rhymed to death, as is said to be done in Ireland;° yet thus much curse I must send you, in the behalf of all poets, that while you live, you live in love, and never get favour for lacking skill of a sonnet; and, when you die, your memory die from the earth for want of an epitaph.

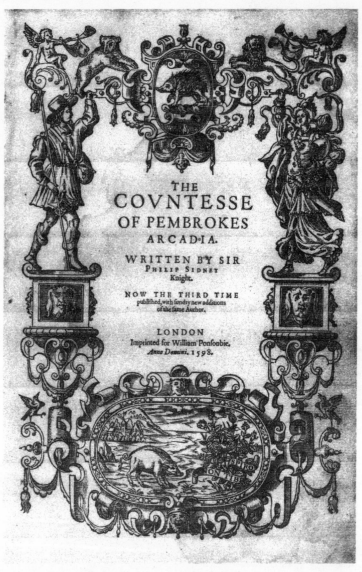

THE
COVNTESSE
OF PEMBROKES
ARCADIA.

WRITTEN BY SIR
PHILIP SIDNEY
Knight.

NOW THE THIRD TIME
published, with sundry new additions
of the same Author.

LONDON
Imprinted for William Ponsonbie.
Anno Domini. 1598.

Title-page of the third edition of the composite *Arcadia* (1598), the first 'complete Sidney'. Reproduced by permission of the Bodleian Library, Oxford.

THE NEW ARCADIA

*The pitiful story of the Paphlagonian
unkind king*

SCARCELY were they out of the confines of Pontus but that, as they rid alone armed (for alone they went, one serving the other), they met an adventure, which though not so notable for any great effect they performed, yet worthy to be remembered for the unused examples therein, as well of true natural goodness, as of wretched ungratefulness.

'It was in the kingdom of Galatia,° the season being (as in the depth of winter) very cold and (as then) suddenly grown to so extreme and foul a storm that never any winter, I think, brought forth a fouler child; so that the princes were even compelled by the hail that the pride of the wind blew into their faces to seek some shrouding place, which, a certain hollow rock offering it unto them, they made it their shield against the tempest's fury. And so, staying there till the violence thereof was passed, they heard the speech of a couple, who not perceiving them (being hid within that rude canopy), held a strange and pitiful disputation—which made them step out, yet in such sort as they might see unseen. There they perceived an aged man, and a young (scarcely come to the age of a man), both poorly arrayed, extremely weather-beaten; the old man blind, the young man leading him. And yet, through all those miseries, in both there seemed to appear a kind of nobleness not suitable to that affliction. But the first words they heard were these of the old man.

'"Well, Leonatus," said he, "since I cannot persuade thee to lead me to that which should end my grief and thy trouble, let me now entreat thee to leave me. Fear not. My misery cannot be greater than it is, and nothing doth become me but misery. Fear not the danger of my blind steps; I cannot fall worse than I am. And do not, I pray thee, do not obstinately continue to infect thee with my wretchedness, but fly, fly from this region only worthy of me."

'"Dear Father," answered he, "do not take away from me the only remnant of my happiness. While I have power to do you service, I am not wholly miserable."

'"Ah, my son!" said he—and with that he groaned, as if sorrow strave to break his heart, "How evil fits it me to have such a son; and how much doth thy kindness upbraid my wickedness!"

'These doleful speeches, and some others to like purpose well showing they had not been born to the fortune they were in, moved the princes to go out unto them and ask the younger what they were. "Sirs," answered he with a good grace—and made the more agreeable by a certain noble kind of piteousness, "I see well you are strangers that know not our misery, so well here known that no man dare know, but that we must be miserable. Indeed, our state is such, as though nothing is so needful unto us as pity, yet nothing is more dangerous unto us than to make ourselves so known as may stir pity. But your presence promiseth that cruelty shall not overrun hate. And if it did, in truth, our state is sunk below the degree of fear.

' "This old man whom I lead was lately rightful prince of this country of Paphlagonia; by the hard-hearted ungratefulness of a son of his deprived not only of his kingdom, whereof no foreign forces were ever able to spoil him, but of his sight, the riches which nature grants to the poorest creatures; whereby (and by other his unnatural dealings) he hath been driven to such grief as even now he would have had me to have led him to the top of this rock, thence to cast himself headlong to death; and so would have made me, who received my life of him, to be the worker of his destruction. But, noble gentlemen," said he, "if either of you have a father and feel what dutiful affection is engraffed° in a son's heart, let me entreat you to convey this afflicted prince to some place of rest and security. Amongst your worthy acts, it shall be none of the least that a king of such might and fame, and so unjustly oppressed, is in any sort by you relieved."

'But before they could make him answer, his father began to speak. "Ah, my son," said he, "how evil an historian are you, that leave out the chief knot of all the discourse—my wickedness! My wickedness! And if thou dost it to spare my ears, the only sense now left me proper for knowledge, assure thyself thou dost mistake me. And I take witness of that sun which you see," with that, he cast up his blind eyes as if he would hunt for light, "and wish myself in worse case than I do wish myself —which is as evil as may be—if I speak untruly, that nothing is so welcome to my thoughts as the publishing of my shame. Therefore know you, gentlemen, to whom from my heart I wish that it may not prove ominous foretoken of misfortune to have met with such a miser as I am, that whatsoever my son (O God! That truth binds me to reproach him with the name of *my son!*) hath said is true. But besides those truths, this also is true: that having had in lawful marriage, of a mother fit to bear royal children, this son (such one as partly you see, and better shall know by my short declaration), and so enjoyed the expectations in the world of him till he was grown to justify their expectations (so as I needed envy no father for the chief comfort of mortality, to leave another oneself after me), I was carried by a bastard son of mine, if, at least, I be bound to believe the words of that base woman, my concubine—his mother, first to mislike, then to hate, lastly to destroy—to do my best to destroy—this son, I think you think undeserving destruction. What ways he used to bring me to it, if I should tell you, I should tediously trouble you with as much poisonous hypocrisy, desperate fraud, smooth malice, hidden ambition, and smiling envy as in any living person could be harboured. But I list it not. No remembrance, no, of naughtiness delights me, but mine own; and methinks the accusing his trains° might in some manner excuse my fault, which certainly I loathe to do. But the conclusion is that I gave order to some servants of mine, whom I thought as apt for such charities as myself, to lead him out into a forest, and there to kill him.

'"But those thieves (better natured, to my son, than myself) spared his life, letting him go to learn to live poorly, which he did, giving himself to be a private soldier in a country hereby. But as he was ready to be greatly advanced for some noble pieces of service which he did, he heard news of me—who drunk in my affection to that unlawful and unnatural son of mine, suffered myself so to be governed by him that all favours and punishments passed by him, all offices and places of importance distributed to his favourites, so that, ere I was aware, I had left myself nothing but the name of a king; which he shortly weary of too, with many indignities (if anything may be called an indignity which was laid upon me) threw me out of my seat, and put out my eyes; and then, proud in his tyranny, let me go, neither imprisoning nor killing me, but rather delighting to make me feel my misery—misery indeed, if ever there were any—full of wretchedness, fuller of disgrace, and fullest of guiltiness. And as he came to the crown by so unjust means, as unjustly he kept it by force of stranger soldiers in citadels, the nests of tyranny and murderers of liberty; disarming all his own countrymen, that no man durst show himself a well-willer of mine—to say the truth, I think few of them being so, considering my cruel folly to my good son, and foolish kindness to my unkind bastard. But if there were any who fell to pity of so great a fall, and had yet any sparks of unslain duty left in them towards me, yet durst they not show it, scarcely with giving me alms at their doors—which yet was the only sustenance of my distressed life, nobody daring to show so much charity as to lend me a hand to guide my dark steps; till this son of mine (God knows, worthy of a more virtuous and more fortunate father), forgetting my abominable wrongs, not recking danger, and neglecting the present good way he was in, doing himself good, came hither to do this kind office you see him perform towards me—to my unspeakable grief, not only because his kindness is a glass even to my blind eyes of my naughtiness, but that, above all griefs, it grieves me he should desperately adventure° the loss of his so well-deserving life for mine, that yet owe more to fortune for my deserts, as if he would carry mud in a chest of crystal. For well I know, he that now reigneth, how much soever and with good reason he despiseth me, of all men despised, yet he will not let slip any advantage to make away him whose just title, ennobled by courage and goodness, may one day shake the seat of a never secure tyranny.

'"And for this cause I craved of him to lead me to the top of this rock, indeed, I must confess with meaning to free him from so serpentine a companion as I am; but he finding what I purposed, only therein since he was born showed himself disobedient unto me. And now, gentlemen, you have the true story which I pray you publish to the world, that my mischievous proceedings may be the glory of his filial piety, the only reward now left for so great a merit. And if it may be, let me obtain that of you which my son denies me, for never was there more pity in saving any than in ending me, both because therein my agonies shall end, and so shall you preserve this excellent young man who else wilfully follows his own ruin."

'The matter in itself lamentable, lamentably expressed by the old prince which needed not take to himself the gestures of pity, since his face could not put off the marks thereof, greatly moved the two princes to compassion, which could not stay in such hearts as theirs without seeking remedy. But by and by the occasion was presented: for Plexirtus (so was the bastard called) came thither with forty horse only of purpose to murder his brother, of whose coming he had soon advertisement, and thought no eyes of sufficient credit in such a matter but his own, and therefore came himself to be actor and spectator; and as soon as he came, not regarding the weak (as he thought) guard of but two men, commanded some of his followers to set their hands to his in the killing of Leonatus. But the young prince, though not otherwise armed but with a sword, how falsely soever he was dealt with by others, would not betray himself; but bravely drawing it out, made the death of the first that assaulted him warn his fellows to come more warily after him.

'But then Pyrocles and Musidorus were quickly become parties (so just a defence deserving as much as old friendship) and so did behave them (among that company more injurious than valiant) that many of them lost their lives for their wicked master. Yet perhaps had the number of them at last prevailed, if the king of Pontus° (lately by them made so) had not come unlooked for to their succour; who having had a dream (which had fixed his imagination vehemently upon some great danger) presently to follow those two princes whom he most dearly loved, was come in all haste, following as well as he could their track with a hundreth horses, in that country which he thought, considering who then reigned, a fit place enough to make the stage of any tragedy. But then the match had been so ill made for Plexirtus that his ill-led life and worse-gotten honour should have tumbled together to destruction, had there not come in Tydeus and Telenor with forty or fifty in their suit to the defence of Plexirtus.

'These two were brothers, of the noblest house of that country, brought up from their infancy with Plexirtus; men of such prowess as not to know fear in themselves, and yet to teach it others that should deal with them, for they had often made their lives triumph over most terrible dangers, never dismayed, and ever fortunate; and truly, no more settled in their valure than disposed to goodness and justice—if either they had lighted on a better friend, or could have learned to make friendship a child, and not the father, of virtue. But bringing up (rather than choice) having first knit their minds unto him (indeed, crafty enough either to hide his faults or never to show them, but when they might pay home), they willingly held out the course rather to satisfy him than all the world, and rather to be good friends than good men; so as, though they did not like the evil he did, yet they liked him that did the evil; and though not counsellors of the offence, yet protectors of the offender.

'Now they having heard of this sudden going out with so small a company, in a country full of evil-wishing minds toward him (though they knew not the cause), followed him; till they found him in such case as they were to venture their lives, or else he to lose his—which they did with such force of mind and body that, truly I may justly say, Pyrocles and Musidorus had never till then found any that could make them so well repeat their hardest lesson in the feats of arms. And briefly, so they did, that if they overcame not, yet were they not overcome, but carried away that ungrateful master of theirs to a place of security, howsoever the princes laboured to the contrary. But this matter being thus far begun, it became not the constancy of the princes so to leave it. But in all haste making forces both in Pontus and Phrygia, they had in few days left him but only that one strong place where he was (for fear having been the only knot that had fastened his people unto him,° that once untied by a greater force, they all scattered from him like so many birds whose cage had been broken); in which season the blind king, having in the chief city of his realm set the crown upon his son Leonatus' head, with many tears both of joy and sorrow setting forth to the whole people his own fault and his son's virtue, after he had kissed him and forced his son to accept honour of him, as of his new-become subject, even in a moment died—as it should seem, his heart, broken with unkindness and affliction, stretched so far beyond his limits° with this excess of comfort, as it was able no longer to keep safe his royal spirits.

The Iberian jousts

'The time of the marrying that queen° was, every year, by the extreme love of her husband and the serviceable love of the courtiers, made notable by some public honours which did as it were proclaim to the world how dear she was to that people; among other, none was either more grateful to the beholders, or more noble in itself, than jousts both with sword and lance, maintained for a seven-night together; wherein that nation doth so excel both for comeliness and ableness that from neighbour countries they ordinarily come, some to strive, some to learn, and some to behold.

'This day it happened that divers famous knights came thither from the court of Helen, queen of Corinth—a lady whom fame at that time was so desirous to honour that she borrowed all men's mouths to join with the sound of her trumpet: for, as her beauty hath won the prize from all women that stand in degree of comparison (for, as for the two sisters of Arcadia, they are far beyond all conceit of comparison!), so hath her government been such as hath been no less beautiful to men's judgements than her beauty to the eyesight; for being brought by right of birth (a woman—a young woman—a fair woman) to govern a people in nature mutinously proud, and always before so used to hard governors as they knew not how to obey without the sword were drawn, yet could she for some years so carry herself among them that they found cause, in the delicacy of her sex, of admiration, not of contempt; and which was notable, even in the time that many countries were full of wars which, for old grudges to Corinth, were thought still would conclude there, yet so handled she the matter that the threatens ever smarted in the threateners —she using so strange and yet so well-succeeding a temper that she made her people (by peace) warlike, her courtiers (by sports) learned, her ladies (by love) chaste; for, by continual martial exercises without blood, she made them perfect in that bloody art; her sports were such as carried riches of knowledge upon the stream of delight; and such the behaviour both of herself and her ladies as builded their chastity, not upon waywardness, but by choice of worthiness: so as, it seemed that court to have been the marriage place of love and virtue, and that herself was a Diana apparelled in the garments of Venus.°

'And this (which fame only delivered unto me, for yet I have never seen her) I am the willinger to speak of to you who, I know, know her better, being your near neighbour, because you may see by her example (in herself wise, and of others beloved) that neither folly is the cause of vehement love, nor reproach the effect; for never, I think, was there any woman that with more unremovable determination gave herself to the counsel of love (after she had once set before her mind the worthiness of your cousin Amphialus), and yet is neither her wisdom doubted of, nor honour blemished; for, O God, what doth better become wisdom than to discern what is worthy the loving? What more agreeable to goodness than to love it, so discerned; and what to greatness of heart than to be constant in it, once loved?

'But, at that time, that love of hers was not so publicly known as the death of Philoxenus and her search of Amphialus hath made it, but then seemed to have such leisure to send thither divers choice knights of her court because they might bring her at least the knowledge, perchance the honour, of that triumph; wherein so they behaved themselves, as for three days they carried the prize; which being come from so far a place to disgrace her servants, Palladius, who himself had never used arms, persuaded the Queen Andromana to be content for the honour sake of her court to suffer us two to have our horse and armour, that he with us might undertake the recovery of their lost honour—which she granted, taking our oath to go no further than her son, and never to abandon him (which she did, not more for saving him than keeping us); and yet, not satisfied with our oath, appointed a band of horsemen to have eye that we should not go beyond appointed limits.

'We were willing to gratify the young prince who, we saw, loved us; and so, the fourth day of that exercise, we came into the field, where, I remember, the manner was that the forenoon they should run at tilt one after the other, the afternoon in a broad field in manner of a battle, till either the strangers, or that country knights, wan the field.

'The first that ran was a brave knight whose device was to come in all chained, with a nymph leading him. His impresa was . . .° Against him came forth an Iberian, whose manner of entering was with bagpipes instead of trumpets, a shepherd's boy before him for a page, and by him a dozen apparelled like shepherds (for the fashion, though rich in stuff) who carried his lances which, though strong to give a lancely blow indeed, yet so were they coloured, with hooks near the morne,° that they prettily represented sheephooks.° His own furniture was dressed over with wool, so enriched with jewels artificially placed that one would have thought it a marriage between the lowest and the highest. His impresa was a sheep marked with pitch,° with this word: "Spotted to be known". And because I may tell you out his conceit, though that were not done till the running for that time was ended, before the ladies departed from the windows—among them there was one, they say, that was the "star" whereby his course was only directed. The shepherds attending upon Philisides went among them and sang an eclogue, one of them answering another, while the other shepherds, pulling out recorders which possessed the place of pipes, accorded their music to the others' voice. The eclogue had great praise. I only remember six verses:° while having questioned one with the other, of their fellow shepherd's sudden growing a man-of-arms, and the cause of his so doing, they thus said:

> Methought some staves he missed—if so, not much amiss,
> For where he most would hit, he ever yet did miss;°
> One said he brake across: full well it so might be,
> For never was there man more crossly crossed° than he;
> But most cried, "Oh, well broke!"° O fool, full gaily blessed,
> Where failing is a shame, and breaking is his best!

'Thus I have digressed, because his manner liked me well; but when he began to run against Lelius,° it had near grown, though great love had ever been betwixt them, to a quarrel; for Philisides breaking his staves with great commendation, Lelius, who was known to be second to none in the perfection of that art, ran ever over his head—but so finely, to the skilful eyes, that one might well see he showed more knowledge in missing than others did in hitting, for with so gallant a grace his staff came swimming close over the crest of the helmet, as if he would represent the kiss, and not the stroke, of Mars. But Philisides was much moved with it, while he thought Lelius would show a contempt of his youth; till Lelius (who therefore would satisfy him because he was his friend) made him know: that to such bondage he was, for so many courses, tied by her;° whose disgraces to him were graced by her excellency; and whose injuries he could never otherwise return, than honours.°

'But so, by Lelius' willing missing, was the odds of the Iberian side, and continued so in the next by the excellent running of a knight, though fostered so by the muses as many times the very rustic people left both their delights and profits to hearken to his songs, yet could he so well perform all armed sports, as if he had never had any other pen than a lance in his hand. He came in like a wild man° (but such a wildness as showed his eyesight had tamed him), full of withered leaves which, though they fell not, still threatened falling. His impresa was a mill-horse, still bound to go in one circle, with this word: "Data fata sequutus".°

'But after him, the Corinthian knights absolutely prevailed, especially a great nobleman of Corinth, whose device was to come without any device, all in white like a new knight (as indeed he was) but so new as his newness shamed most of the others' long exercise; then another from whose tent,° I remember, a bird was made fly with such art to carry a written embassage among the ladies that one might say, "If a live bird, how so taught? If a dead bird, how so made?"; then he, who hidden (man and horse) in a great figure lively representing the phoenix, the fire took so artificially as it consumed the bird, and left him to rise, as it were, out of the ashes thereof; against whom was the fine Frozen Knight° (frozen in despair), but his armour so naturally representing ice, and all his furniture so lively answering thereto, as yet did I never see anything that pleased me better.

'But the delight of those pleasing sights have carried me too far in an unnecessary discourse. Let it then suffice, most excellent lady, that you know the Corinthians that morning in the exercise, as they had done the days before, had the better—Palladius neither suffering us, nor himself, to take in hand that party till the afternoon, when we were to fight in troops—not differing otherwise from earnest, but that the sharpness of the weapons was taken away; but in the trial, Palladius—especially led by Musidorus, and somewhat aided by me—himself truly behaving himself nothing like a beginner, brought the honour to rest itself that night of the Iberian side.°'

Temptations to love and marriage

Cecropia° seeing her son's safety depend thereon, though her pride much disdained the name of a 'desire', took the charge upon her, not doubting the easy conquest of an unexpert virgin, who had already with subtilty and impudency° begun to undermine a monarchy; therefore, weighing Philoclea's resolutions by the counterpeise of her own youthful thoughts (which she then called to mind), she doubted not at least to make Philoclea receive the poison distilled in sweet liquor, which she with little disguising had drunk up thirstily. Therefore she went softly to Philoclea's chamber. And peeping through the side of the door, then being a little open, she saw Philoclea sitting low upon a cushion, in such a given-over manner that one would have thought silence, solitariness, and melancholy were come there (under the ensign of mishap) to conquer delight and drive him from his natural seat of beauty. Her tears came dropping down like rain in sunshine, and she not taking heed to wipe the tears, they ran down upon her cheeks and lips as upon cherries, which the dropping tree bedeweth. In the dressing of her hair and apparel, she might see neither a careful art nor an art of carelessness, but even left to a neglected chance, which yet could no more unperfect her perfections than a die any way cast could lose his squareness.

Cecropia, stirred with no other pity but for her son, came in; and haling kindness into her countenance, 'What ails this sweet lady?', said she. 'Will you mar so good eyes with weeping? Shall tears take away the beauty of that complexion which the women of Arcadia wish for, and the men long after? Fie of this peevish sadness! In sooth, it is untimely for your age. Look upon your own body, and see whether it deserve to pine away with sorrow. See whether you will have these hands', with that, she took one of her hands and, kissing it, looked upon it as if she were enamoured with it, 'fade from their whiteness (which makes one desire to touch them and their softness (which rebounds again a desire to look on them) and become dry, lean, and yellow, and make everybody wonder at the change, and say, that sure you had used some art before, which now you had left—for, if the beauties had been natural, they would never so soon have been blemished. Take a glass and see whether these tears become your eyes—although, I must confess, those eyes are able to make tears comely.'

'Alas, madam,' answered Philoclea, 'I know not whether my tears become mine eyes, but I am sure mine eyes, thus beteared, become my fortune.'

'Your fortune,' said Cecropia, 'if she could see to attire herself, would put on her best raiments! For I see—and I see it with grief, and, to tell you true, unkindness—you misconstrue everything that only for your sake is attempted: you think you are offended, and are indeed defended; you esteem yourself a prisoner, and are in truth a mistress; you fear hate, and shall find love. And truly, I had a thing to say to you—but it is no matter. Since I find you are so obstinately melancholy as that you woo his fellowship,° I will spare my pains and hold my peace'—and so stayed, indeed thinking Philoclea would have had a female inquisitiveness of the matter.

But she (who rather wished to unknow what she knew than to burden her heart with more hopeless knowledge) only desired her to have pity of her, if indeed she did mean her no hurt, then to grant her liberty, for else the very grief and fear would prove her unappointed executioners.

'For that,' said Cecropia, 'believe me, upon the faith of a king's daughter, you shall be free so soon as your freedom may be free of mortal danger, being brought hither for no other cause but to prevent such mischiefs as you know not of. But if you think indeed to win me to have care of you, even as of mine own daughter, then lend your ears unto me, and let not your mind arm itself with a wilfulness to be flexible to nothing—but if I speak reason, let reason have his due reward, persuasion.

'Then, sweet niece,' said she, 'I pray you, presuppose that now, even in the midst of your agonies (which you paint unto yourself most horrible), wishing with sighs and praying with vows for a soon and safe delivery; imagine, niece, I say, that some heavenly spirit should appear unto you and bid you follow him through the door that goes into the garden, assuring you that you should thereby return to your dear mother, and what other delights soever your mind esteems delights—would you, sweet niece, would you refuse to follow him, and say that, if he led you not through the chief gate, you would not enjoy your over-desired liberty? Would you not drink the wine you thirst for, without it were in such a glass as you especially fancied? Tell me, dear niece—but I will answer for you, because I know your reason and will is such as must needs conclude, that such niceness° can no more be in you to disgrace such a mind, than disgracefulness can have any place in so faultless a beauty; your wisdom would assuredly determine how the mark were hit, not whether the bow were of yew or no wherein you shot.

'If this be so (and thus, sure, my dear niece, it is), then I pray you imagine that I am that same good angel, who, grieving in your grief, and in truth not able to suffer that bitter sighs should be sent forth with so sweet a breath, am come to lead you not only to your desired and imagined happiness, but to a true and essential happiness; not only to liberty, but to liberty with commandment. The way I will show you, which, if it be not the gate builded hitherto in your private choice, yet shall it be a door to bring you through a garden of pleasures as sweet as this life can bring forth—nay, rather, which makes this life to be a life.

'My son—let it be no blemish to him that I name him my son, who was your father's own nephew, for you know I am no small king's daughter —my son, I say, far passing the nearness of his kindred with the nearness of goodwill, and striving to match your matchless beauty with a matchless affection, doth by me present unto you the full enjoying of your liberty—so as, with this gift, you will accept a greater (which is this castle, with all the rest which you know he hath in honourable quantity), and will confirm his gift, and your receipt of both, with accepting him to be yours. I might say much both for the person and the matter—but who will cry out, "The sun shines!"? It is so manifest a profit unto you as the meanest judgement must straight apprehend it; so, far is it from the sharpness of yours thereof to be ignorant. Therefore, sweet niece, let your gratefulness be my intercession, and your gentleness my eloquence, and let me carry comfort to a heart which greatly needs it.'

Philoclea looked upon her, and cast down her eye again. 'Aunt,' said she, 'I would I could be so much a mistress of my own mind as to yield to my cousin's virtuous request—for so I construe of it. But my heart is already set', and staying a while on that word, she brought forth afterwards, 'to lead a virgin's life to my death, for such a vow I have in myself devoutly made.'

'The heavens prevent such a mischief!' said Cecropia. '"A vow", quoth you? No, no, my dear niece. Nature, when you were first born, vowed you a woman; and as she made you child of a mother, so, to do your best to be mother of a child; she gave you beauty to move love, she gave you wit to know love, she gave you an excellent body to reward love—which kind of liberal rewarding is crowned with unspeakable felicity; for this, as it bindeth the receiver, so it makes happy the bestower: this doth not impoverish, but enrich the giver. Oh, the sweet name of a mother! Oh, the comfort of comforts! to see your children grow up, in whom you are as it were eternized. If you could conceive what a heart-tickling joy it is to see your own little ones with awful love come running to your lap, and like little models of yourself still carry you about them, you would think unkindness in your own thoughts that ever they did rebel against the mean unto it. But perchance I set this blessedness before your eyes as captains do victory before their soldiers, to which they might come through many pains, grieves, and dangers. No, I am content you shrink from this my counsel if the way to come unto it be not, most of all, pleasant.'

'I know not', answered the sweet Philoclea, fearing lest silence would offend her sullenness, 'what contentment you speak of, but I am sure the best you can make of it, which is marriage, is a burdenous yoke.'

'Ah, dear niece,' said Cecropia, 'how much you are deceived! A yoke indeed we all bear, laid upon us in our creation, which by marriage is not increased, but thus far eased that you have a yoke-fellow to help to draw through the cloddy cumbers° of this world. O widow-nights, bear witness with me of the difference! How often, alas, do I embrace the orphan side of my bed, which was wont to be imprinted by the body of my dear husband, and with tears acknowledge that I now enjoy such a liberty as the banished man hath, who may, if he list, wander over the world, but is forever restrained from his most delightful home; that I have now such a liberty as the seeled dove° hath, which, being first deprived of eyes, is then by the falconer cast off. For believe me, niece, believe me, man's experience is woman's best eyesight. Have you ever seen a pure rose-water kept in a crystal glass?° How fine it looks! How sweet it smells, while that beautiful glass imprisons it! Break the prison, and let the water take his own course: doth it not embrace dust, and lose all his former sweetness and fairness! Truly, so are we, if we have not the stay—rather than the restraint—of crystalline marriage. My heart melts to think of the sweet comforts I in that happy time received when I had never cause to care, but the care was doubled; when I never rejoiced but that I saw my joy shine in another's eyes. What shall I say of the free delight which the heart might embrace—without the accusing of the inward conscience, or fear of outward shame? And is a solitary life as good as this? Then can one string make as good music as a consort; then can one colour set forth a beauty.

'But it may be the general consideration of marriage doth not so much mislike you as the applying of it to him. He is my son. I must confess I see him with a mother's eyes, which if they do not much deceive me, he is no such one over whom contempt may make any just challenge. He is comely; he is noble; he is rich. But that which in itself should carry all comeliness, nobility, and riches—he loves you; and he loves you, who is beloved of others. Drive not away his affection, sweet lady, and make no other lady hereafter proudly brag that she hath robbed you of so faithful and notable a servant.'

Philoclea heard some pieces of her speeches no otherwise than one doth when a tedious prattler cumbers the hearing of a delightful music, for her thoughts had left her ears in that captivity and conveyed themselves to behold, with such eyes as imagination could lend them, the estate of her Zelmane—for whom, how well, she thought, many of those sayings might have been used with a far more grateful acceptation! Therefore, listing not to dispute in a matter whereof herself was resolved, and desired not to inform the other, she only told her that whilst she was so captived she could not conceive of any such persuasions (though never so reasonable) any otherwise than as constraints; and as constraints, must needs even in nature abhor them, which at her liberty, in their own force of reason might more prevail with her; and so, fain would have returned the strength of Cecropia's persuasions, to have procured freedom. But neither her witty words, in an enemy, nor those words (made more than eloquent with passing through such lips) could prevail in Cecropia—no more than her persuasions could win Philoclea to disavow her former vow, or to leave the prisoner Zelmane for the commanding Amphialus; so that both sides being desirous, and neither granters, they brake off conference.

The aunt's atheism refuted by the niece's divinity

Cecropia (threatening in herself to run a more ragged race with her) went to her sister Pamela, who that day having wearied herself with reading, and with the height of her heart disdaining to keep company with any of the gentlewomen appointed to attend her, whom she accounted her jailers, was working upon a purse certain roses and lilies, as by the fineness of the work, one might see she had borrowed her wits of the sorrow that then owed them, and lent them wholly to that exercise—for the flowers she had wrought carried such life in them that the cunningest painter might have learned of her needle, which with so pretty a manner made his careers to and fro through the cloth as if the needle itself would have been loath to have gone fromward such a mistress, but that it hoped to return thenceward very quickly again, the cloth looking with many eyes upon her, and lovingly embracing the wounds she gave it. The shears also were at hand to behead the silk that was grown too short, and if at any time she put her mouth to bite it off, it seemed that, where she had been long in making of a rose with her hands, she would in an instant make roses with her lips—as the lilies seemed to have their whiteness rather of the hand that made them than of the matter whereof they were made, and that they grew there by the suns of her eyes, and were refreshed by the most, in discomfort, comfortable air which an unwares sigh might bestow upon them. But the colours for the ground were so well chosen (neither sullenly dark nor glaringly lightsome) and so well-proportioned (as that though much cunning were in it, yet it was but to serve for an ornament of the principal work) that it was not without marvel to see how a mind, which could cast a careless semblant upon the greatest conflicts of fortune, could command itself to take care for so small matters.

Neither had she neglected the dainty dressing of herself, but, as if it had been her marriage time to affliction, she rather seemed to remember her own worthiness than the unworthiness of her husband; for well one might perceive she had not rejected the counsel of a glass, and that her hands had pleased themselves in paying the tribute of undeceiving skill to so high perfections of nature—the sight whereof, so diverse from her sister who rather suffered sorrow to distress itself in her beauty than that she would bestow any entertainment of so unwelcome a guest, made Cercropia take a sudden assuredness of hope that she should obtain somewhat of Pamela, thinking, according to the squaring out of her own good nature, that beauty carefully set forth would soon prove a sign of an unrefusing harborough.°

Animated wherewith, she sate down by Pamela; and taking the purse, and with affected curiosity looking upon the work, 'Full happy is he', said she, '—at least if he knew his own happiness—to whom a purse in this manner, and by this hand wrought, is dedicated; in faith, he shall have cause to account it not as a purse for treasure, but as a treasure itself, worthy to be pursed up in the purse of his own heart.'

'And think you so indeed!' said Pamela, half smiling. 'I promise you, I wrought it but to make some tedious hours believe that I thought not of them; for else, I valued it but even as a very purse.'

'It is the right nature', said Cecropia, 'of beauty to work unwitting effects of wonder.'

'Truly,' said Pamela, 'I never thought till now that this outward glass entitled beauty, which it pleaseth you to lay to my, as I think, unguilty charge, was but a pleasant mixture of natural colours, delightful to the eye as music is to the ear, without any further consequence, since it is a thing which not only beasts have, but even stones and trees—many of them do greatly excel in it.'

'That other things', answered Cecropia, 'have some portion of it takes not away the excellency of it where indeed it doth excel, since we see that even those beasts, trees, and stones are in the name of beauty only highly praised. But that the beauty of human persons be beyond all other things, there is great likelihood of reason, since to them only is given the judgement to discern beauty—and among reasonable wights (as it seems) that our sex hath the pre-eminence, so that, in that pre-eminence, nature countervails all other liberalities wherein she may be thought to have dealt more favourably toward mankind.

'How do men crown, think you, themselves with glory for having either by force brought others to yield to their mind, or with long study and premeditated orations persuaded what they would have persuaded. And see, a fair woman shall not only command without authority, but persuade without speaking. She shall not need to procure attention, for their own eyes will chain their ears unto it. Men venture lives to conquer; she conquers lives without venturing. She is served and obeyed (which is the most notable) not because the laws so command it, but because they become laws to themselves to obey her—not for her parents' sake, but for her own sake. She need not dispute whether to govern by fear or by love since, without her thinking thereof, their love will bring forth fear, and their fear will fortify their love; and she need not seek offensive or defensive force, since her lips may stand for ten thousand shields, and ten thousand unevitable° shot go from her eyes. Beauty, beauty, dear niece, is the crown of the feminine greatness; which gift on whomsoever the heavens, therein most niggardly, do bestow, without question she is bound to use it to the noble purpose for which it is created, not only winning, but preserving—since that indeed is the right happiness which is not only in itself happy, but can also derive the happiness to another.'

'Certainly, aunt,' said Pamela, 'I fear me you will make me not only think myself fairer than ever I did, but think my fairness a matter of greater value than heretofore I could imagine it, for I ever till now conceived these conquests you spake of rather to proceed from the weakness of the conquered than from the strength of the conquering power. As they say, the cranes overthrow whole battles of Pygmies, not so much of their cranish courage, as because the other are Pygmies;° and that we see, young babes think babies° of wonderful excellency, and yet the babies are but babies. But since your elder years and abler judgement find beauty to be worthy of so incomparable estimation, certainly, methinks, it ought to be held in dearness according to the excellency; and no more than we would do of things which we account precious, ever to suffer it to be defiled.'

'Defiled!' said Cecropia. 'Marry, God forbid that my speech should tend to any such purpose as should deserve so foul a title! My meaning is to join your beauty to love, your youth to delight; for truly, as colours should be as good as nothing if there were no eyes to behold them, so is beauty nothing without the eye of love behold it, and therefore, so far is it from defiling it, that it is the only honouring of it, the only preserving of it; for beauty goes away, devoured by time; but where remains it ever flourishing, but in the heart of a true lover? And such a one (if ever there were any) is my son, whose love is so subjected unto you that, rather than breed any offence unto you, it will not delight itself in beholding you.'

'There is no effect of his love', answered Pamela, 'better pleaseth me than that! But as I have often answered you, so resolutely I say unto you that he must get my parents' consent, and then he shall know further of my mind; for without that I know I should offend God.'

'O sweet youth!' said Cecropia. 'How untimely subject it is to devotion! No, no, sweet niece! Let us old folks think of such precise considerations. Do you enjoy the heaven of your age, whereof you are sure; and like good householders which spend those things that will not be kept, so do you pleasantly enjoy that—which else will bring an over-late repentance when your glass shall accuse you to your face what a change there is in you. Do you see how the springtime is full of flowers, decking itself with them, and not aspiring to the fruits of autumn? What lesson is that unto you, but that in the April of your age you should be like April? Let not some of them for whom already the grave gapeth, and perhaps envy the felicity in you which themselves cannot enjoy, persuade you to lose the hold of occasion while it may not only be taken, but offers, nay, sues to be taken; which, if it be not now taken, will never hereafter be overtaken. Yourself know how your father hath refused all offers made by the greatest princes about you—and will you suffer your beauty to be hidden in the wrinkles of his peevish thoughts?'

'If he be peevish,' said Pamela, 'yet is he my father; and how beautiful soever I be, I am his daughter, so as God claims at my hands obedience, and makes me no judge of his imperfections.'

These often replies upon conscience in Pamela made Cecropia think that there was no righter way for her than, as she had in her opinion set her in liking of beauty with persuasion not to suffer it to be void of purpose, so, if she could make her less feeling of those heavenly conceits, that then she might easily wind her to her crooked bias. Therefore, employing the uttermost of her mischievous wit, and speaking the more earnestly because she spake as she thought, she thus dealt with her.

'Dear niece (or rather, dear daughter, if my affection and wish might prevail therein), how much doth it increase—trow you—the earnest desire I have of this blessed match, to see these virtues of yours knit fast with such zeal of devotion!—indeed the best bond which the most politic wits have found, to hold man's wit in well doing; for, as children must first by fear be induced to know that which after, when they do know, they are most glad of, so are these bugbears of opinions brought by great clerks into the world to serve as shewels° to keep them from those faults whereto else the vanity of the world and weakness of senses might pull them—but in you, niece, whose excellency is such as it need not to be held up by the staff of vulgar opinions, I would not you should love virtue servilely, for fear of I know not what which you see not, but even for the good effects of virtue which you see.

'Fear—and indeed, foolish fear—and fearful ignorance—was the first inventor of those conceits;° for when they heard it thunder, not knowing the natural cause, they thought there was some angry body above that spake so loud; and ever, the less they did perceive, the more they did conceive. Whereof they knew no cause, that grew straight a miracle—foolish folks, not marking that the alterations be but upon particular accidents, the universality being always one.

'Yesterday was but as today, and tomorrow will tread the same footsteps of his foregoers; so as it is manifest enough that all things follow but the course of their own nature—saving only man, who, while by the pregnancy of his imagination he strives to things supernatural, meanwhile he loseth his own natural felicity.

'Be wise, and that wisdom shall be a god unto thee; be contented, and that is thy heaven; for else, to think that those powers (if there be any such) above are moved either by the eloquence of our prayers or in a chafe by the folly of our actions carries as much reason as if flies should think that men take great care which of them hums sweetest, and which of them flies nimblest.'

She would have spoken further, to have enlarged and confirmed her discourse, but Pamela, whose cheeks were dyed in the beautifullest grain of virtuous anger, with eyes which glistered forth beams of disdain, thus interrupted her:

'Peace, wicked woman! Peace! Unworthy to breathe, that doest not acknowledge the breath giver; most unworthy to have a tongue, which speakest against him through whom thou speakest—keep your affection to yourself, which, like a bemired dog, would defile with fawning! You say yesterday was as today. O foolish woman, and most miserably foolish, since wit makes you foolish, what doth that argue but that there is a constancy in the everlasting governor?° Would you have an inconstant God, since we count a man foolish that is inconstant?

'He is not seen, you say. And would you think him a God who might be seen by so wicked eyes as yours—which yet might see enough, if they were not like such who, for sport sake, willingly hoodwink themselves to receive blows the easier? But though I speak to you without any hope of fruit in so rotten a heart, and there be nobody else here to judge of my speeches, yet be thou my witness, O captivity, that my ears shall not be willingly guilty of my creator's blasphemy.

'You say, because we know not the causes of things, therefore fear was the mother of superstition. Nay, because we know that each effect hath a cause, that hath engendered a true and lively devotion; for this goodly work of which we are, and in which we live, hath not his being by chance (on which opinion it is beyond marvel by what chance any brain could stumble!)—for if it be eternal as you would seem to conceive of it, eternity and chance are things unsufferable together, for that is chance-able which happeneth; and if it happen, there was a time before it happened when it might not have happened, or else it did not happen —and so, if° chanceable, not eternal: as now, being; then, not being.

'And as absurd it is to think that, if it had a beginning, his beginning was derived from chance, for chance could never make all things of nothing. And if there were substances before, which by chance should meet to make up this work, thereon follows another bottomless pit of absurdities—for then those substances must needs have been from ever, and so, eternal; and that eternal causes should bring forth chanceable effects is as sensible as that the sun should be the author of darkness.

'Again, if it were chanceable, then was it not necessary—whereby you take away all consequents. But we see in all things, in some respect or other, necessity of consequence; therefore, in reason, we must needs know that the causes were necessary.

'Lastly, chance is variable, or else it is not to be called chance—but we see this work is steady and permanent. If nothing but chance had glued those pieces of this all, the heavy parts would have gone infinitely downward, the light infinitely upward, and so never have met to have made up this goodly body; for before there was a heaven or an earth, there was neither a heaven to stay the height of the rising, nor an earth which, in respect of the round walls of heaven, should become a centre. Lastly, perfect order, perfect beauty, perfect constancy: if these be the children of chance, or fortune the efficient of these, let wisdom be counted the root of wickedness and eternity the fruit of her inconstancy.

'But you will say, "It is so by nature"—as much as if you said, "It is so, because it is so." If you mean, of many natures conspiring together, as in a popular government, to establish this fair estate—as if the elementish and ethereal parts should in their town-house set down the bounds of each one's office°—then consider what follows: that there must needs have been a wisdom which made them concur; for their natures being absolute contrary, in nature rather would have sought each other's ruin than have served as well-consorted parts to such an unexpressable harmony. For that contrary things should meet to make up a perfection, without a force and wisdom above their powers, is absolutely impossible —unless you will fly to that hissed-out opinion of chance again.

'But you may perhaps affirm that one universal nature, which hath been for ever, is the knitting together of these many parts to such an excellent unity. If you mean a nature of wisdom, goodness, and provi-dence, which knows what it doth, then say you that which I seek of you, and cannot conclude those blasphemies with which you defiled your mouth and mine ears. But if you mean a nature, as we speak of the fire which goeth upward, it knows not why, and of the nature of the sea which in ebbing and flowing seems to observe so just a dance, and yet understands no music, it is but still the same absurdity superscribed with another title. For this word "one", being attributed to that which is all, is but "one", mingling of many and many "ones" (as, in a less matter, when we say "one kingdom", which contains many cities, or "one city', which contains many persons), wherein the under-ones, if there be not a superior power and wisdom, cannot by nature regard to any preservation but of themselves (no more we see they do, since the water willingly quenches the fire and drowns the earth), so far are they from a conspired unity—but that a right heavenly nature, indeed as it were unnaturing them, doth so bridle them.

'Again, it is as absurd in nature that from an unity many contraries should proceed, still kept in an unity, as that from the number of contrarieties an unity should arise. I say still, if you banish both a singularity and plurality of judgement from among them, then (if so earthly a mind can lift itself up so high) do but conceive how a thing whereto you give the highest and most excellent kind of being, which is eternity, can be of the base and vilest degree of being, and next to a not-being—which is so to be as not to enjoy his own being.

'I will not here call all your senses to witness, which can hear nor see nothing which yields not most evident evidence of the unspeakableness of that wisdom. Each thing being directed to an end, and an end of preservation, so, proper effects of judgement, as speaking and laughing, are of mankind; but what mad fury can ever so inveigle any conceit as to see our mortal and corruptible selves to have a reason, and that this universality, whereof we are but the least pieces, should be utterly devoid thereof, as if one should say that one's foot might be wise, and himself foolish! This heard I once alleged against such a godless mind as yours, who being driven to acknowledge these beastly absurdities, that our bodies should be better than the whole world if it had the knowledge whereof the other were void, he sought (not able to answer directly) to shift it off in this sort: that if that reason were true, then must it follow also that the world must have in it a spirit that could write and read too, and be learned, since that was in us so commendable—wretched fool, not considering that books be but supplies of defects (and so are praised because they help our want) and therefore cannot be incident to the eternal intelligence, which needs no recording of opinions to confirm his knowledge, no more than the sun wants wax to be the fuel of his glorious lightfulness.

'This world, therefore, cannot otherwise consist but by a mind of wisdom which governs it, which, whether you will allow to be the creator thereof—as undoubtedly he is, or the soul and governor thereof, most certain it is that whether he govern all, or make all, his power is above either his creatures or his government. And if his power be above all things, then consequently it must needs be infinite, since there is nothing above it to limit it; for beyond which there is nothing must needs be boundless and infinite. If his power be infinite, then likewise must his knowledge be infinite, for else there should be an infinite proportion of power which he should not know how to use (the unsensibleness whereof, I think even you can conceive), and if infinite, then must nothing, no, not the estate of flies (which you with so unsavoury scorn did jest at) be unknown unto him; for if it were, then there were his knowledge bounded, and so, not infinite. If knowledge and power be infinite, then must needs his goodness and justice march in the same rank; for infiniteness of power and knowledge, without like measure of goodness, must necessarily bring forth destruction and ruin, and not ornament and preservation.

'Since, then, there is a God, and an all-knowing God so as he sees into the darkest of all natural secrets, which is the heart of man, and sees therein the deepest dissembled thoughts—nay, sees the thoughts before they be thought; since he is just to exercise his might, and mighty to perform his justice; assure thyself, most wicked woman, that hast so plaguily a corrupted mind as thou canst not keep thy sickness to thyself, but must most wickedly infect others, assure thyself, I say—for what I say depends of everlasting and unremovable causes—that the time will come when thou shalt know that power by feeling it, when thou shalt see his wisdom in the manifesting thy ugly shamefastness, and shalt only perceive him to have been a creator in thy destruction!'º

Thus she said; thus, she ended, with so fair a majesty of unconquered virtue that captivity might seem to have authority over tyranny, so foully was the filthiness of impiety discovered by the shining of her unstained goodness—so far, as either Cecropia saw indeed, or else the guilty amazement of a self-accusing conscience made her eyes untrue judges of their natural object: that there was a light more than human which gave a lustre to her perfections. But Cecropia, like a bat which, though it have eyes to discern that there is a sun, yet hath so evil eyes that it cannot delight in the sun, found a truth but could not love it; but, as great persons are wont to make the wrong they have done to be a cause to do the more wrong, her knowledge rose to no higher point but to envy a worthier, and her will was no otherwise bent but the more to hate, the more she found her enemy provided against her.

PSALMS

Psalm VI: Domine ne in furore

1. Lord, let not me, a worm, by thee be shent,
   While thou art in the heat of thy displeasure;
   Ne let thy rage of my due punishment
   Become the measure.

2. But mercy, Lord, let mercy thine descend,
   For I am weak, and in my weakness languish;
   Lord, help, for even my bones their marrow spend
   With cruel anguish.

3. Nay, even my soul fell troubles do appal;
   Alas, how long, God, wilt thou delay me?
4. Turn thee, sweet Lord, and from this ugly fall
   My dear God, stay me.

5. Mercy, O mercy, Lord, for mercy's sake,
   For death doth kill the witness of thy glory:
   Can of thy praise the tongues entombed make
   A heavenly story?

6. Lo, I am tired, while still I sigh and groan:
   My moistened bed proofs of my sorrow showeth;
   My bed, while I with black night mourn alone,
   With my tears floweth.

7. Woe, like a moth, my face's beauty eats,
   And age pulled on with pains all freshness fretteth,
   The while a swarm of foes with vexing feats°
   My life besetteth.

8. Get hence, you evil, who in my evil rejoice,
   In all whose works vainness is ever reigning;
   For God hath heard the weeping, sobbing voice
   Of my complaining.

9. The Lord my suit did hear, and gently hear;
   They shall be shamed and vexed, that breed my crying;
10. And turn their backs, and straight on backs appear
    Their shameful flying.

Psalm XIII: Usque quo Domine

1. How long, O Lord, shall I forgotten be?
       What? Ever?
   How long wilt thou thy hidden face from me
       Dissever?

2. How long shall I consult with careful sprite
       In anguish?
   How long shall I with foes' triumphant might
       Thus languish?

3. Behold me, Lord! Let to thy hearing creep
       My crying:
   Nay, give me eyes, and light,° lest that I sleep
       In dying.

4. Lest my foe brag, that in my ruin he
       Prevailed,
   And at my fall they joy that, troublous, me
       Assailed.

5. No, no, I trust in thee, and joy in thy
       Great pity;
   Still therefore of thy graces shall be my
       Song's ditty.

Psalm XXIII: Dominus regit me

1. The Lord, the Lord my shepherd is,
       And so can never I
           Taste misery.
2. He rests me in green pasture his;
       By waters still and sweet
           He guides my feet.

3. He me revives; leads me the way
       Which righteousness doth take,
           For his name's sake.
4. Yea, though I should through valleys stray
       Of death's dark shade, I will
           No whit fear ill.

For thou, dear Lord, thou me besett'st;°
 Thy rod and thy staff be
  To comfort me.
5. Before me thou a table sett'st,
 Even when foe's envious eye
  Doth it espy.

With oil thou dost anoint my head,
 And so my cup dost fill
  That it doth spill.
6. Thus, thus, shall all my days be fed;
 This mercy is so sure
  It shall endure,
And long, yea long, abide I shall
 There where the Lord of all
  Doth hold his hall.

Psalm XXIX: Afferte Domino

1. Ascribe unto the Lord of light
 Ye men of power, even by birthright,
 Ascribe all glory and all might.
2. Ascribe due glory to his name,
 And in his ever glorious frame
 Of sanctuary do the same.
3. His voice is on the waters found;
 His voice doth threatening thunders sound,
 Yea, through the waters doth resound.
4. The voice of that Lord ruling us
 Is strong, though he be gracious,
 And ever, ever, glorious.
5. By voice of high Jehovah we
 The highest cedars broken see,
 Even cedars which on Leban be;
6. Nay, like young calves in leaps are born,
 And Leban' self with nature's scorn,
 And Shirion like young unicorn.°
7. His voice doth flashing flames divide;
8. His voice have trembling deserts tried,
 Even deserts where the Arabs bide.

9. His voice makes hinds their calves to cast;
    His voice makes bald the forest waste;
    But in his church his fame is placed.
10. His justice seat the world sustains;
    Of furious floods he holds the reins;
    And this his rule for aye remains.
      God to his people strength shall give,
      That they in peace shall blessed live.

Psalm XXXVIII: Domine ne in furore

1. Lord, while that thy rage doth bide,
    Do not chide,
  Nor in anger chastise me;
2. For thy shafts have pierced me sore,
    And yet more,
  Still thy hands upon me be.

3. No sound part (caused by thy wrath)
    My flesh hath,
  Nor my sins let my bones rest;
4. For my faults are highly spread
    On my head,
  Whose foul weights have me oppressed.

5. My wounds putrefy and stink
    In the sink
6. Of my filthy folly laid;
  Earthly do I bow and crook
    With a look
  Still in mourning cheer arrayed.

7. In my reins° hot torment reigns;
    There remains
8. Nothing in my body sound;
  I am weak and broken sore,
    Yea, I roar,
  In my heart such grief is found.

9. Lord, before thee I do lay
    What I pray;
  My sighs are not hid from thee;

10. My heart pants, gone is my might;
      Even the light
    Of mine eyes abandons me.

11. From my plague kin, neighbour, friend
      Far off wend;
12. But who for my life do wait,
    They lay snares; they nimble be
      Who hunt me,
    Speaking evil, thinking deceit.

13. But I like a man become
      Deaf and dumb,
    Little hearing, speaking less;
14. I even as such kind of wight,
      Senseless quite,
    Word with word do not repress.

15. For on thee, Lord, without end
      I attend;
    My God, thou wilt hear my voice;
16. For I said, 'Hear, lest they be
      Glad on me
    Whom my fall doth make rejoice'.

17. Sure I do but halting go,
      And my woe
    Still my o'erthwart neighbour is.
18. Lo, I now to mourn begin
      For my sin,
    Telling mine iniquities.

19. But the while they live and grow
      In great show,
20. Many mighty wrongful foes
    Who do evil for good, to me
      Enemies be:
    Why? Because I virtue chose.

21. Do not, Lord, then me forsake,
      Do not take
22. Thy dear presence far from me;
    Haste, dear Lord, that I be stayed
      By thy aid;
    My salvation is in thee.

LETTERS

1

To Sir William Cecil

Right honourable: I am forced for better expedition to use an unaccustomed manner° of writing unto you: the cause proceeding from a report of some whom neither can I judge friendly to myself, nor yet indifferent towards him, from whom they seek by malice to prevent and detain his worthy preferment, sued for and obtained by his honourable benefactors, I mean my singular good lord my Lord of Leicester, and especially yourself, by whose favour (attained by the request of my friends, and his deserts towards me, assisted by the worthiness of his life and learning) Mr Thornton, my reader, hath unto him granted the next preferment of a canonry in this college of Christ Church. And sithence it hath pleased God (as I gave you humbly to understand in my last letters) to call unto his mercy one Thomas Day, by mean whereof it resteth in your honourable favour to present (according to your former pretence) him, as well for whose cause as divers others I do account myself no less bound than I ought. For that it is very constantly reported that Mr Toby Mathew's friends should use in his behalf some earnest suit, unworthy their callings (because it was moved before the death of the incumbent, by the which it should seem they sought rather by spite to prevent the one than honestly to prefer the other): these are therefore most humbly to request such your wonted favour as neither your honourable benefit may be revoked, my humble and earnest suit prevented, neither the person himself so discredited, but that he may with your favour enjoy his advowson,° by your means obtained, and yourself promised. Thus humbly commending my duty unto your good opinion, myself prest at your commandment, I humbly end. From Oxford, this 26th of February, *anno* 1569 [70].

> Yours in as humble sort as
> your own
> Philip Sidney.

2

To Hubert Languet

Your last letter was very welcome for many reasons, and especially for the kind love it showed towards me. I am glad that you approve of my decision to give up the study of astronomy; but as to geometry, I don't know what I ought to do. I very much wish to know about it, and all the more because I have always understood that it is much to the purpose in military matters; yet I shall give little attention to it, and shall only look through the lattice (so to say) at the first principles of it. Of Greek I wish to take in only enough for a proper understanding of Aristotle, for though translations are made almost every day I suspect that they do not express the author's meaning clearly and aptly enough. Besides, I am very much ashamed to be following the little sidestreams, as Cicero puts it, while disregarding the main sources.

Among Aristotle's works I think his *Politics* especially worth reading: I say this because your advice is to pay most attention to the *Ethics*.°

Of the German language, my dear Hubert, I absolutely despair, for it has (as you well know) a certain harshness, so that at my age I cannot hope ever to master it, or even to understand it; yet, in order to please you, I shall practise it with our friend Delius°—especially when I drink his health.

I readily admit that I am often more serious than I should be at my age or in my present circumstances, yet I know from experience that I am never less given to melancholy than when I am keenly applying the feeble powers of my mind to some arduous and difficult matter.

But enough of this. I am both pleased that you ask so urgently for my portrait (because this shows the sweet and long known love you have for me) and sad that you feel any doubt about making so trivial a request. For even if there were not between us such true and perfect friendship (which puts in the shade all ordinary affections, as the sun with the lesser lights), yet I have received from you what gives you a right to ask much bigger things than these. As soon as I return to Venice I shall have my portrait painted either by Paolo Veronese or by Tintoretto,° who hold by far the highest place in the art at present. As to your verses, although it is certainly a glorious thing to be praised by one who is so much praised himself, and though they are very pleasing to me, since they will testify to your undying affection for me, yet I am unwilling to be so seriously impudent as to arrange to have inscribed on my portrait such a proclamation of my praises, especially since I don't deserve them. Therefore excuse me from this, but in everything else give me your commands, and I shall satisfy you if I can. (Certainly the will shall not be lacking.)

Forgive a letter so full of blots and erasures, but I have been writing in haste. Farewell. Padua, 4 February 1574.

> Your very loving and respectful
> Philip Sidney.

Meanwhile I am glad to send you the portrait which Abondio made;° I shall send or bring him a gift. Again, farewell.

3   *To the Count of Hanau*

On returning to my own country, most noble lord, nothing seemed to me more important than to inform you of this as soon as I could. For you always showed me such kindness that I could not but think that everything that turned out well for me would be pleasing and welcome to you.

On the last day of May, then, with favourable winds I came to this island nest of ours, where I found all my family well, and the Queen, though a little advanced in years, still in vigorous health. This, since it is the will of God that our safety hangs by so slender a thread, is by our constant prayers commended to the care of the Almighty; for to us it is like the brand of Meleager, with whose extinction all our peace will perish.°

But to pass over these things: I ask and beseech you to believe that wherever I may be, you may be certain that I shall always remain the same in my strong and faithful love towards you.

I shall not detain your Excellency any longer: I have no news, but would ask that you will give my greetings to the good and wise lord Paul von Welsperg,° whom I strongly commend to you again and again, though, both because of his deserts and your good judgement, I know that this is superfluous. From London, 12th June 1575.

Your devoted friend,
Philip Sidney.

4   *To the Earl of Sussex*

Right honourable my very good Lord: I am bold to trouble your lordship with these few words, humbly to crave your lordship's favour so far unto me, as that it will please you to let me understand, whether I may with your lordship's leave, and that I may not offend in want of my service, remain absent from the Court this Christmas time.

Some occasions, both of health and otherwise,° do make me much desire it; but knowing how much my duty goes beyond any such causes makes me bold to beseech humbly your lordship to know your direction, which I will willingly follow, not only in those duties I am tied to, but in anything wherein I may be able to do your lordship service. I will no further trouble your lordship, but with the remembrance of my duty to your lordship and my lady and aunt; and so I humbly leave you both to the Eternal, who always prosper you. From Wilton, this 16th of December 1577.

Your lordship's humbly at comandment,
Philip Sidney.

I was bold of late to move your lordship in the case of the poor stranger musician.°

He hath already so far tasted of your lordship's goodness, as I am rather in his behalf humbly to thank your lordship; yet his case is such as I am much constrained to continue still a suitor to your lordship for him.

5   *To Hubert Languet*

Dearest Hubert: Robert Beale and Daniel Rogers and your friend Beuterich° have arrived together, bringing your most welcome letters, so that, to my very great pleasure, it was as if I both saw and heard you at one and the same time. You accuse me sharply of laziness, and at the same time you fall into the same fault and, indeed, a worse one, for your letters improve me, but mine can only seem empty chatter to you. And, as you can see, I have obviously lost the use of my pen; and my mind itself, even if it was ever of any worth, is beginning, through my wretched idleness, to lose strength without my noticing it. For why should our thoughts be aroused to various kinds of knowledge, unless we have some opportunity of exercising them so that some public benefit may result? But in an age of decay this is too much to be hoped for. Who learns music, except for pleasure? Or architecture, except for putting up buildings? But the mind itself, a particle of the divine mind (you will say) is cultivated in the same way. This, if we admit it, will be a very great advantage. But let us see if we are not giving a beautiful but false look to our splendid mistakes. For while the mind is thus, as it were, drawn out of itself, it cannot turn its keen sight inward to examine itself thoroughly, a task to which no other that men can undertake may be compared. Don't you see that I am playing the Stoic with some elegance? And indeed I shall be a Cynic° too, unless you call me back. And so, if you will, oppose me. I have shown you the field of battle: I now send an open declaration of war.

But I wonder, dearest Hubert, what you are thinking of, that, when I have as yet done nothing of which I can be proud, you wish me to be bound with the chains of matrimony; and yet you don't name any particular lady, but seem rather to extol the state of matrimony itself, though you have not yet given it your personal approval. Of that one of whom I readily admit I am not worthy,° I have already written to give my reasons, briefly indeed, but as well as I could.

At this present time I believe you have other thoughts in mind, and whatever they may be, I earnestly ask you to write to me, for everything that comes from you carries great weight with me. And, to be frank, I wonder whether someone relying on suspicions rather than on good judgement may have whispered to you something unfavourable about me; something which, though it did not convince you, yet you wished to disclose with the caution one expects in a friend, so that I might consider it. If this was so, please write about it to me openly, so that I may clear myself to you, by whom I wish to be most fully approved and acquitted. Even if it was only a joke or a piece of friendly advice, I ask you to let me know, since everything from you will be welcome no less than the things I hold most dear.

There is no news here, except what is new, and almost unheard of in a monarchy, that there is no news. Frobisher's gold has been melted and will not produce the greater wealth that at first it had promised.° However, the islands at 62° N. are not to be despised, but (as you know) they keep this a great secret, to prevent an opportunity being lost. Besides, they hope to be able to cross the straits at this same latitude: such nonsense is the great world as described by the cosmographers. But if there is open water in such a climate, you can see that this will be of the greatest importance.°

I believe the Queen will do what you wrote about to me in thanks to Prince Casimir,° but I do not wish to say much about that at present, since I know it is our disposition not to conclude anything quickly. What else can I write to you—for I am almost half asleep—except to say that I love you as my heart, and that I desire nothing so much as to show you this some time. My friend Greville sends his greetings. Give my humble greetings to Count and Countess Hanau, and let me know if they are pleased with the dogs I sent them. I have written to Lobbet, de Banos, Andreas Paull, Anselm, Metellus° . . . am I then so lazy? Please give my greetings to Charles de l'Ecluse,° and tell master Salvart° that I am much indebted to him for the book he sent me in a French translation. I was very busy when it was given to me, but some time I shall deserve this kindness of his. Give many good wishes to master von Glauberg,° to whom I shall gladly give my thanks. Farewell, dearest Languet. London, 1 March 1578. Yours,

Philip Sidney.

I shall give Beale every friendly service that I can, both for his own deserts, and especially for your recommendation of him.

6 *To Edmund Molyneux*

Mr Molyneux: Few words are best. My letters to my father have come to the eyes of some: neither can I condemn any but you for it. If it be so, you have played the very knave with me; and so I will make you know if I have good proof of it. But that for so much as is past. For that is to come, I assure you before God, that if ever I know you do so much as read any letter I write to my father, without his commandment or my consent, I will thrust my dagger into you. And trust to it, for I speak it in earnest. In the mean time, farewell. From Court, this last of May 1578.

By me

Philip Sidney.

7 *To Robert Sidney*

My good brother: you have thought unkindness, I have not written oftener to you; and have desired I should write something of my opinion touching your travel, you being persuaded my experience therein to be something: which I must needs confess, but not as you take it. For you think my experience grows of the good things I have learned, but I know the only experience I have gotten is to find how much indeed I might have learned and how much indeed I have missed, for want of having directed my course to the right end and by the right means.

I think you have read Aristotle's *Ethics*: if you have, you know it is the beginning and foundation of all his works, the good end to which every man doth and ought to bend his smallest and greatest actions.° I am sure you have imprinted in your mind the scope and mark you mean by your pains to shoot at. For if you should travel but to travel, or to say you had travelled, certainly you should prove a pilgrim to no saint. But I presume so well of you, that though a great number of us never thought in ourselves why we went, but only of a certain tickling humour to do as another man had done; your purpose is, being a gentleman born, to furnish yourself with the knowledge of such things as may be serviceable to your country, and fit for your calling; which certainly stands not in the change of air, for the warmest sun makes not a wise man; nor in learning languages (although they be of good serviceable use), for words are but words, in what language soever they be; and much less in that all of us come home full of disguisements, not only of our apparel, but of our countenances, as though the credit of a traveller stood all upon his outside; but in the right informing your mind with those things which are most notable in those places which you come unto. Of which, as the one kind is so vain, as I think ere it be long, like the magnificoes in Italy, we travellers shall be made sport of in comedies;° so may I justly say, who rightly travels with the eye of Ulysses doth take one of the most excellent ways of worldly wisdom. For hard, sure, it is to know England without you know it by comparing it with others; no more than a man can know the swiftness of his horse without seeing him well matched. For you that are a logician know that as greatness of itself is a quantity, so yet the judgement of it, as of might, riches and all other strengths, stands in the predicament of relation;° so that you cannot tell what the Queen of England is able to do defensively or offensively, but by thorough comparing what they are able to do with whom she is to be matched.

This, therefore, is one notable use of travel, which stands in the mixed and correlative knowledge of things: in which kind comes in the knowledge of all leagues betwixt prince and prince: the topographical description of each country; how the one lies by situation to hurt or help the other; how they are to the sea; well harboured, or not; how stored with ships; how with revenue; how with fortifications and garrisons; how the people, war-like trained, or kept under; with many other such considerations which, as they confusedly come into my mind, so I, for want of leisure, hastily set them down. But these things, as I said, are they of the first kind, which stands in the balancing of one thing with the other.

The other kind of knowledge is of them which stand in the things which are in themselves either simply good, or simply evil; and so either serve for a right instruction, or a shunning example. Of these Homer meant in this verse, *Qui multos hominum mores cognovit et urbes*:° for he doth not mean by '*mores*', how to look or put off one's cap with a new found grace (although truly behaviour is not to be despised: marry, my heresy is that the English behaviour is best in England, and the Italians' in Italy): but '*mores*' he takes for that whereout 'moral philosophy' is so called, which contains the true discerning of men's minds, both in virtues, passions and vices; and when he saith '*cognovit urbes*', if I be not deceived, he means not to have seen towns and marked their buildings (for surely houses are houses in every place—they do but differ *secundum maius et minus*): but he intends the knowing of religions, policies, laws, bringing up of children, discipline, both for war and peace; and such like

I take to be of the second kind, which are ever worthy to be known for their own sakes. As surely, in the Turk, though we have nothing to do with him, yet his discipline in war-matters is *propter se*° worthy to be learned. Nay, even in the kingdom of China, which is almost as far as our Antipodes from us, their good laws and customs are to be learned: but to know their riches or power is of little purpose for us, since it can neither advantage nor hinder us. But in our neighbour countries both these things are to be marked, as well as the latter, which construe things for themselves, as the former, which seeks to know how both those and their riches etcetera may be to us available or otherwise.

The countries fittest for both these are those you are going unto: France, above all other, most needful for us to mark, especially in the former kind; next it Spain and the Low Countries; then Germany, which in my opinion excels all the other, as much in the latter consideration as the other do it in the former; yet neither are void of either. For as Germany (methinks) doth notably excel in good laws and well administering of justice; so yet are we likewise to consider in it the many princes with whom we may have league,° the places of trade, and the mean to draw both soldiers and furniture from thence in time of need. So of the other side, as in France and Spain, we are principally to mark how they stand towards us both in power and inclination; so are they not without good and fit things, even in the generality of wisdom to be known: as, in France, the Courts of parliament, their subaltern jurisdiction, and their continual keeping of paid soldiers; in Spain, their good and grave proceeding, their keeping so many provinces under them, and by what means, with the true points of honour. Wherein, sure, they have the most open conceit, wherein if they seem over curious, it is an easy matter to cut off, when a man sees to the bottom. Flanders likewise, besides the neighbourhood with us, and the annexed considerations thereto, hath divers things to be learned, especially their governing their merchants and other trades. As for Italy, I know not what we have or can have to do with them, but to buy their silks and wines. And as for other provinces (except Venice, whose good laws and customs we can hardly proportion to ourselves, because they are quite of a contrary government) there is little there but tyrannous oppression and servile yielding to them that have little or no rule over them. And for the men you shall have there, although indeed some be excellently learned, yet are they all given so to counterfeit learning, as a man shall learn among them more false grounds of things than in any place else that I know. For from a tapster upward they are all discoursers.° In certain qualities, as horsemanship, weapons, vaulting and such, are better there than in the other countries;

but for the other matters, as well, if not better, you shall have them in those nearer places.

Now resteth in my memory but this point, which indeed is the chief to you of all others, which is the choice of what men you are to direct yourself unto to learn those things: for it is certain no vessel can leave a worse taste in the liquor it contains, than a wrong teacher infects an unskilful hearer with that which hardly will ever after out. I will not tell you the absurdities I have heard some travellers tell, I dare swear, from the mouths of some of their hosts. Be sure therefore of his knowledge, of whom you desire to learn; taste him well before you drink too much of his doctrine. And when you have heard it, try well what you have heard before you hold it for a principle, for one error is the mother of a thousand. But you may say, 'How shall I get excellent men to take pains to speak with me?' Truly, in few words, either with much expense,° or much humbleness.

Your assured loving brother,
Philip Sidney.

8   *To my wellbeloved friend Mr Edward Denny*

My Ned: That you love me is no news unto me, having received so notable proofs of it; but yet is the remembrance always exceedingly grateful. And very willingly do I bear the preferring of Lord Grey,° since so I prefer him to myself, as I will ever be most glad to do him service with affectionate honour, which, truly, I am to very few. And if you should do otherwise, instead of thanking you I should doubt you might in like sort dispense with yourself to set me behind some other, of less both acquaintance and worth. Honour him, therefore, still, and as you match me with him, so therein will I match myself with you. And continue, my good Edward, in loving of me, or else I shall be a loser by you.

You will me to tell you my mind of the directing your studies. I will do it as well as the haste of your boy, and my little judgement, will able me. But first let me rejoice with you, that since the unnoble constitution of our time doth keep us from fit employments,° you do yet keep yourself awake with the delight of knowledge; one of the notablest effects of that which makes us differ from beasts.° Resolve therefore upon that still, and resolve thus: that whensoever you may justly say to yourself you lose your time, you do indeed lose so much of your life: since of life (though the material description of it be the body and soul) the consideration and marking of it stands only in time. Neither let us leave off because perchance the right price of these things is not had, without we should wish ourselves asses because some folks know not what a man means. But to your purpose I must say this: if I should generally discourse of knowledge, what it is, how many kinds, which worthy, which not, I might build upon a large ground, and yet leave you unsatisfied, and myself wander beyond mine own reach. This no doubt is true, that such is to human minds the infiniteness of them, that to swallow them up is impossible. Well may a man be swallowed in them, and fruitlessly, if he have not the better line to guide him in the labyrinth. The consideration therefore must be particular, and particularly bent to yourself; for one thing is fit to be known by a scholar that will read in the schools, and another by Ned Denny: and even in Ned Denny, one way to have been begun if you were a child, and another of this age you now pass in.° If you were young, surely the tongues of Latin and Greek (which be as it were the treasure houses of learning) and the art of logic (which indeed helps much to try the value of each thing) were exactly to be desired: and such like, which now, without a miraculous wit, and blessing of God, would bring forth as vain a labour° as if a man that must fight tomorrow, would only study how to send for a good sword into Spain.° To my Ned Denny therefore, and even so to myself (for I do in this with you, as we do to one another in horsemanship: teach before we have well learned): this I think may be the course, to know what it is we desire to know. And that I think to be double, the one as concerning ourselves, the other an outward application of ourselves. The knowledge of ourselves no doubt ought to be most precious unto us; and therein the Holy Scriptures, if not the only, are certainly the incomparable lantern in this fleshly darkness of ours. For (alas!) what is all knowledge, if in the end of this little and wearisome pilgrimage, Hell become our schoolmaster? They, therefore, are diligently to be read. To them if you will add as to the help of the second table (I mean that which contains the love of thy neighbour, and dealing betwixt man and man) some parts of moral philosophy, I think you shall do very wisely. For in truth oftentimes we err, thinking we do well, as long as we mean well, where indeed want of knowledge may make us do as much wickedness (though not so wickedly) as they which even pretencedly commit all naughtiness. Thereout, therefore, may we seek what it is to be truly just, truly valiant, rightly temperate, and rightly friendly, with their annexed qualities and contraries. And thereof are many books written; but to my pleasing Aristotle's *Ethics*° pass;° but he is something dark, and hath need of a logical examination. Tully's *Offices*° next, if not equal, and truly for you and myself, beyond any. With him you may join some of Plutarch's discourses,° as of *Refraining anger*, *Of*

Curiosity, Of the Tranquillity of the mind, Of the Flatterer and the Friend, Of Moral Virtue, and so by pieces, as your leisure serves. But let Tully be for that matter your foundation, next to the foundation of scripture. And when you have read these, we will confer further. The second part consists, as it were, in the trade of our lives. For a physician must study one thing, and a lawyer another; but to you that with good reason bend yourself to soldiery, what books can deliver stands in the books that profess the art, and in histories. The first shows what should be done, the other what hath been done. Of the first sort is Languet in French and Machiavel in Italian,° and many other whereof I will not take upon me to judge; but this I think, if you will study them, it shall be necessary for you to exercise your hand in setting down what you read, as in descriptions of battalions, camps, and marches, with some practice of arithmetic, which sportingly you may exercise. Of them I will say no further, for I am witness of mine own ignorance. For historical matters, I would wish you before you began to read a little of Sacrobosco's *Sphere*,° and the geography of some modern writer, whereof there are many, and is a very easy and delightful study. You have already very good judgement of the sea maps,° which will make the other much the easier; and provide yourself of an Ortelius,° that when you read of any place, you may find it out, and have it as it were before your eyes, for it doth exceedingly confirm both the judgement and memory. So much of this as I account necessary for you is to be done in a month space, or little more, for I do not wish an artificer's wading into it. Then, for the histories themselves, gladly I would wish you should read the Greek and Roman writers, for they were the wisest and fullest of excellent examples, both of disciplines and stratagems; and then would I tell you, you should begin with Philip Melanchthon's Chronology, so to Justin, then to Herodotus, Thucydides, Xenophon, Diodorus Siculus, Quintus Curtius, Polybius, Livy, Dionysius, Sallust, Caesar, Dion, Tacitus, and then the Emperor's lives, gathered together in a volume by Henricus Stephanus.° Then to take Zonaras and Nicetas, for the Greek parts, and Procopius; and from thence, to fall lower, to the particular chronicles of each country, as Paulus Aemilius for France, Polydore for England, and so of the rest. But because this might seem too long, though indeed not so long as a man would think, my counsel to you is even to begin with our English *Chronicle*,° set out by Holinshed, which you should read through until you came to Edward the Third's life; then to take Froissart, after him Anguerard of Monstrelet,° written in old French; after him, Philippe de Commines, and then Guicciardin, who reacheth almost to our time. And these will serve your turn for historical matters.

But now may you ask me: 'What shall I do first?' Truly, in my opinion, an hour to your Testament, and a piece of one to Tully's *Offices*, and that with study. Plutarch's discourses you may read with more ease. For the other matters, allot yourself another hour for Sacroboscus and Valerius,° or any other of geography, and when you have satisfied yourself in that, take your history of England, and your Ortelius to know the places you read of; and so in my conceit you shall pass both pleasantly and profitably. Your books of the art of soldiery must have another hour, but before you go to them you shall do well to use your hand in drawing of a plot, and practice of arithmetic. Whether now you will do these by piecemeal, all in a day, or first go through with one, you must be your own judge, as you find your memory best serve. To me, the variety rather delights me than confounds me.

Thus, not as a general doctrine, but as I think it best for thee, my own Ned, have I spent more lines than I thought to have done words; but good will carries me on to this impudence, to write my counsel to him that (to say nothing of yourself) hath my Lord Grey's company;° which now I will end with these two remembrances:

1. that you forget not to note what you conceive of that you read; and

2. that you remember with your good voice to sing my songs,° for they will one well become another.

My Lord of Pembroke, my sister, and your charge thank you with many thanks, and your cakes are reserved against all the parish come to dinner. Remember your last promise, and farewell from my heart. At Wilton, this Whit Sunday. 1580.

> Your master in name but true friend indeed,
> Philip Sidney.

9   *To the Earl of Leicester*

Right honourable and singular my good Lord: I have now brought home my sister, who is well amended both of her pain and disease. For myself, I assure your lordship upon my troth, so full of the cold as one cannot hear me speak: which is the cause keeps me yet from Court, since my only service is speech, and that is stopped. As soon as I have gotten any voice I will wait on your lordship, if so it please you. Although it be contrary to that I have signified to her Majesty of her want, I doubt not her Majesty will vouchsafe to ask for me, but so long as she sees a silk doublet upon me her Highness will think me in good case. At my departure I desired Mr Vice Chamberlain he would tell her Majesty necessity did even banish me from the place. And, always submitting myself to your judgement and commandment, I think my best, either constantly to wait, or constantly to hold the course of my poverty,° for coming and going neither breeds desert, not witnesseth necessity. Yet if so it please your lordship, I hope within three or four days this cold will be passed, for now truly I were a very unpleasant company keeper. My Lord and my sister do humbly salute you, and I remain to do your commandment as far as my life shall enable me. God preserve your lordship in all happines. At Clarendon,° this 2nd of August, 1580.

> Your lordship's most humble and most obedient
> Philip Sidney.

10   *To Robert Sidney*

My dear brother: for the money you have received, assure yourself (for it is true) there is nothing I spend so pleaseth me as that which is for you. If ever I have ability you will find it; if not, yet shall not any brother living be better beloved than you of me. I cannot write now to H. White,° do you excuse me. For his nephew,° they are but passions in my father, which we must bear with reverence; but I am sorry he should return till he had the fruit of his travel, for you shall never have such a servant as he would prove, use your own discretion therein. For your countenance,° I would for no cause have it diminished in Germany; in Italy your greatest expense must be upon worthy men, and not upon householding. Look to your diet (sweet Robin), and hold up your heart in courage and virtue. Truly, great part of my comfort is in you. I know not myself what I meant by bravery in you, so greatly you may see I condemn you; be careful of yourself, and I shall never have cares. I have written to Mr Savile,° I wish you kept still together, he is an excellent man; and there may if you list pass good exercises betwixt you and Mr Neville,° there is great expectation of you both.

For the method of writing history, Bodin hath written at large; you may read him, and gather out of many words some matter.° This I think in haste: a story is either to be considered as a story, or as a treatise, which besides that addeth many things for profit and ornament. As a story, he is nothing but a narration of things done, with the beginnings, causes, and appendences thereof. In that kind, your method must be to have *seriem temporum*° very exactly, which the chronologies of Melanchthon, Tarchagnota, Languet and such other will help you to. Then to consider by that . . . as you not yourself, Xenophon to follow Thucydides, so doth

Thucydides follow Herodotus, and Diodorus Siculus follow Xenophon. So generally do the Roman stories follow the Greek, and the particular stories of present monarchies follow the Roman. In that kind you have principally to note the examples of virtue or vice, with their good or evil successes; the establishment or ruins of great states, with their causes; the time and circumstances of the laws they write of; the enterings and endings of wars, and therein the stratagems against the enemy, and the discipline upon the soldier, and thus much as a very historiographer. Besides this, the historian makes himself a discourser, for profit, and an orator, yea, a poet, sometimes, for ornament: an orator, in making excellent orations *e re nata*,° which are to be marked, but marked with the note of rhetorical remembrances; a poet, in painting forth the effects, the motions, the whisperings of the people, which though in disputation one might say were true, yet who will mark them well shall find them taste of a poetical vein, and in that kind are gallantly to be marked, for though perchance they were not so, yet it is enough they might be so. The last point which tends to teach profit is of a 'discourser', which name I give to whosoever speaks *non simpliciter de facto, sed de qualitatibus et circumstantiis facti*:° and that is it which makes me and many others rather note much with our pen than with our mind, because we leave all these discourses to the confused trust of our memory, because they being not tied to the tenor of a question; as philosophers' use sometimes plays the divine in telling his opinion and reasons in religion, sometimes the lawyer, in showing the causes and benefits of laws; sometimes a natural philosopher, in setting down the causes of any strange thing which the story binds him to speak of; but most commonly a moral philosopher, either in the ethic part, when he sets forth virtues or vices and the natures of passions; or in the politic, when he doth (as often he doth) meddle sententiously with matters of state. Again, sometimes he gives precept of war, both offensive and defensive; and so lastly, not professing any art, as his matter leads him he deals with all arts; which, because it carrieth the life of a lively example, it is wonderful what light it gives to the arts themselves, so as the great civilians help themselves with the discourses of historians, so do soldiers, and even philosophers and astronomers. But that I wish herein, is this: that when you read any such thing, you straight bring it to his head, not only of what art, but by your logical subdivisions, to the next members and parcel of the art.° And so as in a table, be it witty words, of which Tacitus is full; sentences, of which Livy; or similitudes, whereof Plutarch; straight to lay it up in the right place of his storehouse, as either military, or more specially defensive military, or more particularly defensive by fortification; and so lay it up. So likewise in politic matters; and such a little table you may easily make, wherewith I would have you ever join the historical part, which is only the example of some stratagem, or good counsel, or such like.

This write I to you in great haste, of method, without method; but with more leisure and study (if I do not find some book that satisfies) I will venture to write more largely of it to you. Mr Savile will with ease help you to set down such a table of remembrance to yourself, and for your sake I perceive he will do much; and if ever I be able I will deserve it of him. Only one thing, as it comes unto my mind, let me remember you of: that you consider wherein the historian excelleth, and that to note: as Dionysius° in the searching the secrets of government; Tacitus, in the pithy opening the venom of wickedness; and so of the rest. My time exceedingly short will suffer me to write no more leisurely. Stephen° can tell, who stands with me while I am writing.

Now, dear brother, take delight likewise in the mathematicals, Mr Savile is excellent in them. I think you understand the sphere; if you do, I care little for any more astronomy in you. Arithmetic and geometry I would wish you well seen in, so as both in number and measure you might have a feeling and active judgement. I would you did bear the mechanical instruments wherein the Dutch . . .

I write this to you as one that, for myself, have given over the delight in the world; but wish to you as much if not more than to myself. So you can speak and write Latin not barbarously, I never require great study in Ciceronianism, the chief abuse of Oxford, *Qui dum verba sectantur, res ipsas negligunt.*° My toyfull book° I will send, with God's help, by February, at which time you shall have your money. And for 200£ a year, assure yourself, if the state of England remain, you shall not fail of; use it to your best profit. My Lord of Leicester sends you forty pounds, as I understand by Stephen, and promiseth he will continue that stipend yearly, at the least, and that is above commons. In any case write largely and diligently unto him, for in truth I have good proof that he means to be every way good unto you. The odd 30£ shall come with the hundred, or else my father and I will jarl.

Now, sweet brother, take a delight to keep and increase your music; you will not believe what a want I find of it in my melancholy times. At horsemanship, read Grison, Claudio, and a book that is called *La gloria del cavallo*° withal, that you may join the thorough contemplation of it with the exercise, and so shall you profit more in a month than others in a year; and mark the bitting, saddling and curing of horses. I would, by the way, your worship would learn a better hand, you write worse than I, and I write evil enough. Once again, have a care of your diet, and consequently of your complexion: remember, *gratior est veniens in pulchro corpore virtus.*°

Now, sir, for news, I refer myself to this bearer; he can tell you how idly we look on our neighbours' fires, and nothing is happened notable at home, save only Drake's return,° of which yet I know not the secret points; but about the world he hath been, and rich he is returned. Portugal we say is lost.° And to conclude, my eyes are almost closed up, overwatched with tedious business. God bless you, sweet boy, and accomplish the joyful hope I conceive of you. Once again, commend me to Mr Neville, Mr Savile and honest Harry White, and bid him be merry. When you play at weapons I would have you get thick caps and bracers,° and play out your play lustily, for indeed ticks and dalliances° are nothing in earnest; for the time of the one and the other greatly differs; and use as well the blow as the thrust, it is good in itself, and besides exerciseth your breath and strength, and will make you a strong man at the tourney and barriers. First, in any case, practise the single sword, and then with the dagger; let no day pass without an hour or two such exercise; the rest study, or confer diligently, and so shall you come home to my comfort and credit.

Lord, how I have babbled! Once again, farewell, dearest brother. At Leicester House this 18 of October 1580.

Your most loving and careful brother
Philip Sidney.

11   *To William Temple*

Good Mr Temple: I have received both your book and letter, and think myself greatly beholding unto you for them. I greatly desire to know you better, I mean by sight; for else your writings make you as well known as my knowledge can reach unto; and this assure yourself, Mr Temple, that while I live you shall have me ready to make known by my best power that I bear you good will, and greatly esteem those things I conceive in you. When you come to London or Court I pray you let me see you; meanwhile use me boldly, for I am beholding. God keep you well. At Court this 23th of May 1584.

Your loving friend
Philip Sidney.

12   *To Sir Francis Walsingham*

Right honourable: I receive divers letters from you, full of the discomfort which I see, and am sorry to see, that you daily meet with at home,° and I think, such is the good will it pleaseth you to bear me that part of my trouble is something that troubles you: but I beseech you, let it not. I had before cast my count of danger, want and disgrace, and before God, sir, it is true that in my heart the love of the cause doth so far over-balance them all that, with God's grace, they shall never make me weary of my resolution. If her Majesty were the fountain, I would fear, considering what I daily find, that we should wax dry;° but she is but a means which God useth, and I know not whether I am deceived, but I am faithfully persuaded that if she should withdraw herself other springs would rise to help this action. For methinks I see the great work indeed in hand, against the abusers of the world, wherein it is no greater fault to have confidence in man's power, than it is too hastily to despair of God's work. I think a wise and constant man ought never to grieve while he doth play, as a man may say, his own part truly, though others be out;° but if himself leave his hold because other mariners will be idle, he will hardly forgive himself his own fault. For me, I cannot promise of my own course, no, nor that of the mi . . . , because I know there is a higher power that must uphold me, or else I shall fall; but certainly I trust I shall not by other men's wants be drawn from myself.

Therefore, good sir, to whom for my particular I am more bound than to all men besides, be not troubled with my trouble, for I have seen the worst in my judgement beforehand, and worse than that cannot be. If the Queen pay not her soldiers she must lose her garrison, there is no doubt thereof.

But no man living shall be able to say the fault is in me. What relief I can do them, I will. I will spare no danger if occasion serve; I am sure no creature shall be able to lay injustice to my charge, and for further doubts, truly, I stand not upon them. I have written by Adams° to the Council: plainly thereof let them determine. It hath been a costly beginning unto me this war, by reason I had nothing proportioned unto it; my servants unexperienced, and myself every way unfurnished, and no helps; but hereafter, if the war continue, I shall pass much better through with it. For Bergen op Zoom, I delighted in it, I confess, because it was near the enemy, but especially having a very fair house in it,° and an excellent air, I destinied it for my wife. But finding how you deal there, and that ill payment in my absence thence might bring forth some mischief, and considering how apt the Queen is to interpret everything to my disadvantage, I have resigned it to my lord Willoughby, my very friend, and indeed a frank and valiant gentleman, and fit for that place. Therefore I pray you to know that so much of my regality is fallen. I understand I am called very ambitious and proud at home: but certainly if they knew my heart they would not altogether so judge me.° I wrote to you a letter by William, my Lord of Leicester's jesting player,° enclosed in a letter to my wife, and I never had answer thereof; it contained something to my Lord of Leicester, and counsel that some way might be taken to stay my Lady there.° I since find that the knave delivered the letters to my Lady of Leicester, but whether she sent them to you or know I know not, but earnestly desire to do, because I doubt there is more interpreted thereof. Mr Errington° is with me at Flushing, and therefore I think myself more at rest, having a man of his reputation; but I assure you sir, in good earnest, I find Borlas° another manner of man than he is taken . . . I expected. I would to God Burnham° could obtain his suit. He is honest, but somewhat discomforted with consideration of his estate. Turner° was good for nothing, and worst for the sound of the harquebuse.° We shall have a sore war upon us this summer, wherein if appointment had been kept and these disgraces foreborne, which have greatly weakened us, we had been victorious. I can say no more at this time, but pray for your long and happy life. At Utrecht, this 24th of March 1586.

Your humble son
Ph. Sidney.

I know not what to say to my wife's coming till you resolve better; for if you run a strange course I may take such a one here as will not be fit for any of the feminine gender. I pray you make much of Nichol Gorge.° I have [been] vilely deceived for armours for our horsemen. If you could speedily send me any . . . of your armoury, I will send them you as soon as my own be finished. There was never so good a father had a more troublesome son.

Send Sir William Pelham,° good sir, and let him have Clerk's place,° for we need no clerks here, and it is most necessary to have such a one in the Council.

13   *To Justus Lipsius*

Dear Lipsius: I am sorry that you are leaving us, and all the more because I am afraid that the reason for this lies rather in boredom with those affairs than in your health. If this is so, and if you don't entirely give up hope of this England of ours, I beg you in the name of our friendship that you will think about moving there. The terms which I once obtained for you I shall get confirmed, so that even if I die they will not lapse. I know that you will be most welcome to our Queen and to many others —indeed, to all others—and that you may rely on my good faith. The journey will not be unpleasant for you; if only for the sake of your health you visit those spas, may the Muses themselves attend you so that you may return, and not leave us who truly love you. When you have returned as we wish we shall discuss things further. At present I am almost overwhelmed by the floods of those affairs. I have acted for Buys° and will continue to do so since this is your wish. Certainly I am sorry for the man, though I am under no obligation to him. I would be glad to think him restless rather than faithless.

We struggle against many difficulties. I believe it is the will of God to temper things for his people so that we have neither triumph nor disaster.

My pen and I cannot stay any longer with you. Love me, and farewell. Yours sincerely,

Ph. Sidney.

Deventer 14 September 1586.

14   *To Sir Francis Walsingham*

Right honourable: this bearer, Richard Smith, her Majesty's old servant, hath my Lord of Leicester his letters directed unto you in his favour, for his suit to her Majesty, and therewithal requesteth mine, hoping your honour will the rather help him. I beseech you therefore the rather at my request to help him, and be the good mean for the poor man's prefer-ment, having so long served, and now being aged and weak, hath such need of this or such other good mean for his relief, as without it he may rest, as I hear, in more misery than the desert of so long service requireth. I commend him and his cause to your honour good favour and help; and so I humbly take my leave. From the camp at Zutphen this 22 of September 1586.

Your humble son
Ph. Sidney.

15   *To Johan Wyer*

My dear Wyer: Come. Come. My life is in danger and I long to see you. Whether I live or die I shall not be ungrateful. I cannot write more but with what strength I have I beg you to hasten to me. Farewell. Arnhem. Yours

Philip Sidney.

APPENDICES

A. [Henry Goldwell], *A Declaration of the Triumph showed before the Queen's Majesty and the French ambassadors on Whitsun Monday and Tuesday.*

TO BEGIN particularly to write of these attempts, and briefly to run over each several action, the cause of the same is first to be considered. After the arrival of the French ambassadors,° and upon their coming to the English Court, the nobles and gentlemen of the same, desirous to show them all courtesy possible, fittest for such estates, and to sport them with all courtly pleasure, agreed among them to prepare a Triumph, which was very quickly concluded; and being devised in most sumptuous order, was by them performed in as valiant a manner, to their endless fame and honour. The chief, or challengers, in these attempts, were these:

The Earl of Arundel, the Lord Windsor, Master Philip Sidney, and Master Fulke Greville, who, calling themselves the 'Four foster children of Desire', made their invention of the foresaid 'Triumph' in this order and form following.

The gallery, or place at the end of the Tiltyard adjoining to her Majesty's house at Whitehall, whereas her person should be placed, was called, and not without cause, the Castle or Fortress of Perfect Beauty, for as much as her highness should be there included; whereto the said foster children laid title and claim, as their due by descent to belong unto them. And upon denial or any repulse from that their desired patrimony they vowed to vanquish and conquer by force who so should seem to withstand it. For the accomplishing whereof they sent their challenge or first defiance to the Queen's Majesty, which was uttered by a boy on Sunday, the sixteenth of April last, as her Majesty came from the Chapel; who, being apparrelled in red and white,° as a martial messenger of Desire's fostered children, without making any precise reverence at all, uttered these speeches of defiance from his masters to her Majesty, the effect whereof ensueth:

'O Lady, that doth entitle the titles you possess with the honour of your worthiness, rather crowning the great crown you hold, with the fame to have so excelling an owner, than you receiving to yourself any increase, keeping that outward ornament: vouchsafe with patient attention to hear the words which I by commandment am here to deliver unto you, wherein, if your ears (used to the thanksgiving of your people and the due praises of the earth) shall feel a stately disdain to hear once the sound of a defy, yet dare I warrant myself so far upon the reply-deceiving show of rare beauty, as that malice cannot fall from so fair a mind upon the silly messenger, whose mouth is a servant to others' direction. Know ye, therefore, all-only Princess, that hereby (for far off they are never) there lies encamped the four long hapless, now hopeful, fostered children of Desire: who, having been a great while nourished up with that infective milk, and too too much care of their fiery fosterer (though full oft that dry nurse, Despair, endeavoured to

wean them from it) being now as strong in that nurture, as they are weak in
fortune, encouraged with the valiant counsel of never fainting Desire, and by the
same assured that by right of inheritance, even from ever, the Fortress of Beauty
doth belong to her fostered children; lastly, finding it blazed by all tongues,
engraved in all hearts, and proved by all eyes, that this fortress built by nature is
seated in this realm: these four I say, and say again, thus nourished, thus
animated, thus entitled, and thus informed, do will you by me, even in the name of
Justice, that you will no longer exclude virtuous Desire from perfect Beauty.
Whereto if you yield (O yield, for so all reason requireth!) then have I no more to
say, but rejoice that my sayings hath obtained so rightful, and yet so blissful, a
request. But if (alas, but let that not be needful!) Beauty be accompanied with
disdainful Pride, and Pride waited on by refusing Cruelty: then must I denounce
unto you (woe is me, answer, before it be denounced!) that they determine by
request to accomplish their claim. And because they will better testify to the world
they have been brought up under the wings of honourable Desire, this honourable forewarning they send you: that upon the 24 day of this month of April they
will besiege that fatal Fortress, vowing not to spare (if this obstinacy continue) the
sword of faithfulness, and the fire of affection. Now, if it so fall out the worthy
knights of your Court (moved with passion in themselves) disdain of my sender's
boldness, or partial liking (which I most doubt) to the majesty of your eyes will
either bid them battle before they approach, or, suffering them to approach,
will after labour to levy the siege; they protest to meet them in what sort they will
choose, wishing only it may be performed before your own eyes, whom they know
as even in judging, as dainty in choosing where if so they list: first at the tilt, in so
many courses as yourself shall please to appoint. And then if any will call them to
the course of the field with lance and sword,° they hope to give such true proofs of
their valour as at least shall make their desires more noble, vowing, on the other
side, that if before the night part the fray they do not overcome all them that come
in against them, they will yield themselves slaves unto you for ever.

Thus° therefore, O Queen (greater in that you are queen of yourself, than in
passing the whole compass of the earth) have I delivered my charge, not as a
challenge to your knights, against whom (but in so just a cause) they acknowledge
themselves unable to match the meanest, but as a plain proclamation of war,
unless the Fortress of Beauty, that hath won so many to lose themselves, be
speedily surrendered. And now it shall be seen what knights you have whom
Beauty may draw to resist a rightful title. And I, for my part, moved by that I see in
you (though I serve your enemies) will daily pray that all men may see you, and
then shall you shall not fear any arms of adversaries: or, if enemies you must have,
that either they may have the minds of them that send me, or their fortunes in that
they have long desired.'

At which day abovesaid, for certain urgent occasions, the said challenge and
Triumph by her Majesty's commandment was deferred till the first day of May; at
which day for like causes it was further deferred till the next Monday following,
being the eighth day of May; and so till Whitsun Monday, when they first began to
perform it.

The said day being come, the four foster children had made preparation to besiege the Fortress of Beauty: and thereto had provided a frame of wood which was covered with canvas, and painted outwardly in such excellent order as if it had been a very natural earth or mould, and carried the name of a 'rolling trench',° which went on wheels which way soever the persons within it did drive it. Upon the top whereof was placed two cannons of wood, so passing well coloured as they seemed to be in deed two fair field pieces of ordnances; and by them was placed two men for gunners, clothed in crimson sarcenet, with their baskets of earth for defence of their bodies by them. And also there stood on the top of the trench an ensign bearer, in the same suit with the gunners, displaying his ensign; and within the said trench was cunningly conveyed divers kind of most excellent music against the Castle of Beauty. These things thus all in readiness, the challengers approached, and came from the stable toward the tiltyard, one after another in brave and excellent order. And the manner of their several entering was as followeth:

First, the Earl of Arundel° entered the tiltyard, all in gilt and engraven armour, with caparisons and furniture richly and bravely embroidered, having attendant on him two gentleman ushers, four pages riding on four spare horses, and twenty of his gentlemen: all which aforesaid were apparrelled in short cloaks and Venetian hose° of crimson velvet, laid with gold lace, doublets of yellow satin, hats of crimson velvet with gold bands and yellow feathers, and yellow silk stocks. Then had he six trumpeters that sounded before him, and thirty-one yeomen that waited after him, apparrelled in cassock coats and Venetian hose of crimson velvet, laid on with red silk and gold lace; doublets of yellow taffaty; hats of crimson taffaty with yellow feathers; and yellow worsted stockings.

After him proceeded the Lord Windsor° in gilt and engraven armour, with caparisons and furniture richly embroidered with gold, having attendant on him four pages riding on four spare horses, and four and twenty gentlemen all apparrelled in short cloaks of scarlet, lined through with orange tawny° taffaty, and laid about with silver lace; doublets of orange tawny satin, Venetian hose of orange tawny velvet; black velvet caps with silver bands and white feathers; and silvered rapiers and daggers with scabbards of black velvet. Four trumpeters and two footmen, in cassock coats and Venetian hose of orange tawny velvet, and black velvet caps with silver bands and white feathers, four grooms of his stable leading of his four horses, in cassock coats and Venetian hose of orange tawny taffaty, and orange tawny felts with silver bands and white feathers. Then had he three score yeomen in coats of orange tawny cloth, with the Unicorn of silver plate° on their sleeves, and orange tawny felts with silver bands and white feathers.

Then proceeded Master Philip Sidney, in very sumptuous manner, with armour part blue, and the rest gilt and engraven,° with four spare horses having caparisons and furniture very rich and costly, as some of cloth of gold embroidered with pearl, and some embroidered with gold and silver feathers, very richly and cunningly wrought. He had four pages that rode on his four spare horses, who had cassock coats and Venetian hose all of cloth of silver laid with gold lace, and hats of the same with gold bands and white feathers, and each one a pair of white buskins. Then had he a thirty gentlemen and yeomen and four trumpeters, who were all in cassock coats and Venetian hose of yellow velvet laid with silver lace, yellow velvet caps with silver bands and white feathers, and every one a pair of white buskins: and they had upon their coats a scroll or band of silver which came scarf-wise over the shoulder and so down under the arm, with this posy° or sentence written upon it, both before and behind: *Sic nos non nobis.*°

Then came Master Fulke Greville, in gilt armour, with rich and fair caparisons and furniture, having four spare horses with four pages riding upon them, and four trumpeters sounding before him, and a twenty men, gentlemen and yeomen, attending upon him, who with the pages and trumpeters were all apparelled in loose jerkins of tawny taffaty, cut and lined with yellow sarcenet, and laid with gold lace, and cut down the arm and set with loops and buttons of gold: Venetian hose of the same lined as aforesaid, laid with gold lace down the side with loops and buttons of gold, with each a pair of yellow worsted stockings; and hats of tawny taffaty with gold bands and yellow feathers.

Having thus all entered the tiltyard, they proceeded on with the rolling trench before them, which stayed against the Queen, and they passed by as though they would behold the Fortress of Beauty, and so went about the tilt. At last the boy that uttered the first defiance pronounced these speeches to her Majesty:

'If the message lately delivered unto you had been believed and followed, O Queen, in whom the whole story of virtue is written with the language of beauty, nothing should this violence have needed in your inviolate presence. Your eyes, which till now have been only wont to discern the bowed knees of kneeling hearts, and, inwardly turned, found always the heavenly peace of a sweet mind, should not now have their fair beams reflected with the shining of armour, should not now be driven to see the fury of Desire, nor the fiery force of fury. But since so it is (alas, that so it is!) that in the defence of obstinate refusal there never groweth victory but by compassion: they are come. What need I say more? You see them, ready in heart, as you know, and able with hands, as they hope, not only to the assailing, but to prevailing. Perchance you despise the smallness of the number: I say unto you, the force of Desire goes not by fullness of company. Nay, rather, view with what unresistable determination themselves approach, and how not only the heavens send their invisible instruments to aid them, but also the very earth, the dullest of all the elements, which with natural heaviness still strives to the sleepy centre, yet for advancing this enterprise is contented actively, as you shall see, to move itself upon itself, to rise up in height, that it may the better command the high and high-minded Fortress. Many words, when deeds are in field, are tedious both to the speaker and hearer. You see their forces, but know not their fortunes. If you be resolved, it boots not, and threats dread not. I have discharged my charge: which was, even when all things were ready for the assault, then to offer parley:° a thing not so much unused as gracious in besiegers. You shall now be summoned to yield, which, if it be rejected, then look for the affectionate alarm to be followed with desirous assault. The time approacheth for their approaches. But no time shall stay me from wishing that, howsoever this succeed, the world may long time enjoy her chiefest ornament, which decks it with herself, and herself with the love of goodness.'

Which speech being ended, the rolling trench or mount of earth was moved as near the Queen's Majesty as might be; which being settled, the music played very pleasantly, and one of the boys being then accompanied with cornets summoned the Fortress with this song:

> Yield, yield, O yield, you that this fort do hold,
>   Which seated is in spotless honour's field;
> Desire's great force no forces can withold;
>   Then to Desire's desire, O yield, O yield!
>
> Yield, yield, O yield! Trust not on beauty's pride;
>   Fairness, though fair, is but a feeble shield
> When strong Desire, which virtue's love doth guide,
>   Claims but to gain his due. O yield, O yield!
>
> Yield, yield, O yield! Who first this fort did make
>   Did it for just Desire's true children build:
> Such was his mind; if you another take,
>   Defence herein doth wrong. O yield, O yield!
>
> Yield, yield, O yield! Now is it time to yield,
>   Before th'assault begin! O yield, O yield!

When that was ended, another boy, turning himself to the foster children and their retinue, sung this alarm:

> Alarm, alarm! Here will no yielding be;
>   Such marble ears no cunning words can charm.
> Courage, therefore, and let the stately see
>   That naught withstands Desire. Alarm, alarm!
>
> Alarm, alarm! Let not their beauties move
>   Remorse in you to do this Fortress harm;
> For since war is the ground of virtue's love
>   No force, though force be used. Alarm, alarm!
>
> Alarm, alarm! Companions, now begin
>   About these° never conquered walls to swarm;
> More praise to us we never look to win;
>   Much may° that was not yet; alarm, alarm!
>
> Alarm, alarm! When once the fight is warm,
>   Then shall you see them yield: alarm, alarm!

Which ended, the two cannons were shot off, the one with sweet powder, and the other with sweet water, very odoriferous and pleasant, and the noise of the shooting was very excellent concent of melody within the mount. And after that was store of pretty scaling ladders, and the footmen threw flowers and such fancies against the walls, with all such devices as might seem fit shot for Desire; all which did continue till time the defendants came in.

Then came the defendants in most sumptuous manner, with every one his servants, pages and trumpeters (having some more, some less) in such order as I have here under placed them, with every one his sundry invention, which, for that some of them be mystical and not known to many, I omit therefore for brevity's sake to speak of any, yet such speeches as were spoken or presented for them to her Majesty, so many as were, or at the least as I could come by, I have here in their order placed them, whereby their inventions for whom they were spoken are therein plainly declared. Therefore I refer you to the reading of them hereafter. But thus the defendants entered the tiltyard, one after another, as followeth:

First, Mr Henry Grey, Sir Thomas Perrott, Mr Antony Cooke, Mr Thomas Ratcliffe, Mr Henry Knollys, Mr William Knollys, Mr Robert Knollys, Mr Francis Knollys, Mr Ralph Bowes, Mr Thomas Kelway, Mr George Goring, Mr William Tresham, Mr Robert Alexander, Mr Edward Denny, Mr Hercules Meautus, Mr Edward Moore, Mr Richard Skipwith, Mr Richard Ward, Mr Edward Digby, Mr Henry Nowell, Mr Henry Brouncker: and afterwards, in the middest of the running, came in Sir Henry Lee, as unknown, and when he had broken his six staves went out in like manner again.

So passing on one after another, when Sir Thomas Perrott and Mr Cooke came to the end of the tilt, over against the Queen's Majesty, one of their pages arrayed like an angel uttered these speeches unto her:

'Despair, no, not Despair (most high and happy Princess) could so congeal the frozen knight° in the air but that Desire (ah sweet Desire!) enforced him to behold the Sun on the earth; whereon as he was gazing with twinkling eye (for who can behold such beams steadfastly?) he begun to dissolve into drops, melting with such delight that he seemed to prefer the lingering of a certain death before the lasting of an uncertain life. Such is the nature of engraven loyalty that it chooseth rather to have the body dissolved than the mind disliked. Thus, consuming with content (a sweet sickness is conceit) and pining with more than speakable passions, he suddenly beheld that Sun to be besieged, which he so devoutly served; wherewith boiling in no less disdain, than surprised with immoderate pensiveness, he uttered these words: "O Jove, if thou mean to resolve nature into contraries, why do I live to see it? If into nothing, why do I live at all? If the foot overshoot the head, there is no rest; if desire overshoot duty, there is no reason; and where either of these are, there can be no rule". And so, fetching more sighs than may be numbered by ciphers, this present time (ah, grief!) this present time, that honest and fair hearted frozen knight died. What said I? Even that which again with grief I must say: died, whose ghost making speedy passage into the Elysian Fields (for what more swift than a soul?) in the middest of the infernal multitude, with screeches, cries and clamours, made both Heaven and Hell to redouble this echo: "O times! O men! O corruption of manners!° The Sun° is besieged! The Sun (O mischief!) the Sun is besieged!" Which strange and unacquainted terms caused not only murmuring amongst the ghosts beneath, but a musing amongst the Gods above, who, as well to repress the tumults which might have risen among the shadows, as to revenge the pride which began to grow on the earth, sent down an angel with this commandment: "Go, descend, and cause Adam and Eve° to appear upon the earth in that sort as they were in Paradise, that the world may know them and wonder at them; for seeing out of their loins have issued those preposterous limbs, I know none more fit to correct them—certes none more willing. They will attempt anything for thy sake and service of that earthly, and yet (O strange conceit!) most heavenly Sun, for as they were before driven from their Desire, because they desired to know the best, so now shall they be driven to their Desire which they covet to honour most. This shall be their reward: they shall come near, and yet shall not search; and be they far off, it shall warm. A cloud may sometimes bar their sight, but nothing shall deprive them the safeguard. Yet command them to be humble in affection, though fervent, lest they seem to disdain that pride in others, which they desire themselves. The Sun in the highest delighteth in the shadow which is shortest, and nourisheth the tree whose root groweth deepest, not whose top springeth loftiest". This commission and counsel ended, all things were in a moment accomplished with such celerity (for to the Gods time is tied) that they were sped as soon as they were spoken. And now, most renowned and divine Sun, Adam and Eve being present, vouchsafe to hear somewhat in their behalfs pronounced. Sir knights, if in besieging the Sun ye understood what you had undertaken, ye would not destroy a common blessing for a private benefit. Will you subdue the Sun? Who shall rest in the shadow where the weary take breath, the disquiet rest, and all comfort? Will ye bereave all men of those glistering and gladsome beams? What shall then prosper in the shining, but you will climb it by the rays? O rare exhalations! Brothers ye may be to Desire, but sons ye are to ill hap, which thinks you cannot sink deep enough into the sea, unless you take your fall from the Sun. Desist, you knights, desist, sith it is impossible to resist! Content yourselves with the Sun's indifferent succour; suffer the juniper shrub to grow by the lofty oak, and claim no prerogative where the Sun grants no privilege; for being of the same metal that others are, the Sun will work the like effect as she doth in others. The giants would have been gods, if they could have scaled the heavens; and you no less than stars, could you conquer the same. But as throwing hill upon hill did manifest their pride, but nothing further their pretence, so your laying challenge upon claim, and conquest upon challenge, may well prove a will, but no worthiness; a desire to reach, but no possibility to recover; in which your soaring attempts if you chance to fall, they only comfort you have is to cry with Phaeton, *Magnis excidimus ausis.*° But if no persuasions may move your minds, know ye, proud knights, there are that have hearts as big as mountains, and as far above you in prowess, as ye are above all in presumption; yet not so vain (which ye term "valiant") to assault the Sun. And why? Because it is impregnable. We content to enjoy the light, ye to eclipse it; we to rest under the feet, ye to run over the head; we to yield to that which nothing can conquer, you to conquer that which maketh all men captives. But were it possible that head could devise, courage attempt, or hand execute anything that might show the depth of our unspotted loyalty, soon should be seen (and for yourselves too soon) that your enterprise should be of as small account then, as now they are of likelihood. So deep an impression is engraven in our thoughts, for the majesty of that Sun which now piercing our eyes hath fully subdued our hearts, that we are prest in her defence to offer the whole world defiance. In proof whereof I am charged to throw down his° gauntlet: which who so dareth take up, shall feel both the heat of their just conceived quarrel, and the reproach of their own deserved folly, not only by° riding in breaking a few staves to end the strife, but at tourney or what else so ever they can devise or dare adventure for to win the benefit of Beauty. Thus, most renowned and divine Beauty, whose beams shine like the Sun, have Adam and Eve adventured to defend the Sun: the same I call Beauty, the light of the world, the marvel of men, the mirror of nature: on which their encounter, if those favourable gleams may fall, they will not only think to have done good herein, but to be restored again to Paradise. The one meaneth to repose his trust in a woman who like Eve cannot be beguiled; the other to rest on a Saint° which by a serpent will not be tempted. Thus, being placed in the garden of your graces, O of all things most gracious, where virtues grow as thick as leaves did in Paradise, they will take heed to taste of the forbidden fruit, contented to behold, not coveting to take hold. And for that it hath been long argued, and no arguing can end, whether the first offence came by the crudity° of Adam, or the simplicity of Eve, the one defending his fault by sound arguments, the other excusing hers by sharp answers, they most humbly sue for this: that either by six courses between them the quarrel may be ended, or by your Highness' peremptory sentence determined. For they both being in the world are desirous that one might bear the blame of both. And what herein your excellency shall set down, there is none shall gainsay. For whensoever the question shall be moved, no other reason shall be allowed than this: *Elizabetha dixit.*'

This speech being thus ended, Sir Thomas Perrott and Mr Cooke proceeded backward on the other side of the tilt. And when Mr Ratcliffe came likewise against the Queen, one of his pages pronounced these speeches in his master's behalf to her Majesty:

'So many were the misfortunes (most renowmed and beautiful Princess) of the desolate knight my master, as neither the shortness of time will suffer me to repeat, nor the greatness of the mystery to remember. But let this suffice: that some there were, and so manifold, that geometry whereon the body of man hangeth could not bear, being intolerable, nor the mind which consisteth in arithmetic number, being infinite. Thus, always crossed by Fortune, whose crossing is no blessing, he determined to separate himself as far from society as his actions were from success. Who, wandering through many deserts, yet finding, as he thought, no place desolate, happened at the last to come to a cliff adjoining to the main sea, covered all with moss,° whereon he was walking. Much delighted with the solitary seat, but not well liking the cold situation, he suddenly sunk into a hollow vault. Surprised at the first with fear, but seeing it at the last a place of succour, he accounted his former miseries meetly appeased by this present fortune. In this den he used for his bed moss, for his candle moss, for his ceiling moss, and unless now and then a few coals, moss for his meat. A dry food,

God wot, and a fresh, but so moistened with wet tears, and so salt, that hard it was to conjecture whether it were better to feed or to fast. Here he gave himself to continual meditation, separating his mind from his body, his thought from his heart; yea, divorcing himself from himself, in so much that with his strange diet and new conceits he became so enchanted that neither the remembrance of others, nor a thought touching himself, could enter into his mind. An alteration seldom heard of, that the place whereas he was shrouded in, should make him forget who he is. Living thus for a long time, for that no time should seem short, rising, according to his manner, in the grisping° of the day, he espied upon the shore certain men either cast away by shipwreck, or cast overboard by pirates, unto whom he went; and perceiving by their plaints one which lay dead amongst them° to be their master, enquired whence they were? But they, not willing to repeat their misfortunes, opened the bosom of the gentleman, and pulled out a scroll containing a claim, a challenge, nay, a conquest, of Beauty. At the sight whereof, suddenly (quoth he) "Beauty!" and therewithal paused, entering by little and little out of his present melancholies into his former misfortunes, who as one awaked out of a long dream began thus to debate: "O Beauty, where thy fortress is founded, I know; but what these brethren should mean, I marvel. For as I am assured that to win thee none could be so fortunate, so did I think that to claim thee none could be so fond; when as thou, O divine Beauty, art of everyone to be desired, but never to be conquered of Desire. But, as the eagle beholding the sun, coveteth to build her nest in the same, and so dimmeth her sight; so they, viewing the brightness of Beauty, are incensed to conquer it by Desire. And what then? Because she is invincible, shall I be indifferent? No, I will forsake this caitiffly cottage, and will take arms to defend that Beauty's castle. Nothing shall remove me from mine attempt, which being performed, nothing can move me. Yea, but she hath servants already a number? Aye, but unless I be there, not the whole number. But many were famous? But none more faithful. Yet, alas, if thou go, thou shalt ever be infortunate? Better always infortunate, than once° disloyal." Which words being ended, he demanded whether they would in like case adventure with one of no less courage than their master, but certainly of greater affection. Whose service he having upon small entreaty obtained, for that belike they were desirous to see the event for the which they had suffered such adventures, he departed to his cave, hewing a shield out of the hard cliff, enriched only with soft moss: a double sign of his desire, thinking that nothing could manifest Beauty so well as Pythagoras' walnut, a tender rind and a hard shell. And now, most excellent and divine Beauty, divine it must needs be that worketh so heavenly, sith he is called from his solitary cave to your sumptuous Court, from bondage to liberty, from a living death to a never dying life, and all for the sake and service of Beauty: vouchsafe his shield, which is the ensign of your fame, to be the instrument of his fortune. And for prostrating himself at your feet, he is here ready prest to adventure any adventures for your gracious favour.'

Which speech being ended, he retired back as the rest. And after him came the four sons of Sir Francis Knollys, one after another, according to their age, and all in like armour: who, coming to the end of the tilt, stayed till these speeches were uttered by one of their pages, who, being apparrelled like unto Mercury, pronounced these speeches in the knights' behalfs to her Majesty:

'Report hath bruited all abroad, that desperate Desire, with a wonderful army of affections, hath laid his siege against the invincible Fortress of Peerless Beauty, and that the chiefest champions of this most famous enterprise are four of fancy's fellows, foster brothers to Desire, and dry-nursed by despair; valiant knights, and honourable personages, whose haughty hearts deserve renown, at least, for venturing to win the Golden Fleece without Medea's help.° The giants long ago did scale the clouds, men say, in hope to win the fort of Jupiter. The wanton youth,° whose waxed wings did fry with soaring up aloft, had 'scaped unscorched if he had kept a meaner gale below. So falls it out in this attempt. Desire vaunts to conquer Beauty's Fort by force, wherein the goddess keeps continually watch and ward, so that Desire may despair to win one inch of her against her will. Her stately seat is set so high, as that no level can be laid against her walls; and sooner may men undertake to hit a star with a stone than to beat her brave bulwarks by battery. No undermining may prevail, for that her fort is founded upon so firm a rock as will not stir for either fraud or force. And is there any hope to win by famine such a fort as yields continual food to all her foes? And though they feed not fat therewith, yet must they either feed thereon, or fast, for Beauty is the only bait° whereon Desire bites, and love the chief restorative that lady Beauty likes, so that she can no more be left without meat than men can live without minds. Of all affections that are, Desire is the most worthy to woo, but least deserves to win Beauty; for in winning his saint, he loseth himself. No sooner hath Desire what he desireth, but that he dieth presently. So that when Beauty yieldeth but once to desire, then can she never vaunt to be desired again. Wherefore of force this principle must stand: it is convenient for Desire ever to wish; necessary also that he always want. O rare and most renowmed Beauty, O goddess, to be honoured of all, not to be equalled of any, become not now a prisoner! Your Fortress is invincible; no doubt Desire will content himself with a favourable parley, and wait for grace by loyalty, not challenge it by lance. Although he make ne'er so brave, the world doth know that lady Beauty needs no rescue to raise this siege, for that she sits above all reach; her heavenly looks, when she list, can dazzle all men's eyes. But though she list not use those means, yet it is meet that all her servants come and show themselves devout to do her will. Perchance her pleasure is to see the forts tried of those four foster friends. O happy, ten times happy, they whose hap shall be with favour of her deity to take in hand this brave attempt! In hope whereof these four legitimate sons of Despair, brethren to hard mishap, suckled with sighs, and swathed up in sorrow, weaned in woe, and dry-nursed by Desire, long time fostered with favourable countenance and fed with sweet fancies, but now (alas!) wholly given over to grief, and is disgraced by disdain, are come with ready hearts and hands to prove against these other four that Desire doth not deserve one wink of good favour from Lady Beauty's smiling eyes for threatening to win her fort by force. They doubt not the victory, if only they may find some little show from their saint in favour of their enterprise. If Mercury have said amiss, blame those bright beams which have bereft him of his wit; if well, vouchsafe one beck to bid him pack away.'

These speeches being ended, both they and the rest marched about the tilt, and so going back to the nether end thereof prepared themselves to run, every one in his turn, each defendant six courses against the challengers: who performed their parts so valiantly on both sides that their prowess hath demerited perpetual memory, and worthily won honour both to themselves and their native country, as Fame hath the same reported.

When this day's sport was thus accomplished, the boy that uttered the defiance in these few speeches took his goodnight of the Queen:

'In the trial of this debateful question (O yourself) then with what can be said more, you see that seeing begins to fail. Night,° the ordinary truce-maker, though no truce be treated (if at least your presence make it not lightsome to wrap all in her black and mourning weeds) perchance mourning that since night first was, the noblest Desires° have been subject to undeserved torments; and therefore these knights by th'authority of darkness very undesirously are compelled to depart from whence they came. Never part yet ere they go. Thus much they command me in their names to confess, that such excellency they find in your knights, and in comparison of them, such unableness in their selves, that if Desire did not banish Despair as a traitor out of his kingdom, it would already have undermined their best grounded determination. But no inward nor outward wound, no weakness, no weariness, can daunt Desire, nor take away the natural effects that follow it. Therefore, having left them no other courage than Desire, no other strength than Desire, no other beginning or ending cause but Desire, they will continue this hard and hardy enterprise tomorrow. In the mean time they can find no place in their hearts that doth not wish you as sweet rest as Psyche was conveyed unto by the gentle Zephyrus; and if it be possible, by the same guest° visited. They wish that when your lids lock° up their jewels, they may preserve them to see tomorrow a better day than this: and yet not so singular success, so as you may long, freely and joyfully enjoy yourself, to the delight of lookers and wonder of markers.'

This said, the knights, in order as they came, departed.

The second day's sport

The next day's show was done in this order: the four foster children of Desire entered in a brave chariot (very finely and curiously decked), as men forewearied and half overcome. The chariot was made in such sort as upon the top four knights sat, with a beautiful lady representing Desire above° them: whereunto their eyes were turned, in token what they desired. In the bulk of the chariot was conveyed room for a full consort of music, who played still very doleful music as the chariot moved. The chariot was drawn by four horses according to the four knights, which horses were apparrelled in white and carnation silk, being the colours of Desire; and as it passed by the upper end of the tilt a herald of arms was sent before to utter these speeches in the knights' behalf to her Majesty:

'No confidence in themselves, O most unmatched Princess, before whom envy dieth, wanting all mereness of comparison to sustain it, and admiration is expressed, finding the scope of it void of conceivable limits; nor any slight regarding the force of your valiant knights, hath encouraged the foster children of Desire to make this day an inheritor of yesterday's action. But the wing of Memory, alas, the sworn enemy to the woeful man's quietness,° being constantly held by the hand of perfection, and never ceasing to blow the coal of some kindled Desire, hath brought their inward fire to blaze forth this flame, unquenchable by any means, till by death the whole fuel be consumed. And therefore, not able to master it, they are violently borne whither Desire draws. Although they must confess (alas! that yesterday's brave onset should come to such a confession) that they are not greatly companied with hope, the common supplier to Desire's army: so as now, from summoning this Castle to yield, they are fallen lowly to beseech you to vouchsafe your eyes out of that impregnable Fortress to behold what will fall out betwixt them and your famous knights. Wherein, though they be so overpressed with the others' valour that already they could uneath have been able to come hither, if the chariot of Desire had not carried them; yet will they make this whole assembly witnesses so far of their will, that sooner their souls shall leave their bodies than Desire shall leave souls. In that only stands their strength, that gave them their first courage, and must be their last comfort. For what resistance is there, where not only they are met with foreign enemies, such as stately Disdain, which looks from so high a tower to poor Despair: that, though in itself it be great, yet in her eyes, so seated, it seems small: or such on the other side as unfortunate Despair, which makes the country so barren where they lay their siege, that it would take away all the food of fancy; but even civil war yesterday grew betwixt them and others, who bears the same badge of Desire: that they do so, as thus bestead they are brought to this fair pass, to desire no more, but that this death or overthrow may be seen by those eyes who are only unhappy, in that they can neither find fellows nor see themselves.'°

Which speech being done, the defendants came in, in such order as they came in the day before, therefore I shall not need to make a new repetition of the same, sith all hath been touched already. Then went they to the tourney, where they did very nobly, as the shivering of the swords might very well testify; and after that to the barriers, where they lashed it out lustily, and fought courageously, as if the Greeks and Trojans had dealt their deadly dole. No party was spared, nor estate excepted, but each knight endued to win the Golden Fleece, that expected either fame or the favour of his mistress: which sport continued all the same day. And towards the evening, the sport being ended, there was a boy sent up to the Queen, being clothed in ash coloured garments in token of humble submission, who having an olive branch in his hand, and falling down prostrate on his face, and then kneeled up, concluded this noble exercise with these words to her Majesty:

'Most renowmed Princess of Princes, in whom can nothing obtain victory, but virtue: the foster children of Desire (but heirs only to misfortune) send me to deliver, in such words as sorrow can afford, their most humble hearted submission. They acknowledge this Fortress to be reserved for the eye of the whole world, far lifted up from the compass of their destiny, they acknowledge the blindness of their error, in that they did not know Desire (how strong soever it be) within itself to be no stronger without itself than it pleased the desired. They acknowledge they have degenerated from their fosterer in making violence accompany Desire. They acknowledge that Desire received his beginning and nourishment of this Fortress, and therefore to commit ungratefulness in bearing arms (though desirous arms) against it. They acknowledge noble Desire should have desired nothing so much as the flourishing of that Fortress, which was to be esteemed according to itself's liking. They acknowledge the least determination of virtue (which stands for guard of this Fortress) to be too strong for the strongest Desire; and therefore they do acknowledge themselves overcome, as to be slaves to this Fortress for ever: which title° they will bear in their foreheads, as their other name is engraven in their hearts. For witness thereof they present this olive branch to your presence, in token of your triumphant peace, and of their peaceable servitude, whereby they present themselves as bondmen by those bonds, which the loss of life only can loose. Only, from out of that which was theirs, they crave thus much: to give some token to those knights which may be judged to have done best in each kind of weapon, or who by his device hath come in best sort in this desirous strife. This being done, they being now slaves (in whom much duty requires) for fear of offence dare say no further, but wish from the bottom of their captived hearts, that while this realm is thus fortified and beautified, Desire may be your chiefest adversary.'

Which speech being ended, her Majesty gave them all praise and great thanks, which they esteemed so well, and thought themselves rewarded according to their own wishing. And so they departed each one in order, according to their first coming in.

B. From [Edmund Molyneux], *Historical Remembrance of the Sidneys, the father and the son*, in Holinshed, *The third volume of Chronicles*, 1588

HE WAS sent ambassador to the Emperor when he was not above twenty-one years old (as his father at like age was to the French King°), in which journey, by the way, he had on her Majesty's behalf to visit and treat with sundry princes, other potentates and great ones: which he performed in such exquisite order, and advised wise course, omitting nothing he should do, nor supplying anything he should not do, in ceremony or otherwise, as he exceedingly therein satisfied her Majesty, both by his letters and report, and won to himself great credit and singular commendation.

Not long after his return from that journey,° and before his further employment by her Majesty, at his vacant and spare times of leisure (for he could endure at no time to be idle and void of action) he made his book which he named *Arcadia*, a work (though a mere fancy, toy and fiction) showing such excellency of spirit, gallant invention, variety of matter, and orderly disposition, and couched in frame of such apt words without superfluity, eloquent phrase and fine conceit with interchange of device, so delightful to the reader, and pleasant to the hearer, as nothing could be taken out to amend it, or added to it that would not impair it, as few works of like subject hath been either of some more earnestly sought, choicely kept, nor placed in better place, and amongst better jewels than that was; so that a special dear friend he should be that could have a sight, but much more dear that could once obtain a copy of it.

This right worthy and thrice renowned knight Sir Philip Sidney, Lord Governor of Flushing, having spent some time in her Majesty's service in the Low Countries with great honour, special credit and estimation; and withal, having obtained by his virtue, valour and great policy such an entry of entire good will, trust and authority with the States,° as his counsels and persuasions could much more prevail and work singular effect with them, than any one man's could do in any cause whatsoever that happened to fall in question or debate amongst them: therefore earnestly following the course he then took in hand for the advancement of that service, and to win fame (the only mark true nobility doth or ought to level at) he embarked himself at Flushing, accompanied only with three thousand footmen, and bending his course to Axel,° which lieth in the county of Flanders, used both such diligence and secrecy in this expedition, as he surprised the town, before they could have intelligence of his coming, without loss or hurt of any one of his company. By means whereof, the forts and sconces there near abouts adjoining, being stricken upon the sudden into such a fear and amazement, as doubting some further perils to them intended, than any at the present well appeared, voluntarily and simply gave themselves and their holds into his hands, and yielded to his disposition and mercy. And so after he had well refreshed himself and his company in this town he had thus new taken, he departed thence, and remained in the country not far off ten or twelve days next following, till he had victualled the same and put in a garrison, and left Monsieur Pernon there governor.

Now in the mean time of his state attending these services, and because he would always be occupied in some honourable action, he brake a sluice, forced a trench, and cut out a bank, that made such an open passage and entrance to the sea, as since it hath drowned and destroyed the whole country (being well near now worn into a channel), the same having been the best and most fertile soil in those parts, and far exceeding any territory near thereabouts, to so great a prejudice and annoyance of the enemy, as by common and well grounded opinion, neither by sluice, or lightly any other drain or device, that country can possibly be recovered or regained. And this enterprise was achieved without making head or other offer of offence, invasion or resistance by Mondragon, who was of purpose employed with sufficient force to defend the country, and to have empeached all these attempts and actions.

Moreover, his advice for the service intended at Gravelines° (dissenting in opinion from others, who were thought the most expert captains and best renowned and sorted soldiers) gave such a sufficient proof of his excellent wit, policy and ripe judgement, as his only act and counsel, with the loss of a very few of his company, wrought all their safeties, which otherwise by treachery had been most likely to have been entrapped. And so consequently going forward in other services, at an encounter with the enemy not far from Zutphen, where he that day most valiantly served (for he bare the invincible mind of an ancient Roman,° who ever where he came made account of victory) he received hurt by a musket shot a little above the left knee, which so brake and rifted the bone, and so entered the thigh upward towards the body, as the bullet could not be found before his body was opened. Of which hurt notwithstanding he lived (though in great pain and extreme torment) six and twenty days following, and died the seventeenth day of October between two and three of the clock in the afternoon at Arnhem in Guelderland. By whose untimely death (to the hearty and inward sorrow of many) in the most flourishing and prime time of his years (for he was scarcely complete one and thirty years old) there is presented unto us a very rare example, and that in no common case; that father, mother and son (in line of blood and society in that nearness, as none can be nearer) should come to their fatal ends and fall of name and family within the compass of less than six months:° and that each died so far off by distance of place one from another, as where they died they were but strangers, where by birth and property they could pretend no interest. Whereby we may note a notable lesson to our good (though in this example we be taught to our grief): the variableness of fickle fortune, and the small security in all human and worldly things whatsoever: *Et quod Deus solus in omnibus est suspiciendus.*°

The night before he departed, leaning upon a pillow in his bed, he wrote a line or two by way of letter to Wierus, a very expert and learned physician, to pray him to come unto him. And because it may thereby the better appear how sound and perfect he remained in sense and memory, notwithstanding his most extreme grief and pain, till he rendered his debt to nature, I thought it not inconvenient in this place to remember:

Mi Wiere veni, veni, de vita periclitor, et te cupio: nec vivus nec mortuus ero ingratus, plura non possum, sed obnixe te oro ut festines. Vale.

Tuus P. Sidneius.°

Not many days before he sent these words here before recited, he wrote a large epistle to *Belerius*, a learned divine,° in very pure and eloquent Latin (in like sort as many times he had done before to some great ones, upon occasions, and to others of learning and quality) the copy whereof was, not long after, for the excellency of the phrase, and pithiness of the matter, brought to her Majesty's view. And surely rare he was, as well in that kind, as in many others of equal rarity. Yea, most rare and rarest undoubtedly he would have proved, if so it might have pleased God to have left us so rare a jewel of virtue and courtesy.°

He greatly abounded in sundry good virtues, which ever, where he came, procured him love; but chiefly in justice and liberality (a worthy and most special note in a governor) which gained him hearty love coupled with fame and honour. For the which especially those under his late charge and government so greatly loved, esteemed, honoured, and in a sort adored him, when he was alive, as they made earnest means and entreaty to have his body remain there still with them for memory when he was dead; and promised that (if they might obtain it) to erect for him as fair a monument as any prince had in Christendom, yea, though the same should cost half a ton of gold the building. As his life was most worthy, so his end was most godly. The love men bare him hath left fame behind him; his friendly courtesy to many procured him good will of all. God hath taken him, we hope to his comfort; we have lost him, we feel to our grief. His divine will is done, our human minds must be satisfied, and humbly wish (for it were a presumption to hope) to have his life. For he had that great care and regard to the conservation of his fame and honour entire, when he was gone, that he made a most bountiful and liberal will,° which if the same be performed according to his simple, sincere and good meaning, it will appear that he died not indebted to any, neither to those that were near his person, familiars or domestics, nor to any other he was indebted unto by bond or borrowing, nor otherwise in credit for wares or merchandise, or in other degree whatsoever, he had to treat or deal with him in; yea, not so much as for common courtesy and good will: but he ordered and appointed him satisfaction and honourable contentment.

His body was most honourably conveyed from Arnhem to London, where it remained at the Minories certain days, and from thence brought and removed to the place of his interment; where, with great solemnity and funeral honour, amongst the monuments of his most renowned parents and worthy ancestors, he was buried.°

And here behold the end of two worthy persons, who for that their devices answered in a sort the state of both their fortunes, I think it not impertinent in this place to speak of. The father bare for his device, placed under his arms: *Quo me fata vocant*:° applying the same to his good hap in his younger years when fortune smiled, and time and friends flattered, and none more accounted of and esteemed than he. The son, suspecting future haps, and not trusting over much in present fortune, bare for his device, placed in like manner under his arms: *Vix ea nostra voco*:° signifying thereby, that he would not call those his own, which he knew not how worthy he was to bear, nor how long he should enjoy and keep them, sith that both states and persons are subject to time and mutation, as by his untimely death appeared. And albeit this was his last word and device, which accompanied his funeral: yet not seldom before, as occasion fell out, and as time wrought alteration in his deep and noble conceit, at jousts, triumphs, and other such royal pastimes (for at all such disports he commonly made one) he would bring in such a lively gallant show, so agreeable to every point,° which is required for the expressing of a perfect device (so rich° was he in those inventions) as, if he surpassed not all, he would equal or at least second the best. Wherein, as he rightly deserved, he ever gained singular commendation. There grew some diversity of opinion, amongst their well affected friends, in one point of comparison touching the helps of nature that were distinctly placed in both. Some gave commendation to the father for his gallant tongue, and others to the son for his ready pen. Both were rare gifts in them both, and both two gifts placed in both.

C. Anon, *The Manner of Sir Philip Sidney's Death*

THE loss of a worthy man, enabled and qualified every way for the defence of religion, his country and prince, as it is great, so can it not but work much grief in all good minds, especially in those where the bonds of nature and friendship were fast knit and tied. Yet this grief is greatly assuaged when it is well known that the party so well beloved hath received no damage by death, but by many degrees hath bettered his estate: which moves me, being with Sir Philip Sidney for the space of seventeen or eighteen days before his death, and even unto his last breath, to write, for the comfort of those who did dearly love him, a brief note, not of all—for then I should write a large book—but of the most special things whereby he declared his unfeigned faith, and special work of grace, which gave proof that his end was undoubtedly happy.

After he had received the deadly stroke, being come back into the camp, and lying in a tent, he lift up his eyes to heaven, not imputing it to chance: but with full resolution affirmed that God did send the bullet, and commanded it to strike him. Being told that such sharp correction doth come from God for sin, and that a man so chastised is to humble himself, and to seek to assuage God's displeasure, and to be reconciled unto him: he did not only with fixed eyes upon the heavens confess the same, but also acknowledged it a singular favour and mercy of God, in that he did not strike him dead at once, but gave him space to seek repentance and reconciliation. Hereupon he did not only enter into a deep consideration of those things wherewith he had offended God, but also with great remorse sought how to turn away his displeasure, and to mitigate his anger.

Eight days after he was stricken (at which time he sent for me) the guilt of sin, the present beholding of death, the terror of God's judgement seat (who seemed in hot displeasure to cut him down) concurring, did work in him a fear and an astonishment in mind, which he did overcome, after conference had both touching doctrine and examples of the Scriptures in that matter, where it was proved unto him that the great servants of God were astonished with horror and fear of God's wrath in their outward afflictions. Otherwise, how should they be taught obedience and reverence, to stand in awe of their father? How should they be made conformable to Christ in sufferings, if they should feel no terror of God's wrath in soul for sin? The more natural a child is, the sooner is he abashed at the appearance of God's anger. That now, therefore, he was received into the school of God, and must suffer him to work upon him, to fashion him to his will; nothing happening unto him that was strange and unwonted to those whom God did most dearly love. And so with great cheerfulness he did often lift up his eyes and hands, giving thanks to God that he did chastise him with a loving and fatherly correction, and to his singular profit, whether he should live or die.

Being also advertised that David, and other holy men of God, in time of their extreme dangers, did call to God for help, and solemnly vowed to set forth his praises when he should deliver them; and if he should do the like, it were good: that is, to vow with an unfeigned heart and full purpose, if God should give him life, to consecrate the same unto his service, and to make his glory the full mark of all his actions. To this he answered: 'I beg no life but according to his will. It is not in man to perform further than God shall enable him by his grace. But assure yourselves, I have with unfeigned purpose of heart vowed, if God give life, to addict° myself wholly to his service, and not to live as I have done. For I have walked in a vain course.' And this he spake with great vehemency, both of speech and gesture, and doubled° it, to the intent it might be manifest how unfeignedly he meant to turn more thoroughly unto God than ever before.

Continuing thus certain days, very desirous of conference out of the holy Scriptures, he desired that some godly book might be gotten to be read unto him, which might, as he said, increase mortification, and confirm his mind. He did also sundry times complain that his mind was dull in prayer, that his thoughts did not ascend up so quick as he desired; for having before in manful sort entreated the Lord with fervent prayers, he thought he should at all times feel that fervency, and was grieved when he found any thoughts interrupting the same. 'And for the power of God's word, how great knowledge', said he, 'is there; and how little do men feel the power and inward working of the same.' At another time, being silent, of a sudden he brake out into this speech: 'What is man, that God should so regard him? He is but a poor worm; and yet God hath respect unto him. The Lord himself is an infinite spirit, and his providence reacheth unto all things. He is a most good spirit; for otherwise how should the world continue in the beauty it hath?'° This he spoke with vehement gesture and great joy, even ravished with the consideration of God's omnipotency, providence and goodness, whose fatherly love in remembering him, to chastise him for his soul's health, he did now feel; adding further: 'How unsearchable are the mysteries of God's word unto man's reason and understanding!'°

Here he grew weaker in body, and thereby gathered that he should die: which caused him yet to enter into a more serious consideration of his state, what assurance he had of his salvation. And having by the promises of God, and testimonies of his grace, which he felt working in him, gathered an assurance of God's favour unto eternal life, who made him perceive that he did chastise him as a most loving father, to fashion him unto his own will, and to kill and mortify sin in him; he feared not to die, but he feared that, being a man of a sound and strong heart, and in his flourishing years, the pangs of death would be so grievous that he should lose his understanding; and this fear did remain in him still, notwithstanding any persuasion that might be used.

Being demanded whether he did not desire life to glorify God only, if he should now give him his life (which were in a manner all one as to raise him from the dead), he answered: 'I have vowed my life unto God; and the Lord cut me off and suffer me to live no longer than I shall glorify him, and give myself up to his service.'

The night before he died, towards the morning, I asked him how he did. He answered, 'I feel myself more weak.' 'I trust', said I, 'you are well and throughly prepared for death, if God shall call you?' At this he made a little pause; and then he answered: 'I have', said he, 'a doubt: I pray you resolve me in it. I have not slept this night. I have very humbly and earnestly besought the Lord to give me some sleep; he hath denied it. This causeth me to doubt that God doth not regard nor hear any of my prayers. This doth much trouble me, and I pray you give me your resolution.' Answer was made, that for matters touching salvation and pardon of our sins through Christ, we have an absolute promise; but for things concerning this life, God hath promised but with condition. That which he hath absolutely promised, we may assuredly look to receive, craving it in faith; that which he hath promised but with condition, we may earnestly beg, and not obtain, unless it be best for his glory and our profit, which we know not; and therefore we must ask it with that condition, and leave it to his will and pleasure. 'I am', said he, 'fully satisfied and resolved with this answer. No doubt it is even so. Then I will submit myself to his will in these outward things.' He added further: 'I had this night a trouble in my mind: for searching myself, methought I had not a full and sure hold in Christ. After I had continued in this perplexity a while, observe how strangely God did deliver me—for indeed it was a strange deliverance that I had! There came to my remembrance a vanity wherein I had taken delight, whereof I had not rid myself. It was my Lady Rich.° But I rid myself of it, and presently my joy and comfort returned.'

Within few hours after, I told him that I thought his end did approach; which indeed he well perceived, and with deep meditations prepared himself for it. His fear that the pangs of death would take away his understanding did still remain, for upon some occasion of speech he uttered this: 'I do', said he, 'with trembling heart most humbly beg of the Lord that the pangs of death may not be so great as to take away mine understanding, but that my faith may continue to the end.' When I had proved to him, by testimonies and infallible reasons of the Scriptures, that although his understanding and senses should fail, yet that faith which he had now could not fail, but should hold still the power and victory before God: yea, in that respect all one as if he had sense and understanding: at this he did with a cheerful and smiling countenance put forth his hand, and clapped me softly on the cheek.

Not long after, he lift up his eyes and hands, uttering these words: 'I would not change my joy for the empire of the world.' For the nearer he saw death approach, the more his comfort seemed to increase. After this, for the space of three or four hours, he did still call to be spoken unto out of the word of God. So long as it was not grievous unto him to speak, he would make answer, and if any testimony alleged seemed hard, he would ask the meaning; and if there were any inter-mission of speech, he would by and by call and say: 'I pray you speak still to me.' And in the midst of these speeches, which were for the confirmation of faith, to gather a full assurance of God's love; also touching the vanity of this life, and happiness of the life to come; of the victory of Christ over death and Satan; of the glory which the body shall have at the Resurrection; of that present felicity which his soul should be carried into by the holy angels; and of many other things, whereof present necessity did minister occasion; he did ever and anon lift up his hands and eyes. For as the light of a lamp is continued by pouring in of oil, so he sought to have the burning zeal and flame of his prayers, upon which his heart was still bent, cherished by the comfort of the holy word, accounting it a great injury if we did not still speak, to give wings to his faith, to carry up his prayers speedily; uttering grief when he felt any thought interrupt the same.

And although he had professed the Gospel, loved and favoured those which did embrace it, entered deeply into the service of the Church, taken good order and very good care for his servants and soldiers to be taught and to be brought to live accordingly; yet entering into deep examination of his life, now in the time of his affliction, and feeling those inward motions and workings which he now had: even as the sun when it shineth brightest, though it do not extinguish, yet it doth, as it were, drown the light of a candle, that it is not perceived: so in comparison of God's grace now in him, his former virtues seemed to be nothing, for he wholly condemned his former life. For there being with him a learned man which could speak no English, he spake to him in Latin,° and amongst other things uttered this: that godly men, in time of extreme afflictions, did comfort and support themselves with the remembrance of their former life, in which they had glorified God. 'It is not so,' said he, 'in me. I have no comfort that way. All things in my former life have been vain, vain, vain.'

Perceiving that death did approach, he did with a few and short speeches (for it was grievous for him to speak much) exhort his two brothers° in an affectionated manner, giving them instruction in some points, and namely° to learn by him that all things here are vanity. His speech failing, he made sign with his hands to be still spoken unto, and could then less endure that I should make any intermission. Even as one that runs a race, when he comes near to the end, doth strain himself most vehemently, so he would have all the help that might be, to carry him forward now to the very end of this his race unto God.

When he was so far changed that his eyes were shut up; his breath seemed to come but even from the upper part of his breast; his hands so cold, that all natural heat and life seemed almost utterly gone out of them; we supposed that his senses and understanding had failed, and that it was for no purpose to speak any more unto him. But it was far otherwise; for I spake thus unto him: 'Sir, if you hear what we say, let us by some means know it, and if you still have your inward joy and consolation in God, hold up your hand.' With that, he lifted up his hand, and, and, and stretched it forth on high, which we thought he could scarcely have moved; which caused the beholders to cry out with joy, that his understanding should be still so perfect, and that the weak body, beyond all expectation, should so readily give a sign of the joy of his soul.

After this, requiring of him to lift up his hands to God, seeing he could not speak, nor open his eyes, that we might see that his heart did still pray to the Almighty: he lifted both his hands, and set them together at his breast, and held them upwards, after the manner of those which make humble petition: and so his hands remained, and were so stiff that they would have so continued standing up, being once so set, but that we took them the one from the other.

Thus, his hearing going away, we commended him to God divers times by prayer. And at the last, even with the end of the prayer, he yielded his spirit into the hands of God, to his eternal comfort, the 17th of October 1586, at Arnhem in Guelderland.

D. Three Elegies on Sidney from *The Phoenix Nest*, 1593

[1]   An Elegy, or friend's passion for his Astrophil: written upon the death of Sir Philip Sidney, knight, Lord Governor of Flushing.

> As then no wind at all there blew;
> No swelling cloud accloyed° the air;
> The sky, like glass of watchet° hue,
> Reflected Phoebus' golden hair;
> > The garnished tree no pendant stirred;
> > No voice was heard of any bird.
>
> There might you see the burly bear,
> The lion king, the elephant,
> The maiden unicorn was there,
> So was Actaeon's horned plant,°   10
> > And what of wild or tame are found
> > Were couched in order on the ground.
>
> Alcides' speckled poplar tree,
> The palm, that monarchs do obtain,
> With love-juice stained the mulberry,°
> The fruit that dews the poet's brain,
> > And Phillis' filbert there away
> > Compared with myrtle and the bay.
>
> The tree that coffins doth adorn,°
> With stately height threatening the sky,   20
> And for the bed of love forlorn
> The black and doleful ebony:
> > All in a circle compassed were,
> > Like to an amphitheatre.
>
> Upon the branches of those trees
> The airy winged people sat,
> Distinguished in odd degrees,
> One sort in this, another that:
> > Here Philomel, that knows full well
> > What force and wit in love doth dwell.   30
>
> The sky-bred eagle, royal bird,
> Perched there upon an oak above;
> The turtle by him never stirred,
> Example of immortal love;
> > The swan that sings about to die
> > Leaving Meander,° stood thereby.

Sidney's hearse borne in funeral procession 16 February 1587, accompanied by friends and kinsmen, from Lant, *Roll*, plate 16. Reproduced by permission of the Governing Body of Christ Church, Oxford.

And that which was of wonder most,
The Phoenix° left sweet Araby,
And on a cedar in this coast
Built up her tomb of spicery;   40
    As I conjecture by the same,
    Prepared to take her dying flame.

In midst and centre of this plot
I saw one grovelling on the grass:
A man, or stone, I knew not that;
No stone, of man the figure was:
    And yet I could not count him one
    More than the image made of stone.

At length I might perceive him rear
His body on his elbow end;   50
Earthly and pale, with ghastly cheer,
Upon his knees he upward tend,
    Seeming like one in uncouth stound
    To be ascending out the ground.

A grievous sigh forthwith he throws,
As might have torn the vital strings;
Then down his cheeks the tears so flows
As doth the stream of many springs:
    So thunder rends the cloud in twain
    And makes a passage for the rain.   60

Incontinent, with trembling sound,
He woefully gan to complain;
Such were the accents as might wound
And tear a diamond rock in twain.
    After his throbs did somewhat stay,
    Thus, heavily, he gan to say:

'O Sun', said he (seeing the sun),
'On wretched me why dost thou shine?
My star is fall'n, my comfort done;
Out is the apple of my eyne;   70
    Shine upon those possess delight,
    And let me live in endless night.

'O grief, that lyest upon my soul
As heavy as a mount of lead,
The remnant of my life control,

Consort me quickly with the dead:
  Half of this heart, this sprite and will,
  Died in the breast of Astrophil.

'And you, compassionate of my woe,
Gentle birds, beasts, and shady trees,   80
I am assured ye long to know
What be the sorrows me aggrieves:
  Listen ye then to that ensu'th
  And hear a tale of tears and ruth.

'You knew (who knew not?) Astrophil:
(That I should live to say, "I knew",
And have not in possession still!)
Things known permit me to renew:
  Of him you know his merit such
  I cannot say, you hear, too much.   90

'Within these woods of Arcady
He chief delight and pleasure took,
And on the mountain Partheny
Upon the crystal liquid brook
  The Muses met him every day
  That taught him sing, to write, and say.

'When he descended down the mount
His personage seemed most divine;
A thousand graces one might count
Upon his lovely cheerful eyne: 100
  To hear him speak and sweetly smile
  You were in Paradise the while.

'A sweet attractive kind of grace;
A full assurance given by looks;
Continual comfort in a face,
The lineaments of Gospel books;
  I trow that countenance cannot lie
  Whose thoughts are legible in the eye.

'Was never eye did see that face,
Was never ear did hear that tongue,   110
Was never mind did mind his grace,
That ever thought the travel long:
  But eyes, and ears, and ev'ry thought
  Were with his sweet perfections caught.

'O God, that such a worthy man,
In whom so rare deserts did reign,
Desired thus, must leave us than,
And we to wish for him in vain!
     O could the stars that bred that wit
     In force no longer fixed sit.   120

'Then being filled with learned dew
The Muses willed him to love;
That instrument° can aptly show
How finely our conceits will move:
     As Bacchus opes dissembled hearts,
     So love sets out our better parts.

'Stella, a nymph within this wood,
Most rare and rich of heavenly bliss,
The highest in his fancy stood,
And she could well demerit this: 130
     'Tis likely they acquainted soon,
     He was a sun, and she a moon.

'Our Astrophil did Stella love:
O Stella, vaunt of Astrophil!
Albeit thy graces gods may move,
Where wilt thou find an Astrophil?
     The rose and lily have their prime,
     And so hath beauty but a time.

'Although thy beauty do exceed
In common sight of every eye,   140
Yet in his poesies when we read
It is apparent more thereby:
     He that hath love and judgement too
     Sees more than any other do.

'Then Astrophil hath honoured thee;
For when thy body is extinct
Thy graces shall eternal be,
And live by virtue of his ink;
     For by his verses he doth give
     To short-lived beauty aye to live.   150

'Above all others, this is he
Which earst approved in his song
That love and honour might agree,

And that pure love will do no wrong:
   Sweet saints, it is no sin nor blame
   To love a man of virtuous name.

'Did never love so sweetly breathe
In any mortal breast before;
Did never Muse inspire beneath
A poet's brain with finer store: 160
   He wrote of love with high conceit,
   And beauty reared above her height.

'Then Pallas afterwards attired
Our Astrophil with her device,
Whom in his armour heaven admired,
As of the nation of the skies:
   He sparkled in his arms afars
   As he were dight with fiery stars.°

'The blaze whereof when Mars beheld
(An envious eye doth see afar)   170
"Such majesty", quoth he, 'is seld;°
Such majesty my mart may mar;
   Perhaps this may a suitor be
   To set Mars by his deity."

'In this surmise he made with speed
An iron cane, wherein he put
The thunder that in clouds do breed;
The flame and bolt together shut
   With privy force burst out again,
   And so our Astrophil was slain.'   180

This word 'was slain' straightway did move,
And nature's inward life-strings twitch;
The sky immediately above
Was dimmed with hideous clouds of pitch;
   The wrastling winds from out the ground
   Filled all the air with rattling sound.

The bending trees expressed a groan
And sighed the sorrow of his fall;
The forest beasts made ruthful moan;
The birds did tune their mourning call;   190
   And Philomel for Astrophil
   Unto her notes annexed a 'phill'.

The turtle dove with tunes of ruth
Showed feeling passion of his death:
'Methought', she said, 'I tell the truth,
Was never he that drew in breath
   Unto his love more trusty found
   Than he for whom our griefs abound.'

The swan that was in presence there
Began his funeral dirge to sing: 200
'Good things', quoth he, 'may scarce appear,
But pass away with speedy wing;
   This mortal life as death is tried,
   And death gives live'—and so he died.

The general sorrow that was made
Among the creatures of kind
Fired the Phoenix where she laid,
Her ashes flying with the wind:
   So as I might with reason see
   That such a Phoenix ne'er should be.   210

Haply the cinders driven about
May breed an offspring near that kind;
But hardly a peer to that, I doubt;
It cannot sink into my mind
   That under branches e'er can be
   Of worth and value as the tree.

The eagle marked with piercing sight
The mournful habit of the place,
And parted thence with mounting flight
To signify to Jove the case,   220
   What sorrow nature doth sustain
   For Astrophil, by envy slain.

And while I followed with mine eye
The flight the eagle upward took
All things did vanish by and by,
And disappeared from my look;
   The trees, beasts, birds and grove was gone,
   So was the friend that made this moan.

This spectacle had firmly wrought
A deep compassion in my sprite;   230
My melting heart issued, methought,

In streams forth at mine eyes aright:
And here my pen is forced to shrink,
My tears discolours so mine ink.

[2]   An Epitaph upon the right honourable Sir Philip Sidney, knight,
Lord Governor of Flushing.

To praise thy life, or wail thy worthy death,
And want thy wit, thy wit, high pure, divine,
Is far beyond the power of mortal line,
Nor any one hath worth that draweth breath.

Yet rich in zeal, though poor in learning's lore,
And friendly care obscured in secret breast,
And love, that envy in thy life suppressed,
Thy dear life done, and death hath doubled more.

And I, that in thy time and living state
Did only praise thy virtues in my thought,   10
As one that seld the rising sun hath sought,
With words and tears now wail thy timeless fate.

Drawn was thy race aright from princely line,
Nor less than such, by gifts that nature gave,
The common mother that all creatures have,
Doth virtue show, and princely lineage shine.

A king gave thee thy name;° a kingly mind
That God thee gave, who found it now too dear
For this base world, and hath resumed it near
To sit in skies, and sort with powers divine.   20

Kent thy birth days, and Oxford held thy youth;
The heavens made haste, and stayed nor years, nor time;
The fruits of age grew ripe in thy first prime,
Thy will, thy words; thy words, the seals of truth.

Great gifts and wisdom rare employed thee thence
To treat from kings, with those more great than kings:°
Such hope men had to lay the highest things
On thy wise youth, to be transported hence.

Whence to sharp wars sweet honour did thee call,
Thy country's love, religion and thy friends;   30

Of worthy men the marks, the lives and ends,
And her defence, for whom we labour all.

There didst thou vanquish shame and tedious age,
Grief, sorrow, sickness, and base fortune's might;
Thy rising day saw never woeful night,
But passed with praise from off this worldly stage.

Back to the camp by thee that day was brought
First thine own death, and after, thy long fame;
Tears to the soldiers; the proud Castilians' shame;
Virtue expressed, and honour truly taught.   40

What hath he lost, that such great grace hath won?
Young years, for endless years; and hope unsure
Of fortune's gifts, for wealth that still shall dure;
O happy race, with so great praises run!

England doth hold thy limbs that bred the same;
Flanders thy valour, where it last was tried;
The camp thy sorrow, where thy body died;
Thy friends, thy want; the world, thy virtue's fame.

Nations thy wit, our minds lay up thy love;
Letters thy learning, thy loss years long to come;   50
In worthy hearts sorrow hath made thy tomb;
Thy soul and sprite enrich the heavens above.

Thy liberal heart embalmed in grateful tears;
Young sighs, sweet sighs, sage sighs, bewail thy fall;
Envy her sting, and spite hath left her gall;
Malice herself a mourning garment wears.

That day their Hannibal° died, our Scipio fell;
Scipio, Cicero and Petrarch of our time;
Whose virtues, wounded by my worthless rhyme,
Let angels speak, and heavens thy praises tell.   60

[3] Another of the same, excellently written by a most worthy
gentleman.

Silence augmenteth grief, writing increaseth rage;
Stalled are my thoughts, which loved, and lost, the wonder of our age;
Yet quickened now with fire, though dead with frost ere now,
Enraged, I write, I know not what; quick, dead, I know not how.

Hard-hearted minds relent, and rigour's tears abound,
And envy strangely rues his end, in whom no fault she found;
Knowledge her light hath lost; valour hath slain her knight;
Sidney is dead, dead is my friend, dead is the world's delight.

Place pensive wails his fall, whose presence was her pride;
Time crieth out, 'My ebb is come! His life was my spring-tide.'   10
Fame mourns, in that she lost the ground of her reports;
Each living wight laments his lack, and all in sundry sorts.

He was (woe worth that word!) to each well-thinking mind
A spotless friend, a matchless man, whose virtue ever shined;
Declaring in his thoughts, his life, and that he writ
Highest conceits, longest foresights, and deepest works of wit.

He only like himself, was second unto none;
Whose death (though life) we rue, and wrong, and all in vain do moan;
Their loss, not him, wail they, that fill the world with cries;
Death slew him not, but he made death his ladder to the skies.   20

Now sink of sorrow I, who live, the more the wrong;
Who wishing death, whom death denies, whose thread is all too long,
Who tied to wretched life, who looks for no relief,
Must spend my ever-dying days in never-ending grief.

Heartsease and only I like parallels run on,°
Whose equal length keep equal breadth, and never meet in one;
Yet for not wronging him, my thoughts, my sorrow's cell,
Shall not run out, though leak they will, for liking him so well.

Farewell to you, my hopes, my wonted waking dreams;
Farewell, sometimes enjoyed joy, eclipsed are thy beams;   30
Farewell, self-pleasing thoughts, which quietness brings forth;
And farewell, friendship's sacred league, uniting minds of worth.

And farewell, merry heart, the gift of guiltless minds,
And all sports which for life's restore variety assigns;
Let all that sweet is, void;° in me no mirth may dwell;
Philip, the cause of all this woe, my life's content, farewell!

Now rhyme, the son of rage, which art no kin to skill,
And endless grief, which deads my life, yet knows not how to kill,
Go seek that hapless tomb, which if ye hap to find
Salute the stones that keep the limbs that held so good a mind.   40

E. Extract from Fulke Greville, *The Life of Sir Philip Sidney*, 1652, 'The water bottle story'

WHEN that unfortunate stand was to be made before Zutphen to stop the issuing out of the Spanish army from a strait, with what alacrity soever he went to actions of honour, yet, remembering that upon just grounds the ancient sages describe the worthiest persons to be ever best armed, he had completely put on his; but, meeting the marshal of the camp° lightly armed (whose honour in that art would not suffer this unenvious Themistocles° to sleep), the unspotted emulation of his heart to venture without any inequality made him cast off his cuisses,° and so, by the secret influence of destiny, to disarm that part where God, it seems, resolved to strike him. Thus they go on, every man in the head of his own troop, and, the weather being misty, fell unawares upon the enemy, who had made a strong stand to receive them near to the very walls of Zutphen; by reason of which accident, their troops fell not only unexpectedly to be engaged within level of the great shot that played from the rampires, but, more fatally, within shot of their muskets, which were laid in ambush within their own trenches.

Now whether this were a desperate cure in our leaders for a desperate disease, or whether misprision, neglect, audacity or what else induced it, is no part of my office to determine, but only to make the narration clear, and deliver rumour as it passed then, without stain or enamel.

Howsoever, by this stand an unfortunate hand out of those fore-spoken trenches brake the bone of Sir Philip's thigh with a musket-shot. The horse he rode upon was rather furiously choleric than bravely proud, and so forced him to forsake the field, but not his back, as the noblest and fittest bier to carry a martial commander to his grave. In which sad progress, passing along by the rest of the army where his uncle—the general—was, and being thirsty with excess of bleeding, he called for drink, which was presently brought him; but as he was putting the bottle to his mouth he saw a poor soldier carried along, who had eaten his last at the same feast, ghastly casting up his eyes at the bottle; which Sir Philip perceiving, took it from his head before he drank, and delivered it to the poor man with these words: 'Thy necessity is yet greater than mine'.

And when he had pledged this poor soldier, he was presently carried to Arnhem where the principal chirurgeons of the camp attended for him; some mercenarily out of gain, others for honour to their art, but the most of them with a true zeal (compounded of love and reverence) to do him good, and, as they thought, many nations in him.°

NOTES

Aesop, *Fables*	J. R. Turner (ed.), *The Works of William Bullokar*, vol. iv, *Aesops Fablz 1585* (1969)
AS	*Astrophil and Stella*
Buxton	John Buxton, *Sir Philip Sidney and the English Renaissance* (1964)
CS	*Certain Sonnets*
CSP	Calendars of State Papers
Death	Anon, *The Manner of Sir Philip Sidney's Death*
De L'Isle MSS	Felix Hull, *De L'Isle MSS: Catalogue* (3 vols, 1974)
Diana	Judith M. Kennedy, *A Critical Edition of Yong's translation of George of Montemayor's Diana and Gil Polo's Enamoured Diana* (1968)
DNB	*Dictionary of National Biography*
DP	*The Defence of Poesy*
Dyer	Ralph M. Sargent, *At the Court of Queen Elizabeth: The Life and Lyrics of Sir Edward Dyer* (1935)
ELH	*English Literary History*
ELR	*English Literary Renaissance*
Feuillerat	Albert Feuillerat (ed.), *The Works of Sir Philip Sidney* (4 vols, 1912–26); repr. as *Prose Works* (1962)
Fraunce	Abraham Fraunce, *The Arcadian Rhetorike [1588]*, ed. Ethel Seaton, Luttrell Society Reprints 9 (1950)
Greville, *Prose Works*	John Gouws (ed.), *The Prose Works of Fulke Greville, Lord Brooke* (1986)
Historical Remembrance	Edmund Molyneux, *Historical Remembrance of the Sidneys, the father and the son*, from R. Holinshed, *The third volume of Chronicles* (1588)
HMC	Calendars of manuscripts published by the Historical Manuscripts Commission
JWCI	*Journal of the Warburg and Courtauld Institutes*

Kay	Dennis Kay (ed.), *Sir Philip Sidney: An Anthology of Modern Criticism* (1987)
'Lady Rich'	Katherine Duncan-Jones, 'Sidney, Stella and Lady Rich', in J. van Dorsten, D. Baker Smith, and A. Kinney (eds), *Sir Philip Sidney: 1586 and the Creation of a Legend* (Leiden 1986)
Lant, *Roll*	Thomas Lant, *Sequitur celebritas et pompa funebris* (1587), reproduced in A. M. Hind, *Engraving in England in the Sixteenth and Seventeenth Centuries* (1952), vol. i.
LM	*The Lady of May*
Misc. Prose	K. Duncan-Jones and J. van Dorsten (eds), *Miscellaneous Prose of Sir Philip Sidney* (1973)
Moffet, *Nobilis*	V. B. Heltzel and H. H. Hudson (eds), *Thomas Moffet: Nobilis, Or, A View of the Life and Death of a Sidney* (San Marino, 1940)
NA	V. J. Skretkowicz (ed.), *The Countess of Pembroke's Arcadia (The New Arcadia)* (1987)
Nichols, *Progresses*	John Nichols (ed.), *The Progresses and Public Processions of Queen Elizabeth* (3 vols, 1823)
North's *Plutarch*	W. E. Henley (ed.), *Plutarch's Lives of the Noble Grecians and Romans Englished by Sir Thomas North anno 1579*, Tudor Translations vii (6 vols., 1895)
OA	Jean Robertson (ed.), *Sir Philip Sidney: The Countess of Pembroke's Arcadia (The Old Arcadia)* (1973)
OED	*The Oxford English Dictionary*
OP	*Other Poems* (Ringler)
Osborn	James M. Osborn, *Young Philip Sidney 1572–1577* (New Haven and London, 1972)
Ottley	Peter Beal, 'Poems by Sir Philip Sidney: The Ottley Manuscript', *The Library*, fifth series, xxxiii (1978), 284–95
PN Elegies	Elegies on Sidney from *The Phoenix Nest* (1593)
PP	*Poems Possibly by Sidney* (Ringler)
PQ	*Philological Quarterly*
RES	*Review of English Studies*

Ringler	W. A. Ringler (ed.), *The Poems of Sir Philip Sidney* (1962)
Robert Sidney	Sir Robert Sidney, *Poems*, ed. P. J. Croft (1984)
Sannazaro	Jacopo Sannazaro, *Arcadia* [1504], translated by R. Nash (Detroit, 1966)
Shepherd	Geoffrey Shepherd (ed.), *Sidney: An Apology for Poetry* (1965)
Temple, *Analysis*	John Webster (ed.), *William Temple's Analysis of Sir Philip Sidney's Apology for Poetry* (New York, 1984)
Tilley	Morris Palmer Tilley, *A Dictionary of Proverbs in England in the Sixteenth and Seventeenth Centuries* (Ann Arbor, 1950)
Triumph	Henry Goldwell, *A brief declaration of the shows performed before the Queen's Majesty and the French ambassadors* (1581) (also called *The Triumph of the Four Foster Children of Desire*)
Wallace	Malcolm W. Wallace, *The Life of Sir Philip Sidney* (1915)
Woudhuysen	H. R. Woudhuysen, *Leicester's Literary Patronage: A Study of the English Court, 1578–1582*, unpublished D.Phil. thesis, University of Oxford (1980)
Young	Alan Young, *Tudor and Jacobean Tournaments* (1987)

1 *A dialogue between two shepherds, uttered in a pastoral show at Wilton.* This poem (Ringler *PP* 1) was first printed in the 1613 edition of the *Arcadia*, the last with independent textual authority. The Countess of Pembroke was still alive, and could possibly have furnished the editors with this text. Sidney's visits to Wilton, following his sister's marriage to the Earl of Pembroke on 21 April 1577, were frequent, and Ringler (517) notes evidence that Sidney had a hand in arranging entertainments near Wilton in February 1583/4. However, the English names and setting and the old-fashioned metre (poulter's measure) suggest an early date for the Dialogue, possibly even during Sidney's first visit to Wilton in August and September 1577, when he was there with his younger brother Robert (Wallace 189).

l. 2. *grudge.* Complain, grumble; cf. *AS* 70.1.

l. 8. *lustless.* Listless, joyless.

l. 10. *stoolball.* A primitive version of cricket, played chiefly by young women.

l. 12. *those lightsome sights we see.* No doubt a reference to the splendidly dressed ladies and gentlemen assembled at Wilton.

l. 16. *tar-box.* A 'box used by shepherds to hold tar as a salve for sheep' (*OED*).

2   l. 29. *Remembrance is the chest.* Cf. the emphasis on 'over busy remembrance' in the opening of *NA* (3).

l. 31. *'plained'st.* Complained.

l. 39. *if so our downs be sped:* 'If that is the current state of affairs on the Wiltshire Downs.'

l. 48. *which even dogs do hate.* Cf. 'Lamon's Tale', 519, 'With that, his dog he henced'.

Two songs for an Accession Day Tilt. Classified by Ringler as 'Wrongly Attributed Poems' (AT19 and AT21). However, their presence in Ottley alongside authentic early poems of Sidney's, with a linking sentence in the first person and a final *impresa*, suggests that they are genuine early work. They must belong to a year when Accession Day, 17 November, fell on a Sunday. The two possible years are 1577 and 1584: the 'Philisides' persona and reference to 'Mira' point to the earlier date. They appear, therefore, to be Sidney's earliest datable poems, relating to an Accession Day Tilt at Whitehall, 17 November 1577 (Young, 157–8).

l. 1. *Philisides.* Sidney's pastoral name for himself, based on the Latinization of his own name: Phili[ppus] Sid[n]e[iu]s, which also encompassed a pun on the Greek *philein* and Latin *sidus*, yielding the sense 'star-lover'. The role of Philisides, prominent in *OA*, was considerably scaled down in *NA*.

l. 2. *Menalcas.* Pastoral name deriving from Theocritus and Virgil. He could here stand for any of many courtiers who had London houses. In *OA* and *NA* Menalcas is an Arcadian shepherd who helps Musidorus to gain access to the retired court by lending him clothes and money; Musidorus pretends to be his younger brother.

l. 3. *Mira.* Ringler (481 and *passim*) postulated the existence of a group of early poems relating to the love of Philisides for Mira, some of which, like this, were not gathered up into later work, but others of which were assimilated into *OA* or *AS*. Attempts have been made to identify 'Mira' with a real woman in Sidney's life, such as his sister 'Mari', who was addressed as 'Mira' by T. Moffet in *The Silkewormes and their Flies* (1599). But all that can be said for certain is that her name means 'Wonder'.

3   l. 9. *The chief of Cupid's Sabbath days.* As the following poem makes clearer, this poem relates to one of the 'Accession Day Tilts' held on 17 November to commemorate Elizabeth's accession and the beginning of a new regnal year.

l. 10. *Samos' isle.* It is hard to know why Sidney identified England with Samos, birthplace of Pythagoras, unless he had already adopted the practice of calling England 'Samothea' and here uses 'Samos' as shorthand (see below, p. 353).

l. 24. *till horse.* A heavy horse used for tilling, or ploughing—not the sort of steed normally ridden to tilt.

l. 25. *When he runs well.* Cf. *AS* 41 and 53.

l. 30. *once to miss.* Cf. *OP* 1.2, 'where he most would hit, he ever yet did miss'.

l. 32. *freeman's song.* 'The name applied C16 to a certain class of vocal compositions of a lively character' (*OED*).

l. 42. *Good Lord deliver us.* Refrain from the Prayer Book Litany, as in 'From battle, murder and sudden death/Good Lord, deliver us'.

4 l. 55. *Her day, on which she entered.* The Accession Day was often referred to as Elizabeth's 'entry day'.

l. 57. *adventured.* Jeopardized, exposed to risk.

l. 63. *like for no mo.* As if for ever.

l. 73. *impresa.* An emblematic device with a picture and motto painted on a shield for display at tournaments.

ll. 73–4. *Nec habent occulta sepulchra.* Young (154) translates this as 'Graves have no secrets'; it may, however, mean 'nor are their burial places hidden'.

5 *The Lady of May*, untitled in early texts, was included as the final item in all the folio editions of the *Arcadia* from 1599 onwards. There is also a manuscript text, formerly at Helmingham Hall, Norfolk, now BL Add. MS 61821, which is the sole source for Rombus's final speech. The setting of the entertainment, Wanstead Manor in Essex, had been bought from Lord Rich by Sidney's uncle, the Earl of Leicester, in 1577. The Queen visited him there in May 1578 and May 1579, and it is impossible to determine to which year *LM* belongs. If it was performed in the latter year it must surely have some bearing on Leicester's marriage to the widowed Countess of Essex, Lettice Knollys, of which the Queen had learned in January, and possibly also, as Stephen Orgel and others have argued, on the Queen's own courtship by the Duke of Alençon.

ll. 2–3. *one apparelled like an honest man's wife.* Leicester is described by Rombus, 346 below, as 'an honest man'; if *LM* belongs to 1579 it is possible that it was designed by Sidney as a vehicle for the presentation to the Queen of Leicester's new wife and her eldest daughter, Penelope Devereux (later to become Lady Rich). 'One apparelled like' may hint that the woman suitor's true identity is more exalted than her rustic dress suggests.

l. 4. *desiring all the lords and gentlemen to speak a good word for her.* The new Countess of Leicester was much in need of such support.

l. 16. *honesty.* Chastity.

l. 20. *partakers.* Supporters, seconds.

l. 24. *infectious.* Destructive.

Supplication. The Supplication is really contained in the preceding speech, rather than in this verse address.

6 l. 42. *fosters.* Foresters.

l. 44. *Master Rombus*. From *rhombus*, a figure whose four sides and opposite angles are equal. Fielding used the same idea of angularity and pedantry in calling one of Tom Jones's tutors 'Square'.

l. 49. *startle*. Start with surprise or alarm.

ll. 49–50. *old father Lalus*. In the Third Eclogues of *OA* the marriage of young Lalus to Kala is celebrated; perhaps his father is to be imagined as having the same name.

l. 56. *minsical*. Mincing.

l. 58. *featioust*. Best formed, most handsome; cf. Latin *facticius*.

l. 58. *By my mother Kit's soul*. An invented oath, like those of Dametas in *OA* 32 and *passim*.

l. 59. *fransical*. Frenzied. Sidney preferred the spelling 'franzy'; cf. *CS* 30.

l. 62. *loquence*. Fluency of speech.

l. 63. *bashless*. Bold, shameless, but used here in the reverse sense.

l. 68. *transfund his dotes*. Pour out his gifts, perhaps also with some play on Jove's thundering 'darts'.

l. 72. *juvental fry*. Young infants.

l. 73. *mansuetude*. Gentleness.

7 l. 75. *Parcere subjectis et debellare superbos*. Virgil, *Aeneid*, vi. 853, 'to spare the humble and cast down the proud'.

l. 77. *solummodo*. Alone.

l. 78. *sanguinolent*. Bloody.

l. 79. *Pecorius Asinus*. For *pecus asininus*, asinine brute.

l. 80. *Dixi. Verbum sapiento satum est*. 'I have spoken; a word to the wise is enough' (Tilley W781).

l. 81. *sulks of the sandiferous seas*. Furrows of the sand-bearing seas.

ll. 81–2. *Haec olim meminisse iuvabit*. Virgil, *Aeneid*, i. 203, 'one day we shall enjoy the recollection of these things'.

l. 82. *ad propositos revertebo*. 'I shall return to the matter in hand.'

l. 85. *quodammodo*. In some manner.

l. 86. *a cast*. Technical term from hawking for the number of hawks cast off at one time, i.e. two.

l. 93. *O Tempori, O Moribus*. Garbled from '*O tempora, o mores*', 'O times! O manners!' (Cicero, *Contra Catilinam*, I. i.)

l. 94. *turpify*. Befoul.

l. 103. *a certain gentleman hereby*. Leicester.

l. 110. *that wherein*. In beauty.

8 l. 116. *With me have been*. The parenthesis suggests a mild innuendo.

l. 117. *Therion*. The name means 'wild creature'.

l. 118. *Espilus*. 'Felt-presser'; hence, one who handles wool.

l. 142. *baldrics*. Belts worn across the shoulder.

9 l. 162. *Them can I take, but you I cannot hold.* Therion uses the traditional comparison of an elusive lady to a deer, frequent in medieval poetry, and no doubt familiar to Sidney from Petrarch, Wyatt, and others; cf. 'and wild for to hold, though I seem tame' (Wyatt, *Poems*, ed. R. A. Rebholz (1978), 77).

l. 173. *Dorcas . . . Rixus*. 'Gazelle' (i.e. gentle) and 'quarrelsome'.

l. 178. *the harlotry*. The harlot.

l. 179. *the sheep's rot*. Liver disease still known to farmers. The implied identification of the lady with a sheep parallels Therion's identification of her with a deer, above.

l. 181. *O Midas*. The idea is presumably that the ass's ears of Midas would be appropriate for listening to drivel.

l. 183. *blaying*. Bleating; cf. *AS* ix.49–50.

10 ll. 199–200. *Heu, Ehem, Hei, Insipidum, Inscitium vulgorum et populorum*. A Latin tag may underlie this semi-gibberish— 'Woe on you, ignorant rabble'—but it has not been traced.

l. 200. *nebulons*. From *nebulo*, paltry, worthless fellow.

l. 201. *edify*. Establish.

l. 202. *throw your ears to me*. A literal rendering of Latin idioms such as *praebere aures, admovere aures*, 'lend me your ears'.

l. 203. *indoctrinated your plumbeous cerebrosities*. Instructed your leaden brains.

ll. 205–06. *prius . . . gratia*. 'First a speech must be divided, before it is defined; for instance'; '*exemplum gratia*' is an error for *exempli gratia*, or 'e.g.'.

11 l. 224. *templer*. Probably intended to suggest 'one who contemplates', as well, perhaps, as 'knight templar', suggesting religious zeal, or 'barrister', or inhabitant of the Inner or Middle Temple, suggesting diligent study.

l. 241. *dilucidate*. Elucidate; for once, a correct usage.

l. 243. *equitate*. This should mean 'ride, as on a horse'; presumably Rombus means 'make a confusing equation'.

l. 245. *an enthymeme a loco contingentibus*. An argument from proximity of position.

ll. 247–8. *Darius King of Persia*. A reference to the mnemonic word 'Darii' in formal logic, denoting the mood 'in which the major premiss is a universal affirmative (*a*), and the minor premiss and the conclusion particular affirmatives (*i*)' (Thomas Wilson, *The Rule of Reason* (1567), f. 27). The first four 'modes' or 'moods' are denoted by the words *barbara, celarent, Darii, ferio*.

l. 250. *his major . . . is a fool*. Terms from logic, for the major and minor premiss in a syllogism.

l. 251. *et ecce homo blancatus quasi lilium*. 'And behold a man lily-white!' Perhaps a quotation, but not traced. The implication may be that Dorcas will turn white with dismay.

12 l. 289. *Sylvanus.* The god of foresters. George Gascoigne appeared as Sylvanus in Leicester's Kenilworth entertainment, at which Sidney was present, in 1575 (Nichols, *Progresses*, ii. 515).

l. 295. *Pan.* The god of shepherds. Sidney used the story of Pan mistaking the bed of Hercules for that of his mistress Omphale in *OA* 225.

13 l. 316. *round agates.* Agates were commonly carved, sometimes into human figures, as references in Shakespeare show (*2 Henry IV*, I. ii. 90; *Much Ado*, III. i. 65). But these were presumably smoothly rounded. Agates are only semi-precious, and Sidney and Leicester may have exploited the rustic fiction of *LM* to give the Queen a cheaper present than would normally have been acceptable.

l. 317. *barbarons.* Barbarians, perhaps on the (false) analogy of nebulons, above, 200.

l. 318. *vapilated.* Whipped.

l. 320. *Juno, Venus, Pallas et profecto plus.* A reference to the Judgement of Paris, implying that the Queen has the virtue of all three goddesses and more as well. Cf. the picture of Queen Elizabeth at Hampton Court (by Hans Eworth, *c.*1569) in which Elizabeth, confronting the three goddesses, awards the apple to herself; also George Peele, *The Arraignment of Paris* (1584).

l. 324. *ædicle.* From Latin *aediculum*, small house.

l. 324. *oves, boves et pecora campi.* From the Vulgate, Psalms 8:8. The Prayer Book version is 'All sheep and oxen: yea, and the beasts of the field'.

l. 326. *O heu Aedipus Aecastor.* Perhaps a garbled version of some exclamation in Seneca's *Oedipus* (translated by Alexander Neville in 1563), or *Thebais* (translated by Newton in 1581), or even Gascoigne's *Jocasta* (1575). The uncertainties of this part of the text, based on a single manuscript version, are too great to warrant emendation to 'Oedipus, Jocasta'.

ll. 330–1. *saith 'and Elizabeth'.* The suggestion may be either that Leicester concludes the Lord's Prayer 'In the name of the Father, the Son, the Holy Ghost and Elizabeth', or that he substitutes a prayer to Elizabeth for *Ave Maria.*

l. 332. *secundum the civil law.* According to the civil law. The three categories are natural law, the law of nations, and civil law.

ll. 332–3. *nine hundredth paragroper of the 7.ii. code in the great Turk Justinian's library.* A reference to the *Codex Justinian*; 'code' was the usual term for the collections of statutes of Justinian or Theodosius (*OED*). Lib. vii., tit. ii is *De testamentaria manumissione*, which seems appropriate; Rombus is not always as muddled as he seems. 'Nine hundredth paragroper' is probably an invented reference intended to increase the impressiveness of the citation.

ll. 333–4. *deponed all his juriousdiction.* Relinquished all his rights.

l. 334. *tibi dominorum domina.* To you, mistress of masters.

ll. 335–6. *iure gentiorum.* By the law of nations.

l. 338. *valeamus et plauditamus.* We bid you farewell and applaud; cf. the final lines of Plautus, *Epidicus, Menaechmi, Bacchides,* etc.

14 *Certain Sonnets.* This collection, so entitled in printed texts of *Arcadia* from 1598 onwards, appears to be Sidney's own assemblage of miscellaneous poems written over a number of years, probably between 1577 and (at latest) 1581 (Ringler 423). Attempts have been made to find coherence in the arrangement of the poems, notably by Germaine Warkentin, who suggests that Sidney revised the order several times, the present text representing its penultimate state ('Sidney's *Certain Sonnets*: Speculations on the Evolution of the Text', *The Library,* sixth series, ii (1980), 430–4). Undoubtedly the sequence has a beginning—the two sonnets yielding to love—and an end—love's funeral, followed by the two sonnets rejecting desire in favour of 'higher things'. But variety of tone and verse form may be the chief organizing principle behind the arrangement of the intervening poems and translations. Whereas in *AS* Astrophil is isolated from his friends by his obsession with Stella, *CS* has a high proportion of light, easy lyrics with a manifest or implicit social setting—the four sonnets 'made when his lady had pain in her face' (8–11), the sonnet written to complement one by his friend Dyer (16), the 'Seven Wonders' poem which takes its bearings from his sister's house at Wilton (22), and a scattering of translations in which he may have been trying his hand alongside friends and relations. Sidney's injunction to his friend Edward Denny 'that you remember with your good voice to sing my songs' (290) may well relate to some of the 'To the tune of' lyrics in *CS* (3, 4, 6, 7, 23, 24, 26, 27).

1 ll. 1–7. 'Nine passages of oxymoron to illustrate the contrarious nature of love, in the tradition of Petrarch's earlier "*Pace non trovo, e no ho da far guerra*" (134) and Romeo's later "feather of lead, bright smoke, cold fire, sick health" (I. i. 186.)' (Ringler 426).

1 ll. 11–12. *hardly used . . . made no breach.* Those who have received unjust treatment in prison are entitled to escape.

1 l. 13. *grateful guardian.* Kindly gaoler.

15 3 This song was later used in *NA* (392–3), where Amphialus causes it to be sung to the imprisoned Philoclea from the lake; the music is 'five viols and as many voices'. On the evidence of MS circulation it was popular among contemporaries; they may have liked its use of *correlatio,* in which eight components set out in the first verse are recapitulated in the second. The Italian tune on which this and 4 are based was discovered by F. J. Fabry in a MS at Winchester College ('Sidney's verse adaptations to two Italian art-songs', *RQ* xxiii (1970), 237–55).

4 The song's theme is the nightingale into which Philomela was metamorphosed after being raped by her brother-in-law Tereus (Ovid, *Metamorphoses,* vi. 438 f.): according to a later tradition she had a thorn at her breast with which she pricked herself to keep herself awake. There are many other Elizabethan lyrics on the theme, e.g. one in *The Passionate Pilgrim* (1599), probably by Richard Barnfield, beginning 'As it fell upon a day'.

16 4 l. 20. *wanting is more woe than too much having*. A Sidneian sophistry, implying that rape—'too much having' for its victim—is a manifestation of excessive love.

5 Omitted from early printed texts, but added by Ringler from MS texts, the position being that in which it appears in the Clifford MS. It is Sidney's only piece of rhymed quantitative verse—sapphics. Fulke Greville's rhymed sapphics in *Caelica* vi were probably written in emulation.

17 6 The only poem of Sidney's to survive in his own hand, inscribed on the last leaf of a copy of Jean Bouchet, *Les Annales d'Aquitaine* (Poitiers, 1557), now in the Biblioteca Bodmeriana, Cologny, Geneva (Reproduced and discussed in P. J. Croft, *Autograph Poetry in the English Language* (1973), i. 14–15). Sidney's inscription of the lyric in a book apparently belonging to someone else is added evidence of the 'social' quality of *CS* (see above). There are many settings of the Italian song '*Basciami vita mia*' from 1543 onwards, and it is impossible to know which Sidney had in mind.

6 l. 3. *Way*. Go away; but also an onomatopoeic suggestion of the baby's cry.

6 l. 9. *for that*. For food, i.e. satisfaction of desire.

7 The tune of this Spanish *villancico* has not been traced. The meaning of the title is 'If you, lady, have no pity on me'.

19 7 l. 8. *though tongue to roof be cleaved*. Cf. Psalm 31: 15, translated by Sidney as 'My cleaving tongue close to my roof doth bide'.

20 8 *had pain in her face*. Elizabethan dentistry, or lack of it, must have made this a common affliction. Ringler (428) prefers the suggestion made in one MS text that the lady was suffering from smallpox, citing 'cruel stains' in l. 12. If this is right, the lady could not be Penelope Rich, who had smallpox in 1597 (HMC, *De L'isle and Dudley*, ii. 265, 268). However, nothing in the sonnets suggests that the lady's pain is symptomatic of a life-threatening disease, and Sidney, whose own mother was severely scarred by smallpox in 1562 when nursing the Queen (Wallace 22), seems unlikely to have taken that disease lightly. Toothache/neuralgia seems most probable; lady's identity unknown.

9 l. 7. *child-like love*. Cf. 'baby mine desire' in *CS* 6.

21 11 l. 5. *all pain the mind forebears*. That only the mind, not the body, is capable of suffering.

12 A close translation of Horace, *Carmina*, ii. x, consisting of a catalogue of prudent commonplaces, many of which had acquired proverbial force by the Renaissance. *Tottel's Miscellany* (1557) contained three distinct versions of this Ode (28, 194, 295).

22 12 l. 9. *The highest hills the bolt of thunder cleaves*. The original of this line, *Feriuntque summos fulgura montes*, was used for an *impresa* known to Sidney (Paolo Giovio, *Dialogo dell'Imprese*, Lyons 1574, p. 13; copied by Abraham Fraunce in a MS dedicated to Sidney, Bodleian MS Rawl. D. 345, fo. 19).

13 This seems to be the earliest English translation from Catullus, and is taken from *Carmina* lxx.

14 Paraphrased from Seneca, *Oedipus*, 705–6, which Sidney also quoted in *DP* (230) and in his letter of advice to the Queen (*Misc. Prose*, 56).

23 15 These verses for an *impresa* may be associated with one of Sidney's tiltyard appearances. Birds had their eyes 'seeled', or sewn up, in order to tame them; in *NA* (90) Pyrocles/Zelmane takes the royal family to see 'a seeled dove, who the blinder she was, the higher she strave'. The quotation is from Petrarch's Sonnet 134, referring to the tyranny of Cupid, who 'does not want me for his own, nor does he release me from my trouble'.

15 l. 5. *his.* Cupid's.

16a This lyric by Sidney's friend Edward Dyer (1543–1607) is included in *CS* in this position in all the printed texts; it also appears in several contemporary MSS. The fable of the satyr who kissed fire is told by Plutarch, *De capienda ex inimicis utilitate*, 2, and occurs also in some editions of Aesop's *Fables*.

16a l. 6. *Wood.* Mad.

24 16 Perhaps suggested by Alciati's emblem *In subitum terrorem*, showing a satyr, or Pan, blowing a horn and frightening people away. There is a lively four-part setting of the first four lines by John Ward. *The First Set of English Madrigals* (1613).

16 l. 11. *maybe.* A possible contingency (*OED*).

17 A clumsy and old-fashioned poem by a lover who claims (40) to be a novice at poetry.

17 l. 6. *even by the Stygian lake.* Cf. *OA* 73.161.

17 ll. 16–20. *knotted straw . . . debate.* The 'knotted straw' refers to a classical proverb, *nodum in scirpo quaerere*, 'to seek a knot in a bulrush'. The wooden horse led to the destruction of Troy. The tripod from which the Delphic priestess pronounced the Oracle determined the course of wars; and Demosthenes, to prove the triviality of the interest the Athenians took in his speeches, told of a man who, trying to sit in the shade of an ass he had hired, was told that he had hired the ass only, not its shadow (Plutarch, *Moralia* 848A; Tilley K168).

17 ll. 26–30. Cf. *AS* 54.

25 17 l. 34. *dump.* Melancholy ditty.

17 l. 45. *Think Hannibal did laugh when Carthage lost.* Consider that Hannibal laughed when Carthage was lost. Cf. Petrarch's *Canzoniere* cii. 5–8, translated by Wyatt as:

> And Hannibal eke, when fortune him shut
> Clean from his reign and from all his intent
> Laughed to his folk whom sorrow did torment,
> His cruel despite for to disgorge and quit.

(Sir Thomas Wyatt, *Poems*, ed. R. A. Rebholz (1978), 76.)

17 l. 47. *found.* To be found.

17 l. 48. *in cloudy hue.* In dark clothes.

17 l. 52. *Choler adust.* Dry choler, or melancholy.

26 **18,19** Examples of 'correlative' verse, in which a succession of elements are set out and then recapitulated in the same order.

18 l. 12. *do in my tears augment.* Are swollen by my tears.

27 **20** An example of what Fraunce (46–9) calls 'Epanodos, regression, turning to the same sound', the sound here being 'part', repeated eleven times.

21 l. 12. *corse.* Body.

22 The poem resembles Petrarch's *canzone* cv, in which he describes his love in six exotic similes; but the formula was also imitated by sixteenth-century followers, such as Desportes, who adapted a sonnet by Serafino comparing his mistress to a monster with seven heads (*Amours de Diane*, 1. lxvii). Sidney's seven wonders 'appear to have been drawn as much from observation and conversation as from reading' (Ringler, 430); one of those with whom he might have discussed them is William Camden, who was at Christ Church with him.

22 l. 1. *Near Wilton sweet.* Stonehenge is about 8 miles from Wilton, where Sidney's sister lived. The question of how the stones were transported is still unanswered. William Harrison in his *Description of Britain* says that they are 'very difficult to be numbered' (Holinshed, *First and second volumes of Chronicles* (1577), fo. 97; Camden, *Britannia*, tr. Holland (1610), 251–3).

28 22 l. 11. *The Breretons have a lake.* The story that the lake at Brereton, in Cheshire, sends up dead trees when the head of the family is about to die is told by Camden in *Britannia* (tr. Holland (1610), 609). No personal connection between Sidney and the Breretons is known to exist, but members of the family may have coincided with him either at Shrewsbury School or at Oxford.

22 l. 21. *We have a fish.* Ottley (291) reads 'Thames breeds a fish', which makes a more precise transition from Cheshire to the next location; however, while the status of Ottley is under investigation emendation cannot be justified. The fish in question is the pike, similarly described by Harrison in the final version of his *Description of Britain*, and also by Drayton in *Polyolbion* (1613), iii. 261–72, which is a recapitulation of Sidney's six wonders (Holinshed, *First and second volumes of Chronicles* (1587), 224).

22 l. 31. *Peak hath a cave.* Possibly a reference to the cave near Buxton called Poole's Hole, which has a small entrance and large caverns within, though there are many other caves in the Peak District with stalactites and stalagmites. Buxton was a favourite Elizabethan spa, much frequented by Sidney's uncle, the Earl of Leicester.

29 22 l. 41. *A field there is.* A reference to the ruins of Winburn monastery, near Bath; the phenomenon is described by William Harrison (Holinshed, *First and second volume of Chronicles* (1587), 130).

22 l. 54. *A bird.* The barnacle goose, thought to be hatched from barnacles clinging to shipwrecks, is a wonder credited by travellers from Mandeville to Ralegh.

30   23 The tune to which the poem is set was originally that of a French Catholic song composed in mockery of the Huguenot Prince Louis de Condé in 1568; it was adopted by the Prince de Condé's own troops, became the song of the House of Orange, and is now that of the Dutch National Anthem. Sidney 'may have heard the song during his visit to the Prince of Orange in 1577' (Ringler, 431). The theme, unusually for Sidney, seems to be Neo-Platonic.

31   24 The tune, perhaps a folk melody, has not been traced.

24 l. 24. *eagle-eyed truth.* The eagle was supposed to be capable of looking directly at the sun (Tilley E3).

24 l. 27. *Phoenix' fire.* Cf. Robert Sidney, Song 4.54, 'Phoenixlike joy and burn' (171).

25 The 'Aristophanic' metre is one used by Horace in alternate lines of his *Carmina*, I. viii. Theodore Spencer singled out this poem as 'one example of Sidney's versifying which is successful almost throughout' ('The Poetry of Sir Philip Sidney', *ELH* xii (1945), 260).

32   25 l. 25. *the flower that aye turns.* Heliotrope or girosol.

26 The Italian tune was discovered by F. J. Fabry in a MS at Winchester College; see note on *CS* 3.

33   26 l. 27. *whom.* He whom.

27 The tune has not been traced.

34   28 A translation of the first song in Montemayor's *Diana*. It was also translated by Thomas Wilson, Bartholomew Yong, and Southey (*Diana*, 12–13, 423), and the last stanza was translated by Robert Sidney (268–9) as follows:

> She whom I loved, and love shall still,
> Sitting on this then blessed sand
> Wrate with to me heaven-opening hand
> 'First will I die ere change I will.'
> O unjust force of love unjust!
> That thus a man's belief should rest
> On words conceived in woman's breast
> And vows enrollèd in the dust.

35   28 l. 4. *For hope the colour due.* In *OA* and *NA* Sidney makes great use of the various Renaissance systems of colour symbolism. These systems were by no means consistent, and this poem exploits such an inconsistency: green, which might have stood for Hope, turns out to signify Fickleness. Thomas Wilson, who gave a copy of his translation of Montemayor's *Diana* to Sidney's friend Fulke Greville, had it bound in green in token of his hope that it would be favourably accepted (H. Thomas, ed., '*Diana* de Monte Mayor done out of Spanish by Thomas Wilson (1596)', *Revue Hispanique*, cxvii (Oct. 1920), 367–418).

28 l. 35. '*Sooner die than change my state*'. Montemayor's line, *Antes muerta que*

mudada, was used (altered to the masculine gender) as an epigraph to the portrait of Donne prefaced to his poems in 1635.

28 l. 40. *written in the sand*. A traditional image of fragile aspiration; cf. Spenser, *Amoretti*, lxxv.

36 29 This poem comes in *Diana* soon after the previous one; it is recalled by Silvano, friend of the forsaken Sireno, who recites it (*Diana*, 19–20).

30 One of Sidney's most popular poems, which was already in manuscript circulation during his lifetime (Ringler 555) and was included in *England's Helicon* (1600). Its enduring popularity is shown by Tennyson's protest at source-hunters who 'will not allow one to say "Ring the bell" without finding that we have taken it from Sir P. Sidney' (Hallam Tennyson, *Alfred Lord Tennyson: A Memoir* [1897], i. 258).

30 l. 1. *mourning shows*: black cloths.

30 l. 7. *ungrateful*: cf. *AS* 31.14.

30 l. 10. Cf. The refrain of the second 'Song for an Accession Day Tilt' (2).

37 30 l. 21. *trentals*. A sequence of thirty requiem masses.

30 l. 33. *Love is not dead, but sleepeth*. Cf. 'the maid is not dead, but sleepeth' (Matthew 9: 24).

31 l. 3. *Band*. Swaddling band.

31 l. 4. *web*. 'Cloth in the process of being woven, suggesting Penelope's web' (Ringler, 434).

38 32 l. 6. *sweet yoke*. Image which identifies the alternative to love which 'reachest but to dust' as divine, since it refers to Christ's words 'my yoke is easy, and my burden light' (Matthew 11:30). Sidney also knew an *impresa* consisting of a picture of a yoke with the motto *Suave* (Sweet), used by Pope Leo X (Paolo Giovio, *Dialogo dell'Imprese* (Lyons, 1574), 45; Bodleian MS Rawl, D. 345, fo. 28).

32 l. 15. *Splendidis longum valedico nugis*. The source of this motto, 'I bid a long farewell to splendid trifles', has not been traced. In Ottley (292) *CS* 32 is followed by a motto known to have been used elsewhere by Sidney, *Virtus secura sequatur*, 'let virtue follow in safety' (K. Duncan-Jones, 'Sidney's Personal *Imprese*', *JWCI* xxxiii (1970), 323).

The lad Philisides. Classified by Ringler as OP 5; probably written in 1577–80, when Sidney wrote other poems about Philisides and Mira. It appears to be located somewhere in Eastern England, reached by wind from 'Holland' (106). Wanstead, at Essex, the setting for *LM*, is to the east of London. It was first printed in the 1593 *Arcadia*, inserted, somewhat inappropriately, in the Third Eclogues. It is the first *canzone* to be written in English, being based, rather loosely, on Ecloga 3 of Sannazaro's *Arcadia*. Whereas Sannazaro's *canzone* is sung on 3 March, Sidney's appears to belong to high spring, and might therefore belong to May celebrations at Wanstead in 1578 or 1579.

39 l. 42. *make*. Mate.

l. 45. *engender children high*. Probably referring to the idea that bees were born from the dew on flowers.

40 l. 78. *bea-waymenting*. Lamenting with bleats.

41 l. 113. *willow's bark*. Willow was worn by forsaken lovers; cf. *OA* 13.118.

l. 125. *westward eyeing*. Mira is to the West of Philisides (see above); but this does not really tell us much about her identity or location.

42 *The Old Arcadia*. Probably begun by Sidney in the summer of 1577, after his return from his embassy to the Holy Roman Emperor (cf. Molyneux, 311). According to one of the nine MSS of the romance, it was completed in 1580, and a letter from Sidney to his brother Robert on 18 October 1580 (293) may confirm this, when he says that he hopes to complete his 'toyful book' by February (*OA* xvi and xlii). Even before Sidney undertook the major work of revision which transformed *OA* into the long but unfinished *NA*, there is evidence that certain passages and poems underwent several stages of revision (*OA* lii–lvi). The work consists of five 'Books or Acts' divided by four sets of Eclogues, which alone are included here. The separation of the Eclogues from the main body of the romance is given some warrant by Ringler (xxxviii):

> The eclogues . . . form an isolable unit with a structure of its own that can perfectly well stand by itself . . . Sidney's four sets of eclogues, containing twenty-seven poems totalling more than 2,500 lines, form a more extensive and varied pastoral work than Spenser's [*Shepheardes Calender*] and one that equally deserves attention for its artistic merit. One of the most striking things about Sidney's eclogues is their carefully integrated structure. Each of the four groups develops a situation and explores a theme: the first presents the pangs of unrequited love, the second the struggle between reason and passion, the third the ideals of married love, the fourth the sorrows of lovers and the sorrows of death; and through them all moves the figure of Philisides (Sidney himself), whose identity and story are not revealed until the very end.

The First Eclogues. Book 1 of *OA* shows Arcadia's ruler, Duke Basilius, spurning the advice of his counsellor Philanax and consulting the Delphic Oracle. In order to prevent the troubles foretold him he retires to a 'solitary place' where he, his wife Gynecia, and their two daughters will live for a year in two specially built lodges. The elder daughter Pamela, heir to the throne, is entrusted to the guardianship of the boorish herdsman Dametas. Two young princes, Pyrocles from Macedon and Musidorus from Thessaly, after a year of adventure and heroism in 'Asia, Syria and Egypt', arrive in Arcadia. Pyrocles, seeing a portrait of Basilius and Gynecia with their younger daughter, Philoclea, falls in love with the latter. In order to gain access to her he disguises himself as an Amazon, and succeeds in charming both her and her parents. Musidorus meanwhile has fallen in love with the elder princess, Pamela, and has disguised himself as a shepherd, 'Dorus', bribing and lying his way into the service of Dametas. The whole company, royal and rustic, go out into a meadow surrounded by trees for the 'pastorals', but have no sooner sat down than 'a monstrous lion, with a she-bear of little less fierceness' run out from the trees and disperse the company in terror. Pyrocles, now called Cleophila, grapples with the lion, which wounds him on the shoulder, but eventually he cuts off its head and presents it to Philoclea. Meanwhile Dorus has thrust his shepherd's knife into the heart of the bear. He embraces the swooning Pamela, and when she comes round and throws him off presents her with its severed forepaw. Cleophila receives general praise and thanks; and encouraged by Cleophila, Basilius tells Dametas to accept Dorus into his household. By this time Basilius, his wife Gynecia, who has seen through the Amazon disguise, and Philoclea, who has not, are all beginning to fall in love with Cleophila/Pyrocles. Day is spent, but the interrupted pastorals—'The First Eclogues'—are performed by torchlight.

the very owners of the sheep themselves. Cf. the parable of the hireling shepherd, John 10: 12–16.

43 *corrosive.* Exacerbation of grief.

44 l. 1. *Come, Dorus, come.* One of the earliest singing competitions in English. The more modest one in *LM* may have been written a year or so earlier, as may the August Eclogue in Spenser's *Shepheardes Calender* (1579). Theocritus and Virgil offered models, but Sidney was more immediately influenced by the Second Eclogue in Sannazaro, and the Third Song in the Sixth Book of *Diana* (224–7). The exacting three- and two-syllable rhymes set up by Lalus for Dorus to follow conform with Sidney's praise in *DP* of English as a language rich in such rhymes (249).

l. 7. *the pie.* Magpie.

l. 9. *mattereth.* Festers, exudes matter.

l. 23. *historify.* Relate the history of.

45 l. 35. *how nice to touch, how all her speeches peised be!* How squeamish she is of being touched, and how carefully weighed her words are.

l. 55. *glasseth.* Reflects.

l. 62. *harnished.* Harnessed, armed.

46 l. 74. *enlarged.* Set free, not confined in stays.

l. 85. *Once, O sweet once.* A dramatic projection into the past of Pamela falling 'flat upon her face' at the sight of the she-bear only a little while before the interrupted 'pastorals'.

47 l. 128. *myrtle.* A shrub associated with love and marriage; cf. 68.

48 *eclogue.* Here used in the sense of 'dialogue'.

49 *Argus.* The herdsman transformed to a many-eyed dog by Juno and set to watch over Jove's mistress, Io, transformed to a cow (Ovid, *Metamorphoses*, i).

Pan . . . Syrinx. Pan pursued the nymph Syrinx who was transformed into a reed, from which he made the seven-reeded pan-pipe (Ovid, *Metamorphoses*, i).

l. 1. *Poor painters oft.* Cf. Thomas Watson, *Hekatompathia* [1581/2] xix, in which he 'reproveth the usual description of love ... and proveth by probabilities that he neither is a child ... nor blind, nor winged'.

50 l. 12. *horny head.* The horns traditionally worn by the cuckold.

51 *this pitiful story.* The Erona story, the only major digression in *OA*, is placed in the First Eclogues probably for two reasons: it illustrates the political chaos and personal misery which can be brought about by 'cupidinous' love in a person of royal status; and it shows Pyrocles and Musidorus as active agents of heroic goodness, who are at that moment urgently needed to rescue Erona from prison and death; her story implicitly reproaches them for the frivolity of their sojourn in Arcadia.

52 *satrapas.* Satrap; governor of a province under the ancient Persian monarchy.

53 *camisado.* Night attack; originally one in which night shirts were worn over armour.

vindicative. Vindictive.

55 *undecent.* Inappropriate.

Philisides. See p. 344, ft. *The Old Arcadia.*

56 l. 29. *Ruin's relic.* The old spelling 'relique' may indicate pronunciation here.

l. 53. *He water ploughs, and soweth in the sand.* A classical commonplace; cf. Ovid, *Heroides*, v. 115–16. Sidney's immediate source, however, was lines 10–12 of Sannazaro's Eighth Eclogue which he translates in 53–5:

> Nel'onde solca e nel'arene semena
> E'l vago vento spera in rete accogliere
> Chi sue speranze fonde in cor de femina.

57 l. 62. *the loveliest shepherd.* Probably Sidney's friend Dyer, who wrote in 'A Fancy':

> O frail, unconstant kind, and safe in trust to no man!
> No women angels be, and lo! My mistress is a woman.
>
> (Dyer 186)

l. 63. *plainful.* Plaintful, querulous.

58 l. 108. *malapert.* Impudent, presumptuous.

l. 122. *other sports.* For this catalogue of activities which restrain love, cf. Ovid, *Remedia Amoris*, 715–16, 178–210.

59 l. 10. *brim.* Fierce.

l. 19. *Grew.* Greek.

l. 20. *tway.* Two.

l. 22. *sneb.* Snub.

l. 23. *red.* Advised.

l. 26. *saddest.* Most serious.

60 l. 34. '*I con thee thank*'. Old-fashioned phrase for 'Thank you'.

l. 47. *blow point, hot cockles, or else at keels.* Three rustic games: in the first small pieces of wood were blown through a tube, the second was a form of blind man's buff, and the third ninepins.

l. 58. *cocklings cockered.* Pampered children.

l. 60. *manwood.* Fierce like a man.

61 l. 73. *swan's example.* This fable, explaining the swan's muteness by its former biting tongue, appears to be Sidney's invention.

l. 9. *choler adusted.* Dry choler, melancholy.

62 l. 12. *Heraclitus.* The early Greek philosopher who wept for man's weakness; cf. *DP* 229.

Nota. This list of rules for writing quantitative verse in English is found in only one *OA* MS, that at St John's College, Cambridge, which was Jean Robertson's copy-text. A slightly different version, entitled 'Rules in measured verse in English which I observe', is in Ottley. For an account of Sidney's theories, see Derek Attridge, *Well-weighed syllables* (1974), 173–6.

63 *sapphics.* It is appropriate that the first poem sung by Pyrocles while he is disguised as a woman should be in the verse form associated with the earliest Greek poetess.

66 l. 71. *None can speak of a wound with skill, if he have not a wound felt.* Proverbial; cf. *Romeo and Juliet,* II. ii. 1, 'He jests at scars, that never felt a wound'.

67 l. 78. *emmet.* Ant.

68 l. 114. *these trees.* The tree catalogue was a commonplace going back to classical poetry; e.g. Ovid, *Metamorphoses,* x. Familiar English examples are Chaucer's *Knight's Tale,* 2920–4, and Spenser's *Faerie Queene,* I. i. Sidney's immediate model may have been the opening prose of Sannazaro's *Arcadia.* In *NA* a hiatus marks a place where Sidney seems to have intended to insert a tree catalogue (188).

69 l. 153. *hostry.* Hostelry, inn.

71 *The Second Eclogues.* Book Two shows the love intrigues thickening. Basilius and Gynecia have both declared their passion to Cleophila, who meanwhile attempts to gain access to Philoclea. Dorus pretends to woo Dametas's daughter Mopsa while actually explaining his real identity and love to Philoclea. As Cleophila is parrying the advances of Gynecia they are overtaken by a drunken mob; Dorus hears the noise, and with the help of Philisides and others the princes drive the mob away, killing many of them, and shut the doors of Pamela's lodge against them. The rabble still rage outside, but Cleophila steps out and persuades them, with an eloquent speech, to declare loyalty to Basilius and disperse quietly. Basilius mistakenly believes that the oracle is now fulfilled, and after a hymn to Apollo calls for fresh pastorals, it being his birthday.

The Second Eclogues give the dominant speakers—Dorus, Cleophila, and Philisides—another opportunity to express their various passions, while suggesting also the unsophisticated innocence of the genuine rustics, in the dialogue of Niso and Pas, and the tragic undercurrents to the situation of the princes, in the dialogue of Plangus and Boulon.

forlorn hope. 'Lost troop', body of men detached to the front to initiate attack.

72 l. 1. *Dorus, tell me.* An extended use of trisyllabic rhyme, or 'that, which the Italians term *sdrucciola*' (249): literally, 'sliding rhyme'. Though not a formal singing contest, the exacting rhymes initiated by Dicus and followed by Dorus give the debate about love a strongly competitive feel.

73 l. 17. *muett.* Mute.

74 l. 74. *that construction.* Dicus introduces fresh complication into the verse by initiating internal rhymes, though abandoning the triple terminal rhymes in favour of single ones; Dorus, however, introduces double rhymes twelve lines later, which Dicus builds up to triple rhymes again ten lines on.

76 *assistants.* Audience.

Nico Pas Dicus. A comic singing contest, parodying Virgil's third Eclogue; cf. 345.

l. 9. *rayed.* Diseased.

l. 13. *crouch.* Crutch.

77 l. 25. *by my hat.* Cf. Chaucer, *Parlement of Fowles*, 589.

l. 33. *curbed.* Curved, bent.

78 l. 69. *barleybreak.* Cf. 356 l. 208.

l. 77. *rathe.* Early.

79 l. 105. *tine.* A very short time.

l. 106. *beauties from her fell.* Beauties which fell from her.

80 ll. 141–6. *Tell me . . . foregoes.* Virgil's third Eclogue also contained two riddles. Sidney's have not been satisfactorily explained.

81 l. 24. *With cries first born.* Combined with the previous image of players on a 'filthy stage', this line must have contributed to *King Lear* IV. iv. 184–5, 'When we are born, we cry, that we are come / To this great stage of fools'.

83 l. 106. *Phaethon's dam.* 'Clymene, the mother of Phaethon by Phoebus the sun god' (Ringler).

l. 111. *witold.* Cuckold, i.e. Vulcan or Fire is implored to spare Erona, who is fairer than his wife Venus.

84 l. 136. *but a baiting place.* At the beginning of *OA* (5) Basilius, visiting the Delphic Oracle, is described as misguidedly 'making a perpetual mansion of this poor baiting place of man's life'.

l. 147. *let my life long time.* Cf. the final line of Petrarch's *Trionfo della Morte*, as translated by Sidney's sister, the Countess of Pembroke, in which Laura tells her lover 'Thou without me long time on earth shall stay' (text ed. by

F. B. Young, *PMLA*, xxvii (1912), 52–75). Like Sidney's poem, Petrarch's *Trionfo* is a philosophical dialogue in *terza rima*.

85 l. 184. *The ass did hurt*. A reference to one of Aesop's *Fables*, in which an ass, competing for favour with a young dog, fawns on his master and kicks him (No. 13).

86 *monthly they should send him*. Story perhaps based on that of Theseus and the Minotaur, the Cretan monster which devoured seven youths and seven maidens every year until Theseus killed him. Plutarch opens his *Lives* with the life of Theseus, no doubt well known to Sidney (North's *Plutarch*, i. 29–67).

a horse-load of a mast. A very heavy pole.

partage. Share.

90 *refelled*. Refuted.

93 l. 41. *creatures*. Metre demands that this is pronounced as three syllables.

Anacreon's kind of verses. Not only in an 'anacreontic' metre, but thematically based on the first poem in the *Anacreontea*, in which the poet wants to sing of heroic subjects, but finds that his lyre will sound nothing but love, Cf. K. Duncan-Jones, 'Sidney's Anacreontics', *RES* xxxvi (1985), 226–8.

l. 27. *The sleepy kiss the moon stale*. Referring to the love of Diana (the moon) for the mortal Endymion.

95 *phaleuciacs*. A term apparently invented by Sidney for 'Phaleucian hendecasyllabics', a metre used by Catullus. The military imagery of this poem links it with *AS* 29.

96 *asclepiadics*. A difficult metre, which Sidney is unable to adhere to consistently, originated by the Greek poets Sappho and Alcaeus and extensively used by Horace. The first two lines were used as the beginning of No. 10 in John Dowland's *Second Book of Songs or Airs* (1600). Together with Philisides' echo poem, this is thought by Ringler (404) to be an early poem, imperfectly revised and blended into the Second Eclogues.

l. 20. *humorists*. Fantasists, persons governed by 'humours'.

97 *The Third Eclogues*. Book Three has shown the princes advancing their pursuit of the two princesses by a series of stratagems. Musidorus plays on the avarice of Dametas, the jealousy of his wife Miso, and the naïvety and amorousness of their daughter, Mopsa, to get them all out of the way on false trails while he elopes towards the coast with Pamela. Pyrocles pretends to respond to the loves of both Basilius and Gynecia, tricking them into a midnight assignation in a cave with each other; meanwhile he visits Philoclea, who is alone in her chamber and miserable with sexual confusion and jealousy of her own mother, makes his identity and love known to her, and seduces her. While the noble characters are 'either sleeping or otherwise occupied', the narrator draws his audience of 'fair ladies' to Lalus's marriage celebrations, which comprise the Third Eclogues, offering many ironic points of contrast to the behaviour of the princes.

98 *Coredens.* A mysterious figure, who has been identified with Sidney's friend Dyer, or, by Ringler, with Edward Wotton, who travelled back to England from Vienna with Sidney in 1575—'*cored[i]ens*'. However, *OA* 64.40 suggests that Coredens stood in a tutelary relation to Philisides, which suits Dyer better than Wotton. Since, like Philisides and others, he is a melancholy lover, his name may be construed rather as '*cor edens*', or 'heart-eater', one who is eating his heart out.

99 l. 1. *Let mother earth.* One of the earliest epithalamia in English. The verse form is based on that of a wedding poem in *Diana* (378–9). We should notice that Cupid, who dominates the extra-marital loves of the princes and the Arcadian royal family, is here firmly banished, in favour of Hymen. This is consistent with Dicus's bitter attack on Cupid in the First Eclogues (49–50).

102 *Sentences, sentences.* Sententiae, or, in this case, 'empty aphorisms'.

    l. 1. *A neighbour mine.* It is appropriate to Nico's coarse-grained rusticity that his discourse is in the form of a *fabliau*, a genre not used by Sidney elsewhere.

103 l. 31. *chumpish.* Sullen, grumpy.

104 l. 91. *pistle.* Epistle, letter.

105 *dicker.* Half a score.

106 *Actaeon's ornament.* Horns.

    l. 1. *As I my little flock on Ister bank.* This poem reflects Sidney's friendship with the Huguenot statesman Hubert Languet, who instructed him in political wisdom. Sidney and Languet were together on 'Ister bank', i.e. in Vienna, on the Danube, in August 1573 and August 1574, but there is no way of knowing either which year the poem refers to or when it was written. It is the poem which brings him closest to Spenser, being written in 'old rustic language', such as he was to criticize in *DP* (242). Specifically, it is analogous to the February Eclogue of *The Shepheardes Calender* (1579), a beast fable taught to the poet Thenot in his youth by an older poet, Tityrus.

    l. 2. *couthe.* Knew.

107 l. 24. *naught.* Evil.

    l. 29. *thilk.* Those.

    l. 30. *jump.* Exact, perfect.

    l. 33. *old true tales.* Writing to Sidney in 1579 Daniel Rogers referred to Languet as he who 'guided you through the histories and origins of states' (*OA* 463).

    l. 40. *worthy Coredens.* Probably Dyer; see above.

    l. 43. *Such manner time there was.* This passage derives partly from Ovid's accounts of the Golden Age (*Metamorphoses*, i and xv) and partly from Isaiah 11: 6–8. Greville recalls Sidney's myth in 'A Treatise of Monarchy', stanza 122 (*Remains*, ed. G. Wilkes (1965), 65). *I not.* I know not.

    l. 45. *woned.* Inhabited.

l. 51. *nis.* Is not.

108 l. 58. *envy harb'reth most in feeble hearts.* A parody of the Chaucerian commonplace, 'Pittee renneth sone in gentil herte'.

l. 66. *pewing.* Plaintive crying.

l. 68. *seech.* Seek.

l. 74. *swink due to their hire.* Labour which is their responsibility.

l. 80. *ounce.* Lynx.

110 l. 133. *foen.* Foes.

l. 148. *But yet, O man.* This has generally been seen to have a political application, though opinion has been divided as to whether Sidney endorses rebellion against tyranny. According to Ringler (413) 'the general moral is clear—a powerful aristocracy is the best safeguard of the common people against tyranny'. Later commentators have not found the message so clear, and have discussed in detail the relation of Sidney's ideas to those of Languet and other Calvinist political thinkers (cf. Martin Bergbusch, 'Rebellion in the *New Arcadia*', *PQ* liii (1974), 29–41; Richard McCoy, *Rebellion in Arcadia* (1979): Martin N. Raitiere, *Faire Bitts: Sir Philip Sidney and Renaissance Political Theory*, Pittsburgh (1984)). However, the political application of the fable, whatever it may be, has force only if the plea for tenderness towards animals is also accepted on a literal level. Exceptionally for an Elizabethan, Sidney seems to have disliked hunting; according to Sir John Harington he 'was wont to say; that next hunting, he liked hawking worst' (*A New Discourse of a Stale Subject* [1596], ed. E. S. Donno, 1962, 108).

l. 149. *gloire.* Glory.

l. 154. *or know your strengths.* William R. Drennan points out that Sidney's friend Fulke Greville used this phrase in a speech in the House of Commons in 1593 in a context that makes it clear that it refers to justified resistance to oppression ('Or know your strengths: Sidney's attitude to rebellion in "Ister Banke"', *N&Q*, ccxxxi (1986), 339–40). This may resolve some of the uncertainties about the political application of the fable.

113 l. 73. *Thy father justly may of thee complain.* Cf. Shakespeare, *Sonnets*, 13, 14.

a lady. Gynecia, from whom Basilius has seized a cup of what she believed to be a love potion; the body which she laments over is his.

114 *The Fourth Eclogues.* In Book Four Dametas returns from the fool's errand for gold on which Musidorus has sent him to find his house empty. After a violent squabble with his wife and daughter, he searches for Pamela in the other lodge, and discovers Cleophila and Philoclea in bed together. Meanwhile Basilius and Gynecia have met together in the cave, and Basilius believes that he has made love to Cleophila; however, Gynecia discovers herself to him and reproaches him for his fickleness. As they are on the point of being reconciled Basilius sees a golden cup which Gynecia had filled with what she believed to be an aphrodisiac; he impulsively drinks it up and

immediately changes colour and falls down lifeless. Gynecia is overcome with shame and self-hatred, and a crowd of shepherds begin to lament the death of their Duke. Philanax arrives with a troop of horsemen to put down the rebellion (dealt with in the previous Book); he is astonished to find Basilius dead and is fiercely vengeful against Gynecia. Inside the house Pyrocles wakes up to find his sword gone and himself and Philoclea locked in. He attempts to kill himself with an iron bar. Philoclea eloquently dissuades him. Philanax and some of the Arcadian aristocracy arrive; Pyrocles is taken off to be held prisoner, and Philoclea is kept under house arrest. Musidorus meanwhile had been just about to rape the sleeping Pamela when some villains, relics of the earlier rebellion, interrupt him; he kills some and drives others away, but the remainder decide to take him and Pamela back to Basilius. On the way they meet some of Philanax's soldiers, who take them prisoner. A rival counsellor, Timautus, proposes the release of Gynecia and her daughters, and Kerxenus, who had entertained them on their first arrival in Arcadia, champions the princes. None of these counsels prevail, and the day ends with the main characters still prisoners and the leading noblemen of Arcadia locked in dispute about what to do with them.

115 *Strephon and Klaius would require a whole book.* Various attempts have been made to explain the significance of the gentlemen-shepherds Strephon and Klaius and their lost mistress, Urania (see for instance K. Duncan-Jones, 'Sidney's Urania', *RES* xvii (1966), 124–32; Alastair Fowler, *Conceitful Thought* (1975), 56–8). Whatever their precise significance in neo-Platonic terms, it is clear that these companionable lovers of an unattainable and absent mistress represent a higher kind of love than that of Pyrocles and Musidorus. Sidney himself came near to writing 'a whole book' on their sorrows in *Lamon's Tale* (138–52), and it may be to this that he refers in saying 'another place will serve perchance for the declaring of them'.

116 l. 42. *serene.* Harmful summer dew. Evening and morning dews were thought to bring fatal diseases with them; cf. *Julius Caesar*, II. i. 261–3.

117 l. 67. *she, with whom compared the Alps are valleys.* A hyperbole perhaps not here intended to be ridiculous, as it is in the Red Queen's remark in Lewis Carroll's *Through the Looking Glass*: 'I've seen hills, compared with which this is a valley'.

dizain . . . crown. 'Dizains', or ten-line stanzas ending in couplets, seem to have been first referred to by Gascoigne in *Certain Notes of Instruction* (1575). This appears to be the first English reference to the 'crown', a sequence of stanzas or sonnets in which the first line of each repeats the final line of its predecessor, the last line of all repeating the first. Sidney's brother was to attempt a 'Crown of Sonnets' (Robert Sidney, 174–81; cf. also Donne's 'La Corona').

119 l. 63. *the fish torpedo fair.* In *NA* (367) the torpedo fish, or electric ray, is used as an *impresa* on his shield by the accident-prone Amphialus.

l. 72. *crowned basilisk.* A mythical crowned serpent whose gaze was fatal; cf. Pliny, *Natural History*, viii. 33.

l. 80. *spent*. Destroyed.

120 l. 103. *stroys*. Destroys.

Samothea. Sidney probably took this name for Ancient Britain from Harrison's *Description of Britain* prefaced to Holinshed's *Chronicles* (1577), though there were many other places where he could have come across it. He recommended the reading of Holinshed to Edward Denny in 1580 (289). (Cf. K. Duncan-Jones, 'Sidney in Samothea', *RES* xxv (1974), 174–7). This passage is the nearest Sidney ever came to autobiography.

121 *accompanable*. Fit to accompany (others).

123 l. 69. *Meagre cheer*. Sour expression.

l. 80. *jarred*. Deviated, dissented from.

125 l. 141. *crown of amber fair*. Perhaps signifying 'amber' coloured hair, which Sidney admired; cf. *AS* 91.6.

l. 147. *smirkly*. Simperingly.

126 *Coredens*. Cf. 350. Like Urania, Mira has two lovers, an older and a younger. Dyer's 'Amaryllis', in which Amaryllis, a waiting woman of Diana, is unsuccessfully wooed by 'Coridon' and 'Charamell', who are metamorphosed respectively into the flower heartsease and an owl, may relate in some way to Sidney's stories about friendly rivals (Dyer, 192–5).

128 l. 86. *farewell, long farewell*. Cf. the motto subscribed to *CS* (14).

129 *Agelastus*. MSS of earlier versions of *OA* show that Sidney originally intended Dicus to utter this lament. Along with the November Eclogue in Spenser's *Shepheardes Calender* it is one of the earliest pastoral elegies in English. It is partly modelled on the Eleventh Eclogue in Sannazaro's *Arcadia*, which is also in *terza rima* (Ringler, 419–21).

l. 29. *ai*. The letters imagined by Greek poets as inscribed on the hyacinth after the metamorphosis of the young Hyacinthus; cf. Moschus, *Elegy on Bion*, v. 5 ff.; Ovid, *Metamorphoses*, x. 215; and Milton's 'Lycidas', 106, 'that sanguine flower inscrib'd with woe'.

130 l. 61. *Philomela*. The nightingale, imagined as pricking her breast against a thorn; cf. *CS* 4.

131 l. 86. *produce*. Draw out, extend.

l. 106. *O elements, by whose (they say) contention*. Renaissance commonplace; cf. Marlowe, *Tamburlaine*, *1*. II. vii. 18–20.

l. 111. *Atropos*. The Fury who cuts off the thread of man's life.

132 l. 116. *Aesculapius*. The god of medicine.

l. 127. *in turn of hand*. 'In the twinkling of an eye.'

l. 1. *Farewell O sun*. The first stanza was quoted by C. S. Lewis as an example of 'Golden' poetry, but his use of the 1593 text, in which 'woeful's' in line 4 appears as 'joyful's', led him to dismiss the line as 'vapid' and the whole poem as 'empty': a striking example of the need for sound texts as a foundation for criticism (*English Literature in the Sixteenth Century* (1954), 326–7).

l. 8. *queint*. Quenched.

134 '*What tongue can her perfections tell*'. This poem (*OA* 62) comes near the end of Book Three of *OA*, where it is described as 'a song the shepherd Philisides had ... sung of the beauties of his unkind mistress'. The lyric comes into the mind of Pyrocles as he lays Philoclea on her bed; while the audience of 'fair ladies' enjoy this poetic celebration of Philoclea's body, Pyrocles enjoys the real thing. *OA* MSS show that Sidney worked hard over this light, easy-seeming Ovidian *blason*, or catalogue of beauties, revising it several times. It quickly became one of his most popular poems, occurring in many MS commonplace books and, for instance, in *England's Parnassus* (1600). Puttenham described it as 'excellently well handled' (*Arte of English Poesy*, ed. G. D. Willcock and A. Walker (1936), 244), and many later poets imitated it; see, for instance, Lord Herbert of Cherbury, *Poems*, ed. G. C. Moore Smith (1923), 2–5; Thomas Carew, *Poems*, ed. Rhodes Dunlap (1949), 99–101.

l. 17. *Their matchless praise*. This is the reading of *OA* MSS. Robertson follows the 1590 edition in giving 'The matchless pair'; however, this may be a case of early editorial emendation. 'Matchless praise' fits in with the next four lines, in which no simile of 'praise' is adequate to 'praise' her eyes; cf. also *AS* 35. 13–14.

l. 26. *queen-apple*. A kind of red apple.

135 l. 51. *a say*. An assay, a foretaste.

l. 57. *porphyry*. A reddish crystal.

136 l. 97. *bought incaved*. Inbent curve.

l. 98. *like cunning painter*. Perhaps a reference to miniature painting, in which density was given to colour by the use of white.

l. 99. *the gart'ring place*. Just above the knee, where garters were tied.

l. 103. *Atlas*. The ankle, which supports her heavenly body, as Atlas was supposed to support the heavens.

l. 110. *mews*. Moults.

l. 116. *the hate-spot ermelin*. The white ermine was thought to hate dirt so much that it would die rather than allow its coat to be stained. There is an *impresa* of an ermine with the motto '*Rather dead than spotted*' in *NA* (101).

137 '*Since nature's works be good*'. In Book Five of *OA* Pyrocles and Musidorus, in prison and awaiting trial on capital offences, patiently discuss the afterlife in terms derived from Plato and Du Plessis Mornay. After Pyrocles has expounded the nature of memory after death, 'when, void of sensible memory or memorative passion, we shall not see the colours but the lives of all things that have been or can be', Musidorus, 'looking with a heavenly joy upon him, sang this song unto him he had made before love turned his muse to another subject' (*OA*, 373–4, 479–80).

139 *Lamon's Tale.* First published at the end of the First Eclogues in the 1593 *Arcadia*, where Basilius commands 'one Lamon, who had at large set down their country pastimes and first love to Urania to sing the whole discourse, which he did in this manner' (Ringler *OP* 4, 493–4). In the Fourth Eclogues (115) readers are told that Strephon and Klaius 'would require a whole book to recount their sorrows and the strange causes of their sorrows—another place perchance will serve for the declaring of them'. *Lamon's Tale* (title not authorial), the longest poem Sidney wrote, though unfinished, may be this 'book', written probably after *OA* was finished, and near in time to the early stages of *AS* (Ringler, 494).

l. 3. *plain-singing.* Not merely stylistically plain, but bearing the technical sense of 'unaccompanied singing', as in 'plainsong'.

l. 20. *clouted shoe.* Shoe studded with clouts, or nails, equivalent to modern 'hob-nailed boot'.

l. 25. *Epirus.* In the north-west Peloponnese, south of Macedonia.

l. 26. *Aeol's land.* 'Island of Aeolus between Sicily and Sardinia, far to the West of Epirus' (Ringler).

l. 33. *Klaius for skill of herbs.* It may be relevant that in 1577 John Frampton dedicated his translation of Nicholas Monardes's *Joyfull Newes*, on the medicinal qualities of New World plants, to Edward Dyer (Dyer 56).

140 l. 43. *form.* The technical name for the hare's nest, in long grass or rushes.

l. 48. *keels.* Also called kayls or kills—a form of nine-pins.

l. 53. *green gowns.* Girls were 'given green gowns' by being rolled in the grass.

l. 56. *quintain.* Post used as a mark for tilting.

l. 64. *they in themselves did reign.* 'Content is a kingdom' (Tilley, C623); cf. also Dyer's best known poem, 'My mind to me a kingdom is' (Dyer, 200–1).

l. 67. *cark.* Care.

l. 70. *His mark a pillar was devoid of stay.* It may be significant that we first see Klaius as a 'dyer', marking his flock; also, Dyer's New Year's gift to the Queen in 1578/9 was 'a pillar of gold enamelled, garnished with small opals and small rubies' (Dyer 54). However, other courtiers used this motif (Ringler, 495).

l. 73. *laurel tree.* Laurel may imply that Strephon is identifying himself as a poet as much as a May Lord. In 1586 Geffrey Whitney, addressing an emblem on poetic fame to Sidney and Dyer, assigned a 'laurel leaf' to Sidney and a 'golden pen' to Dyer (*A choice of emblems* (1586), 196–7). For the background to Strephon's role as 'village lord', see E. K. Chambers, *The Mediaeval Stage* (1906), i. 160–181 and *passim*.

141 l. 86. *his milk-white.* As Ringler (495) points out, Skelton's Philip Sparrow 'is white with a black cap and rests between his mistress's breasts'.

l. 103. *snugging.* Snuggling.

l. 110. *on elbow leaned.* Pose signifying melancholy.

l. 118. *In whom no ill did reign, nor good appear.* Resembling the May Lady's shepherd suitor Espilus, who 'as his fortune hath not been to do me great service, so hath he never done me any wrong' (8).

142   l. 131. *his triumph bad.* Perhaps a reference to Petrarch's *Trionfo d'Amore.*

l. 152. *the tyrant threatens blood.* Cf. *AS* 73.11.

143   l. 174. *fur.* Archaic form of 'far', retained for the rhyme.

l. 181. *babery.* Grotesque ornament.

144   l. 201. *but a babe.* Cf. *CS* 6, 'Sleep, baby mine, desire'.

l. 206. *in Lion's cave.* The Sun enters Leo in late July, so about two months have passed since Strephon, a Whitsuntide Lord, first fell in love.

l. 208. *barley-break.* 'In the country game of barley-break the two couples at either end of the field attempt to change partners without being caught by the couple in the middle (called hell). The couple in the middle must hold hands while chasing the others, and if they catch any one member of an opposing couple before they meet as partners, that pair must take their place in hell' (Ringler, 495). The game described by Sidney proceeds as follows:

Round 1

Geron	Nous	Strephon
Cosma	Pas	Urania

Round 2

Nous	Urania	Cosma
Pas	Geron	Strephon

Round 3

Geron	Strephon	Pas
Urania	Nous	Cosma

As the game breaks up, Urania is caught, after a zigzag pursuit, first by the spectator Klaius, then by Strephon also (ll. 384–416); then she breaks away from their double embrace and goes home.

l. 214. *self-'gard.* Self-regard.

l. 240. *frembed.* Enemy.

145   l. 264. *somedel.* Somewhat.

146   l. 291. *Numid lions.* Cf. Pliny, *Natural History*, viii. 50.

l. 313. *Nous with him must dwell.* Strephon seeks to encompass his love, Urania, but gets only Nous, whose name may allude phonetically ('noose') to Sidney's fable of Cupid as hangman, *OA* 8; cf. also *OA* 29.92.

147   l. 342. *near Wilton fair.* Ringler (494) thought this poem too English and Elizabethan to be included in the *Arcadia*. The allusion to the Wiltshire Downs links it with *A Dialogue between two shepherds* (1–2); both poems may be associated with entertainments at Wilton.

l. 359. *dear she.* Cf. *AS* 1.2.

148   l. 370. *girosol.* Heliotrope, flower that turns to the sun.

149 l. 410. *Creon's child.* 'Creusa, whom the jealous Medea destroyed by sending her a poisoned robe and necklace' (Seneca, *Medea*, 570 ff.) (Ringler, 496).

l. 443. *jade.* Worthless or worn-out horse.

150 l. 448. *an ugly cat.* Ill omen, perhaps a witch's 'familiar'.

151 l. 512. *piecing.* Here, incomplete or partial devotion.

l. 515. *murrain.* Plague, especially in farm animals.

l. 519. *henced.* Banished with the word 'hence'; cf. *A Dialogue between two shepherds*, 2 ll. 47–8.

152 l. 544. *thus breathed out.* A lament equivalent in length and intensity to Strephon's is presumably meant to follow. If Klaius was modelled on Dyer, it is possible that Sidney intended him to take up the writing at this point. However, Dyer's poetic fluency seems never to have matched Sidney's.

153 *Astrophil and Stella.* Written, probably, between 1 November 1581 (when Penelope Devereux, on whom 'Stella' is modelled, married Robert, Lord Rich) and the end of 1582 (Ringler 438–9). However, the sequence may well incorporate poems or sonnets written earlier, and Ringler's argument that 'it is scarcely probable' that the composition of the sequence extended into 1583 or later because 'it was carefully planned' is not conclusive. If we knew the nature of 'this great cause' (*AS* 107.8) in the penultimate sonnet we might be in a better position to suggest a terminal date. It may be reasonable, however, to conjecture that *AS* was completed before 1 September 1583, when Sidney married Frances Walsingham, daughter of the Secretary of State. There is no evidence that the title is authorial (Ringler 458). It derives from the first printed text, the unauthorized quarto edition published by Thomas Newman (1591). Newman may also have been responsible for the consistent practice in early printings of calling the lover persona 'Astrophel'. Ringler emended to 'Astrophil' on the grounds of etymological correctness, since the name is presumably based on Greek *aster philein*, and means 'lover of a star'; the 'phil' element alluding also, no doubt, to Sidney's Christian name. Some, but by no means all, of the writers close in time and association to Sidney also spell it thus: e.g. Matthew Roydon (319), Thomas Watson, Gabriel Harvey, and Sir John Harington. *AS* is the first sonnet sequence in English, and formed the model for the many that were to follow during the 1590s. However, few of its successors approached its range, coherence, and variety.

1 Sidney opens the sequence with a metrical innovation (in English): a sonnet in alexandrines, or twelve-syllable lines. Lines 1–4 are quoted by Fraunce (39) as an example of 'Climax . . . a reduplication continued by divers degrees and steps, as it were, of the same word or sound.' l. 2. *she* (*dear she*). Metre, and Sidney's habitual use of parenthesis, support this reading from the 1598 folio, rather than 'the dear she', the reading of the quartos and MSS, adopted by Ringler.

2 l. 1. *dribbed.* Ineffectual, random. l. 3. *known worth.* Whereas Dante, Petrarch, and most of the French Petrarchizers described love at first sight,

Sidney denies it, exploiting this to the greater glory of Stella. It is not clear whether Sidney met Penelope Devereux before her arrival at Court in the autumn of 1581, but he might have known of her 'worth' before meeting her, and her father's dying wish in 1576 for a match between his daughter and Sir Henry Sidney's son makes it likely that he did. Penelope was then 13 (Wallace, 169, 244–5; cf. also *AS* 33). l. 10. *slave-born Muscovite*. The Russians—Slavs—were believed by the Elizabethans to enjoy the oppressive rule of their tsar, at this time Ivan the Terrible. They were also thought comically clumsy and barbaric, as in the Muscovite disguise of the four lovers in *Love's Labour's Lost*, v. ii, which probably alludes to this sonnet. l. 14. *paint*. Probably in *OED* sense 5, 'To give a false colouring or complexion to'.

3 ll. 1–8. Sidney catalogues four current ways of ornamenting or elaborating verse: invocation of Muses; imitation of Pindar and other Greek poets, as professed by Ronsard and the other Pléiade writers; logical and rhetorical elaboration, introduced into English notably by Thomas Watson in his *Hekatompathia* (1582); and the use of exotic similes from natural history, initiated in English prose by Lyly, but already employed in poetry by Petrarch and his European followers. Sidney himself uses all four kinds of elaboration in *OA* poems; rhetorical and logical complexity is the only one used persistently in *AS*.

154 4 l. 5. *old Cato's breast*. Cato the Censor, who lived to the age of 85, was known as 'a bitter punisher of faults' (238). l. 8. *thy hard bit*. Astrophil is imagining himself to be a horse: cf. *AS* 49 and the opening passage of *DP*.

155 5 l. 11. *Which elements with mortal mixture breed*. Reference to Plato's theory that mortal beauty, clothed in the physical elements, is only a shadow of absolute virtue; the elements combine in a perishable way (cf. *Republic*, x). l. 13. *up to our country*. Cf. Du Plessis Mornay, tr. Mary Herbert, Countess of Pembroke, *A Discourse of Life and Death*: 'Man is from heaven: heaven is his country and his air' (1592), sig. D3v.

6 Another sonnet in alexandrines. ll. 1–4. Reference to Petrarchan paradox and oxymoron; 'wot not what' refers to his repeated phrase '*non so che*', which became the French '*je ne sais quoi*'. 'Freezing fires' are the most often quoted Petrarchan oxymoron; cf. Leonard Forster, *The Icy Fire* (1969). ll. 5–6. Ronsard used Jove's metamorphoses—into a bull for love of Europa, swan for Leda, and shower of gold for Danäe—as metaphors for his love, e.g. in the sonnet translated by Ralegh as 'Would I were changed into that golden shower' (Ronsard, *Amours*, xx; Ralegh, *Poems*, ed. A. Latham (1951), 81–2). But many other poets of the period used them too. ll. 7–8. An allusion to pastoral poetry, possibly in particular to the work of Spenser, whose *Shepheardes Calender* (1579) was dedicated to Sidney. However, the reference might equally well be to numerous Continental pastoral poets, such as Sannazaro in Italy or Marot in France. ll. 9–11. Perhaps a reference to the *dolce stil nuovo* of the Italian poets of the fourteenth century. l. 12. *I can speak what I feel*. Six emphatic monosyllables underlining Astrophil's blunt truth-telling.

7 Penelope Devereux is known to have had dark eyes and fair hair; but there is also a long tradition of praise of black beauty underlying both *AS* and Shakespeare's 'Dark Lady' sonnets. l. 6. *strength*: strengthen.

8 l. 2. *Turkish hardened heart*. Sidney is thinking of Cupid in contemporary Greece, which was part of the Ottoman Empire, and sees him as a refugee from the proverbially cruel Turks; cf. *AS* 30. Cyprus, birthplace of Aphrodite, was taken by the Turks in 1573.

156 9 ll. 12–14. *Of touch . . . straw*. Elaborate punning metaphor, perhaps reflecting the influence of recent Spanish poets, playing on three or four senses of 'touch'. Stella's eyes are of touch-stone (black marble), which without 'touching' 'touch', or move, those who see them. The last line introduces yet another reference, to touch-paper or touchwood, which sets the straw, Astrophil, alight.

10 l. 2. *brabbling*. Quarrelling, quibbling.

157 11 l. 11. *pit-fold*. 'Pitfall, a trap for birds' (Ringler).
12 l. 2. *day-nets*. 'A net used by day in daring [=fascinating] larks or catching small birds' (*OED*). l. 11. *got up a breach*: broken into the enemy's defences.

13 ll. 1–6. The coats of arms refer to amorous exploits: Jove's, to his taking the shape of an eagle to carry off the fair youth Ganymede; Mars's, to his
159 love affair with Venus. l. 3. *eagle sables*. Black eagle. l. 4. *talents*. Talons. l. 6. *vert field*. Green field. l. 11. *Where roses gules are borne in silver* field. Possibly a reference to the Devereux arms, *argent, a fesse, gules in chief three torteaux*, or three red discs on a silver background, as well as to Stella's rosy cheeks. Sidney refers to his own crest in *AS* 65. l. 13. *blaze*. Technical term for spelling out or describing heraldic accoutrements, but also an appropriate word for the activity of Phoebus.

14 First of many sonnets showing Astrophil with an uncomprehending or disapproving friend; cf. 20, 21, 23, 27, 51, 88, 92 and 104. l. 3. *him who first stale down the fire*. Prometheus, who stole fire from heaven and was punished by having his entrails continually torn by a vulture. Cf. *CS* 16a. l. 5. *rhubarb*. Bitter purgative.

15 Another sonnet on contemporary poetic styles; cf. 3, 6. ll. 1–4. *You . . . poesy wring*. Those who rifle classical poets for phrases and images, or imitate other poets who have done the same, gathering stale, not 'sweet', flowers of poetry. ll. 5–6. *You . . . rattling rows*. Poets who use alliteration, mimicked in the phrase 'running in rattling rows', such as those early Tudor poets whom C. S. Lewis called 'Drab'. ll. 7–8. Imitators of Petrarch, of whom there had been many in French, Italian, and Spanish; an English imitator close in time to Sidney was Thomas Watson, whose *Hekatompathia* was dedicated to Sidney's enemy the Earl of Oxford. l. 8. *denizened*. Naturalized, i.e. originally foreign.

16 l. 9. *while I thus with this young lion played*. Reference to Greek fable of a shepherd who brought a pet lion cub into his family which when it grew up

destroyed his flocks; the story was applied by Aeschylus to Helen of Troy (*Agamemnon*, 717–36).

17 l. 6. *prove*. Test, provoke.

18 l. 1. *With what sharp checks I in myself am shent*. With what sharp rebukes I 160 am inwardly shamed. l. 5. *Unable quit ... rent*. Unable even to get clear—'quit' is an abverb—of my debt to nature. There may also be a reference to 'quit-rent', the small rent paid by a freeholder in lieu of services. The wider sense is that Astrophil is barely capable of staying alive. ll. 9–10. *my knowledge ... defend*. Possibly alluding to *OA*, Sidney's 'toyful book', and *DP*, in which, having 'slipped into the title of a poet', he proceeded to defend the art.

19 ll. 9–10. *who fare ... doth fall*. Commonplace comment on astronomers, deriving from an anecdote about the Greek scientist Thales who fell into a well while gazing at the stars; cf. *DP* 219.

20 l. 6. *level*. Aim. l. 7. *black*. Stella's eye, but also an archery term for black ring surrounding inmost circle on a target.

161 21 l. 1. *caustics*. Burning substances used in surgery. l. 2. *windlass*. Ambush, ensnare. l. 7. *coltish gyres*. Youthful gyrations, probably with allusion to Plato's image of reason as a charioteer to the passions, identified with horses. l. 9. *mad March great promise made of me*. Probably refers to Sidney's early travels and reputation in Europe, and in particular his embassy to the Holy Roman Emperor in the spring of 1577.

22 l. 2. *from fair twins' golden place*. The zodiacal sign of Gemini, which the sun leaves in late June. l. 5. *by hard promise tried*. Suggests that the ladies rode out to keep an important appointment, and may indicate, *pace* Ringler (468), that the sonnet is based on a real incident.

162 23 l. 5. *how my spring I did address*. Cf. *AS* 21.9–10; perhaps alludes to Sidney's studiousness during his three years of European travel. l. 7. *the prince my service tries*. The monarch makes use of me. Sidney had been appointed Royal Cup-bearer in 1576 (Wallace, 165), but the allusion here may be to some more significant court duty. l. 9. *harder judges judge ambition's rage*. Still a concern of Sidney's in the last year of his life, when he wrote to his father-in-law: 'I understand I am called very ambitious and proud at home, but certainly if they knew my heart they would not altogether so judge me' (296).

24 Unlike the miser, ll. 1–8, who at least appreciates the value of his gold, the possessive husband may subject his wife to 'foul abuse'. Presumably an invective against Penelope Devereux's husband, Lord Rich, though J. G. Nichols has suggested that Sidney and Lord Rich may actually have been 'very friendly', and the attacks on him no more than rough banter (*The Poetry of Sir Philip Sidney* (1974), 96).

25 ll. 1–4. *the wisest ... would raise*. Plato, scholar of Socrates, who had been adjudged wisest of men by the Delphic Oracle ('Phoebus' doom'), did indeed say that if we could see the true form of virtue we should instinctively

love it (Plato. *Apology*, 21). But Sidney may be deriving Plato's idea from Cicero (*De Officiis*, 1.15), as suggested by the allusion in *DP* (231) to 'the saying of Plato and Tully . . . that who could see virtue would be wonderfully ravished with the love of her beauty'.

163 **26** A light treatment of a weighty Renaissance question: whether the stars were placed simply for our delight, or, as in the medieval view, as pervasive influences on human character and behaviour. Sidney, as distinct from Astrophil, was probably one of the 'dusty wits'. He had a horoscope cast in 1570, perhaps at the behest of his uncle, Leicester, but seems not to have taken the trouble to take it away from Oxford (Bodleian MS Ashmole 356 (5); Osborn, 517–22). Two of his *imprese* celebrate the sheer beauty of the stars: Phalantus's starry shield with a motto 'signifying that it was the beauty which gave it the praise' (*NA* 94), and a pennon carried in his funeral procession showing a fish gazing up at the stars with the motto *Pulchrum propter se* (Lant, 6). Moffet (75) recorded that Sidney particularly disliked judicial astrology, though his anecdote of the 3-year-old Sidney worshipping the new moon (70) confirms his appreciation of celestial beauty.

27 l. 9. *Yet pride, I think, does not my soul possess*. Sidney, like Astrophil, was conscious of being thought proud; cf. *AS* 23.9 and note. l. 12. *overpass*. Ignore.

28 This address to laborious interpreters of his poems to 'Stella' suggests that Sidney imagined an audience for his sequence.

164 **29** A complex military metaphor is applied to Stella in ll. 1–12: she allows Cupid to keep arms in every part of her body except her heart, so that the heart itself, her capital city, may be kept free of love. This is succeeded in ll. 13–14 by the idea that Astrophil, simply because he has looked at her outward beauty, has been taken captive by love for her.

30 The seven topical questions to which Astrophil is indifferent place the sonnet in the summer of 1582 (Ringler, 470–1). ll. 1–2. The Turks were a threat to Western Europe well into the seventeenth century, and in the early summer of 1582 an attack on Spain was expected. ll. 3–4. Stephen Bathory, the elected king of Poland, invaded Muscovy (Russia) in 1580 and besieged Pskov until December 1581. By the summer of 1582 a treaty had been signed, but Sidney may not have heard of this. l. 5. The three parts are the Catholics, the Huguenots, and the moderate Politiques, who struggled for control of France until the accession of Henri de Navarre in 1589. l. 6. A reference to the Germans (Deutsch), not Dutch (who come in the next line). The Diet of the Holy Roman Empire was held at Augsburg from early July to September 1582 (cf. paper by E. G. Fogel referred to by Ringler, 471). ll. 7–8. The towns of Breda, Tournay, Oudenarde, Lier, and Ninove were won by the Spaniards during 1581–2; the hope of the Dutch lay in William of Orange. ll. 9–10. Sir Henry Sidney subdued the province of Ulster during his third term of office as Lord Deputy Governor of Ireland, 1576–8, partly by dividing it into shires, and partly by imposing a 'cess', or land-tax, on the great lords; this may be referred to in the 'golden bit'. l. 11. The confusion of the political situation in Scotland is suggested by the word 'weltering' (editions of *AS* during James I's reign tactfully emend to 'no weltering'). During the summer of 1582 there were complex intrigues leading up to the Raid of Ruthven on 22 August.

165 31 l. 14. *Do they call virtue there ungratefulness?* Inversion of the order of subject and object makes it hard to determine whether this means 'Do ladies in heaven call their lovers' virtue "ungratefulness"', i.e. 'unpleasingness', or 'Do ladies in heaven call their own ungratefulness virtue?' The second sense is the likelier, however; and cf. *AS* v.42 and note.

32 ll. 1-2. *Morpheus . . . living die.* Morpheus, son of Somnus, had the special function of bringing human images to dreamers (Ovid, *Metamorphoses*, xi. 735). Sidney may be particularly recalling Chaucer's *Book of the Duchess*, in which the dreamer reads of Morpheus bringing the drowned King Ceyx to his wife Alcyone, and subsequently himself has a dream of death and living death. l. 3. *an history*: presumably 'a story teller', though not in *OED* in this sense. l. 9. *of all acquaintance.* Probably, 'for friendship's sake'.

33 Somewhat obscure, but presumably alludes to the abortive scheme to betroth Sidney to Penelope Devereux in 1576 (cf. *AS* 2 note). It makes better sense if we believe, with Wallace (156), that Sidney had seen her some years before her marriage to Lord Rich, rather than, with Ringler (436 ff.), that he first saw her about the time of her marriage in 1581: 'rising morn' would then refer to Penelope's appearance as a child of twelve or so, 'fair day' to her fully developed beauty. The meaning of the last line is probably: 'Would that I had been foolish enough to fall in love with Stella when I first saw her, or wise enough never to fall in love at all'.

166 34 Dialogue between the passionate Astrophil and his 'wit', or reason. l. 4. *oft cruel fights well pictured forth do please.* Refers to Aristotle's *Poetics*; cf. *DP* (227). l. 7. *fond ware*: 'foolish trifles' (Ringler). l. 8. *close.* 'Kept private, not allowed to circulate' (Ringler).

35 l. 4. *nature doth with infinite agree.* 'Stella, though a product of finite nature, is goddess-like and therefore infinite' (Ringler). l. 5. *Nestor's counsels.* Nestor was the praeternaturally aged counsellor who gave advice to the Greeks in Homer's *Iliad*.

167 36 l. 2. *yelden.* Yielded. ll. 12-14 *not my soul . . . from thee.* Not only Astrophil's soul, which has sense, but stones and trees, which lack it, are enchanted by Stella's voice. Astrophil had already been conquered through one sense, that of sight; now he is conquered through another in hearing her singing voice. For evidence that Lady Rich was indeed musical, see 'Lady Rich' 185-8. There is an implicit allusion to Orpheus, whose power to enchant stones and trees was described in Ovid, *Metamorphoses*, x. xi; cf. also *AS* 3.1-6.

37 Appears in only one MS, and in neither of the quarto editions; first printed in 1598 folio. It may have been suppressed from circulated texts because the attack on Lord Rich was too explicit. Though the language is distanced and romance-like—as in 'lordings'—the allusions are clear. The

seat of the Riches was in Eastern England, Leighs, in Essex, which is presumably indicated by the fairy-tale like phrase 'Towards Aurora's court'; there may also be a sense of 'near Queen Elizabeth's court', though Aurora was not one of her usual names. The 'riddle' posed by the nymph's 'misfortune' would pose little difficulty to contemporary readers aware of Penelope Devereux's forced marriage, at which, it was later said, 'she did protest at the very solemnity and ever after' (Wallace, 247).

38 l. 2. *hatch.* Close. *unbitted.* Unrestrained. l. 5. *error.* wandering. l. 7. *so curious draught.* Such painstaking workmanship, or drawing. l. 8. *not only shines, but sings.* Cf. Strephon's vision of Urania in *Lamon's Tale*, 505–7. l. 14. Stella has murdered sleep; cf. *Macbeth*, II. ii. 35.

168 **39** l. 5. *press.* Crowd. ll. 9–14. *Take thou . . . weary head.* The offer of gifts to Morpheus is conventional, but a specific source may be Chaucer's *Book of the Duchess* 240–69; cf. *AS* 32 note. The 'rosy garland' probably means a garland of secrecy, as in the phrase *sub rosa*.

40 l. 14. *thy temple.* Sidney's brother was also fond of the image of the lover's heart as a temple to his lady's love: cf. Robert Sidney, 139, 183, 207.

169 **41** Probably refers to *Triumph* (299–311). Though Sidney took part in other tournaments in 1581–2, this was much the most striking one at which a French delegation was present. l. 6. *daintier.* 'More precise' (Ringler). l. 7. *sleight which from good use doth rise.* Dexterity achieved by plenty of practice. l. 11. *nature me a man of arms did make.* Sidney's father and grandfather, Sir Henry and Sir William Sidney, were both tilters in their youth; so were his mother's brothers, the Earls of Leicester and Warwick (Young, 55, 126–7, and *passim*). The phrase 'man of arms' refers specifically to one who fought in the semi-medieval armour of the tilt; cf. the description in *NA* (91) of Phalantus as 'the fair Man-of-Arms'.

42. l. 14. *Wracks triumphs be, which love (high set) doth breed.* Cf. Petrarch. *Canzoniere*, cxl. 14, translated by Surrey as 'Sweet is his death, that takes his end by love'.

170 **44** l. 7. *overthwart.* 'Perverse, contrary' (Ringler).

45 l. 3. *cannot skill.* Is not able. l. 14. *pity the tale of me.* A use of the Aristotelian paradox that objects represented in art may have an emotive effect that they lack in life. *AS* as a whole may constitute 'the tale of me'.

171 **47** l. 2. *burning marks.* 'Brands indicating slavery' (Ringler).

48 l. 14. *A kind of grace it is to slay with speed.* The French *coup de grace* may underlie this; cf. also Petrarch, '*Un modo di pietate, occider tosto*' (Ringler).

172 **49** There are parallels to the image of the lover as a horse ridden by love in Petrarch (Ringler, 476); it has a particular appropriateness to a poet whose first name means 'horse-lover', and who was elsewhere almost persuaded 'to wish myself a horse' (*DP* 212). l. 7. *boss.* Metal knob on the bit. l. 14. *manage.* Technical term for the movements of a highly trained horse. Astrophil presumably takes delight both in his horse's 'manage' and in his own, guided by Cupid.

50 A self-sustaining artefact: Stella's name, which opens the sonnet, preserves it from deletion. Perhaps imitated by Shakespeare in *The Two Gentlemen of Verona*, I. ii. 195–30, where Julia shows tenderness to the name 'Proteus' written on scraps of a letter she has just torn up. l. 8. *portrait*. Portray. l. 11. *babes*. His newborn thoughts.

173 **51** Apparently addressed to a fellow-courtier whose solemn talk of politics, court intrigues and quests for favour Astrophil finds tedious and incongruous with his pleasant reflexions on Stella. l. 5. *silly*. Innocent, naïve. l. 7. *in steed*. Instead. l. 10. *most troubled streams*. An image often used for the flowing channels of the Queen's bounty; cf. Ralegh:

> Those streams seem standing puddles, which before
> We saw our beauties in, so were they clear.
> Belphoebe's course is now observed no more.

(*Poems*, ed. A. Latham (1951), 34).

52 'Love asserts his right of possession ("title") to Stella by citing facts—that she outwardly wears his badge or livery; Virtue enters a demurrer—admits the facts but denies that they establish legal title by raising the question whether the essential Stella is her inside or her out; this stops the action (stays the suit) until the court can decide the legal point' (Ringler).

53 Contrast with *AS* 41; whether Astrophil does well or badly in the tiltyard, he attributes the outcome to Stella. l. 2. *staves*. Plural of (tilting) staff. The object of tilting was to break one's staff on the opponent's shield. l. 11. *to*
174 *rule*. To control (the horse). l. 12. *trumpet's sound*. A trumpet signalled the beginning of each fresh course in the tilt.

54 l. 13. *Dumb swans, not chattering pies, do lovers prove*. Quoted by Nashe in *Summer's Last Will and Testament* (1592/3):

> Well sung a shepherd that now sleeps in skies
> 'Dumb swans do love, and not vain chattering pies'.
> (*Works*, ed. McKerrow (1958), iii. 271).

55 l. 8. *How their black banner might be best displayed*. A military version of the paradox expressed in *AS* 2.14, 'While with a feeling skill I paint my hell'. Astrophil's sad words are led by a black banner both because they are written in black ink and because they are associated with destruction (cf. Marlowe, *1 Tamburlaine*, IV. i and *passim*).

175 **56** l. 3. *a whole week without one piece of look*. If it is remarkable that Astrophil has had a week without sight of Stella we may perhaps imagine a good many habitual encounters between the two. l. 11. *phlegmatique*. Cold and moist; spelling retained for the sake of metre.

57 ll. 10–11. *But them . . . darkness clear*. Probably the suggestion is that Stella sings the actual sonnets of the sequence we are reading, and in so doing sweetens them and drains them of pathos.

58 l. 1–8. *Doubt . . . rudest brain*. Refers to a controversy in classical oratory about whether the words or the manner of delivery have more influence on the audience (Cicero, *De Oratore*, ii. 223; Quintilian, XI. xi. 2–4). The image of rhetoric's golden chain is traditional, employed, for instance, in the emblem in which Hercules is shown leading crowds by golden chains from his mouth (Alciati, *Emblemata* (Antwerp, 1574), 458).

176 60 l. 1. *my good angel.* Refers to the classical theory that every human being is accompanied by two spirits, one good, one bad, which prompt him accordingly; cf. Shakespeare, *Sonnets* 144, and the Good and Bad Angels in Marlowe's *Doctor Faustus.*

177 61 l. 7. *selfness.* Selfishness, egotism (a coinage of Sidney's).

62 l. 5. *thus watered was my wine.* So my hopes were moderated; cf. Isaiah 1: 22. l. 6. *a love not blind.* Refers to the neo-Platonic theory of two Venuses and two Cupids, earthly and heavenly (Ficino). The earthly Cupid, or Desire, is blind; the heavenly, or Platonic, is sighted. The divine Cupid is often shown in emblems (e.g. Alciati, *Emblemata* (Antwerp, 1574) 297).

63. l. 3. *dove.* 'An appellation of tender affection' (*OED*). Astrophil is becoming increasingly possessive in his ways of speaking of Stella. l. 14 *in*
178 *one speech two negatives affirm.* A rule applying to Latin, not English, grammar, but Astrophil adapts it to his purpose, the question 'to grammar who says nay?' neatly repeating the idea of a negative reply. The refrain of *AS* 4 ('No, no, no, no, my dear, let be') shows that in English doubled negatives may emphasize, not affirm.

First song. l. 22. *Who long-dead beauty with increase reneweth?* Presumably implies that Stella calls ancient beauties, such as Helen or Laura, back to
179 life, but is even more beautiful than they. l. 32. *not miracles are wonders.* Wonders are not miracles; i.e. wonders in you appear as a matter of course, they are not contrary to nature.

64 l. 1. *no more these counsels try.* Stella seems to have been talking to Astrophil, trying to dissuade him from love.

65 ll. 5-8. *For when . . . mine eyes.* The fable of the runaway Cupid given refuge ('harbour') by the lover derives from the *Anacreontea*, 33, imitated also by Greville. *Caelica*, 12. l. 14. *Thou bear'st the arrow, I the arrow head.* Refers to the Sidney arms, *or, a pheon azure*, a blue arrow head on a gold background.

180 66 l. 8. *stilts.* Crutches.

67 l. 8. *What blushing notes dost thou in margin see?* The 'text' is Stella's eyes, the 'margin' her cheeks, blushing, as in the preceding sonnet.

181 68 *Amphion's lyre.* Thebes was built with his music; cf. *AS* 3.4. l. 14. *to enjoy.* With sexual undertone.

69 ll. 7-8. *Gone is the winter of my misery/My spring appears.* Perhaps echoed by Shakespeare, *Richard III,* i. i. 1-2.

70 l. 4. *I Jove's cup do keep.* Ganymede mixed nectar for Jove, and Astrophil is promoted to heavenly favour by Stella's promise; it may also be relevant that Sidney held the office of Royal Cup-bearer.

182 71 l. 7. *night-birds*. 'Vices (the owl, for instance, is used variously to pictorialize avarice, envy, sloth, and gluttony)' (Ringler),   l. 14. T. P. Roche has pointed out that this line, a vivid expression of the reason why Astrophil's virtuous covenant with Stella will not hold, comes at the numerical mid-point of the sequence, if all the lines are counted ('*Astrophil and Stella*: A Radical Reading', *Spenser Studies*, iii (1982), 144, 186).

72 l. 8. *Virtue's gold now must head my Cupid's dart*. Cf. *AS* 65.14; the blue arrow head of the Sidneys must now be tipped with gold.

Second song. Makes Astrophil's desire more explicit than in the preceding sonnets, where it is to some extent veiled in double meaning (cf. *AS* 68.14). Stella's awakening and anger prevent seduction; cf. *OA* (202), where Musidorus's assault on the sleeping Pamela is interrupted by 'a dozen
183 clownish villains'.   l. 14. *Cowards love with loss rewardeth*. Love rewards cowards with loss, i.e. 'None but the brave deserve the fair'.   l. 26. *Louring*. Scowling.

73 l. 4. *so soft a rod*. The worst Cupid has to fear is an angry look from his mother Venus.   l. 11. *Those scarlet judges, threatening bloody pain*. Stella's lips, like High Court judges, are robed in scarlet; Astrophil's offence is serious.

184 74 l. 1. *Aganippe well*. Fountain in Greece dedicated to the Muses.   l. 2. *Tempe*. Valley in Thessaly where Apollo pursued Daphne and she was changed into laurel.   ll. 5-6. *Some . . . mean by it*. Consistent with Sidney's dismissal of the idea of poetic inspiration in *DP* (240).   l. 7. *blackest brook of hell*. Styx; cf. *OA* 73.161 and *CS* 17.6.   l. 11. *my verse best wits doth please*. Astrophil does not seem to have reserved his sonnets for Stella's eyes only.

75 Apparently oddly placed among the group of sonnets reflecting on Astrophil's stolen kiss and its aftermath, this sonnet survives in a MS belonging to Sir John Harington (H. R. Woudhuysen, '*Astrophel and Stella* 75: A 'new' text', *RES* 37 (1986), 388-92).   l. 4. *imp*. Graft.   ll. 5-8. *Nor . . . did late obtain*. Edward IV usurped the throne in 1461, after his father, the Duke of York, was killed while fighting against the Lancastrians: the later years of his reign were tranquil and well ordered.   ll. 9-11. *Nor that . . . a tribute paid*. In 1474 Edward invaded France, and was persuaded by Louis XI to withdraw with a payment of 75,000 crowns. France was not, in fact, 'hedged', or protected, at this time by the 'bloody lion' (Scotland, represented by a red lion).   l. 14. *To lose his crown, rather than fail his love*. In 1464 Edward married Lady Elizabeth Grey, widow of Sir Richard Grey. Warwick, the 'King-maker', who had been negotiating a French match for him, drove Edward into exile in 1470, though he recovered his throne in the following year. Cf. Shakespeare's *3 Henry VI*, III. ii and *passim*.

185 76 Another sonnet in alexandrines.   l. 13. *walking*. With agitated thoughts, mind 'racing'.

77 In alexandrines.   l. 2. *whose lecture*. The reading of which.

78 A characterization of the monster Jealousy, comparable with the monster

Cupid anatomized in *OA* 8. It is presumably directed towards Lord Rich, as suggested in the final wish that he should be cuckolded.

186 79 ll. 1–2. *Sweet . . . sweetest sweetener art.* A use of 'polyptoton', when a single word with 'divers fallings or terminations' is frequently repeated (Fraunce, 51–2).

80 l. 8. *honour's grain*: 'The purple of political dignity' (Ringler). l. 12. *resty.* Restive.

187 82 l. 1. *Nymph of the garden.* The garden is Stella's own body; the cherry tree is her lips. Cf. Thomas Campion's song 'There is a garden in her face' (*Works*, ed. W. R. Davis (1967), 174). l. 3. *His who till death looked in a watery glass.* Narcissus drowned while gazing at his own reflection in a river. l. 4. *hers whom naked the Trojan boy did see.* Paris saw Venus naked.

83 l. 1. *Good brother Philip.* Stella's sparrow is 'brother' to Astrophil both because they are rivals for her favour and because they share a Christian name. The sparrow, traditionally identified with lechery, is partly an image for Astrophil's own desire; cf. Gascoigne's *The praise of Phillip Sparrowe*, where the innuendo is inescapable (*Posies*, ed. J. W. Cunliffe (1907), 455–6). Other sources are Catullus's elegy on Lesbia's sparrow and Skelton's *Philip Sparrow*. l. 3. *your cut to keep.* To behave with modesty, restraint. l. 14. *sir Phip.* 'Sir' is used here 'With contemptuous, ironic or irate force' (*OED* 6b). Sidney's knighthood, which he received in January 1583, is unlikely to be relevant.

Third song l. 1–4. For Orpheus and Amphion, cf. *DP* (217). ll. 7–10. *If love . . . endless night.* Alludes to two anecdotes in Pliny's *Natural History* (viii. 61, x. 18). Thoas, an Arcadian, was rescued from robbers by a dragon (lizard) to which he had been kind; and a maiden of Sestos nurtured an eagle which loved her so much that it flew into her funeral pyre and was consumed.

84 Addressed to the road leading to Stella's house. Mona Wilson suggested that this was the Whitechapel Road, leading to Wanstead (*Sir Philip Sidney* (1950), 191); but the Rich seat, Leighs, in Essex, or Penelope Devereux's brother's house, Essex House, in London, seem slightly more likely destinations. l. 2. *to some ears not unsweet.* Another hint that these poems are being read and appreciated by readers other than Stella; cf. *AS* 74.11. ll. 3–4. *Tempers . . . chamber melody.* According to a great-uncle of John Aubrey's, Sidney 'was often wont, as he was hunting on our pleasant plains, to take his table book out of his pocket and write down his notions as they came into his head' (Aubrey, *Brief Lives*, ed. A. Clark (1898), ii. 248).

85 ll. 3–4. *joy . . . strain.* In *OA* (229) Pyrocles, on his way to Philoclea's chamber, 'found that extremity of joy is not without a certain joyful pain, by extending the heart beyond his wonted limits'. l. 6. *Not pointing to fit folks each undercharge.* Not assigning secondary duties to appropriate underlings. l. 14. *Thou but of all the kingly tribute take.* Astrophil's heart, the addressee here, should take possession of Stella's.

189 Fourth song l. 15. *These sweet flowers on fine bed too.* Presumably flowers

190 embroidered on a bedspread, since the lovers are indoors. l. 37. *Your fair mother is abed.* Penelope Devereux's mother, Lettice Knollys, had been married to the First Earl of Essex (d. 1576); she then married Sidney's uncle, the Earl of Leicester, in 1578, thus making Sidney a step-cousin of her children. She seems to have been at least as remarkable a personality as her daughter, whom she outlived by nearly thirty years. l. 39. *you do letters write.* Unlike many less well educated Elizabethan ladies, Penelope Devereux was a fluent and accomplished letter writer ('Lady Rich', 188–9).

86 l. 5. *like spotless ermine.* The ermine was believed to die rather than allow its skin to be spotted; cf. *OA* 62.116 (136).

191 **Fifth song** Astrophil punishes Stella for her rejection of him by offering her
192 a clumsy and old-fashioned poem ('Lady Rich', 178). l. 31. *Your client poor my self shall Stella handle so?* Can Stella, exalted by Astrophil's muse, get away with treating him so badly? l. 36. *Sweet babes must babies have.* Nice children must have dolls. l. 42. *Ungrateful who is called, the worst of evils is spoken.* 'Ingratitude comprehends (is the worst of all) faults (vices)' (Tilley, 166). l. 46. *rich in all joys.* No doubt another pun on Stella's married name.
193 ll. 89–90. *such skill in my muse . . . shall be proved.* If Stella will only be kind to Astrophil, he will again write skilful poetry in her praise, instead of the present inelegant abuse.

Sixth song Included in William Byrd's *Psalms, Sonnets and songs of sadness*
194 *and piety* (1588). l. 4. *former.* First, higher. l. 43. *common sense.* Shared or community feeling or judgement (*OED*, sense 3).

195 **Seventh song** Quoted by Fraunce (46) as an example of 'Epanodos, regression, turning to the same sound, when one and the same sound is repeated in the beginning and middle, or middle and end'.

Eighth song Imitated by many later poets; e.g. Fulke Greville, *Caelica* lxxv; Edward, Lord Herbert of Cherbury, 'Ode upon a question moved: whether love should endure for ever'. There is a setting by Robert Dowland in *A Musical Banquet* (1610). l. 1. *In a grove most rich of shade.* The suggestion may be that the shade is made rich by Lady Rich's presence, and not necessarily that the meeting occurs in the garden of one of Lord Rich's
196 houses. l. 19. *arms crossed.* The pose of melancholy, or like effigies on
198 tombs. l. 104. *my song is broken.* The attempt at objectivity represented by third person narration collapses here; cf. the complementary shift from first to third person in the following song, ll. 26–30.

Ninth song There is a setting by Robert Dowland in *A Musical Banquet*
199 (1610): also in Christ Church, Oxford, MS 439, fo. 9. l. 23. *caitiff.* Wretched, miserable.

200 87 l. 4. *iron laws of duty.* Not identifiable. l. 5. *she with me did smart.* She shared my pain.

88 Astrophil is tempted to unfaithfulness by the flirtatious approaches of another lady, but maintains his devotion to Stella through inward recollection. l. 6. *sun.* Consistent with identification of Stella elsewhere with the

sun rather than, as her name might suggest, a star. l. 8. *cates*. Choice victuals.

201 **89** Only two 'rhyme' words are used, 'night' and 'day', but in a pattern approximating to the Petrarchan form. Fraunce (48) quoted ll. 5–14 as an example of '*epanodos*, regression'.

90 Perhaps Stella has accused Astrophil of using her as a pretext for enhancing his own reputation through poetry; this would be consistent with other hints, in this part of the sequence, of incipient disintegration of the relationship. l. 9. *laud*. Praise, credit.

91 l. 1. *honour's cruel might*. Presumably the same as the 'iron laws of duty'
202 which called Astrophil away in *AS* 87.4. l. 11. *Models such be wood-globes of glistering skies*. 'Wood-globes' must be globes showing the constellations, which were in use throughout the sixteenth century. Sidney studied the 'sphere' during his year in Italy, and he recommended its study to his brother Robert and to Edward Denny in 1580 (290).

92 l. 1. *Indian ware*. Ware from the Indies, proverbially scarce and expensive. In *The Defence of Leicester* Sidney says that, given his noble ancestry, Leicester's want of gentility 'would seem as great news as if they came from the Indies' (*Misc. Prose*, 133). l. 3. *cutted Spartans*. The Spartans were notorious for their 'cutted', or concise, pithy, mode of rhetoric. l. 5. *total*. Brief.

Tenth song Set by William Byrd in *Songs of sundrie natures* (1589) and by Robert Dowland in *A Musicall Banquet* (1610). ll. 19–48. *Thought ... nectar drinking*. Fulke Greville's *Caelica*, xlv, 41–50, seems to comment on this passage in which Astrophil sends his 'Thought' off on a journey of sexual exploration:

> But thoughts, be not so brave
> With absent joy;
> For you with that you have
> Yourself destroy.
> The absence which you glory
> Is that which makes you sorry
> And burn in vain:
> For thought is not the weapon
> Wherewith *thought's-ease* men cheapen:
> *Absence is pain.*

> ('Lady Rich', 191).

204 **93** ll. 6–8. *my foul stumbling ... did miss*. The exact nature of Astrophil's offence is as obscure as the 'fault' of the young man in Shakespeare's *Sonnets*; but he seems to claim that he has been trying too hard to do or say the right thing. l. 11. *'quit*. Acquit.

205 **96** l. 9. *mazeful*. Bewildering.

97 The full moon (Diana) accompanied by stars makes a brilliant night, but the night would prefer the sun (Phoebus); likewise, another, unidentified lady ('Dian's peer', or equal) tries to console Astrophil for the absence of

Stella (the sun). l. 4. *standing*. Shooting position (archery term). l. 8. *dight*. Dressed.

206 **98** As Ringler says, 'Addresses to the bed were frequent in Renaissance love poetry', but 'Sidney's handling is, as usual, entirely original'. l. 4. *lee shores*. Shores facing away from the wind. l. 11. *when Aurora leads out Phoebus' dance*. When dawn leads in day. l. 13. *wink*. Close.

99 l. 3. *mark-wanting shafts*. Arrows lacking a target. l. 9. *charm*. Sing in unison.

100 l. 1. *O tears, no tears, but rain from beauty's skies*. An example of epanorthosis, or 'correction . . . when anything passed is called back' (Fraunce, 78–9). Perhaps imitated by Kyd, *Spanish Tragedy*, III. ii in the speech beginning 'O eyes, no eyes, but fountains fraught with tears', which in turn was mocked by Jonson in *Every Man in his Humour*, I. v. 57–8. Sidney's own model was probably Petrarch or one of the Pléiade poets who

207 used the device. l. 9. *conserved in such a sugared phrase*. Refers to the preservation of fruits in sugar.

101 l. 11. *prest*. prompt, ready. l. 14. *heaven stuff*. 'Heavenly material, her bodily beauty' (Ringler).

102 Another sonnet in alexandrines; cf. 1, 6, 8, 76, 77. l. 5. *vade*. Disappear. l. 9. *Galen's adoptive sons*. 'Followers of Galen, old-fashioned physicians unaware of the new Paduan school' (Ringler). l. 10. *hackney on*. Ride stumblingly, as on a worn-out horse.

208 **103** l. 2. *with many a smiling line*. Cf. *NA* (7), where blood has 'filled the wrinkles of the sea's visage'. l. 9. *Aeol's youths*. Breezes, sons of Aeolus, god of winds.

104 l. 10. *If I but stars upon my armour bear*. Sidney may have worn starry armour in tournaments. A star-spangled banner is shown in Lant's *Funeral Roll* (5), and Nathaniel Baxter describes a posthumous vision of him in blue armour covered with silver stars (*Sir Philip Sidneys Ouránia* (1606)). Cf. also *NA* (412) for a description of a knight whose clothes were 'all cut in stars, which made of cloth of silver and silver spangles, each way seemed to cast many aspects'.

Eleventh song First printed in the 1598 folio of Sidney's works. There is a
209 setting by Thomas Morley, *The First Booke of Aires* (1600). l. 27. *such minds*. Such states of mind. l. 42. *Argus' eyes*. Argus was a many-eyed monster set by Juno to watch over Jove's mistress, Io.

210 **105** Astrophil has missed an opportunity of seeing Stella by night, but the circumstances are obscure. 'Dead glass' in l. 3 has been variously identified as Astrophil's eye, a telescope, or his tears; Ringler (490) thinks it is Astrophil's eyes, which were not to blame for not seeing Stella. However, 'dazzling race' may suggest a lantern or torch, as in l. 11; and the Bright MS version of l. 1, 'Unhappy light', suggests that this object may be the main addressee throughout.

106 l. 3. *Bare me in hand*. 'Deceived me, promised me falsely' (Ringler).

l. 5. *dainty cheer.* Comfort, choice provisions. l. 10. *conversation sweet.* A phrase used of Stella in *AS* 77.

211 107 l. 8. *this great cause.* May refer either to public duty or a literary project, such as the translation of Du Bartas, which Stella herself wishes to see accomplished ('what thy own will attends'). Ringler thinks the reference is to 'public service in general', but the phrase sounds allusive and specific.

108 A reversion to Astrophil's previous self-absorbed obsession; perhaps placed as a final snapshot of 'Astrophil' before Sidney directs his 'wit' to the 'cause' mentioned in the previous sonnet. The paradoxes and oxymora make it clear that he can go no further as 'Astrophil'. l. 10. *Phoebus' gold.* Sunlight.

212 *The Defence of Poesy.* Written some time after December 1579, when Spenser's *Shepheardes Calender* was dedicated to Sidney (cf. *DP*, 1244–5). Some stimulus may also have been given by the dedication earlier in the same year of Stephen Gosson's *The schoole of abuse*, a Puritan attack on plays and players for which Spenser claimed that Gosson had been 'scorned' by Sidney (*Two Letters*, 1580). However, Gosson dedicated another book to Sidney a few months later, and was apparently promoted by Sidney's future father-in-law, Sir Francis Walsingham, after another attack on the stage, *Playes Confuted* (1582) (A. F. Kinney, *Markets of Bawdrie: The Dramatic Criticism of Stephen Gosson*, Salzburg (1974), 43–51). Van Dorsten suggested that *DP* was written while Sidney was completing *OA* during 1580, as 'a summary of his views before the early experiments were over' (*Misc. Prose*, 63), but it may equally well belong to the interval between the two *Arcadias*, overlapping, perhaps, with *AS*, as hinted by verbal and metaphoric links and a possible allusion in *AS* 18.10. Shepherd (4) assigned it to 1581–3; the date limits may be even wider, from early 1580 to 1585, when William Temple became Sidney's secretary and prepared his *Analysis* of the work.

Among Sidney's models were Aristotle's *Rhetoric* (which he is said to have translated); Horace's *De arte poetica*; J. C. Scaliger's *Poetices libri septem* (1561); Serranus's edition of Plato (1578); Amyot's preface to his translation of Plutarch's *Lives* (translated by North in 1579); and various Italian theorists such as Minturno (*De Poeta*, 1559). As Shepherd (12–16) has shown, the treatise is cast in the form of a classical oration, though designed for silent reading, not delivery. Its title is unstable. As van Dorsten says, 'Sidney may never have contemplated giving his discourse a proper title' (*Misc. Prose*, 69); however, his extraction from *DP* of the phrase 'a . . . defence of . . . poetry' seems editorially dubious, since his copy-text was *The Defence of Poesy*, published by Ponsonby in 1595. Olney published the work under the title *An Apology for Poetry* in the same year, and in his manuscript *Analysis* Temple referred to it as '*tractatio de Poesi*'. In the present edition the Ponsonby title, adopted in the 1598 and later editions of Sidney's works, is restored, along with about twenty readings from his text rejected by van Dorsten.

ll. 1–2. *When . . . together.* Edward Wotton (1548–1626) was secretary to the

English embassy in Vienna at the court of the Holy Roman Emperor, Maximilian II, while Sidney was there in the autumn of 1574, and travelled back to England with him in the spring of 1575 (Osborn, 235, 307–8, and *passim*). He was one of the pall-bearers at Sidney's funeral, and was bequeathed 'one fee-buck to be taken yearly out of my park at Penshurst' in Sidney's will (*Misc. Prose*, 149, 218).

ll. 2–3. *John Pietro Pugliano . . . stable.* The office of 'Esquire of the stable' was a dignified one.

l. 10. *faculty.* Profession.

l. 15. *pedanteria.* Italian word for 'pedantry', or heavy-footed book learning, perhaps quoted from Pugliano's native tongue.

l. 19. *a piece of a logician.* One of his Oxford contemporaries, Richard Carew, testified to Sidney's early skill in disputation (*The Survey of Cornwall* (1602), 102v), and his protégé Abraham Fraunce shared with him an interest in the latest developments in Ramist logic (cf. Bodleian MS Rawl. D.345). However, another logician in his entourage, his secretary William Temple, made a logical *Analysis* of *DP* which showed its arguments to be in several respects deficient (see Abbreviations).

ll. 26–7. *having slipped into the title of a poet.* This may refer to *OA*, or to Sidney's lyric poetry in general including the poems in *OA* and *CS*; it can refer to the work which reads most like a 'spontaneous overflow of powerful feelings', *AS*, only if, *pace* van Dorsten, we date *DP* after 1582 (see headnote, above).

l. 36. *is fallen to be the laughing stock of children.* The mid-Tudor period —called by C. S. Lewis 'the Drab Age'—was not a very distinguished phase of English poetry, but even so Sidney is probably exaggerating for effect.

ll. 41–2. *the hedgehog . . . host.* Aesop, *Fables*, 184–5.

213 ll. 42–3. *vipers . . . parents.* Pliny, *Natural History*, x. lxxxii. 2.

ll. 45–6. *Musaeus, Homer, and Hesiod, all three nothing else but poets.* Musaeus, whose *Hero and Leander* was translated by Marlowe (published 1598), was believed by the Elizabethans to be an even earlier poet than Homer, though he actually wrote in the fifth century AD. Hesiod, author of *Theogonia* and *Opera et Dies*, really was ancient, writing in the eighth century BC.

l. 47. *Orpheus, Linus.* The archetypal Greek poet Orpheus was believed in the Renaissance to be the author of the 'Orphic hymns'; Linus was supposedly his teacher, so more ancient still.

ll. 53–4. *Amphion . . . Thebes.* Thebes was said to have been built by the power of Amphion's music; cf. *AS* 3.2–3.

ll. 54–5. *Orpheus . . . beastly people.* Sidney may imply that it was more remarkable that Orpheus moved the hearts of barbarous people than that he moved beasts.

l. 56. *Livius Andronicus and Ennius.* Livius Andronicus (d. 204 BC), a Greek, was thought to be the earliest Latin poet; Ennius (239–169 BC) wrote *Annales*, a history of Rome, in verse.

l. 57. *Dante, Boccaccio, and Petrarch . . . Gower and Chaucer.* Sidney's emphasis is on the encyclopaedic character of these five poets, as well as their early date.

ll. 64–6. *Thales, Empedocles, and Parmenides . . . Pythagoras and Phocylides . . . Tyrtaeus . . . Solon.* Seven early Greek thinkers: Thales (fl. 585 BC) was believed to have composed poems on astronomy and physics; Empedocles (fl. 450 BC) wrote poems *On Nature* and *Purifications*; Parmenides (fl. 475 BC) founded the Eleatic school of philosophy; Pythagoras (fl. 530 BC) was believed to be the author of *Aurea Carmina*; Phocylides (fl. 560 BC) wrote gnomic verses; Tyrtaeus (fl. 670 BC) was a lame schoolmaster who inspired the Spartans to victory by his verses; and Solon (fl. 600 BC), the great Athenian legislator, was the supposed author of a lost epic on Atlantis (Plato, *Timaeus*, 20e). Sidney probably knew these fragments of early Greek poetry from Henri Estienne's collection *Poesis Philosophica* (1573), whose preface included eulogies of poetry which may have influenced *DP*.

ll. 76–7. *the well ordering of a banquet, the delicacy of a walk, with interlacing mere tales, as Gyges' ring.* Supper arrangements are described in Plato's *Symposium*; an outdoor walk in the *Phaedrus*; and the fable of Gyges' ring of invisibility in *Republic*, ii. 359.

214 l. 79. *historiographers.* Writers of history.

ll. 81–2. *Herodotus entitled his History by the name of the nine Muses.* Herodotus was not himself responsible for naming each of his nine books after a Muse, but Sidney may not have known this. Valla's translation of Herodotus into Latin was corrected by Sidney's friend Henri Estienne (1566).

ll. 92–3. *In Turkey . . . poets.* Like most Elizabethans, Sidney took a keen interest in the Turks, whose Ottoman Empire extended to Cyprus (cf. *AS* 8) and deep into Hungary. T. Washington's *Navigations into Turkey* (1585, but probably completed four years earlier), translated from Nicolas de Nicolay, was dedicated jointly to Sidney and his father. This included plates depicting both 'law-giving divines' and poets, or minstrels.

ll. 93–4. *In our neighbour country Ireland . . . in a devout reverence.* Sidney here uses the power of the Irish bards to support his case for the archetypal nature of poetry, though their activities were actually seen as dangerous and anarchic by his father, as Lord Deputy Governor; cf. John Derrick, *The Image of Ireland* (1581), fo. 2r–v.

l. 96. *areytos.* 'Rhymes or ballads' celebrating ancestral valour, accompanied by dancing and music, performed by New World Indians on Haiti (Peter Martyr, *Decades of the newe worlde or West India* tr. Richard Eden (1555), III. vii).

ll. 102–7. *In Wales . . . long continuing.* Sidney had a particular knowledge of Wales and Welsh antiquity through his father, who was Lord President of the Marches of Wales from 1559, and supported the completion by David Powell of the learned antiquary Humfrey Lhuyd's *Commentarioli Brittanicae* (*The historie of Cambria* (1584), dedicated to Sidney).

215 ll. 119–23. *whereof . . . performed it.* Julius Capitolinus, *Vita Albini*, in

Scriptores Historiae Augustae, tells this anecdote; line from Virgil, *Aeneid*, II. 314, tr. by T. Phaer (1580) as 'With anger wood [=mad], and fair me thought in arms it was to die.'

ll. 127–8. *the oracles of Delphos and Sybilla's prophecies were wholly delivered in verses.* The Pythian priestess at Delphi declared Apollo's oracles in hexameters; the original Sibylline oracles of early Greece hardly survive, but a large body of 'Sibylline' verses was gathered up from late antiquity onwards.

ll. 137–8. *as all learned Hebricians . . . not yet fully found.* Hebrew scholars from Jerome onwards agreed that the Psalms were in verse, and until the work of Lowth in the eighteenth century it was thought that some pattern of quantity or stress or rhyme might be discovered in them.

l. 140. *prosopopoeias.* Personifications.

ll. 141–2. *his telling of the beast's joyfulness and hills leaping.* Psalm 29.

l. 155. *a maker.* Obsolete word for 'poet', current in the Renaissance.

216 l. 179. *Cyclops, Chimeras, Furies.* The Cyclops were one-eyed monsters; Chimeras were winged, goat-like animals; Furies or Erinyes were savage, malign creatures concerned with retribution.

ll. 188–90. *so true a lover as Theagenes . . . Virgin's Aeneas.* Theagenes was the young hero of Heliodorus's *Aethiopica*, a late Greek romance (translated by Underdowne, ?1569) which was one of the sources of *OA*; Pylades was the faithful friend of Orestes in Euripides's *Oresteia*; Orlando was the hero of Ariosto's *Orlando Furioso* (1532); Cyrus the young prince whose education was described in Xenophon's *Cyropaedia*; and Aeneas, hero of Virgil's *Aeneid*, was seen by Renaissance readers as virtually faultless.

l. 194. *idea or fore-conceit.* Sidney uses Plato's word 'idea' and his own phrase 'fore-conceit' to denote the original conception in the artist's mind to which he attempts to give expression in poetry.

l. 196. *imaginative.* Fanciful, with derogatory connotations.

l. 198. *a Cyrus.* Another reference to Xenophon's *Cyropaedia*; see above, l. 220. As the archetypal *bildungsroman*, Xenophon's work was regularly used in the education of young princes, such as Edward VI and James VI of Scotland, as well as forming part of the curriculum of Shrewsbury School when Sidney was there (T. W. Baldwin, *Small Latine and Lesse Greeke* (1944), 237, 543, 391, and *passim*).

217 l. 221. *a speaking picture.* The saying, much quoted in the Renaissance, that poetry is a speaking picture and painting a silent poetry, was attributed by Plutarch ('*De gloria Atheniensum*', *Moralia*, 346) to the poet Simonides of Ceos.

ll. 227–8. *Emanuel Tremellius and Franciscus Junius.* Tremellius and Junius called these books poetical in their joint translation of the Bible into Latin (Frankfurt, 1575, ii. 4). When previously published by Henri Estienne in 1569 Tremellius's *New Testament* had been dedicated to Queen Elizabeth.

ll. 232–3. *St James's counsel.* James 5: 13: 'Is any among you afflicted? let him pray. Is any merry? let him sing psalms.'

ll. 238-40. *Tyrtaeus . . . Lucan.* Tyrtaeus (cf. ll. 73-8 note) praised martial valour; Phocylides wrote verse precepts: 'Cato' at this time denoted the moral distichs gathered up by Erasmus, much used in the first and second form at grammar schools; Lucretius's *De Rerum Natura* treats of the nature of the physical world, and Virgil's *Georgics* of farming; Manilius was the author of *Astronomica*, a poem in five books; Joannes Jovius Pontanus, the only post-classical author in this list, wrote *Urania*, a neo-Latin astronomical poem, in the late fifteenth century; and Lucan's *Pharsalia*, much admired by the Elizabethans, described the wars between Caesar and Pompey.

l. 245. *this question.* The question of how effectively they teach virtue.

ll. 249-50. *the constant though lamenting look of Lucretia.* Depictions of Lucretia's suicide were extremely common in Renaissance Europe, and found their way into the houses of many Elizabethan noblemen.

ll. 257-8. *waited on . . . poets.* That is, the best writers in the best languages call these writers 'poets', not 'prophets' or 'seers' ('vates').

ll. 266-7. *the heroic, lyric, tragic, comic, satiric, iambic, elegiac, pastoral.* This list of eight poetic genres, in what appears to be descending order of magnitude, derives from Horace, Quintilian, and others, but is unusual in assigning the second highest place to the 'lyric'. The 'iambic' was a form of satire written in iambic metre associated with the early Greek writers Archilochus and Hipponax.

l. 270. *numbrous.* Rhythmical, measured; probably a coinage of Sidney's.

l. 276. *as Cicero saith of him.* In his *Epistola ad Quintus*, I. i. 23, Cicero praised Xenophon's *Cyropaedia* as an exemplary fiction, not a history.

ll. 277-8. *Heliodorus . . . Chariclea.* Heliodorus's *Aethiopica*; see above, ll. 188-90.

219 ll. 309-10. *the astronomer, looking to the stars, might fall in a ditch.* Plato, *Theaetetus,* 174A, described the astronomer Thales falling into a well; cf. *AS* 19.10.

l. 316. *architektoniké.* 'The master-art or science which prescribes to all beneath it' (Liddell and Scott, *Greek Lexicon*).

220 l. 327. *the moral philosophers.* This account of the futility of philosophy owes much to Cornelius Agrippa, *De incertitudine et vanitate Scientiarum et Artium* (1530), which had been translated into English by James Sanford in 1569.

ll. 352-3. *I am testis temporum, lux veritatis, vita memoriae, magistra vitae, nuntia temporis.* Misquotation of a well-known passage in Cicero, *De Oratore,* II. ix. History claims to be 'the witness of the ages, the light of truth, the life of memory, the governess of life, the herald of antiquity' (cf. North's *Plutarch,* i. 16).

ll. 356-7. *in the battles of Marathon, Pharsalia, Poitiers, and Agincourt.* The Athenians defeated the Persians at Marathon in 490 BC; Caesar defeated Pompey at Pharsalia in 48 BC; Edward, the Black Prince, captured the King of France at Poitiers in 1356; and Henry V defeated the French at Agincourt in 1415.

221 l. 364. *Brutus, Alphonsus of Aragon.* According to Plutarch, Marcus Brutus spent his time before the battle of Pharsalia studying history: 'when others slept, or thought what would happen the morrow after, he fell to his book, and wrote all day long, till night, writing a breviary of Polybius'; and Alphonsus of Aragon was said to have cured himself of sickness by reading about Alexander the Great (North's *Plutarch*, vi. 185; i. 17–18).

l. 368 *moderator.* Judge, arbitrator.

l. 378. *rather formidine poenae than virtutis amore.* Through fear of punishment rather than love of virtue; cf. Horace, *Epistles*, i. xvi. 52–3.

l. 389. *halt.* Limp, proceed defectively.

222 ll. 406–7. *a man that had never seen an elephant or a rhinoceros.* This included most Elizabethans; however, Dürer's woodcut (1515) gave sixteenth-century readers an idea of the rhinoceros, and Sidney would have been familiar with *imprese*, copied by Abraham Fraunce from Paolo Giovio, showing an elephant and a rhinoceros (K. Duncan-Jones, 'Two Elizabethan Versions of Giovio's treatise on *imprese*', *English Studies*, lv (1971), 120–1).

l. 408. *the architecture.* The structure (cf. *OED* senses 3, 5).

ll. 420–1. *Tully . . . the force love of our country hath in us.* A common theme in Cicero; cf. *De Officiis*, i. xxiv. 83–4; xlv. 159–60; iii. xxiv. 93; xxv. 95; xxvii. 100; *De oratore*, i. 196–7; *De finibus* iii. 64.

l. 422. *old Anchises . . . Troy's flames.* Virgil, *Aeneid*, ii. 634–50.

ll. 422–4. *Ulysses . . . Ithaca.* Homer, *Odyssey*, v. 149ff., 215.

l. 424. *Anger . . . a short madness.* 'Ira furor brevis est', Horace, *Epistles*, i. ii. 62.

ll. 424–5. *let but Sophocles bring you Ajax on a stage.* Actually, this is reported, not shown; Sophocles, *Ajax*, 1061. Sidney probably knew the play from J. C. Scaliger's translation of it into Latin.

l. 428. *the schoolmen.* The scholastic philosophers of the Middle Ages; academics who taught in 'schools', or university lecture halls.

ll. 429–30. *Ulysses . . . Euryalus.* All examples from the history of Troy, but not precise enough to be identified with particular passages in Homer, Virgil, or later writers.

ll. 432–4. *Oedipus . . . Agamemnon . . . Atreus . . . the two Theban brothers . . . Medea.* These are all subjects of Greek tragedy, though Sidney and his readers may have been more familiar with them from the tragedies of Seneca, which had been translated into English between 1559 and 1567.

l. 435. *the Terentian Gnatho.* From Terence, *Eunuchus*; the word 'gnatho' was used to mean 'sycophant, parasite' during the sixteenth and seventeenth centuries.

l. 435. *our Chaucer's Pandar.* The word 'pandar', for a go-between, derives from the character in Chaucer's *Troilus and Criseyde*.

l. 442. *Sir Thomas More's Utopia.* More's *Utopia* (1516) had been translated into English by Ralph Robinson in 1551. Sidney's reservations about the work may derive—as suggested by the phrase 'it was the fault of the man'—from More's political and religious standpoint. However, a distant kinsman, George More, travelled with Sidney on his 1577 embassy, and was the occasion of a eulogy of Sir Thomas More to which Sidney was a witness at a social gathering at Nuremberg (cf. K. J. Höltgen, 'Why are there no wolves in England? Philip Camerarius and a German version of Sidney's table-talk', *Anglia*, 99 (1981), 60–82).

l. 444. *absolute.* Perfect, complete.

223   ll. 449–50. *Mediocribus ... columnae.* Horace, *De arte poetica*, 372–3, translated by Ben Jonson as

> But neither men, nor gods, nor pillars meant
> Poets should ever be indifferent.

'That is, mediocrity in poets is rejected by all, including their booksellers (whose wares were displayed in Rome around the columns of buildings)' (Shepherd, 174).

l. 455. *Dives and Lazarus.* Luke 16: 19–31.

l. 456. *the lost child and the gracious father.* The parable of the Prodigal Son, Luke 15: 11–32.

l. 475. *Aristotle ... in his discourse of poesy. Poetics*, IX. 1451b. The Greek terms which follow are accurately glossed by Sidney.

224   l. 487. *Vespasian's picture right as he was.* Vespasian, as described in Suetonius's *Vita Vespasiani*, xx, was coarse-looking and ugly. Sidney could have seen images of him both in England and on the Continent (cf. K. Duncan-Jones, 'Sidney and Titian', in *English Renaissance Studies: Presented to Dame Helen Gardner* (1980), 9–10).

ll. 490–1. *the feigned Cyrus in Xenophon ... the true Cyrus in Justin.* Xenophon's *Cyropaedia* (translated into English by W. Barker, 1560) was a fictionalized account (see above, l. 276); Justin's *Histories*, a compilation made from the earlier Greek history of Trogus Pompeius, had been translated by Arthur Golding (1564), and were recommended by Sidney to Edward Denny (289).

l. 492. *the right Aeneas in Dares Phrygius.* The account of the Trojan War by 'Dares Phrygius' was believed by medieval writers, such as Chaucer, to be more authentic than Homer or Virgil; if Sidney had doubts about its authenticity, it would not serve his purpose to air them here.

ll. 495–6. *Canidia... was full ill-favoured.* Horace, *Epodes*, v, described the ugly witch Canidia trying to regain her beauty; cf. also *Satires*, I. viii; *Epodes*, III. xvii.

l. 500. *Alexander or Scipio himself.* Quintus Curtius wrote a life of Alexander; Livy in his *Histories*, xxi–xxxii wrote about the mainly admirable, but latterly faulty, Scipio Africanus. Cf. also North's *Plutarch*, iv. 298–386 and vi. 395–431.

l. 504. *doctrine.* Learning, knowledge.

l. 504. *the history.* The historian; cf. *AS* 32.3.

l. 508. *a gross conceit.* 'An undiscriminating understanding' (Shepherd).

ll. 518–23. *Herodotus and Justin . . . Darius.* Herodotus, *History*, III. 153–60; Justin, *Histories*, I. x.

l. 524. *Livy . . . his son.* Livy, *Histories*, I. iii–iv.

225 ll. 525–6. *Xenophon . . . Cyrus' behalf. Cyropaedia*, VI. i. 39 has such an anecdote of Araspas, whom Sidney has confused with Abradatas.

l. 535. *from Dante's heaven to his hell.* This is one of the earliest references to Dante in English literature; see also below, l. 1522.

l. 545. *Ulysses in a storm, and in other hard plights. Odyssey*, V and *passim*.

l. 548. *the tragedy writer.* Euripides, as described by Plutarch. '*Quomodo adolescens poetas audire debeat*' (*Moralia*, 19); the example was of Ixion, who ended up 'manacled' to a wheel.

ll. 552–3. *see we not valiant Miltiades rot in his fetters?* Miltiades, who had won the battle of Marathon for the Greeks, was imprisoned by his own people; cf. Cicero, *Republic*, I. iii. 5.

ll. 553–4. *The just Phocion and the accomplished Socrates put to death like traitors?* Cf. North's *Plutarch*, v. 108, where the execution of Phocion by the Athenians is compared with that of Socrates.

ll. 554–5. *The cruel Severus live prosperously?* The Emperor Lucius Septimus Severus (d. AD 211).

l. 555. *The excellent Severus miserably murdered.* 'Alexander Severus, Emperor AD 222–35, murdered in his thirtieth year by mutineers' (Shepherd).

ll. 555–6. *Sulla and Marius dying in their beds?* 'Lucius Sulla (138–78 BC), dictator of Rome, whose bitter struggles with Caius Marius (157–86 BC) and the Marian party filled all Italy with strife and terror for twenty years' (Shepherd).

ll. 556–7. *Pompey and Cicero . . . a happiness?* Pompey fled to Egypt after his defeat at Pharsalia, and was killed there (48 BC); Cicero tried to escape from Rome after being proscribed by Mark Antony in 43 BC, and was put to death.

ll. 557–9. *See we not . . . highest honour?* Cato, who continued to resist Caesar after his victory at Pharsalia, was finally driven to suicide at Utica, in Africa; Caesar, the rebel, has given his name to future monarchs (cf. 'Kaiser', 'Tsar'). The Holy Roman Emperor was referred to in Latin as 'Caesar', Sidney's 1577 embassy being '*ad Caesarem*'.

l. 561. *Caesar's own words.* 'He was ignorant of letters', reported by Suetonius, *Julius Caesar*, 77, and extracted by Erasmus as an apothegm.

226 ll. 565–7. *Cypselus, Periander, Phalaris, Dionysius . . . usurpation.* Cypselus and Periander were long-reigning tyrants of Corinth in the 7th century BC; Phalaris was a tyrant of Sicily in the 6th century BC; and Dionysius was

tyrant of Syracuse in the 4th century BC.

l. 577. *philophilosophos*. A lover of the philosophers.

l. 583. *not gnosis but praxis*. Not knowing but doing.

ll. 597–8. *natural conceit*. Innate reason, inclination.

l. 599. *hoc opus, hic labor est*. Virgil, *Aeneid*, VI.129, 'This is the work, this is the toil' (i.e. 'this is the really difficult bit')—words applied by the Sybil to the journey up from the underworld.

l. 600. *human*: secular, not sacred; 'humane learning'.

227 l. 614. *aloes or rhubarbum*. Two commonly used bitter tasting purgatives.

l. 625. *as Aristotle saith . . . delightful*. *Poetics*, IV. 1448b; cf. *AS* 34.4.

l. 626. *Amadis de Gaule*. A romance, originally Spanish, later translated into French and extended by Herberay and others, which was one of the sources of *OA*.

ll. 628–9. *Aeneas carrying old Anchises on his back*. *Aeneid*, II. 705–84.

ll. 632–3. *Whom doth not . . . miserum est*. Turnus, betrothed to Lavinia, is destined to be defeated and supplanted by Aeneas; his tale is told in the later books of the *Aeneid*, and the quotation comes from XII. 645–6, translated thus by T. Twyne (1584): 'And shall this ground fainthearted dastard Turnus flying view? / Is it so vile a thing to die?'

ll. 637–8. *Plato and Boethius . . . poesy*. Plato's use of poetry has already been cited (ll. 69–78); Boethius, in *De consolatione philosophiae*, personified Philosophy as a female figure, and alternated prose with verse.

l. 640. *indulgere genio*. Persius, *Satires*, V. 151, 'to follow one's natural inclination'.

228 l. 648. *Menenius Agrippa*. This story, told by many Roman historians, is now best known from Shakespeare's adaptation of it in *Coriolanus*, I. i. 95 ff., which may owe something to Sidney's version.

ll. 653–4. *if they were Platonic . . . conceived*. Plato's Academy was said to have 'Let no man enter who is not a geometrician' written over the door.

l. 661. *only words*. Words alone.

l. 664. *Nathan the prophet*. 2 Samuel 12: 1–15.

l. 671. *that heavenly psalm of mercy*. Psalm 51.

l. 676. *end*. Aim, objective.

l. 687. *Sannazaro and Boethius*. Sannazaro's *Arcadia* alternated passage of narrative with poems; so did Boethius's *De consolatione* (see above, ll. 637–8).

229 l. 688. *Some have mingled matters heroical and pastoral*. As Sidney himself did, most notably in *NA*; Montemayor and Ariosto were among those who had previously done so.

l. 695. *Meliboeus*. The name of the speaker in Virgil, *Eclogues*, I, who laments his dispossession. Thomas Watson was to use the name for Sidney's father-in-law, Sir Francis Walsingham, in his elegy *Meliboeus* (1590).

l. 697. *Tityrus.* Meliboeus's interlocutor in *Eclogues*, I, who rejoices in the security afforded him by the reign of Augustus.

ll. 698-700. *sometimes . . . patience.* Cf. Sidney's own beast fable, *OA* 66; Spenser's May Eclogue in *The Shepheardes Calender* and *Mother Hubberds Tale.*

ll. 700-1. *contentions . . . trifling victory.* Exemplified in *OA* 29 (modelled on Virgil, *Eclogues*, III) where the singing competition of Nico and Pas has a dog and cat as prizes.

l. 702. *cock of this world's dunghill.* 'Every cock is proud on his own dunghill' (Tilley, C486).

ll. 704-5. *Haec memini . . . nobis.* Virgil, *Eclogues*, VII. 69-70: 'This I remember, and how Thyrsis, vanquished, strove in vain. From that day it is Corydon, Corydon with us' (i.e. Corydon is the pre-eminent poet).

l. 707. *Heraclitus.* The early Greek philosopher who was said to weep at human folly; cf. *OA* 11.12.

l. 711. *Iambic.* Abusive poem, or lampoon, written in iambic metre, as distinct from the more elaborate and indirect 'satire'.

l. 714. *Omne vafer vitium ridenti tangit amico.* From Persius, *Satires*, I: 'the rascal probes every fault of his friend'.

l. 718. *circum praecordia ludit.* From the following line in Persius: 'he plays with the secrets of the heart.'

l. 721. *Est Ulubris, animus si nos non deficit aequuus?* Horace, *Epistles*, I. xi. 30: '[Contentment] is at Ulubrae, if there fail you not a mind well balanced' (Loeb trs.). Ulubrae was a notoriously unpleasant, marshy provincial town.

ll. 721-2. *naughty play-makers . . . odious.* Perhaps a gesture of assent to the thrust of Gosson's *Schoole of abuse*, as the word 'abuse' in the next sentence may indicate.

230 ll. 732-4. *of a niggardly Demea, of a crafty Davus, of a flattering Gnatho, of a vainglorious Thraso.* Characters from the comedies of Terence: Demea from *Adelphi*, Davus from *Andria*, Gnatho and Thraso from *Eunuchus.*

l. 735. *the signifying badge . . . comedian.* With an art akin to caricature, the comic dramatist makes the dominant vices of these characters vividly apparent; a theory closely approaching Jonson's 'comedy of humours'.

l. 739. *in pistrinum.* 'At the mill', working like a slave.

l. 745. *tissue.* Rich fabrics.

ll. 747-8. *the affects of admiration and commiseration.* Feelings of terror and pity, as in Aristotle's *Poetics*, 6.

ll. 750-1. *Qui sceptra . . . in auctorem redit.* 'The tyrant who rules harshly fears those who fear him; terror returns to its agent'; Seneca, *Oedipus*, III. 705-6; cf. adaptation in *CS* 14.

l. 753. *Alexander Pheraeus.* He 'went out of the theatre . . . because he was ashamed his people should see him weep, to see the miseries of Hecuba and Andromache played, and that they never saw him pity the death of any one man, of so many citizens as he had caused to be slain' (North's *Plutarch*, ii. 323).

l. 762. *Lyric.* For the purposes of his argument Sidney adopts here the limited, classical definition of 'lyric' as 'panegyric', hymn of praise.

231   l. 767. *the old song of Percy and Douglas.* The ballad of *Chevy Chase*, describing the fatal conflict between the Earls of Percy and Douglas.

ll. 768–9. *crowder.* Fiddler. Several documents show Sidney's fondness for popular musicians: for instance, at the age of eleven he gave money to a 'blind harper' (Wallace, 421).

l. 771. *Pindar.* The Greek lyric poet who wrote hymns and accounts of military and sporting triumphs; his notoriously elaborate metres contrast with the simple four-line stanza of the Border ballad.

l. 771. *In Hungary.* Sidney was in Hungary for a few weeks in the late summer of 1573 (Osborn, 102–4). The Hungarians' 'soldierlike' powers were frequently tested in battles with the invading Turks.

l. 774. *The incomparable Lacedaemonians.* The Lacedaemonians, or Spartans, were much admired by the Elizabethans. Plutarch described their warlike music in the *Life of Lycurgus* (North's *Plutarch*, i. 148–50).

ll. 783–4. *Philip of Macedon . . . three fearful felicities.* Cf. North's *Plutarch*, iv. 300; his other 'felicities' were a victory over the Illyrians and the birth of Alexander, all three occurring on the same day.

l. 790. *Tydeus.* One of the 'seven against Thebes' in Statius, *Thebais*.

l. 790. *Rinaldo.* Hero of Tasso's *Gerusalemme Liberata.*

l. 793. *the saying of Plato and Tully.* Plato, *Phaedrus*, 250D; Cicero, *De finibus*, II. xvi. 52 and *De officiis*, I. v. 14; and cf. *AS* 25.1–4.

232   l. 814. *melius Chrysippo et Crantore.* Horace, *Epistles*, I. ii: 'better than Chrysippus and Crantor' (two early Greek philosophers).

l. 824. *prophesying . . . making.* 'Vates', 'poet'.

ll. 835–6. *even our Saviour Christ vouchsafed to use the flowers of it.* In parables, like that of the Prodigal Son; see above, ll. 524–5.

233   l. 848. *the spleen.* Thought to be the seat of hostile laughter.

ll. 853–5. *a playing wit . . . plague.* Three examples of the mock encomium, a favourite humanist genre with which *DP* itself has some kinship. Lucian, Apuleius, and Cornelius Agrippa were among those who eulogized the ass; Francesco Berni (c. 1496–1535) wrote comic poems in praise of debt and plague (*Il primo libro dell'opere burlesche* (Florence, 1558), 9–18, 80–7).

l. 857. *Ut lateat virtus proximitate mali.* Adapted from Ovid, *Ars Amatoria*, II. 662 (Sidney translates the phrase).

ll. 858–60. *Agrippa . . . folly.* Cornelius Agrippa, *De incertitudine et vanitate scientiarum et artium* (1530); Erasmus, *Moriae Encomium* (1511).

ll. 861-2. *for Erasmus . . . promise.* These apparently sportful works were more profound and serious than might be thought (perhaps like *DP*).

ll. 865-6. *scoffing cometh not of wisdom.* Sounds proverbial, but not traced.

l. 873. *Scaliger judgeth. Poetices*, I. ii.

ll. 874-5. *oratio . . . mortality.* Commonplace idea deriving from Cicero and other classical writers that reason and language distinguish man from beasts.

l. 879. *without.* Unless.

l. 883. *memory being the only treasure of knowledge.* Tilley, M870.

234 ll. 892-3. *they that have taught the art of memory . . . known.* Formal theories of the 'art of memory', propounded by Raymond Lull and others, recommended the identification of sections of argument with objects which were then allocated to particular positions in an imaginary building (cf. F. A. Yates, *The Art of Memory* (1966)).

ll. 911-12. *the largest field to ear, as Chaucer saith. Knight's Tale*, 28.

ll. 915-16. *as if they had overshot Robin Hood.* Extravagantly boastfully; cf. Tilley, R148: 'Many speak of Robin Hood that never shot in his bow.'

l. 916. *Plato banished them out of his commonwealth. Republic*, II. iii. 10.

l. 919. *petere principium.* 'Beg the question'.

235 l. 933. *Charon.* The ferryman who rowed dead souls over the River Styx to the underworld.

l. 937. *artists.* Men skilled in 'liberal arts'.

l. 940. *maketh any circles.* Refers to necromancy, in which spirits were summoned into a circle.

l. 962. *John-a-stiles and John-a-Nokes.* John of the stile and John of the oaks; fictitious names used in teaching or debating legal arguments.

236 ll. 971-2. *the principal . . . abuse I can hear alleged.* The stimulus given by drama—especially stage comedy—to sexual licence was the dominant theme of Gosson's *Schoole of abuse* (1579), though a wider reference may be intended, since the other genres are not much dealt with by Gosson.

ll. 974-5. *even to the heroical Cupid hath ambitiously climbed.* For instance, in the mingled epics of Ariosto and Tasso; also Sidney's own *OA*.

ll. 981-2. *Some of my masters . . . the excellency of it.* Perhaps a dig at Plato, among others, who eulogized love in the *Symposium* and the *Phaedrus*.

ll. 989-90. *eikastiké . . . phantastiké.* 'showing forth', or 'picturing'; 'fanciful, imaginative'.

237 l. 1019. *never was the Albion nation without poetry.* In his *Description of Britain* William Harrison gave an account of Britain as a place where the arts flourished even before it was conquered by 'Albion' (Holinshed, *Chronicles* (1577), 1-2).

l. 1021. *chainshot.* Cannon balls linked by a chain; hence, a resounding blow.

l. 1022. *certain Goths.* Continuation of Dio Cassius, *Roman Histories*, LIV. 17.

l. 1023. *hangman.* Villain, rogue.

l. 1035. *iubeo stultum esse libenter.* Adapted from Horace. *Satires*, I. i. 53, 'I willingly tell him to be a fool'. Quoted in this form by Francis Davison in the Preface to *A poetical Rapsody* (1602).

l. 1039. *the quiddity of ens and prima materia.* Terms from scholastic philosophy: 'the essential nature of being and original matter.'

l. 1039. *a corslet.* Body armour.

238 ll. 1048-9. *Alexander . . . took dead Homer with him.* Alexander loved the *Iliad* so much that he 'laid it every night under his bed's head with his dagger' (North's *Plutarch*, iv. 305; cf. also Plutarch's essay *De Fortuna aut virtute Alexandri*).

l. 1058. *the former.* Cato the Censor (234-149 BC), rather than his great grandson, Cato of Utica (see above, l. 641); cf. North's *Plutarch*, iii. 1-47. The story of Cato's dislike of Fulvius's bringing the poet Ennius on campaign with him was often repeated, e.g. by Cornelius Agrippa and Stephen Gosson.

l. 1064. *unmustered.* Unenrolled (as a soldier).

ll. 1065-8. *the other Scipio brothers . . . sepulture.* Cicero, *Pro Archia poeta*, ix. 22, mentions that the poet Ennius was buried in the Scipios' vault.

ll. 1084-6. *they found for Homer . . . to live among them.* Cicero, *Pro Archia poeta*, viii. 19, is among those who said that seven Greek cities competed for the honour of having Homer among them. Empedocles and Protagoras were among Greek philosophers banished from their native cities.

ll. 1086-9. *For only repeating . . . unworthy to live.* The story of some Athenians being saved from slaughter by the Syracusans for reciting lines from Euripides is told by Plutarch in his *Life of Nicias* (North's *Plutarch*, iv. 42-3); there is an allusion in the same work to the banishment of the philosopher Protagoras and the execution of the philosopher Socrates (ibid. 35).

239 ll. 1089-90. *Certain poets . . . a just king.* Hieron I, tyrant of Syracuse, was a patron of art and literature. Simonides reconciled Hieron to his brother Theron, and Pindar celebrated Hieron's achievements.

ll. 1091-2. *where Plato . . . was made a slave.* Cf. Cicero, *Pro Rabirio Postumo*, ix. 23.

l. 1096. *see whether any poet do authorize abominable filthiness as they do.* Like Scaliger (*Poetices*, I. ii) Sidney believes Plato to authorize homosexuality; and in Plutarch's *De amore* (*Moralia*, 751) Protogenes asserts that 'there is only one genuine Love, the love of boys'.

l. 1098. *where he himself alloweth the community of women. Republic*, v.

ll. 1104-5. *St Paul . . . 'their prophet'.* In the Penshurst MS of *DP* this citation is glossed: 'Acts: 17. To Titus: 1'.

ll. 1115–16. *Plutarch ... divine providence.* De Iside et Osiride, *Moralia,* 351–84; De defectu oraculorum, *Moralia,* 410–38; and probably De sera numinis vindicta, *Moralia,* 548–68.

ll. 1122–3. *Qua authoritate... exigendos.* Scaliger, *Poetices,* I. ii, refers to Plato 'whose authority certain barbarous and uncouth men seek to use to banish poets from the commonwealth'.

ll. 1127–9. *who ... unto poetry.* 'Whatever Plato intended, the dialogue [*Ion*] was never taken ironically by 16th century readers, who all found in it many passages commending poetry' (Shepherd). One such commentator was Landino; see below, l. 1524.

240 ll. 1132–3. *under whose lion's skin... poesy.* Refers to Aesop's fable of the ass who put on a lion's skin and passed for a lion until a stranger who had seen real lions unmasked him (Aesop, *Fables,* 120–1).

l. 1135. *more than myself do.* Sidney was unusual among Renaissance theorists in rejecting the idea of divine inspiration for poetry (cf. *AS* 74. 4–5), but conventional in taking Plato's *Ion* to support the notion.

ll. 1140–2. *Laelius ... made by him.* Terence hints in the prologue to the *Heautontimourumenos* ('The man who hurts himself') that parts of it were written by Gaius Laelius, friend of Scipio Africanus the younger.

ll. 1142–4. *even the Greek Socrates ... verses.* Plato, *Phaedo,* 60; Plutarch, *Quomodo adolescens poetas audire debet, Moralia,* 16. For Socrates as 'the only wise man', cf. *AS* 25. 1–2.

l. 1150. *guards.* Borders, decorative trimmings.

l. 1165. *career.* Race course, or running track in the tiltyard; Sidney is imagining himself either on horseback, or as himself a horse.

l. 1171. *Musa ... laeso?* Virgil, *Aeneid,* I. 8, 'Tell me, O muse, the cause, wherein thwarted in will ... ?'

241 ll. 1173–41. *David ... to be poets.* David was both King of Israel and author of the Psalms; Hadrian was Emperor of Rome (AD 117–38) and wrote verses; Sophocles was an Athenian general as well as a dramatist; Germanicus, nephew of Tiberius, conquered Germany and was reputed to write poetry.

ll. 1175–6. *Robert ... King James of Scotland.* Robert II of Anjou (1309–43) was a patron of Petrarch; Francis I of France was patron of many artists and writers, including Rabelais, Erasmus, and Leonardo da Vinci; James I of Scotland (1394–1437) was a patron of letters and author of *The Kingis Quhair.* James VI, future James I of England, was born in 1566, so cannot have been much more than sixteen when Sidney wrote *DP*. However, Sidney alludes to his tutor, Buchanan, further on in the sentence, and may have been aware of James's youthful verses which were to be published as *Essayes of a Prentis* (1584). Shepherd (212) and van Dorsten (59) suggest that the allusion is to James VI, but that it breaks the pattern of pairs in Sidney's list, and may be a later insertion. However, the list proceeds in a fairly orderly fashion, with steady diminution in the number of examples, thus: 4;

3; 2, 2, 2, 2; 1, 1; the overall organization of the sentence does not support the idea of revision and insertion. James VI's contribution of an English sonnet to the Cambridge volume of elegies on Sidney (*Academiae Cantabrigiensis lachrymae* (1587), sig. K1) could reflect some earlier mutual knowledge of literary endeavours. The present allusion may or may not be to him.

ll. 1176–7. *Bembus and Bibbiena.* Pietro Bembo (1470–1547) wrote poems and prose, including a defence of the Tuscan language analogous to Sidney's own defence of English in the succeeding pages; Bernard Dovizi, Cardinal Bibbiena (1470–1520), was secretary to Lorenzo de'Medici and wrote a Plautine comedy.

ll. 1177–8. *Beza and Melanchthon.* Theodore de Bèze (1519–1605) wrote a tragedy, *Abraham sacrifiant,* and an edition of the New Testament. His commentary on the Psalms was drawn on by Sidney in his translation. Philip Melanchthon (1497–1560) was a German humanist poet and educationalist, close associate both of Luther and of Sidney's friend Hubert Languet.

l. 1178. *Fracastorius.* Girolamo Fracastorio (1483–1553), author of medical and scientific works, some in verse.

l. 1179. *Pontanus and Muretus.* Giovanni Pontano (1426–1503), astronomical poet (see above, l. 275); Marc-Antoine Muret (1526–85), French humanist and scholar.

ll. 1179–80. *George Buchanan.* Scottish humanist, tutor to James VI, and translator of the Psalms (cf. I. Macfarlane, *George Buchanan* (1981)).

ll. 1180–1. *that Hôpital of France.* Michel Hurault, de l'Hôpital (1503–73), Chancellor of France 1560–8, whose support for religious tolerance must have commended him to Sidney, was a Latin poet, who wrote six books of verse epistles. Both Buchanan and he may have been personally known to Sidney.

ll. 1187–9. *heretofore . . . did sound loudest.* Sidney is unspecific about when this time was, perhaps deliberately, since he later (l. 1242) refers to Chaucer's period as a 'misty time'.

l. 1190. *strew the house.* Prepare a welcome by spreading fresh rushes and flowers on the floor. Sidney did not regard the peace enjoyed by England in Elizabeth's reign as an unmixed blessing.

l. 1191. *the mountebanks at Venice.* Quick-tongued salesmen, 'mounted on a bench', who made a strong impression on English visitors to Venice such as Thomas Coryate. Jonson's Volpone assumes the role of a mountebank selling quack medicine, *Volpone,* II. ii.

l. 1197. *base men with servile wits.* As in *AS* 3 and 15, Sidney implies that there are a lot of bad, derivative poets among his contemporaries, but names no names.

ll. 1199–1201. *Epaminondas . . . highly respected.* Plutarch, in his *Precepta gerendae reipublicae (Moralia,* 811) describes Epaminondas accepting the office of telearch (which involved organizing street-cleaning) and bringing it distinction (cf. D. A. Russell, *Plutarch* (1973), 14).

l. 1204. *without any commission.* i.e. no one has asked them to write poetry.

l. 1206. *Queis meliore luto finxit praecordia Titan.* Juvenal, *Satires*, XIV. 33–5, 'whose souls informing better clay Prometheus has shaped'.

l. 1208. *knights of the same order.* A jocular or contemptuous phrase; cf. *OED* 12c, 'knight of the pen'.

242   l. 1224. *orator fit, poeta nascitur.* Tilley, P 451, 'Poets are born but orators are made'. Keats adapts the same idea in saying 'That if Poetry come not as naturally as the Leaves to a tree it had better not come at all' (*Letters*, ed. M. Buxton Forman (1952), 107).

l. 1226. *a Daedalus.* In Greek mythology, the originator of the arts, father of the high-flying Icarus whose wings melted in the sun; used here allegorically for 'the foundation of poetry'.

l. 1229. *we.* We 'paper-blurrers'.

l. 1231. *fore-backwardly.* Back to front (a coinage of Sidney's).

l. 1235. *quodlibet.* 'Anything we like'; any question proposed in scholastic debate.

l. 1237. *Quicquid conabor dicere, versus erit.* Ovid, *Tristia*, IV. x. 26, 'whatever I tried to say turned out as poetry'. (Cf. Pope, *Epistle to Dr Arbuthnot*, 128, 'I lisp'd in Numbers, for the Numbers came'.)

ll. 1240–3. *Chaucer ... after him.* The five-book structure of *Troilus and Criseyde*, with the lovers' consummation described in the central book, may have been Sidney's prime model for the structure of *OA*.

ll. 1244–5. *I account the Mirror of Magistrates ... beautiful parts.* The *Mirror for Magistrates* was a cumulative collection of poems, initiated by Thomas Sackville in 1559, on the falls of kings and eminent people. Poems on ancient British monarchs (such as Cordelia) had been added in the 1574 edition. It is a work made up of 'parts', not a coherent whole (cf. edition by L. B. Campbell, 2 vols, 1938, 1946).

ll. 1245–6. *the Earl of Surrey's lyrics ... noble mind.* A substantial proportion of Surrey's lyrics were included in *Tottel's Miscellany* (1557). Some contemporaries saw Sidney as Surrey's poetic heir; cf. G. Whitney, *A choice of emblems* (1586), 196–7.

ll. 1246–8. *The Shepheardes Calender ... deceived.* Spenser's *Shepheardes Calender* (1579) was dedicated to Sidney under the pseudonym 'Immerito'. Perhaps, at the time of writing *DP*, Sidney was unaware that Immerito was Edmund Spenser; but more probably he deliberately respected his pseudonymity. In his dedicatory poem Spenser commends the book to Sidney 'As child whose parent is unkent'. Sidney's criticism of Spenser's language in the succeeding sentence may be proprietorial in tone, rather than dismissive. It is not quite just, since Theocritus did use Doric dialect for many of his *Idylls*: and cf. also *OA* 66. However, the 'marked tendency towards modernization' identified by De Sélincourt in the third edition of the *Calender* (1586) may reflect a response to Sidney's comment (Spenser, *Minor Poems*, ed. E. De Sélincourt (1910), xii).

l. 1249. *allow*. Praise.

243 ll. 1259–64. *Gorboduc . . . might not remain as an exact model of all tragedies.* *Gorboduc*, named on the title-page of the first authorized edition (1571) as *The Tragidie of Ferrex and Porrex*, had been performed at Court in 1561 and was the joint work of Thomas Sackville, later Lord Buckhurst (1536–1608) and Thomas Norton (1532–84). This political fable of the evils ensuing to a divided Britain was a model or reference point for many writers of the period, including Shakespeare. Sidney accords it high praise in finding its style comparable with that of Seneca's tragedies, but finds it deficient in 'circumstances', that is, the Aristotelian unities of place and time.

l. 1269. *inartificially*. Inartistically.

l. 1282. *traverses*. Troubles, difficulties.

l. 1286. *the ordinary players in Italy*. Sidney may have seen such players during 1574, when he was in Venice and Padua (cf. K. M. Lea, *Italian Popular Comedy* (1934), i. 262).

ll. 1287–8. *Yet will some bring in . . . twenty years*. As elsewhere in *DP*, Sidney appears to be writing without checking his citations; Terence's *Eunuchus* occupies a single day, but he may really be thinking of the longer-drawn-out *Heautotontimourumenos* (1141–2) which Scaliger (*Poetices*, VI. iii) described as performed in two parts on two successive days.

l. 1290. *Plautus have in one place done amiss*. Probably another recollection of Scaliger (ibid.), who criticizes the extended action of Plautus's *Captives*.

244 l. 1299. *Peru . . . Calicut*. Sidney imagines remote and recently discovered points West and East: Peru, conquered by Pizarro (1478–1541) and Calicut, in Malabar, India, where Vasco da Gama landed in 1498.

l. 1300. *Pacolet's horse*. The horse belonging to the enchanter Pacolet in the poular late medieval romance *Valentine and Orson*.

l. 1301. *Nuntius*. Messenger.

l. 1303. *ab ovo*. Horace, *De arte poetica*, 147, 'from the egg'.

l. 1314. *Euripides*. In his *Hecuba*, from which there are concealed quotations in the phrases 'for safety's sake, with great riches' and 'to make the treasure his own' (cf. K. O Myrick, *Sir Philip Sidney as a Literary Craftsman* (1935; repr. 1965), 105–7).

ll. 1322–3. *Apuleius did somewhat so*. In his *Golden Ass*, translated by W. Adlington (1566), a source for *OA*; this is not a drama, however, so the example is an odd one.

l. 1325. *Plautus hath Amphitryo*. Scaliger and others regarded this play as the archetypal tragi-comedy.

l. 1326. *daintily*. Reluctantly.

245 ll. 1340–1. *Delight . . . Laughter hath only a scornful tickling*. Sidney's account of comedy is a modified version of the theories of Castelvetro and Trissino; cf. Shepherd, 223–5.

ll. 1347-8. *go down the hill against the bias*. Travel down a slope which counteracts the direction given to a bowl by its bias.

ll. 1351-2. *Alexander's picture well set out*. Alexander was painted by Apelles and others (North's *Plutarch*, iv. 300-1); Signorelli and Giulio Romano are among the many Renaissance artists who depicted him, and there were some pictures of him in Elizabethan houses, e.g. one at Essex House (C. L. Kingsford, 'Essex House', *Archaeologia*, lxxiii (1923), 1-54)

ll. 1352-3. *twenty mad antics*. Referring to the 'antique' or grotesque style of decoration, described thus by Peacham: 'an unnatural or unorderly composition for delight sake, of men, beasts, birds, fishes, flowers & c., without (as we say) rhyme or reason; for the greater variety you show in your invention the more you please' (*The Gentleman's Exercise* (1612), 50).

ll. 1353-5. *Hercules ... spinning at Omphale's commandment*. After the completion of this twelve Labours, Hercules became infatuated with Omphale, Queen of Lydia; Plutarch refers to comic pictures of him in women's clothes (*Moralia*, 785), and similar pictures were fairly common in the Northern European Renaissance, e.g. by Cranach and by Bartholomaeus Spränger, court painter to the Emperor Rudolph.

ll. 1367-8. *Nil habet ... quod ridiculos homines facit?* Juvenal, *Satires*, III. 152-3, 'Poverty contains no sharper misery that that it makes men ridiculous'. We may note that Sidney's comic clowns, the Dametas family in *OA* and *NA*, have been elevated from poverty by royal favour, and so become legitimate butts of merriment.

l. 1369. *Thraso*. A boaster, like the character in Terence's *Eunuchus*.

l. 1370. *A self-wise-seeming schoolmaster*. Like Rombus in *LM*.

246 l. 1372. *the other*. In tragedy. As Shepherd observes (225), 'the complimentary reference to George Buchanan as a model for the writer of tragedies has something of the appearance of an afterthought'.

ll. 1387-8. *so coldly they apply fiery speeches*. The Petrarchan oxymoron of 'icy fire', used here to condemn third-generation Petrarchizers.

l. 1393. *forcibleness or energia*. The word 'energy' was not yet current in English; '*energeia*' (Greek) or '*efficacia*' (Latin) were used by rhetoricians and literary theorists such as Scaliger to denote 'the force of poetry', or the clarity with which the poetic theme has been realized in words.

ll. 1399-1402. *far-fet words ... winter-starved*. List of poetic faults—affected diction, excessive alliteration, Euphuistic similes—which closely parallels *AS* 15.

ll. 1407-10. *the diligent imitators of Tully and Demosthenes ... make them wholly theirs*. This attack on excessive and excessively overt Ciceronianism is consistent with Sidney's advice to his brother in October 1580 (293). 'Nizolian paper-books' were commonplace books of phrases from the classical rhetoricians, named after Marius Nizolius who published *Thesaurus Ciceronianus* (1535). Sidney's friend Henri Estienne wrote an attack on the 'Nizolian' method, *Nizoliodidascalus* (1578). Sidney seems to recommend, rather, absorption in the original writers and a personal transformation ('translation') of their techniques.

247   ll. 1414–16. *Tully, when he was to drive out Catiline . . . Imo in senatum venit &c*. From the opening of Cicero's *In Catilinam*, I: '[What an age we live in! The senate knows it all, the consul sees it, and yet] this man is still alive. Alive did I say? Not only is he alive, but he attends the senate' (Loeb trs.). Sidney quotes from the same well-known passage in *LM* (7).

l. 1420. *too too much choler to be choleric*. Excessive rage to express rage with so much repetition. There may be a pun on 'colour', or figure of rhetoric.

l. 1421. *similiter cadences*. From Latin *similiter cadentiae*, similar endings; Sidney refers to the use of rhyme, assonance, and other figures of repetition by public speakers.

l. 1422. *daintiness*. Discretion. Less imitation of Cicero, more of Demosthenes, is what Sidney seems to recommend.

ll. 1423–5. *the sophister . . . had none for his labour*. A commonplace story about the pitfalls of specious logic, told, for instance, by Thomas More: 'as though a sophister would with a fond argument prove unto a simple soul that two eggs were three, because that there is one, and there be twain, and one and twain make three: that simple unlearned man, though he lack learning to foil his fond argument, hath yet wit enough to laugh thereat, and to eat two eggs himself, and bid the sophister take and eat the third' ('The Confutation of Tyndale's Answer III', in *Works*, Yale edition, viii. 287).

l. 1428. *certain printed discourses*. Perhaps a reference to Lyly's *Euphues, the Anatomy of Wit* (1578) and its sequel, *Euphues and his England* (1580). Sidney's dislike of Lyly's style could have been compounded by the fact that his patron was the Earl of Oxford.

ll. 1437–42. *Antonius and Crassus . . . used these knacks very sparingly*: Cicero, *De Oratore*, II. i.

l. 1444. *curiously*. Elaborately, painstakingly.

l. 1450. *to hide art*. Tilley, A335: 'It is art to hide art.'

l. 1452. *pounded*. Rounded up into a 'pound' or enclosure, like a straying animal; Sidney may be still imagining himself a horse (cf. l. 1349).

l. 1453. *in the wordish consideration*. In matters of diction and style.

248   l. 1461. *it is a mingled language*. Unlike Sidney, other humanist critics regretted the mixed character of English, e.g. 'E.K.', in his Preface to Spenser's *Shepheardes Calender*: 'they have made our English tongue a gallimaufray or hodgepodge of all other speeches.'

l. 1466. *the Tower of Babylon's curse*. Elizabethans identified 'Babylon' with 'Babel' (Genesis 10: 10).

ll. 1469–72. *is particularly happy . . . can be in a language*. Sidney's inventive use of compound words and epithets was recognized by later writers as one of his most distinctive achievements.

l. 1473. *of versifying there are two sorts*. The dialogue between Dicus and

Lalus at the end of two texts of the *OA* First Eclogues (*OA* 89–90) can be seen as an early draft for this passage in *DP*. For a full discussion of the metrical debate and Sidney's role in it, see Derek Attridge, *Well-weighed syllables* (1974).

l. 1484. *vulgar*. Vernacular, not learned.

l. 1485. *the ancient*. The classical, quantitative method of versification.

l. 1486. *the Dutch*. German. Sidney complained of the harshness of the German language in one of his letters to Languet (280).

l. 1490. *dactyls*. Long (strong) syllable followed by two short (weak) syllables.

249 l. 1499. *sdrucciola*. 'Slippery' or 'sliding' rhyme, where the rhyme words are trisyllables, used extensively by Sidney, e.g. in *OA* 7. John Florio defines it differently, as 'a kind of smooth running blank verse' (*Queen Anna's New World of Words* (1611)), but this is not what is meant here.

l. 1508 *poet-apes*. False, imitative poets; cf. *AS* 3.3.

l. 1514. *Aristotle*. As cited by Boccaccio, *De genealogia deorum*, XIV. viii.

l. 1517. *Scaliger. Poetices*, III. xix.

ll. 1518–21. *Clauserus . . . quid non?* Conrad Clauser, preface to his translation of L. Annaeus Cornutus, *De natura deorum gentilium* (Basle, 1543).

l. 1524. *Landino*. Cristoforo Landino, prologue to his edition of Dante's *Divina Commedia* (Florence 1481). We may notice that Sidney is here conjuring his readers to believe in the poet's 'divine fury' though he has himself previously rejected the idea (1314).

l. 1530. *libertina patre natus . . . Herculea proles*. The first phrase is from Horace, *Satires*, I. vi. 6, where in celebrating his friendship with his patron Maecenas he calls himself 'the son of a freedman'; the second phrase means 'descendant of Hercules'.

l. 1531. *Si quid mea carmina possunt*. Virgil, *Aeneid*, IX. 44, 'If my verses can achieve anything'.

250 ll. 1533–4. *the dull-making cataract of Nilus*. The deafening effect of the waterfalls in the upper reaches of the Nile was described by Cicero, *Somnium Scipionis*, V. 13; in the same work he writes of the music of the spheres.

ll. 1536–7. *such a mome as to be a Momus*. Such a dunce ('mome') as to be a carping critic. Momus, son of Night, was a type of the bad-tempered fault finder.

l. 1538. *the ass's ears of Midas*. Awarded to King Midas because he preferred the music of Pan to that of Apollo. (Ovid, *Metamorphoses*, XI. 146ff.).

l. 1538. *Bubonax*. Bupalus, who made a statue of the ugly poet Hipponax, was driven to suicide by Hipponax's verses (Pliny, *Natural History*, XXXVI. v. 4). Sidney has conflated the two names.

ll. 1539–40. *to be rhymed to death, as is said to be done in Ireland*. This example is close to home. Sidney's own father was at one stage threatened with death by Irish bards (cf. K. Duncan-Jones, 'Irish Poets and the Sidneys', *English Studies*, xlix. 424–5). Cf. also Scot, *Discoverie of Witchcraft* (1584), III. xv, 'The Irishmen . . . will not stick to affirm, that they can rhyme either man or beast to death.'

253 *The New Arcadia. The pitiful story of the Paphlagonian unkind king.* From Book 2 of *NA*. Musidorus (disguised as the shepherd Dorus) relates the previous experiences of himself and Pyrocles to the princess Pamela, describing their births, education, shipwreck on the coast of Phrygia, and subsequent adventures. After settling the troubled affairs of the kingdoms of Phrygia and Pontus, the princes decided to move on 'to see more of the world, and to employ those gifts esteemed rare in them to the good of mankind'. The following episode was Shakespeare's source for the Gloucester plot in *King Lear*, and there are verbal reminiscences of it throughout the play (cf. G. Bullough, *Narrative and Dramatic Sources of Shakespeare*, vii (1975), 284–6, 402–14).

the kingdom of Galatia. A province of Paphlagonia, immediately to the East of Pontus (cf. *OA*, Mercator's Map 1).

254 *engraffed.* Implanted.

255 *trains.* Wiles, stratagems.

256 *adventure.* Risk, run in danger of.

the king of Pontus. A nobleman whom Pyrocles married to a sister of the previous king and placed on the throne.

257 *fear having been the only knot that had fastened his people unto him.* Apparently an allusion to Sidney's favourite tag from Seneca (*Oedipus*, 704–5) on the fragility of tyranny based on terror; cf. *Misc. Prose* 56; *CS* 14; *DP* 230; *NA* 320.

258 *his heart . . . stretched so far beyond his limits.* This account may have influenced Shakespeare's rendering of the deaths of both Gloucester and Lear (cf. *King Lear*, v. iii. 196–9; 313–14).

258 *The Iberian jousts.* From Book 2 of *NA*. Pyrocles (disguised as the Amazon Zelmane), alone with his beloved Philoclea, has made his true identity known to her. They seal their love with embraces, and he then takes up the tale of the adventures of himself and Musidorus, the earlier instalment of which she had heard from Pamela. At this point in the related narrative Pyrocles and Musidorus have been put in prison by the lustful and domineering Queen Andromana, who is attracted to both of them. However, her son Palladius releases them under cover of participation in the jousts, here described.

that queen. Andromana; see above.

259 *a Diana apparelled in the garments of Venus.* This passage reads like a eulogy of the court and regime of Elizabeth I, despite plot details that inhibit a complete identification of Helen of Corinth with Elizabeth of England.

His impresa was ... One of four lacunae in the text of *NA*, indicating its unfinished state.

morne: the 'rebated' head of a tilting staff (blunted for safety).

sheephooks. Pastoral array strongly reminiscent of Sidney's own 'rustical music' and shepherdish disguise in the ?1577 Accession Day Tilt (cf. 2–4).

260 *a sheep marked with pitch*. No doubt referring to the proverb (derived from Ecclesiasticus 1–3: 1), 'He that touches pitch shall be defiled' (Tilley P358). Though Philisides is inspired by a lady whom he calls his 'star', we cannot necessarily assume that the pitch-markings on the sheep are star-shaped, though a device of a star-marked sheep is associated with Sidney by Abraham Fraunce (cf. *NA* 552; and see also D. Coulman, 'Spotted to be known', *JWCI* xx (1957), 179–80; K. Duncan-Jones, 'Sidney's Personal Imprese', *JWCI* xxxiii (1970), 321–4; Alan Hager, 'The Exemplary Mirage', Kay 59–60.

six verses. The six lines may correspond with six 'courses' at the tilt, which was the regular number (Young, 81).

Methought ... *One said he brake across*. 'Some thought he missed with his lance; some argued he almost hit; others believed he did not score any of the more difficult hits; perhaps his hits were of the easiest type to score; yet most roared their approval anyway' (E. Malcolm Parkinson, 'Sidney's Portrayal of Mounted Combat with Lances', *Spenser Studies*, v. (1985), 238). The line 'Where he most would hit, he ever yet did miss' is perhaps echoed by Sir John Harington in a line he added to Ariosto, on Astolfo's betrayal by Alcina, 'The mark is missed that I was wont to hit' (*Orlando Furioso* (1591) XXIII. 50).

crossly crossed. Unluckily frustrated.

Lelius. Perhaps an allusion to the Queen's Champion, Sir Henry Lee (1533–1610), who was certainly known as 'Laelius' in later years. Sidney tilted against him at the Accession Day tilt in 1584, and perhaps on earlier occasions (cf. *NA* xiv–xv).

tied by her. Lelius is presumably the chained knight described above. Lee had a notorious love affair with Anne Vavasour, and in a royal entertainment in 1592 alluded to his 'thraldom' to her (E. K. Chambers, *Sir Henry Lee* (1936), 150).

261 *a mill-horse* ... *with this word, Data fata sequutus*. Mill-horses were blindfolded to prevent them deviating from their course; the phrase about the knight whose 'eyesight had tamed him' may imply that the 'wild man' is also blind[folded], in which case his 'excellent running' is the more remarkable. A 'Blind Knight' (perhaps Lee again) took part in the 1584 Accession Day tilt, and was also poetical, reciting a sonnet to the queen (Young, 160). The 'word' means 'following the prescriptions of destiny'.

tent. Decorative pavilions with 'special effects' were features only of the most opulent Elizabethan tournaments (Young, 92–6).

the fine Frozen Knight. Cf. *Triumph*, 304.

brought the honour to rest . . . of the Iberian side. The honours are even; the visiting Corinthians win the tournament in the morning; the home team, the Iberians, helped by Pyrocles and Musidorus, win the tourney 'in troops' in the afternoon. For the tourney, see Young, 32, 34.

261 *Temptations to love and marriage. Cecropia*. Sidney may have taken the name from 'Cecrops', an early Athenian king who was 'two-faced', as Cecropia is.

subtilty and impudency. This is how Cecropia views Philoclea's languid but resolute rejection of Amphialus's courtship.

his fellowship. The company of (personified) Melancholy.

263 *niceness*. Fussiness.

264 *cloddy cumbers*. Earthy impediments.

265 *the seeled dove*. Cf. *CS* 15 and note.

rose-water kept in a crystal glass? Rose water was a frequent ingredient of Elizabethan cooking, as well as being used for cosmetic and medicinal purposes (cf. H. Spurling, ed., *Eleanor Fettiplace's Receipt-Book* (1986)). For marriage as rose water, cf. Shakespeare, *Sonnets*, 5. 9–14.

266 *The aunt's atheism refuted by the niece's divinity*. From Book 3 of *NA*. Cecropia has failed to persuade Philoclea of the nobleness of Amphialus, who has behaved with some courage and magnanimity in a fierce battle against the followers of Basilius. She has already witnessed Pamela's piety, overhearing her prayer for fortitude, and her line of temptation is adjusted accordingly.

267 *harborough*. Harbour, refuge. Cecropia thinks that Pamela would not be so well groomed unless she wanted to attract men.

unevitable. Unavoidable.

268 *the cranes . . . Pygmies*. There are many references in Greek literature to cranes overcoming Pygmies; e.g. Homer, *Iliad*, III. vi.

babies. Dolls; cf. *AS* 5. 36.

269 *shewels*. Scarecrows.

Fear . . . was the first inventor of those conceits. A commonplace argument of atheists; and cf. Chaucer, *Troilus and Criseyde*, IV. 1408.

270 *there is a constancy in the everlasting governor?* Pamela appeals to 'natural reason' in attempting to persuade Cecropia of the existence of God and the operation of providence. Sidney's main source for this passage was probably Philippe Du Plessis Mornay's treatise *De la verité* (1581), which he began to translate; the work was delegated to Arthur Golding, and published in 1587. For a discussion of the wider background to Pamela's speech, see D. P. Walker, *The Ancient Theology: Studies in Christian Platonism from the Fifteenth to the Eighteenth Century* (1972), 132–63.

if chanceable. Emended from the 1590 reading 'of chanceable'.

271 *as if the elementish and ethereal parts . . . of each one's office*. As if the material and immaterial parts of the cosmos should define the mutual limits of their territories.

shalt only perceive him to have been a creator in thy destruction. D. P. Walker (op. cit., 162) thinks that Pamela threatens destruction in this life, not damnation in the next; this may be confirmed by Cecropia's actual death, in which she falls backwards off the roof of her castle and survives long enough to see her beloved son killing himself (*NA*, 440).

274 *Psalms.* Sidney's version of Psalms I–XLIII, which was completed by his sister, the Countess of Pembroke, in the years after his death, was not printed as a whole until 1823 (ed. S. W. Singer), though it circulated widely in manuscript. It is not clear when Sidney made his metaphrases, in which each Psalm is rendered in a different verse form, a procedure followed by his sister. Some critics have identified them as early work, but Wallace (324) and Ringler (500) suggest that 'Sidney began the work late in his career, perhaps not long before his departure for the Netherlands in 1585'. Admirers of the Sidney/Pembroke Psalms have included Donne, who wrote a poem celebrating them; George Herbert, who was strongly influenced by their style and form; and Ruskin, who made a selection from them entitled *Rock Honeycomb. Broken Pieces of Sir Philip Sidney's Psalter* (1877). The most recent and authoritative study is Rivkah Zim, *English Metrical Psalms: Poetry as Praise and Prayer 1535–1601* (1987), 152–202.

Psalm VI. The first of the seven 'Penitential Psalms'. Ruskin (ed. cit.) found this an example of 'the feeblest work attributed to Sidney . . . but . . . still sincere'.

feats. Actions, deeds.

275 Psalm XIII. *give me eyes and light.* Cf. *CS* 32.8.

Psalm XXIII. *besett'st.* Probably in *OED* sense 1 (b) of 'beset', 'surround, encircle'.

276 Psalm XXIX. Ruskin called this 'grand in beat and tone, but absolutely needs music'.

like young calves . . . like young unicorn. Cf. *DP*, 215.

277 Psalm XXXVIII. Another 'Penitential Psalm', which would have lent itself well to use while Sidney was dying.

reins. Kidneys, loins.

279 *Letters.* Most of Sidney's letters are to be found in Feuillerat, iii; much of his correspondence with Languet and other humanists up to 1577 is in Osborn. However, there is as yet no complete edition of Sidney's correspondence.

[1] From B. L. Lansdowne MS 12 (50), autograph. The earliest surviving piece of writing by Sidney in English, this concerns the preferment of his tutor ('reader'), Thomas Thornton, to a canonry of Christ Church. Thornton was successful, and so, later in the year, was Toby Mathew, who was to become Archbishop of York in 1606 (Wallace, 95–7; *DNB*).

unaccustomed manner. Two letters to Cecil from the spring and summer 1569 are in Latin, evidently the language in which the young Sidney normally wrote to him.

advowson. Patronage, right of presentation of a benefice.

[2] From Feuillerat, iii. 84–5, Latin, translated here by John Buxton. Hubert Languet (1518–81) was a diplomat for the Elector of Saxony. Ninety-six letters from Languet to Sidney were published at Frankfurt (1633); some of these, and some of Sidney's letters to Languet, are quoted in translation in Osborn.

pay most attention to the Ethics. Cf. Letter [7].

Delius. Matthaus Delius, a pupil of Melanchthon's and a native of Hamburg. Languet had suggested that he could help Sidney with German 'by playing and jesting with you' (Osborn, 130); Sidney's remark is probably a jest, for to drink his health he needed only to say the Latin word '*Prosit*'.

I shall have my portrait painted either by Paolo Veronese or by Tintoretto. Veronese began to paint Sidney in late February 1574; by early June Languet had received the portrait. He admired it, but thought it made Sidney look too young—no more than 12 or 13 (Osborn, 152–7, 203). The portrait is not known to survive.

281 *the portrait which Abondio made*. Antonio Abondio was a medallist and sculptor in bas-relief who was employed by the Emperor Maximilian. His portrait of Sidney, possibly in the form of a wax medal, is not known to survive (Osborn, 101–2).

[3] From Feuillerat, iii. 103, Latin, translated by John Buxton. The Count of Hanau was a young German nobleman whom Sidney met through Languet, initially in Venice, and with whom he formed a strong friendship (Wallace, 130; Osborn, 308–10 and *passim*).

the brand of Meleager . . . will perish. In Greek mythology Althaea, Queen of Calydon, was told by the Fates at the birth of her son Meleager that he would live only so long as a fiery brand continued to burn.

Paul von Welsperg. 'companion and head of household to the Count of Hanau' (Osborn, 129).

[4] From B. L. Harleian MS 6992 (42), autograph. The endorsement survives only as 'To the Earl of . . .', and Feuillerat identified the addressee as Leicester. However, Sussex, as Lord Chamberlain, was the man whose permission was needed for a courtier's absence, and in the dozen surviving letters from Sidney to Leicester he consistently addresses him as 'my singular good Lord', rather than 'my very good Lord'. Sussex was a fierce rival and enemy of Leicester.

both of health and otherwise. One of the 'occasions' detaining Sidney at Wilton may have been the composition of *OA*, probably begun earlier that year.

my lady and aunt. Sussex's second wife was Frances, sister of Sir Henry Sidney, by whose will Sidney Sussex College, Cambridge, was founded in 1589.

282 *the poor stranger musician*. Not identified, but no doubt one of the many Italian and French musicians of Protestant allegiance who came to England at this period.

[5] From Feuillerat, iii. 119–21, Latin, translated by John Buxton.

Robert Beale and Daniel Rogers and your friend Beuterich. Beale (1541–1601) was secretary to Sir Francis Walsingham; Rogers (?1538–91) was one of the most important of Walsingham's foreign agents; Beuterich was a knight in the retinue of Prince Casimir.

the Stoic... a Cynic too. The ancient Greek Stoic philosophers taught detachment from worldly affairs: the Cynics, at least as popularly understood, despised knowledge and morality.

283 *Of that one of whom I readily admit I am not worthy.* This lady is not identified. Languet was a bachelor.

Frobisher's gold... will not produce the great wealth that at first it had promised. Martin Frobisher (?1535–94), navigator, in whose three major voyages Sidney invested, returned from his second voyage to the New World in September 1577 with two hundred tons of ore which turned out to be worthless. He had also claimed that six nearby islands were rich in gold.

if there is open water... this will be of the greatest importance. Like his contemporaries, Sidney hoped that a North-West Passage would be discovered which would offer a fast sea route from Europe to the Orient.

Prince Casimir. Sidney's friend John Casimir, son of the Elector Palatine, was an enthusiast for the idea of a pan-European Protestant League, in which Sidney managed briefly to interest the Queen (Osborn, 494, 498).

Lobbet, de Banos, Andreas Paull, Anselm, Metellus. Though the specific letters referred to here do not survive, this list suggests the extent of Sidney's habitual European correspondence, of which surviving letters must be only a small sample. Some letters from Jean Lobbet (Professor of Law at Strasbourg), Théophile de Banos (minister of the Huguenot church in Frankfurt), and Andreas Paull (counsellor to the elector of Saxony) are collected in Osborn.

Charles de L'Ecluse. 1526–1609, eminent botanist and director of the Imperial gardens (Buxton, 60–3 and *passim*).

master Salvart. Jean François Salvart, whose *Harmonia confessionum fidei*, reconciling the doctrines of the various reformed churches of Europe, was to be translated into English in 1586. This work would have been an important plank in the Protestant League envisaged by Sidney and his friends. According to Aubrey, Spenser had a similar experience to Salvart's when bringing Sidney some books of *The Faerie Queene*: Sidney was too busy to see him, but later, after reading what he had left, sent for him and gave him money (*Brief Lives*, ed. Clark (1898), ii. 248–9).

master von Glauberg. Johann von Glauberg (1529–1609), 'member of a leading Calvinist family in Frankfurt' (Osborn, 297).

284 [6] From De L'Isle MSS, Z 53/24. Edmund Molyneux became Sir Henry Sidney's secretary in the mid-1570s. Later in the summer of 1578 he convinced Sidney of his integrity, and eight years later paid tribute to his employer and his son in his joint obituary (Appendix B).

[7] From Bodleian MS Rawl. D. 924, fos. 14–16v, emended from other texts in three places. Copies survive in at least nine MSS, all apparently fairly remote from the original, and in one printed text: Essex, Sidney, Davison, *Profitable Instructions: Describing what special observations are to be taken by travellers* (1633). No date is assigned to the letter in any of the texts; Osborn (117) places it in May 1578, about the time Robert Sidney embarked on his European tour.

it is the beginning . . . greatest actions. That is, the 'ends' of actions are the foundation of Aristotle's moral theory.

285 *like the magnificoes in Italy . . . in comedies.* Another hint (cf. *DP*, 243) that Sidney had seen performances of Italian popular comedy. Much-travelled gentleman travellers did indeed become a comic stereotype in later Elizabethan and Jacobean drama.

the predicament of relation. The fourth of ten 'predicaments', or categories, in Aristotle's *Logic*, that of 'relationship' or comparison.

Homer . . . Qui multos hominum mores cognovit et urbes. 'Who knew many customs and cities of men'. Probably quoted from memory from Horace, *Ars Poetica*, 142, *qui mores hominum multorum vidit et urbes*, itself based on the description of Odysseus which opens the *Odyssey*.

286 *propter se.* For its own sake.

the many princes with whom we may have league. At this period Sidney hoped for a league of Protestant princes which might challenge the power of Spain.

discoursers: here used to mean 'wordy talkers'; contrast the more positive use of the word in Letter [10].

287 *much expense.* Cf. Letter [10], 'in Italy your greatest expense must be upon worthy men'.

[8] From Bodleian MS Don. d. 152, fos. 3v–4, a scribal copy by John Mansell, later President of Queens' College, Cambridge. It was ably documented soon after its discovery by John Buxton, 'An Elizabethan reading-list', *TLS*, 24 March 1972, 343–4. Edward Denny (1547–99) seems to have got to know Sidney at Court in the later 1570s; at the time of the present letter he was about to go to Ireland with Lord Grey.

the preferring of Lord Grey. Lord Grey de Wilton (1536–93) was appointed Lord Deputy Governor of Ireland in the summer of 1580, in succession to Sidney's father. Sidney himself had hoped for this post (Kay, 64–5).

the unnoble constitution of our time doth keep us from fit employments. Cf. *DP*, 241.

that which makes us differ from beasts. Reason, which is presumably 'the better line to guide him the labyrinth'.

this age you now pass in. Denny was 33, seven years older than Sidney. Sidney may imply that Denny is not a good Latinist; many of the authors he recommends were available in translation.

288 *labour.* Emended from 'labourer' in MS.

send for a good sword into Spain. Spanish, or 'Toledo', blades were highly prized; cf. *Othello*, v. ii. 253.

Aristotle's Ethics. J. Wilkinson translated Aristotle's *Ethics* (from an Italian version) in 1547.

pass. surpass.

Tully's Offices. An English translation of Cicero, *Thre bookes of duties*, by Nicholas Grimald, was first published by Tottel in 1556, and went through many editions, with the Latin text alongside the English.

Plutarch's discourses. Sidney valued Plutarch so highly that in 1573 he offered Languet five times the normal price for Amyot's translation of Plutarch's essays (Feuillerat, iii. 81).

289 *Languet in French and Machiavel in Italian.* Hubert Languet, *Harangue au roy Charles IX*, printed in *Memoires de l'Estat de France* (1578); probably Machiavelli, *Discorsi*, comments on the first book of Livy, which went through many editions from 1531 onwards, and in 1584 was printed in London by John Wolfe.

Sacrobosco's Sphere. Johannes de Sacro Bosco, *Opus sphericum*, a work which went through many editions, with augmentations and commentaries, throughout the sixteenth century.

you have already very good judgement of the sea maps. Denny had been on several privateering voyages to the New World; cf. Buxton, art. cit.

an Ortelius. Abraham Ortelius's great atlas, *Theatrum Orbis Terrarum* (1570). In 1577 Ortelius visited England, and gave help to Sidney's friend Camden. In an undated letter to Christopher Plantin, Sidney ordered 'Les mappes de lortelius en la plus nouvelle édition' (Feuillerat, iii. 134).

the Emperor's lives gathered together in a volume by Henricus Stephanus. Not traced.

even to begin with our English Chronicle. Perhaps Sidney has just remembered that Denny is not a good Latinist; only a few of the ancient and Byzantine historians mentioned above had been translated, and despite his assurance that the project is 'not so long as a man would think', he seems to drop the whole lot in favour of more recent chronicles in English, French, or Italian.

Anguerard of Monstrelet. Enguerrard de Monstrelet (d. 1453) continued Froissart's *Chronicle* to the year 1444. Froissart, but not Enguerrard, had been translated into English by Lord Berners (1523).

Valerius. Cornelius Valerius, *De sphaera*. There were several editions by C. Plantin in the 1560s and 1570s.

290 *him that (to say nothing to yourself) hath my Lord Grey's company.* Osborn (536) detected an allusion here to Spenser, who had just become secretary to Lord Grey. However, Sidney may simply mean that he is impudent in giving his advice both because Denny may not need it, and because, if he does need it, he can seek it from his companion Lord Grey.

my songs. Impossible to identify these precisely with existing poems, but the reference is significant in showing that some of Sidney's lyrics circulated among his friends at an early date and had musical settings.

[9] From the Cottrell-Dormer MSS, Rousham. Though Sidney doubtless did have a cold, it is possible that the later stages of writing *OA* for his sister were also keeping him at Wilton.

291 *constantly to wait, or constantly to hold the course of my poverty.* To wait at Court continually, which entailed much expense, but might lead eventually to preferment; or to remain in the country, which might signal to the Queen his lack of resources.

Clarendon. Clarendon Park, part of the estate of the Earls of Pembroke, adjacent to Wilton.

[10] From De L'Isle MSS, C 7/8. This letter was admired by Walter De la Mare, who quoted from it in his anthology *Come Hither* (1923), item 286.

H. White. Harry White, a Sidney family servant, who was to receive an annuity of forty pounds in Sidney's Will (*Misc. Prose*, 149, 218).

his nephew. Probably Rowland White, whose correspondence with Robert Sidney during the 1590s is a rich historical source (HMC *De L'Isle and Dudley*).

countenance. Position, dignity established by his retinue.

Mr Savile. Henry Savile (1549–1622), distinguished mathematician and scholar, who taught Greek to Queen Elizabeth, translated Tacitus (1591), worked on the Authorized Version of the Bible, and founded chairs of geometry and astronomy at Oxford (*DNB*).

Mr Neville. Probably Henry Neville (?1564–1615).

Bodin . . . some matter. Jean Bodin, *Six livres de la republique* (1576), which Sidney seems to have considered interesting but diffuse.

seriem temporum. Chronological sequence.

292 *e re nata.* Arising out of the matter in hand.

non simpliciter . . . facti. Not just of the event, but of the nature and circumstances of the event.

bring it to his head . . . next member and parcel of the art. Sidney suggests a division of the material into conceptual sections and sub-sections according to the logical method of Ramus. Some surviving notebooks kept by Robert Sidney later in his life show his attempts to order his historical reading (De L'Isle MSS Z1/1, 2, 3).

Dionysius. Emended from 'Dion Nicoeus'; the reference is probably to Dionysius of Halicarnassus (fl. 20 BC), whose history of Rome from its origins parallelled Livy's.

293 *Stephen.* Probably Stephen le Sieur, who may have returned with Sidney from the Continent in 1575, and was to become a distinguished diplomat. Sidney left him two hundred pounds in his will (*Misc. Prose*, 149–50, 219).

Qui dum verba sectantur, res ipsas negligunt. 'Who, while they pursue the words, neglect the subject matter.' Sidney's own style while an Oxford undergraduate was rather wordy; cf. Letter [1].

My toyfull book. Presumably *OA*.

take a delight to keep and increase your music. Robert Sidney seems to have followed this advice; he was, for instance, godfather to Robert Dowland, who dedicated *A Musicall Banquet* (1610) to him.

Grison, Claudio, and a book that is called La gloria del cavallo. Federico Grisone, *Ordini di cavalcare* (Naples 1550), translated by Blundeville (1560); Claudio Corte, *Il cavalerizzo* (Venice 1573), translated by Bedingfield (1584); Pasquale Caracciolo, *La gloria del cavallo* (Venice, 1566). See also *NA*, xxiii–xxiv.

294 *gratior est veniens in pulchro corpore virtus.* 'Virtue is more pleasing when it comes in a beautiful body', from Virgil, *Aeneid*, v. 344.

how idly we look on our neighbours' fires ... Drake's return. Sidney did not delight in the peacefulness of Elizabethan England; cf. *DP* 241. 'Neighbours' fires' included the English struggle to subdue the 'wild Irish' and the wars of religion in France. Drake returned from his circumnavigation of the world on 26 September 1580.

Portugal we say is lost. Sidney supported the claim of the bastard prince Don Antonio to the throne of Portugal, which had passed to Philip II of Spain in February 1580. In June Don Antonio arrived in England in search of help, but after much prevarication it became clear that the Queen would not commit herself, and Sidney was among those who saw the pretender off English soil in September 1580 (Wallace, 267–9).

bracers. Straps for holding the buckler (a small shield) on the arm.

ticks and dalliances. Light strokes and playful movements.

[11] From Bodleian MS Tanner 79, fo. 229, autograph. Wiliam Temple had sent Sidney a copy of his *P. Rami Dialecticae libri duo* (1584). In 1585 Sidney invited Temple to become his secretary, and he is said to have died in his arms. He received an annuity of thirty pounds in Sidney's will (*Misc. Prose*, 152, 221).

295 [12] From BL MS Harleian 287, autograph, damaged in places.

the discomfort ... that you daily meet with at home. Caused by the Queen's dissatisfaction with Leicester's campaign in the Netherlands and his acceptance of the title of Governor-General; for a detailed documentation, see R. C. Strong and J. A. van Dorsten, *Leicester's Triumph* (1964).

the fountain ... we should wax dry. A euphemistic reference to the Queen's reluctance to release enough money to support Leicester's campaign in the Netherlands. However, much of the responsibility for the failure to pay the soldiers may have laid with the corrupt Treasurer, Richard Huddilston, and some of the captains (cf. C. G. Cruickshank, *Elizabeth's Army* (1966), 148–9 and *passim*).

out. At a fault, in error (*OED*, 20 a, b).

Adams. Possibly the Mr Adams who helped Thomas Digges to map the fortifications at Ostend (*CSP Foreign 1585-6*, 191-2; cf. also 248, 462), who was probably Robert Adams (d. 1595) whose drawings provide the best surviving record of the movements of the Spanish Armada *DNB*).

having a very fair house in it. The Castle of Wou, whose garrison, in Willoughby's absence, mutinied and surrendered to the enemy in the winter following Sidney's death (*CSP Foreign June 1586-March 1587*, 317-18).

296 *I understand . . . so judge me.* Cf. *AS* 23. 9-11.

William, my Lord of Leicester's jesting player. Probably Will Kempe, who was in the Netherlands as part of Leicester's troupe of entertainers, and became a celebrated dancer and clown whose roles included Peter in *Romeo and Juliet* and Dogberry in *Much Ado about Nothing* (DNB).

to stay my Lady there. Rumours of the Countess of Leicester's proposed arrival in the Netherlands with a lavish train enraged the Queen, who feared that a low key, defensive military operation was turning into a jamboree. Sidney clearly hoped that his own wife might be able to join him, but not at the price of encouraging the Countess of Leicester to come too. In the event Francis Sidney came over only after Sidney had been wounded.

Mr Errington. Nicholas Errington, master of the artillery in Leicester's forces, held the garrison at Flushing as deputy-governor in the interregnum after Sidney's death. He was an old man, and impoverished himself by providing food for the English soldiers at his own expense (*CSP Foreign June 1586-March 1587*, 110, 348, 370-1).

Borlas. William Borlas, marshal of the garrison at Flushing.

Burnham. Edward Burnham, water bailiff of Flushing.

Turner. Probably Richard Turner, water bailiff of Brill, who may have been the father of the dramatist Cyril Tourneur (cf. A. Nicoll ed., *The Works of Cyril Tourneur* (1930), 3-4; *DNB*).

harquebuse. Portable field gun.

Nichol Gorge. Described by Leicester as 'an old servant of her Majesty, and well worthy of preferment' when he sued for the office of Serjeant of the Bakehouse in June 1586 (*CSP Foreign June 1586-March 1587*, 28; cf. also *CSP Dom. 1581-90*, 517, 521).

Sir William Pelham. Marshal of Leicester's army; according to Greville, his light arming for the skirmish at Zutphen indirectly caused Sidney's death (cf. 329).

Clerk's place. Bartholomew Clerk (?1537-90) was a Cambridge humanist and lawyer who translated Castiglione's *Il Cortegiano* into Latin (1570). Leicester favoured him, and he came to the Netherlands at the same time as Sidney, as a member of the Council of State. As an elderly non-combatant, he was clearly not esteemed by Sidney, whose dislike may have been compounded by the fact that Clerk had been a tutor to the Earl of Oxford. However, he wrote Leicester a handsome letter of condolence for Sidney's death (BL MS Cotton Galba C.X.73).

[13] From Feuillerat, iii. 182, Latin, translated by John Buxton. The humanist scholar Justus Lipsius (1547–1606) was a professor at Leiden, 1579–90, and in March 1586 had dedicated a treatise on the correct pronunciation of Latin to Sidney. He is said to have called Sidney 'the flower of England' (Buxton, 73, 80). It seems that Sidney hoped to persuade Lipsius to settle in England; however, in 1590 the notoriously changeable Lipsius used the pretext of taking the waters at Spa for a journey to Mainz, where he was reconciled with the Church of Rome.

297 *Buys*. Paul Buys (1531–94), an ambitious lawyer who represented Utrecht on the Council of State of the United Provinces until he was imprisoned in July 1586 on strong suspicion of disloyalty (*CSP Foreign Sept. 1585–May 1586*, 394; *CSP Foreign June 1586–March 1587*, 318, 211–12, and *passim*). Sidney disliked and mistrusted Buys (Feuillerat, iii. 163).

[14] PRO SP Foreign, Holland, X.19 (SP 84/10); autograph. Sidney's letter is accompanied by one from Leicester, dated 20 September, recommending Smith—otherwise unknown—for 'a knight's room at Windsor'. A formal system of pensions for old soldiers did not begin to be set up until 1593 (C. G. Cruickshank, *Elizabeth's Army* (1966), 184–5). If Sidney's letter is correctly dated, he must have written it within hours, or even minutes, of his departure for the skirmish in which he was fatally wounded.

[15] PRO SP Foreign, Holland x. 19 (SP 84/10); autograph. Sidney's last letter, written the night before he died to the elderly physician to the Duke of Cleves. A covering letter from Gisbert Enerwitz, the doctor who was attending Sidney, suggests that his patient is dying, and the letters were probably never sent to Wyer. Both are transcribed and documented by G. F. Beltz, 'Memorials of the Last Achievement, Illness and death of Sir Philip Sidney', *Archaeologia*, xxviii (1840), 27–37.

APPENDICES

299 A. *[Henry Goldwell], A Declaration of the Triumph showed before the Queen's majesty and the French ambassadors on Whitsun Monday and Tuesday [1581]*. Goldwell's *Triumph*, an account of as much as he could gather of the pageantry that took place at Whitehall on 15 and 16 May 1581, has been the subject of an article by Norman Council ('O Dea Certe: The allegory of the Fortress of Perfect Beauty', *HLQ* xxxix (1975–6), 328–42); an unpublished thesis by A. L. Blankenship (University of Colorado Ph.D. 1978); a text is included in Jean Wilson's *Entertainments for Elizabeth I* (1980), 60–85; and both the text and the events themselves are explored in depth by Woudhuysen, 305–50. All these scholars agree that Sidney played a major part in devising the spectacles and writing the speeches, though Blankenship attributes the defenders' speeches to John Lyly. Ringler includes the two sonnets in the *Triumph* as PP4 and PP5, concluding cautiously that they 'are possibly by Sidney' (519). It is clear that the occasion was spectacular, memorable, and so elaborate that neither Goldwell nor a French eye-witness called Nallot (cf. Woudhuysen, op cit.) claims to include all the details, let alone to explain their meaning. However, the essential

context for the *Triumph* must be the presence of the large French legation which came over to negotiate the Queen's marriage with the Duke of Alençon. Sidney's *Letter* arguing strongly against the match was by this time widely circulated in manuscript (*Misc. Prose*, 34). The *Triumph* belongs to the penultimate stage of the Alençon courtship, before Alençon's own arrival in November, when it was clear that the possibility of marriage had evaporated (Woudhuysen, 346–7). It probably had a twofold purpose. Its general function was 'to show the Commissioners that English court culture was as sophisticated as French' (Woudhuysen, 346); but its particular purpose must have been to suggest that the Queen was not to be won in marriage. Four leading courtiers made energetic efforts to conquer the 'Fortress of Beauty' (the Queen), but soon declared themselves defeated. The diplomatic balancing act was as delicate as any in Sidney's career. In *LM* he left it open to the Queen to decide between the 'great services and great faults' of Therion and the 'few services and no faults' of Espilus. Here it was open to the French Commissioners to conclude either that a French prince might succeed where four English courtiers had failed, or, as the Leicester–Sidney party hoped, that the Queen was not to be conquered in marriage by anyone. The present text is based on the Huntington Library copy of the *Triumph* (STC microfilms 384), omitting the preliminaries, the marginal glosses, and Goldwell's conclusion.

the arrival of the French ambassadors. About five hundred French courtiers arrived in London on 20 April (see headnote). A special banqueting house, on the site of the present Inigo Jones banqueting house at Whitehall, was constructed for their entertainment.

red and white. Colours associated with love.

levy. Raise (the siege).

dainty. Discriminating; cf. *AS* 41.6.

300 *first at the tilt … then … with lance and sword.* A mounted tilt on Day 1 followed by a tourney or foot combat on Day 2 was the normal format for court tournaments (Young, 32–3, 195).

Thus. Emended from 'This'.

301 '*rolling trench*'. A large, ornately equipped canvas-covered 'mountain' on wheels, 'trench' here signifying 'ramparts, mound or embankment' (*OED* 3c).

sarcenet. A thin silk of taffeta weave.

the Earl of Arundel. Philip Howard, 1st Earl of Arundel (1557–96), who from 1584 was a Roman Catholic, and from 1585 until his death a prisoner in the Tower. His claim to the Earldom of Arundel had been allowed by the heralds only a few weeks before the *Triumph*, in March 1581 (*DNB*)

Venetian hose. Long, padded breeches which fastened below the knee.

Lord Windsor. Frederick, fourth Baron Windsor (1559–85). His father, a Catholic, had entertained Sidney in Venice in the summer of 1574, and died there some months later (Osborn, 212, 283–6, and *passim*).

orange tawny. A bright, red-gold colour, sometimes associated with pride.

the Unicorn of silver plate. Unicorns on silver discs are shown on the armour of Windsor's brother Frederick in a portrait bearing the date 1588 reproduced in Young (71); there is also an emblematic painting of a unicorn in the top left-hand corner.

blue . . . gilt and engraven. The Sidney crest, 'or, a pheon azure', showed blue on gold. It may or may not be relevant that blue and gold together could signify 'desire of riches'.

302 *posy.* A short motto or quotation, like those engraved inside rings.

Sic nos non nobis. 'We are thus, but not for ourselves.' Perhaps the implication is that Sidney and his companions expose themselves to public defeat and humiliation not for their own sakes, but for the good of the state. Sidney used another version of this motto, *sic vos non vobis*, in *OA*, where it suggested deflected honour (108).

parley. Emended from 'partly'.

303 *these.* Emended from 'this'.

Much may. 'We may win much praise' (Ringler).

the frozen knight. Perrott had already appeared as a Frozen Knight in the 'Callophisus challenge' in January 1581 (Woudhuysen, 312); cf. also the account of the 'Iberian jousts' from *NA* (261).

304 *O times! O men! O corruption of manners!.* From the well known opening of Cicero's *Contra Catilinam*; cf. *LM* (7).

The Sun. 'By the Sun is meant her Majesty, called before the Fortress of Beauty' (marginal note).

305 *Adam and Eve.* 'Sir Thomas Perrott and Mr Cooke were both in like armour beset with apples and fruit, the one signifying Adam and the other Eve, who had hair hung all down his helmet' (marginal note). Cooke's appearance must have been comparable with that of Pyrocles in Amazon guise in *OA*. Woudhuysen (332) points out that a staircase leading to the Queen's Privy Gallery was known as the 'Adam and Eve' stairs.

Magnis excidimus ausis. From Ovid, *Metamorphoses*, II. 327–8, the epitaph on Phaethon, who tried to drive the chariot of his father Phoebus; it is translated thus by Golding:
      Here lies the lusty Phaethon which took in hand to guide
      His father's chariot, from the which although he chanced to slide
      Yet that he gave a proud attempt it cannot be denied.

306 *his.* Presumably that of the Frozen Knight, Perrott.

by. Emended from 'my'.

a woman . . . a Saint. Evidently the Queen in both cases.

crudity. Immaturity. Emended from 'crudelity'.

moss. Perhaps here denoting seaweed (*OED* 3d).

307 *grisping.* Twilight.

one which lay dead amongst them. Possibly an allusion to Edward Knollys, one of the seven sons of Sir Francis Knollys, who had died some time in 1580 (*DNB*).

once. Emended from 'one'.

308 *without Medea's help.* In Greek mythology, Medea helped Jason and the Argonauts to find the Golden Fleece.

The giants ... the wanton youth. In Greek mythology, the giants Otus and Ephialtus tried to reach Olympus (cf. *NA* 289); Icarus tried to fly with wings made by his father Daedalus, but the wax which kept them together melted in the sun.

bait. Food.

309 *Night.* Emended from 'Might'.

Desires. Emended from 'Desire'.

the same guest. Cupid.

lock. Emended from 'look'.

above. Emended from 'about'.

bulk. The hold or interior of the chariot (*OED* 3c).

310 *Memory ... the sworn enemy to the woeful man's quietness.* Cf. *NA* 3–4.

those eyes ... can neither find fellows nor see themselves. Cf. *OA* 62.21–2; and Tilley, E232.

title. Emended from 'tilt'. Slaves were branded on the forehead.

311 *B. [Edmund Molyneux], Historical Remembrance of the Sidneys, the father and the son.* Extract from Molyneux's joint obituary for Sir Henry Sidney and his son in Raphael Holinshed, *The third volume of Chronicles* (1587), 1548–5. Molyneux had been Sir Henry Sidney's secretary from the mid-1570s. His relations with the younger Sidney were not always happy; cf. Letter [6]. Though his comments on the *Arcadia* are often quoted, his account as a whole has not been reprinted in modern times.

as his father was at like age to the French King. Sir Henry Sidney went as ambassador from Edward VI to the King of France in 1552 (*DNB*).

his return from that journey. Sidney got back from his embassy to the Emperor Rudolph in June 1577.

312 *the States.* The States General, 'delegates representing the provinces of Gelderland, Holland, Zeeland, Friesland, Overijssel, Utrecht and Ommelander' (Greville, *Prose Works*, 204).

Axel. The surprise of Axel took place on 7 July 1586. It is described by Greville, *Prose Works*, 72.

the service intended at Gravelines. Sidney was lured to Gravelines by an assurance that it was about to be betrayed to the rebel forces; however, he was rightly suspicious, and released only a small contingent of his soldiers into what turned out to be a trap (cf. Greville, *Prose Works*, 72–4, 212–13).

313 *an ancient Roman.* Julius Caesar, whose claim of *Veni, vidi, vici* ('I came, I saw, I conquered') was a catchword among the Elizabethans (cf. *Cymbeline*, III. i. 24–5).

their fatal ends . . . within . . . less than six months. Sir Henry Sidney died at Worcester on 5 May 1586; Lady Mary Sidney at Penshurst on 9 August.

Et quod Deus in omnibus est suspiciendus. 'God alone is to be looked to in all things.'

Mi Wiere . . . P. Sidneius. For a translation, see Letter [15].

Belerius, a very learned divine. Not identified, nor is Sidney's letter to him known to survive.

courtesy. Molyneux goes on here to quote Henri Estienne's dedicatory epistle to Sidney in his edition of the New Testament in Greek (1576).

314 *a most bountiful and liberal will.* Included in *Misc. Prose*, 147–52. Molyneux's hopes were not fulfilled; Sir Francis Walsingham, who was eventually bankrupted by his attempts to resolve his son in law's financial affairs, observed that 'his goods will not suffice to answer a third part of his debts'.

His body . . . he was buried. A full verbal and visual record of Sidney's funeral is provided by Lant, *Roll.*

Quo me fata vocant. 'Whither the Fates call me.'

Vix ea nostra voco. 'I scarcely call those things my own'—a modest disclaimer of Sidney's personal entitlement to family arms testifying to the nobility of his father and grandfather.

every point. 'There are five special points required in every device to be perfect' (marginal note).

rich. This choice of word may hint that Molyneux was aware of Sidney's poetic courtship of Lady Rich.

315 *C. Anon, The Manner of Sir Philip Sidney's Death.* This account survives in two MSS: BL Cotton Vitellius C. 17, fos. 382–7; and one in the possession of Dr B. E. Juel-Jensen. Date, authorship, and authenticity are all uncertain. The traditional attribution to George Gifford rests on the fragmentary '. . . fford' visible on the endorsement of the (damaged) Cotton MS, combined with Sidney's bequest in his Will of twenty pounds to 'Mr Gifford the minister'. However, the Essex preacher George Gifford does not allude to Sidney in his numerous printed works, even in sermons dedicated to surviving members of Sidney's circle, such as Essex; nor is there any evidence that he accompanied the English forces in the Netherlands (*Misc. Prose*, 161–2; *DNB*). Though the author may have been a minister named Gifford, it seems safest to treat the work as anonymous. The present text is that of *Misc. Prose*, 166–72.

316 *addict*: bind, attach.

doubled: repeated.

otherwise how should the world continue in the beauty it hath? Cf. Pamela's argument to Cecropia in *NA* that 'perfect beauty' cannot be the result of chance (271).

How unsearchable . . . unto man's reason and understanding. Cf. Romans 11: 33, 'how unsearchable are his judgements, and his ways past finding out!'

317 *It was my lady Rich.* This sentence, which occurs only in the (late) Juel-Jensen MS, may have been included 'for the comfort of those who did dearly love him' (see opening paragraph of *Death*) rather than because Sidney actually said it; cf. also 'Lady Rich', 172–4.

318 *He spake to him in Latin.* Molyneux also suggests that Sidney's linguistic proficiency did not desert him at the end; cf. *Historical Remembrance*, 313.

his two brothers. Robert and Thomas, both serving with Leicester's forces. Neither this author nor Greville mentions the presence of Sidney's wife.

namely. Especially.

319 *D. Phoenix Nest Elegies.* These three poems (strictly speaking, an elegy and two epitaphs) open the verse collection *The Phoenix Nest* (1593) compiled by 'R.S.' and prefaced by a posthumous defence of Sidney's uncle, the Earl of Leicester. They were reprinted, with some minor errors, in Spenser's *Colin Clouts come home againe* (1595), and are discussed and annotated in detail in H. E. Rollins's edition of *PN* (1931).

[1] *An Elegy, or friend's passion for his Astrophil.* Little is known of Matthew Roydon, the author of this poem, which is a visionary elegy with an unnamed friend of Sidney's as focus; Roydon does not himself claim friendship. An allusion by Nashe in the preface to Greene's *Menaphon* (1589) suggests that the poem had been written by that date.

l. 2. *accloyed.* Filled, burdened.

l. 3. *watchet.* Blue.

l. 10. *Actaeon's horned plant.* Presumably the stag.

l. 15. *With love juice stained the mulberry.* Stained with the blood of Pyramus and Thisbe (Ovid, *Metamorphoses*, IV).

l. 19. *The tree that coffins doth adorn.* Cypress.

l. 36. *The swan . . . leaving Meander.* From Ovid onwards the dying swan was associated with the River Meander.

321 l. 38. *The Phoenix.* In the title of *PN* the Phoenix rising from her own ashes seems to represent the living Muse of the dead Sidney.

l. 44. *one grovelling on the grass.* This chief mourner could represent Robert Sidney, or Essex, or Dyer, or Greville, or even an amalgam of all of them.

323 l. 123. *That instrument. AS?*

ll. 169–70. *He sparkled . . . fiery stars.* Cf. *AS* 104.10, 'If I but stars upon mine armour bear'.

324 l. 171. *is seld.* Is exceptional.

326 [2] *An Epitaph upon the right honourable Sir Philip Sidney.* By Ralegh, whose

acquaintance with Sidney probably went back to their days at Oxford (Wallace, *Life*, 108–9).

l. 17. *A king gave thee thy name*. Philip II of Spain, husband of Mary Tudor.

l. 26. *those more great than kings*. The Holy Roman Emperors Maximilian and Rudolph.

l. 57. *their Hannibal*. Annibale Gonzaga, a Spanish officer of noble birth also fatally wounded at Zutphen.

327 [3] *Another of the same*. Sargent (Dyer, 198–9) attributes this poem to Dyer; the metre, poulter's measure, is one he uses elsewhere, and the suggestions of perpetual 'dying' in ll. 4, 21–4, 32, may allude to his name.

328 l. 25. *Heartsease and only I, like parallels run on*. He will never again meet with happiness.

l. 37. *void*. Avoid, depart. The phrase is quoted from Spenser, *Shepheardes Calender* (1579), August eclogue, 164.

329 E. '*The water bottle story*'. This famous anecdote, perhaps based on a story told of Alexander the Great (North's Plutarch, iv. 349) comes from Fulke Greville's *A Dedication to Sir Philip Sidney* (formerly known by its title in the first printed edition (1652), *The Life of the Renowned Sir Philip Sidney*), which was probably written between 1604 and 1614—that is, about thirty years after Sidney's death (Greville, *Prose Works*, xxiii–xxiv). Greville was not present in the Netherlands, and none of the earlier biographers, such as Molyneux or Moffet, mentions the incident. The text is that of Greville, *Prose Works*, 76–8.

the marshal of the camp. Sir William Pelham (d. 1587).

unenvious Themistocles. Themistocles envied the renown of Miltiades so much that he could not sleep (North's *Plutarch*, i. 285).

cuisses. Armour protecting the thighs.

the principal chirurgeons . . . in him. Greville goes on to describe Sidney's patience during repeated probing of his wound. The fact that so many doctors (ignorant of modern techniques of sterilization) examined him probably contributed to the infection which killed him.

FURTHER READING

(This list supplements the titles included in the Abbreviations, 330–2 which are not repeated here.)

BOOKS

Attridge, Derek, *Well-weighed syllables* (1974).

Berry, Edward, *The Making of Sir Philip Sidney* (1998).

Connell, Dorothy, *Sir Philip Sidney: The maker's Mind* (1977).

Donow, H. S., *A Concordance to the poems of Sir Philips Sidney* (Ithaca, 1975).

Duncan-Jones, Katherine, *Sir Philip Sidney: Courtier Poet* (1991).

Fowler, Alastair, *Conceitful Thought* (1975).

Hamilton, A. C., *Sir Philip Sidney: A Study of his Life and Works* (1977).

Helgerson, Richard, *The Elizabethan Prodigals* (Berkeley, 1976).

Herbert, Mary Sidney, *The Collected Works of Mary Sidney Herbert, Countess of Pembroke*, ed. M. P. Hannay, N. J. Kinnamon, and M. Brennan, 2 vols. (1998).

Howell, Roger, *Sir Philip Sidney: The Shepherd Knight* (1968).

Kalstone, David, *Sidney's Poetry: Contexts and Interpretations* (Cambridge, Mass., 1965).

Lamb, Mary Ellen, *Gender and Authorship in the Sidney Circle* (Wisconsin, 1990).

McCoy, Richard, *Sir Philip Sidney: Rebellion in Arcadia* (New Brunswick, 1979).

Myrick, K. O., *Sir Philip Sidney as a Literary Craftsman* (Cambridge, Mass., 1935; repr. 1965).

Nichols, J. G., *The Poetry of Sir Philip Sidney* (1974).

Norbrook, David, *Poetry and Politics in the English Renaissance* (1984).

Patterson, Annabel, *Censorship and Interpretation* (Wisconsin, 1984).

Pears, S. A., *The Correspondence of Sir Philip Sidney and Hubert Languet* (1845).

Robinson, F. G., *The Shape of Things Known: Sidney's Apology in its Tradition* (Massachusetts, 1972).

Salzman, Paul, *English Prose Fiction 1558–1700: A critical history* (1985).

Stump, Donald V., *et al.*, *Sir Philip Sidney: An Annotated Bibliography of Texts and Criticism (1554–1984)* (1994).

van Dorsten, J., Baker Smith, D., and Kinney, A. F. (eds), *Sir Philip Sidney: 1586 and the Creation of a Legend* (Leiden, 1986).

Wilson, Mona, *Sir Philip Sidney* (1931, repr. 1950).

Worden, Blair, *The Sound of Virtue: Sir Philip Sidney's 'Arcadia' and Elizabethan Politics* (1996).

Woudhuysen, H. R., *Sir Philip Sidney and the Circulation of Manuscripts 1558–1640* (1996).

Young, R. B., 'English Petrarke' in *Three Studies in the Renaissance* (New Haven, Conn., 1958).

ARTICLES

Bergbusch, Martin, 'Rebellion in the *New Arcadia*', *PQ* liii (1974), 29–41.

Chaudhuri, S., 'The Eclogues in Sidney's *New Arcadia*', *RES* 35 (1984), 185–202.

Craig, D. H., 'A Hybrid Growth: Sidney's Theory of Poetry in *An Apology for Poetry*', *ELR* 10 (1980), 183–201.

Duncan-Jones, K. D., 'Sidney's Urania', *RES* 17 (1966), 124–32.

—— 'Liquid Prisoners: Shakespeare's Re-writings of Sidney', *Sidney Journal and Newsletter* 8/14 (1997), 3–20.

Fabry, F. J., 'Sidney's verse adaptations to two Italian art-songs', *RQ* xxiii (1970), 237–55.

Heninger, S. K., 'Sidney and Serranus' Plato', *ELR* 13 (1983), 146–61.

Höltgen, K. J., 'Why are there no wolves in England? Philip Camerarius and a German version of Sidney's table-talk', *Anglia* 99 (1981), 60–82.

Lanham, Richard A., 'Sidney: The Ornament of his Age', *Southern Review* (Adelaide, 1967).

Levy, F. J., 'Sir Philip Sidney Reconsidered', *ELR* 2 (1972), 5–18.

Marotti, A. F., '"Love is not love": Elizabethan sonnet sequences and the social order', *ELH* 49 (1982), 396–428.

Parker, R. W. 'Terentian Structure and Sidney's Original *Arcadia*', *ELR* 2 (1972), 61–78.

Spencer, Theodore, 'The Poetry of Sidney', *ELH* xii (1945), 251–78.

Warkentin, Germaine, 'Sidney's *Certain Sonnets*: Speculations on the evolution of the text', *The Library*, sixth series, ii (1980), 430–44.

Wilson, Christopher R., '*Astrophil and Stella*: a tangled editorial web', *The Library*, sixth series i (1979), 336–46.

SELECTIVE GLOSSARY

affects, emotions, affections; cf. Latin *affectus*

ambassade, message sent by an ambassador

appassionate (*adj.*), full of passion

baiting place, place for rest and refreshment (food)

bate (*n.*), dispute, debate

bias, irregularity designed to determine the course of a bowl's path (in game of bowls)

brawl, from French *branle*, a kind of dance

cleeves, cliffs

concent, harmony

contentation, contentment

drivel (*n.*), (of a person), drudge

garboils, confusions, tumults

gins, traps

gossips, godparents, or friends generally, especially women

grateful, pleasing, attractive

haling, pulling, dragging

honesty, chastity

jarl (*vb.*), quarrel

jurat, sworn witness

lickerous, greedy, lecherous

mich (*vb.*), play truant; *micher* (*n.*), one who plays truant

moods, rages.

narr, nearer

niggard (*adj.*), miserly, grudging; *niggardly* (*advb.*), grudgingly

painful (*adj.*), taking trouble; *painfulness*, painstakingness.

passenger, traveller, passer-by

peise (*vb.*), weigh; *peised* (*adj.*), weighed, balanced

plot, map, plan

prest, prompt, ready

quintessence, the imagined 'fifth element', which alchemists tried to extract

rampire, rampart, defence

rebeck, three-stringed musical instrument

richess, richness

shrewd, mischievous, vicious

spill, destroy

sublime (*vb.*), extract

suitable, matching, appropriate

table, tablet, notebook or writing tablet

try, experience, enjoy

waymenting, lamenting

winter-starved, killed or famished by cold

wrack (*n.*), destruction

INDEX OF FIRST LINES

American Literature

British and Irish Literature

Children's Literature

Classics and Ancient Literature

Colonial Literature

Eastern Literature

European Literature

Gothic Literature

History

Medieval Literature

Oxford English Drama

Poetry

Philosophy

Politics

Religion

The Oxford Shakespeare

A complete list of Oxford World's Classics, including Authors in Context, Oxford English Drama, and the Oxford Shakespeare, is available in the UK from the Marketing Services Department, Oxford University Press, Great Clarendon Street, Oxford OX2 6DP, or visit the website at www.oup.com/uk/worldsclassics.

In the USA, visit www.oup.com/us/owc for a complete title list.

Oxford World's Classics are available from all good bookshops. In case of difficulty, customers in the UK should contact Oxford University Press Bookshop, 116 High Street, Oxford OX1 4BR.